How To Succeed As An

Independent Consultant

MORE BOOKS FOR CONSULTANTS

How To Succeed As An
Independent Consultant

Second Edition

Herman Holtz

WILEY

John Wiley & Sons, Inc.

New York • Chichester • Brisbane • Toronto • Singapore

Publisher: Stephen Kippur
Editor: Karl Weber
Managing Editor: Ruth Greif
Assistant Managing Editor: Corinne McCormick
Editing, Design, and Production: Publication Services, Inc.

Published by John Wiley & Sons, Inc.

Library of Congress Cataloging-in-Publication Data

Holtz, Herman.
How to succeed as an independent consultant / Herman Holtz. —2nd ed.
p. cm.
Bibliography: p. 387
Includes index.
ISBN 0-471-84729-1
1. Business consultants. I. Title.
HD69.C6H63 1988 88–729
658.4'6'068—dc19 CIP
Printed in the United States of America
10 9 8 7 6
Printed and bound by Courier Companies, Inc.

Preface

Consulting has more than its share of detractors, critics who question both the merits and necessity of consulting in general and the capabilities and integrity of its practitioners.

It is also very difficult to define consulting; the debates and controversies over what it is (and what it is not!) continue to rage as vigorously as ever. However, despite these problems, the markets for consulting and the number of consultants practicing continues to grow.

The growth in markets for consulting and in numbers of specialists "hanging out their shingles" as consultants is the logical and inevitable consequence of several forces, including rapid increases in technological, political, economic, and industrial forces and the rapidly rising average level of education. It is inevitable that consulting will continue to grow and be a force in the business world and in society in general.

Yet, despite this growth, "consulting" is difficult to define. Try, for example, to look up "consultants" in the yellow pages telephone directory of any metropolitan area and you will experience some frustration immediately; there is no such heading. But look it up in the index to the directory, and you will find many consultant listings. The index of the Washington, D.C. directory is a good example:

Consultants

See Advertising Agencies & Counselors

See Agricultural Consultants

See Automation Consultants

See . . .

And so the list continues, alphabetically, to a final entry of "See Wedding Consultants." And even that is not all, for there are a few additional and special consulting services such as "Crisis Consultants" following these, but again under the now familiar "See. . ." direction to look under some primary heading first.

That in itself delivers the clue we need to understanding this difficulty of definition. Consulting is not a profession in itself, it is a way of practicing a profession. The engineer who consults remains an engineer first, and a consultant only after that. The physician who consults does not give up being a physician first, nor do any of the others who turn to consulting change their professions. They change merely the arrangements under which they render their services and often the kind of individuals and organizations to whom they render the services.

That latter aspect, who the clients are, gives us another clue to the nature of consulting and consultants, for we can divide the consultant's clients into two broad classes: peers and others. Most consultants serve one or the other, but some consultants serve both. The physician invariably serves his or her peers when called on to consult. But a public relations consultant would almost invariably serve a client who has a very limited experience with PR. An engineer might serve other engineers as clients, but could easily be called upon by a client who is not an engineer.

This is an important point, because it affects how you conduct your practice and how you do your marketing. It also defines what you do as a consultant. And the necessity for doing that will also become more apparent.

While I was gathering information for and writing the first edition of this book, an extremely important development was taking place—the desktop computer was rapidly coming of age. There was little consciousness of this, and so the first edition of this book was created on a Selectric typewriter, whereas this second edition is being created via a WordStar word processor, running on an IBM-XT clone, and printed out as a manuscript on an NEC printer.

These technology developments have created an entire new class and population of computer consultants who specialize in small (desktop) computers and problems related to desktop computers, such as helping millions of new computer owners and users select, install, and learn to use the machines. It has also placed this priceless tool in the hands of independent consultants, giving them resources that only large and powerful consulting firms enjoyed before. It has given them resources that bring new meaning to "other profit centers," in fact.

Wise consultants will make it their business to be equipped with a suitable desktop computer and to learn all its uses. In this new edition I will try to help you do this.

Herman Holtz
Wheaton, MD

Contents

Introduction

Consulting has been a source of controversy around Washington, D.C. since 1977 when the Carter administration first raised strong objections to allegedly excessive use of consultants by federal agencies. The cause was soon taken up by several members of Congress, but in congressional debates, as in the administration's Office of Management and Budget (OMB), it was soon apparent that those involved were having great difficulty defining what consulting was. To this day, despite the best efforts of the OMB (via its Office of Federal Procurement Policy—OFPP), nothing approaching consensus has been reached. The OMB/OFPP have finally settled on *their* definition of consulting, but many other federal agencies do not agree with the definition and therefore do not comply fully with administration directives on what federal agencies ought and ought not to do about contracting for consulting services.

Anyone familiar with consulting or government contracting could have anticipated this problem, given the ill-defined and loosely used term *consulting*, which is the butt of so many jokes, from the allegation that a consultant is someone who borrows your watch to tell you what time it is (Robert Townsend, in *Up the Organization*, New York, Alfred A. Knopf, 1970) to the general observation in and around Washington, D.C. that a consultant is someone who is out of work but has a briefcase and a three-piece suit. A consultant, however, can be properly defined (if we study the types of work and services provided by those established firms and individuals who represent themselves as consultants) as anyone who can and does render advice and/or related services in any skill area of at least a quasi-professional or technical nature, at some fixed fee or rate, on a contractual basis. Ordinarily the services and skills/knowledge required are somewhat specialized and not commonly available. And contrary to the fondest beliefs of some idealistic purists, only rarely can consultants command substantial fees for advice alone; most clients want specific work done, even if they also want expert counsel and guidance.

A FEW PROBLEMS OF DEFINITION REVISITED

The preceding paragraphs represent generally the introductory words to the first edition of this book, with only minor revision. The original words were written shortly after the Carter administration was succeeded by the Reagan administration, and so reflected the lingering atmosphere of the late Carter administration in Washington, D.C., which is, of course, a center for a great deal of consulting activity to government agencies directly and to the many government contractors in the metropolitan area. I am both surprised and pleased that there is so little reason to make any but the most minor changes to those opening statements of the first edition.

The opponents of consulting in the former administration ran into immediate difficulties when challenged by the agencies to define the term; it proved to be quite easy to devise definitions, especially in governmentese, but very difficult to devise a definition that is acceptable to everyone. The problem is one of too many individual ideas of what kinds of activities constitute consulting and the fact that any definition you can devise also describes services performed under different names. Consulting is, by its very nature, a highly diversified profession, which alone makes it difficult to capture a precise definition or to reach agreement with others on what a precise definition ought to be.

Consulting is not truly a new profession, nor is it confined to the business and professional worlds. When men made themselves the heads of state in various societies they soon found that they could not govern alone; they needed seers, counselors, ministers, even as government heads do today. Consulting, therefore, is certainly among the oldest professions and it has most honorable beginnings in early civilizations and cultures. (We can easily imagine the first primitive man who learned how to sharpen and point a stick to make an early spear, and was soon besieged by others to teach them how to do the same!)

Perhaps the classic or at least best known modern consultant is the medical specialist called in by other medical practitioners to *consult*, which means to examine the patient and/or the medical records established, discuss the case with the client (original practitioner), and offer his or her own expert opinion or diagnosis. This is, of course, a rather common practice in the medical profession when dealing with cases having serious complications and/or depending heavily on the practitioner's judgment. However, note that it is the fact of being *called upon to consult* that is significant here. Had the patient visited the specialist directly (assuming that the specialist maintained a private practice as well as one of consultation), the specialist would not have been a consultant!

The circumstances under which technical/professional or other specialized service is rendered has a great deal to do with whether the service is or is not consulting. Because consulting is not a licensed or controlled profession, although consultants may be specialists in a licensed and controlled profession, there are no absolutes. Job shops that supply technical/professional temporaries (technical writers, engineers, computer programmers, designers, trainers, physicists, illustrators, drafters, and others), sometimes for short-term jobs, such as a week or two, but more often for long-term jobs of many months and even years, often identify themselves as consulting firms and the temporaries they supply as consultants. There are also independent consultants who hire themselves out on the same basis, eliminating the broker. The so-called *job shops* are really brokers dealing in human labor, very much as talent agencies (or booking agents as they are also called) are. These consultants work entirely on the client's premises, functioning very much as temporary employees, albeit usually in specialized work requiring special skills and knowledge, and actually on the payroll of the firm who supplies them, not that of the firm for whom they are doing work. (If they are independents who deal directly with clients, instead of brokers, they are employed as independent contractors, as well as consultants.)

On the other hand, many consultants, both large organizations and independent consultants, work on their own premises or on both the client's and their own premises, usually under contract to do a specific job, rather than under an indefinite-term agreement to work for the client.

There are also many professions that fit the general description of consulting firms but which are not identified as consulting. Lawyers, physicians, dentists, architects, and other professional or technical experts for example, do not call themselves legal consultants or medical consultants. And some, such as lawyers, do not generally use the term "consulting," as physicians do, even in the special circumstances of asking another lawyer to participate in a case. The legal profession uses the term "associate," obviously preferring it to "consultant." In fact, in legal practices, even when bringing in an expert of some sort to depose or testify, he or she becomes an "expert witness," and not a consultant (although consultants may be called upon to become expert witnesses, as I have been.)

Even large firms that are generally recognized as consultant firms do not always identify themselves as such. Scrutinizing the yellow pages of the Washington, D.C. telephone book, for example, reveals that Arthur Young and Company is listed under both "Management Consultants" and "Certified Public Accountants," while some other large firms well known for their management-consulting services (e.g., Peat, Marwick & Mitchell) choose to be listed as accountants only.

It is also interesting to note that there are no listings under "Consultants" per se, but only under "Management Consultants," "Engineering Consultants," etc. Obviously it is the profession in which one consults that is the prime identifier, rather than consulting itself.

That is probably a major clue to defining consulting. It suggests that a consultant is always a specialist within a profession and that consulting is not itself the profession. This appears to be entirely consistent with all other evidence of how consulting appears to others, as well as to how consultants themselves regard and define what they do. In my own case, as an example, I identify myself first as a marketing specialist, second as a specialist in marketing to government agencies, and third as a consultant to others requiring assistance in marketing to government agencies. But I might also regard myself as a writer who consults with others requiring assistance in writing proposals, a must for certain types of ventures. And even those are only two of several possible ways in which I might identify and define what I am and what I do. But the differences are more than semantics; they have a great deal to do with how successful I am in marketing my services.

HOW THAT DEFINITION RELATES TO CONSULTING SUCCESS

What is the importance of this? Why trouble ourselves about defining what we do if we are completely free to call it whatever we wish to, to define it however we wish to, and to practice it however we wish to?

The definition—and the knowledge that consulting is not itself a profession, but is a specialty within a profession—is of critical importance in marketing your services. Later, when we delve deeply into the problems of marketing your services and methods for doing so, you will see the absolute need to know what business you are in, if you are to succeed in the all-important marketing aspect of your chosen field. Marketing, more than anything else, identifies and defines what this book is all about, for that is what *success* is all about.

Independent consultants need to develop a better marketing capability if we are to improve our public image and win clients—that is, we must *sell* our services effectively. The fact that prominent people—those who manage to get the ear of the public, such as Robert Townsend for one—appear to regard consulting as a profession without virtue is a significant indicator of our failure (collectively) to market ourselves effectively. We all need to market so as to improve our public image, as well as to sell our services. (In fact, the two are not separate; they are interdependent.)

Nothing has happened since writing that first book to suggest that the premise and the focus on marketing was a mistake. Quite the contrary, the overwhelming majority of feedback from readers confirmed that the marketing emphasis was most helpful and most needed.

THE CONSULTING MARKET HAS GROWN, RATHER THAN CHANGED

The career prospects for independent consultants have not changed greatly over these few years, except to continue to grow. I perceive a steadily increasing incidence of and business opportunities for the independent consultant. The swift and continuing popularity of the initial edition of this book itself indicates the widespread interest in consulting as an independent career. The demand for consulting services has grown in both the private sector and the public sector. There is a growing amount of literature—articles, newsletters, and other publications—covering the subject as a matter of popular interest. There is an increasing recognition of and references to consulting in contemporary business literature and an increasing number of independent specialists who identify and list themselves as consultants. At the same time, I perceive a significant lessening of the criticisms directed at consultants and consulting, such as those attributed to Robert Townsend and others in the earlier edition. It appears that consulting is becoming more and more widely recognized as a respectable and respected method for practicing one's profession, if not a profession in itself. Evidently we *are* learning to market more effectively.

Defining what you do or propose to do as an independent consultant, then, depends primarily on what you are willing to do and on what kinds of assignments or contracts you wish to accept—not on what you call yourself. You are free to accept only problem-solving jobs, if you wish, although you will probably limit your market considerably if you do so. You may refuse assignments that require you to write lengthy formal reports or make formal presentations to the client's assembled staff. You may confine yourself to assignments only in your local area and refuse to travel, if you prefer to make such conditions. You can, in fact, establish whatever rules you wish to establish for yourself. And, in so doing, you may define for yourself just what the title "consultant" means, as far as you and your own practice are concerned. In fact, *only* you can define the term for yourself.

On the other hand you do not have that control over what a prospective client perceives a consultant and consulting services to be. And that perception matters a great deal if you are to market successfully, for you can sell successfully only to the client's perception, not to your own. Perhaps you can shape the client's perception to some extent; marketers do that—or try to—constantly, sometimes with success, sometimes without it. But it is risky to try to modify the client's perception. It requires great skill to do so (and in many cases it cannot be done at all), and the cost of failure to do so is the loss of the contract. It is usually more practical to determine what the client expects you to be, whether that is scholar, expert, trainer, troubleshooter, mentor, guide, hard worker, resident sage, father confessor, and/or other functionary, and try to conform to that image. Your success in marketing yourself as a consultant depends almost entirely on these three things:

1. How accurately you have assessed the image you must project and how well you have succeeded in projecting that precise image.
2. How effectively you have convinced the prospective client that you—your image—are exactly what he or she is looking for.
3. How effectively you have disseminated that image—made enough prospective clients aware of you, your image, and your availability to help them overcome their problems and magnify their success. (In marketing, statistics and playing percentages are all important.)

Although this is presented in the context of achieving marketing success, these factors are almost equally important to achieving client satisfaction with your work after you have won the contract (which is itself a factor in marketing.) Everything you do after winning the assignment must confirm and reinforce the image you created earlier. As in marketing, truth is whatever the client perceives truth to be. You will always have difficulty satisfying a client who has an adverse impression of you. But you will find it rather easy to please the client who has a favorable image of you. Clients, too, tend to see what they expect (and want) to see.

There are many hazards in consulting independently, many of them peculiar to and the result of being a one-person show. For example, as an independent it is extremely difficult to cope with the feast-and-famine nature of consulting. It is difficult—frequently impossible—to backlog consulting assignments, and yet you have only so many hours a day available. How do you smooth out those peaks and valleys? Some jobs that come your way require several people; how do you cope with that successfully so that you do not lose the contract? Some clients simply cannot afford your regular, direct rates, although they have need of help. How can you help them–and yourself—without cutting rates?

These are among many other problems considered and addressed in these pages. I assume in writing this, as I did in the first edition, that you bring to your independent consulting practice the technical/professional expertise of your special field and need no help or guidance in assisting your clients, but that you can make good use of some suggestions, ideas, and general guidance in all the other areas necessary to establish and operate a successful independent consulting practice—that is, *winning* clients.

One thing I wish to do in this new edition is to report what readers of the first edition had to say and offer as suggestions and experience to others. I wish especially to offer additional and new insights into methods for marketing your services successfully. A large part of this second edition will therefore focus sharply on specific marketing ideas and methods for you to consider and use, as the first edition did, for those are, after all, the true ingredients of your success as an independent consultant. But a few significant things have happened in even the few short years between editions and these issues (i.e., the computer revolution and changes in government procurement) and will be addressed in this edition.

All of this make the second edition of *How To Succeed As An Independent Consultant* necessary, if it is to continue to serve independent consultants properly.

1

What Does (Should) a Consultant Do?

Better to be proficient in one art than a smatterer in a hundred.

—Japanese proverb

BRIEF SURVEY OF THE CONSULTING FIELD

One reason we have so much difficulty identifying or defining consulting services is that the services provided by consultants are themselves not truly remarkable in any way that distinguishes them from other contracted specialist services, such as might be rendered by an interior decorator, image counselor, financial advisor, or free-lance package designer. The only difference between these individuals and the consultants who provide the same services is the name by which the individual identifies himself or herself and what he or she does. In this chapter we'll ignore the facade of names and instead examine some of the most active fields for consulting and discuss several aspects of the consulting industry, especially as it pertains to independent consultants. First, let's look at those consultants who are most often employed on the client's premises on a full-time basis, often long term (many months, and even years), as a quasi employee—a phenomenon of the modern technological age and most in evidence in areas of high technology and large federal contracts.

COMPUTERS AND DATA PROCESSING

The word *computer* has now acquired meaning for the average person, who by now has seen at least one desktop computer, even if he or she has never seen one of the early behemoths, with their desk-sized consoles, spinning tape servos, and other whirring and whirling peripheral equipments. Those early machines created a great many consulting jobs, especially for those specializing in writing custom programs for these machines, since there were few ready-made programs and even the ones that were available rarely were suitable for general applications. So hundreds of thousands of individuals became computer programmers, many of them independent consultants, others evolving into large consulting companies. But not all these computer specialists were programmers in the literal sense. Many were known by other titles, such as systems analysts, systems designers, system engineers, and operators. And there were often gradations within categories, to indicate levels of experience and capability, such as *senior systems analyst* and *junior systems analyst*, or they might be graded numerically. They might even be given other titles—*information analyst* or *data designer*. And as the computer and, especially, the software industries grew, there were more modifiers and qualifiers added to the descriptions of the individual's qualifications and capabilities, so that a programmer would also have to list the various computers and computer languages he or she was familiar with and, finally, the kinds of programs he or she was most experienced in.

There was a steady proliferation of areas of specialization and expertise, as the technologies of the hardware and software evolved. For example, one of the most troublesome areas was that of data storage, and the improvements evolved through several stages—banks of electronic (flip-flop) circuits, tape on large reels, magnetic drums, magnetic cores—before the modern and efficient hard disk and floppy disk systems evolved. At each stage manufacturers were eagerly seeking engineers experienced in the most current method of data storage. Not finding enough qualified applicants to accept jobs, many manufacturers turned to hiring consultants to work on-site as long-term contract labor—temporary employees, in effect.

The picture was the same in the software industry. Companies who could not hire qualified employees turned to technical/professional temporaries—consultants—to fill the gaps.

A great deal of the cost was passed on directly to the federal government via cost-plus contracts, especially in military contracts, but also in others, such as the NASA space program. Hundreds of thousands of such consultants worked for the General Electric Company, RCA, General Dynamics, Boeing, North American Rockwell, McDonnell Douglas, Northrup, Hughes Aircraft, TRW, General

Motors, Ford, and many other supercorporations as well as smaller, less well-known companies developing weapons and space systems. But it was not only contractors and private industry that made use of consultants working as contract labor or temporaries; many government agencies found this an expedient way to get their own projects completed. The NASA bases, for example, employed many such consultants, as did many military bases where a great deal of R&D work was being conducted. Civilian agencies also used this method for hiring hard-to-find specialists. The U.S. Postal Service used contract engineers, technicians, drafters, and designers, and many of the major computer systems in federal agencies were installed by such contract personnel.

The growth of independent consulting took place under the pressure of military needs and the drive to beat the Soviets in the race for space. The pace has abated a great deal today, but although less frantic, there is still large-scale hiring of consultants. For many consultants this type of work has become a way of life, a regular career. It can be a gypsy kind of life because it is difficult to remain permanently in one place and yet pursue this kind of a career; to work regularly one must be willing to go wherever the next job is. But that suits some individuals, especially those who like to keep moving and keep seeing new places. And it suits those, also, who want to make a much greater income than they are likely to make in a permanent job with an organization. Consultants generally can earn up to twice as much as regular employees in the same jobs (and even more, in situations in which specialists are in especially short supply or the assignment involves special hazards and hardships), although with considerably fewer fringe benefits. (They also earn per diem living allowances when more than 50 miles from their official home bases.)

The growth and earning potential is not confined to the computer and data processing industries; it is far more widespread.

THE AEROSPACE AND ELECTRONICS INDUSTRIES

The use of consultant specialists as temporary employees predates the computer industry by some years. As a direct result of World War II, specifically the emergence of the Soviet Union as a major military power and potential threat to the Western world, the U.S. government decided not to follow up the dismantling of our huge military organization by lapsing into its prewar peacetime mode;

instead, the government accepted its new role as one of the only two remaining superpowers on earth and resumed development of new weapons and systems. So, as the Cold War became the status quo, the newly reorganized military organizations were given huge new budgets and authority to begin developing supersystems of all kinds, most of them involving the new high technologies of electronics applications—radar, sonar, missiles, computers, secure communications, jet aircraft, helicopters, and other such advanced systems concentrated principally in the aerospace industries.

A new phenomenon appeared, reflecting a change in the thinking of the military developers. Equipments (this new plural form came into popular and accepted vogue quite quickly) were soon not singular, independent items, but were components of greater entities—of *systems*. For instance, a fighter aircraft was no longer an airplane, but a *weapons system,* an entity involving radar, fire-control mechanisms (which means aiming and tracking systems). This philosophy gradually extended to even larger entities, such as the Navy's destroyers and cruisers and the Air Force's biggest bombers and reconnaissance airplanes. Airplanes became defensive and offensive *systems,* self-contained in capabilities for detecting and neutralizing hostile attacks while carrying out their own attacks in integrated systems of detection, tracking, and attack systems using a variety of weapons—machine guns, light cannon, missiles, napalm, rockets, and bombs—against ground targets. (Even helicopters became "gunships," equipped as systems for specialized kinds of missions in the war we carried on in Southeast Asia.)

The concept of integrated systems spread rapidly and was reflected in what was now identified as "systems engineering," which again called for the services of specialists who were not available in sufficient quantities for direct employment. A great many "systems engineers" thus became consultants. There were many stories of employees who resigned their jobs but never left them. Instead, they joined the ranks of companies supplying consultants as professional temporaries and were assigned to do exactly what they had done as employees of the client company, but now at a far greater rate of compensation as consultants, not employees!

In this milieu a new era had dawned in the world of technology. The concept of "interdisciplinary" specialties had arrived, and new problems of hiring and staffing had to be solved. For example, what mix of specialists is needed, and what kind of specialist should lead a team of different kinds of specialists? Suppose you need a team charged with developing a new missile system. You need to develop the rocket engine, airframe, launch system, guidance system, and warheads, and because this is a highly complex system of many complex components, you must design and manage complex tests to troubleshoot, debug, validate, and ultimately certify the final system. This means mechanical engineers, stress analysts, chemical engineers, electronic engineers, test engineers, and more than a few other specialists will be needed to put the whole system together. Where and how will you get all these expert specialists, and who should lead that team?

The economics of doing business this way are relatively simple. The government might allow the contractor $12 an hour for some given type of specialist. (Remember that we are talking about an earlier, preinflation situation!) The firm supplying the specialists might charge the government contractor $9 an hour for the specialist, and pay the specialist $6 or $6.50 an hour. This would provide the specialist about 50 percent more than the $4/hour he or she might earn as the employee of the client company, while providing the supplier of the specialists some $2.50-3.00 gross profit.

That typical 50 percent differential between what the specialists could earn as the consultant/technical temporary and the direct employee explains why so few of such specialists resisted the many offers they received to "go direct" with the client companies. It was easy to decline.

In fact, those specialists who choose to make a career of being "job shoppers" (the firms who hire them and assign them to client companies are known colloquially as "job shops," although many refer to themselves as consultants) are virtually a subculture of their own, jeering openly among themselves at the thought of "going direct," referring to it almost as an act of betrayal. The majority work for one of the many job shops, but a number are independent even in placing themselves in assignments–that is, contracting directly with the client companies–thereby controlling their own situations entirely. (This generally comes about after the consultant has become well known to many of the client companies and developed a good individual reputation.)

In many cases the situation is quite complex, and the client for such services may be a sub-subcontractor, especially when the project and original contract are large ones. Even the largest corporations cannot do everything, and to perform most of the huge government projects even the largest of the supercorporations must award hundreds of subcontracts, many of which are quite substantial and are awarded to other large corporations. The basic contract for the Atlas Missile System, for example, went to General Dynamics, who awarded a large contract for a supporting subsystem to RCA; IBM was a subcontractor to International Telephone & Telegraph (ITT) on a large Air Force logistics network (the 465L system); and GE developed radar sets for the Ballistic Missile Early Warning System under contract to RCA.

When the contracts total hundreds of millions of dollars, there are usually several hundred subcontracts, many of them rather large. This imposes a temporary labor burden on many of the subcontractors, as well as on the primary contractor. In many cases the contractor does not want to hire permanent employees, knowing that the contract represents a temporary need for more people who would become surplus when the contract is finished. Although consultants are often hired as temporary employees because it is the only way to staff a project rapidly enough with qualified specialists, in many other cases consultants are hired as temporaries because it makes better economic and business sense to do so. It costs money to hire people, especially in the large organization. There is advertising, interviewing, paperwork, relocation, and numerous other costs incurred in recruiting employees. Terminating personnel who are no longer needed also costs money; and there are many legal obligations today in hiring people, as well as problems in terminating them. The technical temporaries represent a way around many of these problems. They can be hired quickly, with little paperwork and little legal obligation, since they work for a contractor not for the client, and they can be terminated as easily when the need ends. Moreover, if and when the work of a temporary is unsatisfactory, there are no complications in terminating that individual's services, whereas it is not always a simple matter today to discharge a permanent employee for cause. (These are among the effective sales arguments employed in selling consultant services as temporary employees.)

The size of programs for temporaries—the number employed and the duration of the assignments—varies widely. NASA has used rather large forces of such personnel, notably in engineering and computer-related work, and General Electric Company has almost traditionally employed large numbers of temporaries in the various engineering functions of their missile and space programs. In fact, when the project requires large numbers of temporaries, it is not unusual to have temporaries from several firms working together on the client's premises.

The duration of the assignment may vary from a few days to several years. A consultant may be employed on an indefinite basis and be kept on for one project after another. For example, many consultant temporaries were assigned to the GE missile and space systems plants in the Philadelphia area for as long as five years. And very much the same situation prevailed at the large training center Xerox Corporation established in Leesburg, Virginia, near Washington, D.C., where they hired several dozen training technologists, many of whom remained on assignment for approximately five years. Those were all "hired"—that is, placed under contract—as self-employed individuals or contractors working on the client's premises.

Most often these assignments are not designed to last so long. Frequently the assignment starts as a relatively short-term one of several months, but when new contracts come in, the consultants are asked to remain. This can continue indefinitely, with the client always acting on the reasonable assumption that the need is temporary.

The practice of bringing in whole staffs of specialists, whether they are called consultants, contract labor, professional temporaries, on-site contractors, or contract labor—and all of these terms are used—has become widespread in all sectors of the economy (e.g., in major government contracts, in commercial or nongovernment industry, and in government itself). Many federal institutions and facilities are staffed and operated by such personnel, especially agencies doing technical work—NASA, the Environmental Protection Agency (EPA), and the Department of Defense (DOD), for example—but not exclusively so. The Air Force has contracted with private industry to manage and operate a warehouse in which it stores the many technical documents required to support its vast array of complex equipment systems. The Postal Service Training and Development Institute awarded a contract to have a private firm administer its correspondence courses in Norman, Oklahoma. The General Services Administration has a private firm running a chain of stores selling personal computers to government buyers. And there are many more such situations, where it is more expedient or more efficient to contract out the management and operation of a government operation.

Most clients who hire consulting specialists as temporary employees have the common problem of needing a temporary force of specialists of one sort or another, usually to staff a special project that represents a nonrepetitive peak load. However, this is not always the case. Some clients have more technical problems that require special expertise beyond the mere recruitment of a staff of specialists on a temporary basis.

One such case was that of Remington-Rand, a computer division of the Sperry Corporation. This organization had built a custom-designed, state-of-the-art computer for a California customer and was approached by the U.S. Navy with an invitation to build another for them, albeit with a few changes, such as a much greater memory. The trouble began when the Navy rejected the user manuals Remington-Rand offered. The Navy refused to pay until an acceptable set of manuals was produced for them, but the publications staff at Remington-Rand had been producing commercial manuals and was not familiar with typical military requirements for technical manuals. To solve this problem, Remington-Rand contracted with four consultant specialists to assist their publications staff in making the manuals acceptable to the customer, a project that consumed several months.

Today we have a great many computer consultants, and the number is growing steadily for two reasons: (1) the number of computers has grown exponentially since the advent of the low-cost personal computer, which has made it possible for almost everyone in even the smallest business or professional practice to own at least one computer; and (2) the computer industry continues to become more and more sophisticated—and that means more and more complex—in both the hardware and software aspects.

When IBM entered the desktop computer market with its IBM PC, it quickly became a dominant force in the market, and the entire industry began a rapid conversion to the production of IBM lookalikes, advertised loudly as "IBM compatible," with the arguments that these IBM-like "me-too" machines would do almost anything an IBM PC would do and for a great deal lower price. But IBM went from its PC to even more sophisticated machines—an XT (for extended technology) and an AT (for advanced technology)—with more to come undoubtedly. And of course the imitators—"IBM clones," in the popular jargon—followed with lower-priced compatibles for those, too.

The growing acquisition of computers and their increasing capabilites means even more complexity. There is a universe of possible configurations of these machines into systems, with various size memories, drives, keyboards, monitors, software, accessories, add-on boards, and operating system versions, so that even an expert is soon confused.

So where the computer consultant of the pre–personal computer days was probably called upon most often to help a client with the programming, or software, problems, many of today's computer consultants find that clients are more likely to either want help in selecting the right system for their needs or are already in trouble. That is, they may be buying a first system, maybe ready to purchase a larger or more sophisticated system (e.g., multitasking, multiuser, or local area network), or may have already bought a system that doesn't do what they need it to do. Software problems are less urgent today because of the wealth of proprietary software available.

This is not to neglect the more classic consulting situation, in which the client not only has a problem to solve, but the problem is so highly specialized that part of the problem lies in finding the right consultant for the job. In one case not long ago one of my own clients found themselves in need of a specialist in Tempest and EMP–hardening technology, areas concerned with data security and system survival under nuclear attack. There are many engineering people who know a great deal about these technologies, but in this case the work involved precise compliance with a highly detailed and sophisticated military technical specification. As esoteric as this subject is, there is enough demand to keep an expert in the subject quite busy advising electronic companies, even the largest ones, about this. They managed to find one such expert who turned in an excellent performance. There are probably not six others quite as knowledgeable as he about this specialized field.

In the same vein, a few years ago NASA commissioned a venerable Japanese scientist to write a definitive work on celestial mechanics because he was considered to be by far the most highly qualified person in the world for this assignment. (In fact, he was quite well along in years, and NASA feared that his great knowledge might be lost if he did not record it for others, and so hastened to initiate his doing so.)

Although there are many consulting specialties that are not in common supply, they are not so rare that it is extraordinarily difficult to find qualified practitioners. My own specialty is one of these. I write, lecture, and consult on marketing generally, but especially on government marketing, and clients call on me often to help them write proposals—the indispensable key to important government contracts. There are not a great many consultants who can boast of an impressive track record in writing winning proposals—good proposal writers must be sought out—but the skill is not so highly specialized that the talented proposal writer is a rare and much sought after expert; it requires work to find fully competent proposal writers, but there is a reasonably abundant supply available—a substantial number with good reputations as competent practitioners. At the same time, the truly outstanding proposal writers are in relatively short supply and because so much depends on the proposal—a proposal that doesn't win is almost always a total loss, although there are exceptions—clients normally seek and engage proposal consultants with great caution.

During the worldwide economic disaster of the Great Depression, there grew up a consulting class known as "efficiency experts." These were individuals who claimed an ability to raise operating efficiency in companies and so reduce costs, an unusually attractive prospect in those times. Businesspeople, even those operating large companies, found it difficult to resist the lure of relieving some of the economic pressure. And so more than a few companies brought teams of efficiency experts aboard to work their magic. However, these efficiency experts ran into opposition from employees and labor unions, many of the latter struggling then to establish their existence. They saw efficiency experts as the enemy who was determined to eliminate jobs, and so they did everything they could to discredit the whole idea of efficiency experts. The term "efficiency expert" was replaced by today's term for the discipline, "industrial engineer," also called at times "methods engineer," specialists in designing work systems for greatest efficiency.

Industrial engineering and methods engineering are respectable professions today. Large industrial firms often have such experts on staff, sometimes serving the firm as internal consultants, but there are still many opportunities for independent industrial engineers to win consulting assignments with firms who have only an occasional need for such capabilities.

THE CONSULTANT ORGANIZATION

There are at least two distinct types of consulting organizations, although there are the inevitable hybrids that blur the distinctions made here. The first type is the supplier of technical/professional temporaries. The second type is the consulting organization that undertakes a project, generally under a contract, with a defined product or service to be delivered and with work done most often on the consulting organization's own site, although on the client's site or on both sites if necessary.

The Job Shop or Supplier of Temporaries

Typically, the job shop must submit a bid for each contract to supply on-site consultants. In most cases the job shop offers its employees as consultants. These employees are usually also temporary, being employed by the job shop only as long as the job shop has a client to send them to and bill. So employment by a job shop is a technicality; it coincides exactly with assignment to a client, and not one hour longer.

The client wants to see résumés of available consultants, and may even ask to see these before asking for quotation of rates, to satisfy himself or herself that the consultants available are suitably qualified. Clients do not scrutinize these résumés quite as closely as they would prospective new hires, but they do study them with care.

Generally the client chooses the résumés of those prospective consultants whom he deems to be satisfactory and asks the job shop to have the selected individuals visit to be interviewed. The actual selection is done by the client. (An exception is made when the client accepts the résumés of consultants known to him or her as capable practitioners, for there is no need to interview those, of course.)

Typically, the job shop quotes consultants by classes, asking the same rate for each person in a given class, although not necessarily paying each person in a given class the same rate! (Beginners in this kind of work almost always sign up too cheaply, but they soon learn what to demand.) The fringe benefits are scant, consisting of a few paid days off and perhaps a group hospitalization plan. And the employee often qualifies for paid days off only when employed for six months or a year, which is far from certain to happen in that work. Most "job shoppers" change employers frequently, as opportunities are presented.

This arrangement permits the job shops to operate at low overhead, an absolute necessity for survival in that field. Typical overhead rates are about 35 to 40 percent, which must cover insurance, taxes, miscellaneous costs, and profit. However, when the job shop is fortunate enough to hire some well-qualified beginners, they may earn considerably more than 35 to 40 percent gross profit on those individuals.

There are some individuals who far prefer the frequent changes of jobs and locales, the financial benefits of job shopping, and the many vacations they are able to take (between assignments), so they make a career of such work, earning at least 50 percent more than they would on salary, and in many cases considerably more than that. There are also some individuals who choose this working arrangement because they are unable to win jobs on the regular payroll of a company, either because they are too old or can't pass a medical examination. (Large companies often have rather rigid policies that seem to bar older people, not necessarily because of their age, but because they cannot pass the insurance examinations.) Job shopping is a boon for many people in these situations.

There are also a great many individuals who turn to job shopping for a short while, attracted by the money or unable temporarily to find a job. Many of these people soon tire of the uncertainty and the constant moving about necessary to work steadily in that field. Seasoned by the experience of a few assignments, they move on to work they find more satisfactory as employees or as independent consultants. In fact, it is not at all uncommon for job shoppers to make such a good impression on clients that the clients offer them permanent employment. All of this results in a steady turnover in the field, making it relatively easy to break into it as a training ground or a starting point in a career.

THE CONSULTANT COMPANY

True consultant companies hire permanent employees to work in the company's own facilities on a project managed by the company and for which the company is responsible. For this reason many people do not consider the job shops to be true consulting organizations nor job shoppers to be true consultants. However, defining consulting in today's business and industrial complex is a difficult task. For example, among the many procurement categories the government employs to classify and organize its purchasing is "H: CONSULTANT AND EXPERT SERVICES." One might expect that anything listed here would be consulting without question. However, among the services requested here are real estate appraisals, computer software programming, technical writing, surveys, and other tasks that we do not normally conceive of as consulting chores.

There are a great many services firms offering "management consulting," among other services, because that term appears to encompass and include virtually any kind of service a business or any other kind of organization might need. Prominent among these are the major accounting firms—Arthur Young and Company; Peat Marwick and Mitchell; Deloitte Haskins and Sells; Price Waterhouse; Coopers and Lybrand; Touche Ross; Ernst and Whinney; and Arthur Anderson. Accounting firms obviously find it expedient, perhaps easy, to make the transition to management consulting and conduct major operations under that business umbrella, judging from the number that have done so successfully.

But it is not only accountants who find that a useful transition. Engineering firms, such as Booz Allen and Hamilton, have also moved into management consulting, as have firms in training development, public relations, and a great many other successful firms in specialized businesses. But it is not only established companies who make such transitions. Individuals launch their independent consulting practices from a base of experience in some given industry, for the potential for practicing as a counselor or consultant in any of today's many specialized fields is almost unlimited. In fact, although no such firms or individual practitioners list themselves under a main heading of "consulting" as their basic category, they do make it clear that they offer consulting services.

HYBRIDS

We have looked at two basic types, which may be considered to be at the extremes of consulting, one considered true consulting, recognized as such by even the purists, and the other barely qualifiying as consulting to some. A great many consultants and consulting firms fall between these extremes of definition. In fact most firms have at least some of the characteristics of each of the extremes.

There is a distinct difference between supplying technical/professional temporaries and carrying out projects on-site (i.e., on the client's premises). In providing technical/professional temporaries you are selling hours of professional effort, normally at a per-hour rate. The contractor (consultant firm) is obligated only to supply qualified personnel, as agreed to and contracted for, and does not incur responsibility for the project, whatever it is. It is up to the client to make best use of this labor—to *manage* the effort and the people. It is the client who is responsible for the result and who must pay the hourly rate for every hour expended by the temporaries, regardless of the result, just as with internal, direct employees. (Of course, the client may terminate summarily the services of the supplying firm or of any individual supplied.) However, in carrying out a project on-site (whether entirely or only partially on-site), the contractor must assume responsibility for the project overall, for its outcome, as well as for the management of the staff, regardless of where they are physically employed. Under federal law, you must always manage your own employees when they are working on-site at some federal facility because the law prohibits civil service employees from giving direct orders to or being given direct orders by contractor personnel. Therefore, the on-site contractor must always provide on-site supervision and management of the staff working on-site. Civil service employees provide only "technical direction" to the contractor's managers.

A great many firms who specialize in supplying professional temporaries also have in-house capabilities for staffing, managing, and carrying out projects on their own premises. But many of those firms whose main enterprise is handling projects in-house are quite willing to carry out projects on the client's premises or to supply professional temporaries, so that distinctions between the two tend to disappear.

THE CONSULTANT AS A SELF-EMPLOYED, INDEPENDENT INDIVIDUAL

As an independent consultant you should be aware of and familiar with all kinds of organizations discussed previously and the markets for their services, for as an independent consultant you can take advantage of all these opportunities for selling your services too.

Whether you find yourself working mostly on clients' premises or in your own office depends largely on the kind of consulting service you provide, and perhaps even more on the basic nature of your clients. If you counsel individuals in personal matters, it is likely that you will have to arrange to receive them in your own offices for at least two reasons: (1) since fees are generally by the hour, usually running an hour or two per consultation and by appointment, you must see several clients a day, making it impractical to call on the clients, and (2) it is usually necessary to have a controlled environment—privacy and quiet, or access to resources such as a library, a computer, or files—something that is often difficult to achieve in a client's home.

On the other hand, if you serve organizations and the nature of your work is such that most of your assignments run to at least several days and are billed by the day, it is likely that you will work largely and perhaps entirely on the clients' premises.

A FEW EXCEPTIONS

There are exceptions to this, of course. The nature of consulting is that it is a custom service and therefore must be tailored to each case. Even dealing with large organizations may result in clients visiting you and working with you on your premises. Such was the case on more than one occasion when I was fortunate enough to work with a large and prominent division of Dun & Bradstreet, with a large hospital in Florida, and with many other such clients. (In fact, except for presenting seminars, it is rarely that I do not carry out part of my consulting work in my own office.)

This does not necessarily mean that you must rent offices in a downtown location or in some office building. Although I did just that for some years, I subsequently discovered that even major companies who were my clients were not dismayed at finding that my offices were in my home, and they were entirely willing to call on me and work with me there. (In fact, some applauded the wisdom of minimizing overhead costs by working from an office at home.)

Overhead reduction and other benefits of working from an office at home are obvious. However, you must decide for yourself whether it is a desirable alternative for you—whether you have suitable facilities for an office at home, whether it is or is not harmful to your practice, and whether there are local ordinances that prevent you from doing so effectively.

WHAT FIELDS ARE SUITABLE FOR CONSULTING?

Many of us have a tendency to assume that what we ourselves know well is common knowledge. The first time I conducted a seminar on how to write proposals for government contracts I stipulated in my advertising that it was a "graduate" course and not at all suitable for beginners in proposal writing. Nevertheless, a generous portion of the 54 attendees who registered for that first session were beginners, lured by my promises to reveal a number of inside tips I had learned over the years. However, there were also a number of thoroughly experienced people, including two senior executives who were in the process of forming a new division of their large corporation. They had come to the seminar to see if they could pick up even a handful of useful ideas.

Until I conducted that session, I had doubts that I could reveal enough little-known information to justify the cost and the full day's time spent by each attendee. I was amazed to discover that even senior, experienced people were unaware of many basic facts that I thought quite fundamental and even obvious about proposal writing, facts that I would have expected senior executives to know as well as I knew them. For example, when presenting the topic of costs—those cost analyses and detailed presentations required in most proposals—I had expected to do little more than mention these briefly in passing, but, to my amazement, that portion of my presentation proved to be one of the greatest areas of interest to the attendees. Even senior people tend to be somewhat confused and uncertain about "direct" and "indirect" costs, overhead, "other direct," and many other basic cost elements and concepts, let alone the concepts such as "G&A" and "expense pools."

This has been an experience repeated in almost every seminar I have conducted, and I am always slightly surprised by it. I can never believe that experienced proposal writers in contracting companies have so little understanding of what costs are, how they are generated, how they proliferate, how they are classified, what they really mean, and how they must be analyzed and presented. That is because I myself found the matter of costs a fascinating and critically important one many years ago when I first became involved in proposal writing. Unlike many other proposal writers, I was not content to surrender this portion of the proposal effort to the accountants; I insisted that I would work out the costs and let the accountants review them. I insisted that I would not submit and be responsible for the success of a proposal until and unless I personally approved of everything in the proposal. I became so knowledgeable about the cost side of the business that I took such knowledge for granted and assumed that everyone writing proposals was equally knowledgeable. Therefore, I was too modest about what I had to offer listeners in this respect.

It's a common enough error. Most of us assume that we have special knowledge or abilities to offer to those unfamiliar with our fields, but not to those who are peers in our fields. However, this is not so. You can probably sell your services to your technical/professional peers too, once you take the time to learn in what areas they most need help or what special knowledge or skills you have in your field that is helpful but not widely known or available in your profession. Examples include shortcuts, methods, ideas, and "tricks of the trade" you have learned from especially knowledgeable "old timers," through extensive special reading and studies, or through your own experience, introspection, and innovation.

This applies to virtually all professions and fields. A list of just some of the fields/areas in which consulting services are offered follows. Even these are, for the most part, generalized items, with various specializations possible within each. Many were derived from the general index to the telephone company's yellow pages directory, which does not list "consultants" as a primary classification, but only as a subclassification within general headings. Study this list to gain an appreciation of the diversity. You may find yourself qualified to consult in more than one field.

Accounting
Advertising
Agriculture/Farming
Arbitration
Audiovisual presentations
Auditing
Automation
Aviation
Banquet planning and management
Building construction
Business
Business writing
Career and vocational counselors
Club management
Communications
Computer advisory services
Contract administration
Convention, conference, meeting
planning/arrangement
Data processing
Design
Drug and alcohol abuse
Editorial services

Educational counselors
Engineering, general
Executive search
Financial management
Fire protection
Food and beverage service
Food facilities
Food preparation
Foreign trade
Grantsmanship
Hearing aids
Hotel management
Immigration and naturalization
Industrial engineering
Industrial methods
Insurance
Labor relations
Lighting
Management
Marketing
Marriage and family relations counselors
Mergers and divestitures
Military specifications
Municipal services
New ventures
Office organization
Office procedures
Organizational development
Personnel
Personal security
Plant security
Public relations
Program
Public utilities
Publications services
Publishing
Recreation program counselors
Restaurant management
Safety
Sales promotion
Social event counselors
Taxes
Technical writing services
Training
Transportation
Weddings and social affairs
Word processing services
Writing services

Even these are often too general. One security consultant, for example, may be a specialist in security *devices*—locks, alarms, barriers, safes, surveillance equipment, and other such items—while another is a specialist in security *forces*—guards, patrolling, background checking, and other security measures based on direct human surveillance. Most of the categories listed can be divided into several subcategories. Career and vocational counselors, for example, may easily specialize in several areas. There are many kinds of engineers (e.g., civil, construction, mechanical, chemical, electrical, electronic, stress, and industrial), and these are all subdivided into many narrower specialties. Designers likewise fit into all kinds of categories (e.g. package designers, lighting designers, presentation designers, etc.) as do most of the specialists listed here. In fact it is a rare field today that will not support a well-experienced specialist as a consultant in that field.

There are many examples of the opportunities to turn your own special knowledge—which does not have to be in a technical field—into a consulting specialty and practice. One such example concerned an administrator of the General Services Administration (GSA) of the federal government, Jay Solomon. One of GSA's major divisions is its Public Buildings Service, which handles much of the construction and real estate management of federal agencies. Solomon's own experience as a businessman who had had many buildings constructed was that a principal maintenance problem was leaking roofs. He believed that if he could develop superior roofing designs and procedures he would have drastically reduced maintenance problems. Accordingly, he launched a major campaign to find roofing specialists, whom he recruited as consultants to support his goal of improving designs and methods for roofing public buildings.

Another example involves an engineering discipline known as value engineering or value analysis. This discipline has been adopted by many government agencies, the Department of Defense, the Public Buildings Service, and the Federal Supply Service, among others. In these latter agencies the discipline has become known as value management to broaden its applications and stress its basic value as a management tool. Value engineering produced an association, the Society of American Value Engineers, known by the acronym SAVE, which summarizes a basic objective of the discipline. SAVE developed a certification program, and many of the resulting certified value specialists set up shop as consultants. Even then, there were specialties within the specialty, as value engineering champions produced "Design to Cost" and "Life Cycle Costing" methodologies, producing specialists in these aspects. And at least one such consultant also publishes a newsletter on the subject.

Résumé services are another example of creating a consulting opportunity. Some of these services advise clients on how to best organize and present their (the clients') experience and other qualifications. Some counsel on careers and job hunting.

Publishing consultants are another example. A former bookstore manager, Hubert Bermont, of Glenelg, Maryland, built a successful consulting practice as a specialist in book publishing. He then went on to take his own advice by building The Consultant's Library, his own publishing firm, specializing in books for and about consultants and consulting.

On the other hand, Marilyn and Tom Ross, of Saguache, Colorado, became consultants in publishing one's own books, but they also conduct seminars and sell books by mail (the *Maverick Mail Order Bookstore*). And to prove that location is not of the essence—that remote locations need not be a bar to success—consider that Marilyn and Tom live in such a remote part of Colorado that they were unable to get a telephone installed unless they were willing to pay about $25,000 to have a line run to them!

One problem in consulting is deciding just how specialized you should be. There is at least a general relationship between the degree to which you specialize and your marketing success. You must be a specialist to be qualified in clients' eyes as a true consultant, and the degree to which you specialize determines how many competitors you have. It also determines the size of your market—that is, how many potential clients, or people with problems matching your specialty, are out there awaiting your services. Choosing the right degree of specialization represents a trade-off, with success depending on your finding the right compromise.

Some individuals who have broad experience and are highly versatile change their specialties, chameleonlike, according to the market opportunities of the moment! This is a fairly common practice among those who devote themselves to accepting temporary assignments as "job shoppers." The typical methods for finding such positions and qualifying for acceptance make this option quite viable. The individual needs to have more than one résumé or the ability to create the right résumé spontaneously for each opportunity. None of the résumés gives false testimony, but each presents a different kind of experience and capability as a consulting specialty.

Actually, the clients inspire and are largely responsible for this because many of them go overboard in the degree of specialization they call for as qualifications. A client seeking technical writers, for example, may demand that applicants be familiar with some given specification. But the competent technical writer usually has no serious problem working with any specification.

For some consultants this "adaptability" poses an ethical problem. Is it honest to be different kinds of a specialist on different occasions? Is that versatility or is it opportunism? These are questions you must answer for yourself.

The evidence suggests that few people ever set out to become consultants; apparently most become consultants as the result of chance circumstances. In fact, in some cases the transition into consulting is so gradual that the individual hardly realizes that he or she has become a consultant until the transition is complete. In many cases there never is a specific decision to become a consultant; circumstances force the decision on the individual.

My own case is such an example. I was a free-lance writer undertaking a variety of writing projects for government agencies and other clients, after a career in high-tech companies contracting with the government. In this career I had served as engineer, technical writer, proposal specialist, director of marketing, and general manager, among other positions. Friends and acquaintances in quest of government and private sector contracts and knowing of my success in winning government contracts over the years often asked my advice and sometimes even asked for assistance in writing proposals and other aspects of pursuing government contracts. Like many people, I always found it difficult to refuse. But eventually this interfered with my writing work, and I was forced to begin begging off, pleading lack of time and the necessity to earn my own living. To my surprise, most requestors immediately offered to pay me for my time to consult with them as an expert! They wanted help enough to pay for it.

Many others become consultants as a result of certain specific developments, some related to the many technological revolutions of recent decades, which created so many consultants in engineering and scientific fields, but others related to other developments. For example, Lyndon B. Johnson's administration, with its War on Poverty projects and related programs, inspired the creation of many new consultants in poverty, education, housing, and a number of other fields and activities related directly and indirectly to combating poverty in the United States. Most of these new consultants were sociologists, psychologists, economists, educators, educational technologists, and others in social sciences and humanities. The other programs launched to further the cause of civil rights and to reduce the worst aspects of discrimination and persecution of minorities also served to foster many new consulting specialties. The advent of the new communications media—TV and orbiting satellites–created new situations (aside from the technological ones), such as the impact of these media on political campaigns. This inspired the rise of a great many political consultants and "image" consultants.

The government's programs to reduce and control environmental pollution, to find new sources of energy while conserving conventional sources, to further the development of houses for everyone, to improve education, and to provide better mass transportation, have been responsible for creating even more consulting specialties. So it is certainly not surprising that consulting is definitely a growth industry; circumstances compel it. It is an industry that is doing more than merely *growing;* it is virtually *exploding.*

WHAT DOES IT TAKE TO BE A CONSULTANT?

As a consultant you need two sets of skills. First, you need that set of skills that relates to your professional field. Remember that consulting is not a profession itself; it is a way of practicing your profession. Second, you need the basic consulting skills (e.g., listening, analyzing, synthesizing, presenting, etc.). If you are an independent consultant, you need two additional sets of skills—those skills relevant to marketing your services and to administering your practice successfully.

I will not address professional skills. I assume here that you are entirely proficient in your own professional field. It is in the other three sets of skills, and especially in marketing, that I offer help in becoming a successful consultant. We will preview those three subjects briefly here and in much greater detail later.

Consulting Skills

The consultant must have or develop certain skills and abilities that are necessary to consulting generally and to independent consulting especially, regardless of those professional skills you also require. For example, the consultant must have good listening, analyzing, and synthesizing skills—that is, the consultant must be able to analyze symptoms, identify the problem, and synthesize a solution or approach to solution. Consulting also requires abilities to make effective presentations, both in person and in writing. And consulting independently also requires an ability to "interface" effectively with a client—that is, to build an image of competence and authority, to win the client's respect, and even to establish a relationship of mutual respect.

All of these are necessary capabilities for success as an independent consultant. However, although I have divided these sets of skills and functions into four sets for purposes of discussion, in practice they are not so easily separated. They are, in fact, intertwined and even interdependent. Some of the skills so necessary to conducting a satisfactory consulting assignment are the same skills that help you market successfully and even administer successfully.

Management and Administration of the Independent Consultancy

Strange as it may seem, management and administration of your practice as an independent consultant are probably the least important of the four sets of skills and functions identified here. That is not to say that they are unimportant; however, the other skills are even more important, especially marketing skills. The reasoning is simple: it is a rare venture that fails when it is achieving a satisfactory volume of sales at prices that enable the taking of at least a modest profit. Profitable ventures can and do usually survive all other problems, even problems of poor management and poor administration. The reverse, however, is not true: no amount of highly able management and administration can save a venture that is not succeeding in making enough sales to cover costs and produce a slight profit. Although marketing is the most important set of skills for success—even for mere survival—all the skills must be brought into play in building and maintaining a successful consulting practice. The following example illustrates this.

One of my valued clients is a conglomerate, headquartered in New York City and comprising 20 or more companies. They had done some business with the government but had never actively pursued government business. However, they decided to look into the prospect of chasing government contracts, which led them to send two people to a seminar I offered in marketing to the government. As a result I was invited to have lunch with the executive appointed by the corporation to head up their new government marketing division to discuss what I might do for them. As an immediate result of that luncheon meeting and *my own aggressive follow up*, several things happened:

1. I was retained to help prepare a capability brochure for the corporation. In fact, they provided a draft, which I was to critique and offer contributions to.
2. I wrote a proposal for one of the companies.
3. I delivered an in-house seminar to a group of marketing people from a number of the companies.
4. I continued to help several of the companies prepare proposals.
5. I was called on periodically for miscellaneous chores.

This means that I was a good listener and analyst. I listened carefully to the client's views, analyzed the real and perceived needs, and responded with offers that I thought were relevant and that the client would agree were relevant. The client never grants you the right to make the decisions, only to make recommendations. It is critically important that you consider the client's orientation–including any biases the client has—in making those recommendations.

Marketing Skills

The marketing challenge appears to be simply finding and winning clients for typical consulting assignments; at least this appears to be true until experience teaches you that this is an idealized view. Novice independent consultants view the marketing problem this way partly because they also view consulting as the practice of advising distressed clients on how to solve their problems. Novices envision sitting with the client in his or her comfortable office, listening to a litany of woes and pleas for help, dictating a substantial daily fee as the price of assistance, and having a grateful client agree immediately, after which a contract is signed and the consultant renders the wisdom that will solve the client's problems.

The marketing process, based on this rationale, consists of finding prospects with appropriate problems, winning the prospect's consent to become a client, and negotiating a suitable daily or hourly rate of compensation.

It seldom works quite that way. Prospects often have a quite different view of what they need than the consultant does. They know they need help of some sort, but they approach consulting with some skepticism and apprehension. They tend to resist agreeing to an hourly or daily rate in what they deem an open-ended arrangement; they want the benefit of consulting services at bargain-counter prices. And even when you succeed in winning a few contracts in this way, they occur irregularly, so that you find yourself in the feast-or-famine cycle.

For example, the corporate client who started by retaining me to help write their capability brochure knew next to nothing of what a capability brochure should normally contain; they were apparently greatly influenced in writing that brochure by the copy in their corporate annual report. The brochure was all wrong for their purposes. Yet, to persuade them to change it to what it ought to be meant criticizing what they had done, hardly an easy thing to do. The conflict is between treating the client with great care and doing your work honestly and ethically. It calls for a great deal of tact to suggest and explain the need for drastic changes without condemning what has been already done.

Note, too, the variety of services I provided. Although perhaps the most valuable direct service I can render in many cases is actual proposal writing, I often find it necessary to spend a great deal of time selling the client on the need to do what I have done or propose to do in and with the proposal. My typical client is an intelligent, capable, and successful executive, scientist, or engineer, with ideas of his or her own. They require me to be honest in my views, but I must also be prepared to explain and justify my recommendations, especially when they clash with the client's ideas!

All of this points to the need for versatility in your capabilities and services and marketing them appropriately. In the case I just cited, had I stubbornly insisted that my consulting service was restricted to advising clients on government marketing, I probably would have received about 20 percent of the work. Even if I had insisted that my services were restricted to advising and/or writing and leading proposal efforts, I would have closed the door on much of the work, and perhaps on all of it, if the client had decided to seek a consultant more amenable to meeting all his needs. This brings up a marketing problem of a special kind: how specialized should you be?

Versatility versus Specialization

Your main specialty as a consultant may be in a subject area, a skill, or some combination of these. All fields grow increasingly diverse as time goes on. I have seen "radio" become "electronics" and grow, along with aeronautical design, into serious and highly respected engineering disciplines of their own, disciplines of growing significance and importance in this increasingly automated world.

There is no doubt that this trend will continue, and other new specialties will evolve, some within a larger and established parent discipline, some based on entirely new fields, which are opening at an ever-increasing rate today. For example, the work of Stanford B. Ovshinsky in Troy, Michigan represents what is now being rapidly accepted as a complete breakthrough into an entirely new and exciting area of solid-state physics. This is almost certain to create a new field for scientists and engineers. And even then engineers and consultants will specialize in different kinds of devices and different applications—that is, in different specialties within the new field.

THE AVENUES OF SPECIALIZATION

The degree to which consultants specialize varies widely. In my own case I tend to generalize within the field of proposal consultation and writing, but I am the exception; most proposal consultants specialize in given subject fields—such as engineering and technical (NASA and military/defense projects, especially), social science projects, training development, health programs, or other specialized areas, based primarily on the consultant's prior career experience. On the other hand, I work almost invariably on proposals submitted in pursuit of contracts, whereas there are consultants who serve clients pursuing grants, which usually also require proposals.

As in all things, there are advantages and disadvantages in versatility as there are in a high degree of specialization. You must be guided in making your choices by your personal judgment, your objectives, your standards, and perhaps most of all by your experience, which is really the final arbiter.

Many Consulting Specialties Evolve

Initial decisions regarding avenues of specialization are or should be always regarded as premises, to be tried and tested by experience—in other words, trial and error. You start at some position, one of the extremes or midstream, and you make adjustments as your experience reveals the need for adjustments, until you achieve the point at which you are satisfied with the results. This means keeping an open mind. Set out at the beginning with the knowledge that your first premises are almost certain to be considerably less than perfect for your purposes and be prepared to learn from experience.

Making mistakes of judgment and learning from them is crucial. For example, after I had begun to offer seminars, I began to build a reputation as something of a specialist in this field of proposal writing and found myself drawing inquiries from large corporations who were interested in having me deliver an in-house training seminar in proposal writing. Each time I received such an inquiry I cheerfully calculated the costs for customizing my seminar to the individual client's needs and quoted accordingly.

The results were disappointing. I failed to win a single contract for an in-house seminar. Obviously I was doing something wrong, and my judgment was that these prospective clients were unwilling to pay the price for customizing my seminar for them. I therefore switched tactics and began to respond to such inquiries with a proposal to deliver my standard seminar, customized for them (but only insofar as I could do so spontaneously in my delivery, and principally through my choice of illustrative anecdotes and case histories), without extra cost.

I immediately began to win virtually all such contracts and still present a number of customized, in-house seminars every year. Moreover, whereas I began doing them at the equivalent of my daily consulting fee, I soon learned that this was a mistake and raised the cost. Interestingly enough, I soon learned that the clients did not object to the cost and apparently never had; they objected only to the idea of paying a fee for customizing the seminar.

It is only from experience that you can learn these things. Remember that no matter what your general specialty as a consultant is, either originally or as it ultimately evolves, you should be alert for opportunities to develop specialties within your consulting framework. In fact, it is not at all unusual for a consultant to eventually come to a specialty quite different from that which he or she embraced in the beginning. For that matter, it is not unusual for any business venture to evolve into something quite different from its origin. Some rather large companies do not today resemble their beginnings even remotely.

A Special Case of Evolutionary Change

Changes in consulting specialties are not always the result of gradual evolution. Other factors bring change also, sometimes rather abruptly. The ability to switch fields rapidly and frequently—having a number of different résumés on hand—is one way some versatile consultants respond to targets of opportunity and maximize their prospects for assignments. Since many consulting specialties are suggested by and spring up out of new developments, such as equal opportunity and civil rights programs, watching for new developments is also important. However, these conditions and circumstances do not always represent permanent change. In many cases the programs and influences prove to be transient and fleeting.

Such has been the case with many federal programs, some of them the pet programs of presidents, but disowned by successor presidents, as in the case of Lyndon B. Johnson's War on Poverty and Great Society programs. In the mid to late sixties the area surrounding 19th and M Streets NW in downtown Washington, D.C. fairly swarmed with consultants specializing in poverty and education programs conducted by government agencies. Even such major corporations as Xerox, General Electric, RCA, and IBM created (and sometimes acquired through mergers and purchases) special divisions (at great expense) to participate in these ventures.

A few years later, with changes in administrations, the excitement subsided, many of the great new business organizations were quietly dismantled and disbanded, and most of the independent consultants found it necessary to move on to other interests, many to new consulting specialties and other ventures.

Very much the same situation was created by the establishment of the U.S. Postal Service as a government corporation. After years of free-spending programs for consulting services to support the Postal Service Training and Development Institute, harsh economic realities—that is, the failure of the Postal Service to pay its own way through revenues—forced the sharp curtailment of the programs and especially of the contracting out for services.

The effects of such events are obvious, of course. The consultant who has been highly specialized must move on or adapt in some other way, while those less highly specialized may well survive such catastrophes. For example, the reading specialist—an educator/-trainer in reading skills for the functionally illiterate—may be totally without resources in the face of an abrupt shutdown of a major government project, whereas the educational technology consultant—a developer of training programs generally—can probably turn to other government training programs, which abound generally.

The Basis for Specialization

A rather lengthy list of consulting specialties offered earlier tended almost entirely to classify consultancies by general industries as fields of activity (e.g., accounting, taxes, travel, club management, etc.) rather than by individual occupations or skills (e.g., accountant, dietician, housewares buyer, conference arranger, etc.) A few such listings are offered here as a comparison with the earlier list to illustrate the difference.

Accountant
Architect
Auditor
Copy writer
Soils chemist
Appraiser
Arbitrator
Automation designer
Banquet planner
Career counselor
Contract administrator
Drug prevention specialist
Editor
Fire-fighting equipment specialist
Grants writer
Hotel manager
Insurance expert
Merger advisor/negotiator
Municipal services expert
Office procedures designer
Public relations writer
Researcher
System Analyst

This focus on individual skill is quite important to resolving your own definition of what you offer to do for clients, for that inevitably becomes the chief focus of all your marketing. Even so, these latter listings are rather broad and could be narrowed further in their focus, taking into account the individual skills you offer to your clients. A technical writer, for example, must sometimes demonstrate to a prospective client that he or she is a "radar writer" or "computer writer," because many clients are convinced that it is necessary to be that highly specialized.

Another important factor to remember is that truth is a subjective quantity, and in marketing the only "truth" that counts is the client's truth. No matter what you do, it is likely that the client will mentally tag and label you. For example, in my mind I am truly a marketing strategist, but clients tend to perceive me as a proposal writer or as a lecturer on the subject, depending on their own needs. Moreover, most of my clients associate me with government marketing only. That is understandable, considering my extensive experience in that field, but the real reason for the perception is that most of my clients do not perceive a need for help in marketing commercially. Government marketing, however, seems to be something of a mystery. However, many prospective clients, especially those in marketing and sales departments, would resist retaining me to help them in marketing commercially because they would regard that as an intrusion into their own domains and a lack of faith in their own abilities. But government marketing is different, and they do not feel it a blow to their egos in admitting to a need in this special and difficult field or to my special qualifications. So in the end it does serve my own best interests to encourage that view of my special abilities.

You are always the victim—and perhaps sometimes the beneficiary—of the client's own biases. One problem is that of being pigeonholed by clients according to their needs, regardless of how you represent your skills and specialties. For example, when doing any kind of custom writing job for engineers or other professional people and executives, I have often encountered the bias most have that they can write as well as any "expert." Many refuse to acknowledge writing as a special skill or talent, and so tend to treat the professional writer's work casually and almost with disdain.

Another typical problem involves fees. One prospect was outraged at the consulting fee I stated. "That's too much money for a hired writer," she stormed.

"But you are not retaining me as a writer," I tried to explain. "I am a specialist in developing marketing strategies for proposals to win government contracts. The writing is incidental and not what people retain me for at all."

It was futile. I was unable to make my point because the other party was simply unwilling to accept it under any circumstances. She insisted that I was a writer for hire and asking too much money for my services as a writer.

What this means is that you must recognize that you do not always have an entirely free choice in deciding what you are and what you offer. You must work at understanding the client's mind set and prejudices, and you may have to tailor yourself and your offerings accordingly, to win the client over.

In short, how you represent yourself and what you offer are not decisions to be made without analysis and deliberation, especially an examination of how the clients tend to perceive you and what you do and—even more important—how clients *prefer* to view you and what you offer.

That is not as cynical as it sounds, and it is not an exhortation to mislead or deceive your clients. It is simple realism to structure your presentations to complement your prospective clients' attitudes.

2

Why Do So Many Consultants Fail? How To Succeed

All you need in this life is ignorance and confidence, and then Success is sure.

—Samuel Clemens (Mark Twain), 1887

THE SHADOW OF FAILURE

I am surprised as much as I am delighted when I find a new independent consultant still in independent practice a year after launching the practice. That I am surprised to hear that yet another independent consultant has survived his or her first year is indicative of the high casualty rate among new, independent consultant practices. The real tragedy is that most of the failures are unnecessary; with just a little foresight and caution most of the consultants could have survived that critical first year.

Every year I receive many handsomely printed and dignified announcements of new consulting practices, along with embossed business cards, brochures, letters, and other trappings of the new practice. I also receive many telephone calls from newly launched independent consultants, advising me of their new ventures and offering to be available to me for future support and/or co-ventures in consulting.

Unfortunately, later in the year I also receive a large number of résumés and offers from many of these newly established consultants, offering me their services to support my own consulting projects. Most such offers are thinly disguised appeals for help, many of them almost in desperation. Such appeals indicate trouble ahead for the individual, suggesting that the individual has no work and therefore no income and few prospects for new assignments. It means, too, that in most cases survival of the individual as an independent consultant is very much in question.

In a great many of each of these cases I learn later that the individual has joined the staff of a company, often that of a former client. Of course, that is not necessarily a tragic fate; many consultants win excellent positions that way and are quite content with the result. In fact, some independent consultants enter consulting with the intention of remaining only temporarily. But it is somewhat tragic for the individual who had counted on building a solid independent consulting practice and who must now admit failure.

There are many reasons for such failures. The Small Business Administration and almost anyone else with substantial entrepreneurial experience will agree that the first year of a new venture is almost always the most critical one, the year that witnesses by far the majority of business failures. This does not guarantee permanent job security, but the failure rate for those ventures that survive the first year is far lower. Survive the first year, and your chances for overall success improve considerably. The third year is the watershed year; survive that and you probably can count yourself a success for the long term.

Even for those who do not survive these critical years, the experiences are not always lost opportunities, as observed by Howard Shenson, a prominent lecturer and writer on the subject of consulting. He reports on a consultant who faltered three times but was back on his feet and trying again a fourth time. This individual observed that his first failed effort taught him the lesson of accounts receivable, or too much credit extended. His second attempt taught him the lesson of accounts payable, or failure to control spending. And his third unsuccessful run taught him the lesson of overhead—too much of it. Now, trying for the fourth time, he was hopeful that the education he had paid so much for—the mistakes he had learned not to repeat—was complete and he would now succeed.

Howard Ruff, author of the best selling book *How to Prosper During the Coming Bad Years,* also believes that failure is a natural step in the process of becoming a successful entrepreneur. He told interviewer Dennis Blank ("Carving a Niche in the Market," *Business*

Age, July/August 1986) that failing "was the best thing that ever happened to me" and that "people who fear failure will never succeed at anything."

There is a great deal of evidence that most of the successful entrepreneurs are individuals who failed a time or two—or even several—before they found their major success. It appears that failure is the school that teaches success. But this is not surprising. Formal education cannot teach success in the business world; here the only education that works reliably is the education of *experience*. Although there are some exceptions (e.g., those who are born successful or have success thrust upon them), the secret of success is usually the experience of and learning from various tries—mistakes, if you wish to call bad guesses and inaccurate estimates by that name. There is no universal and unfailing formula for success; that is, there really is no failure as such, but there are the normal mistakes, sometimes painful, usually costly, but always educational, if you permit them to be. Remember that education is never truly free; it has a cost. But success has a cost also.

WHAT IS FAILURE?

In this philosophy, there is no failure; there are setbacks, and there is experience and education, but these are taken in stride as anticipated events that result in a constant movement toward eventual success.

Failure is easy to define; it is quitting, giving up, surrendering to setbacks. Since it is almost certain that you will have setbacks while you are learning what works and what does not, you can succeed only if you pick yourself up each time you suffer a setback, digest what you have learned in that latest encounter, and go on. Success results from *knowing* that you must eventually learn what does and does not work for you and thus find the right methods and practices.

THE COMMON MISTAKES OF NEOPHYTE CONSULTANTS

There are many scenarios illustrating the start of new consulting practices. Unfortunately, most of them illustrate a pattern of setbacks and frustration. But while setbacks are often positive influences in building a practice, many can be avoided when you know what they are and how they are caused. In any case, let's examine a few typical cases. These are all factual accounts and are absolutely typical of the mistakes a great many consultants make.

Jordan is one of those incurable optimists, unusually naïve and trusting if we judge him by the exceedingly narrow base on which he ventured forth to do battle as an entrepreneur. The base was narrow both in terms of the services he offered potential clients and the market he addressed.

Jordan is a journalist, with experience on several newspapers. As a journalist he had learned a good bit about public relations, writing news releases, and planting stories in newspapers. He offered a few tips to fellow members at the country club where he played golf. As the word got around that he could give some of the professionals and businesspeople good public relations ideas, he found himself besieged with request for free advice. When he begged off, pleading lack of time, several of his friends and acquaintances insisted that they would pay for his time. After a few good experiences, Jordan took the plunge. He quit the paper and became a PR consultant. But he thought he had to "do things right." He spent a great deal of money for a stock of impressive stationery and elaborate brochures, he furnished a plush office suite, with an anteroom for a secretary, in a downtown office building, and he went into considerable debt on the strength of only a single client with a firm contract, and those other, rather vague, prospects.

That one client proved to represent far less business than Jordan had expected, and most of the others who promised him work lost interest rapidly when the advice was no longer free. Jordan soon found himself staring at the walls in his quiet office, wondering where he would get next month's office rent.

Henry is a talented industrial designer, winner of several awards for his excellent work, known to many clients of his employer's company, and especially well known for his creative designs of corporate logos. In fact, many of those clients demanded that Henry be assigned to design their logos and packages; many even made the project conditional on Henry being in charge of it and handling all the creative concepts.

Several times clients hinted to Henry that they would like him to moonlight for them, but Henry never felt right about doing that. One of the major clients said, "Look, Henry, if you ever decide to start your own shop come to me; I'll use your services."

So Henry finally quit and started his own shop to design logos and counsel corporate clients on package design. That first client kept his word, and kept Henry busy for nearly six profitable months. But it finally ended, and Henry went in quest of other clients. He looked first among all those other corporate people he had known and who had wanted him to moonlight for them. However, none of them had any immediate work. And although some could possibly have used him for other kinds of industrial design work, Henry had decided to specialize in logos and packaging, so he did not respond to those leads. Getting new business was not quite as easy as he had thought. He, too, soon found himself studying his dwindling funds and calculating how much longer he could hold out.

John is a somewhat different kind of case. A Ph.D.—really *Dr.* John—he is a computer specialist. Let go by his company when their largest contract ended (quite a common event in high-tech industries, unfortunately), John contacted his business friends and acquaintances to let them know that he was now available on a consulting basis.

It happens that John's skills as a technical/professional specialist who writes really well, thinks clearly, and devises strategies, made him an excellent candidate for helping clients write proposals in search of contracts. He found a number of clients eager to retain him to do just that, after just a few telephone calls, and he was soon busy as many hours a week as he wished to work, at rates he stipulated. He even took in a partner to help him handle the large workload.

It lasted for several months. But proposal writing, while it is a year-around activity, also has its peak seasons, when organizations who normally write many proposals need extra help. Even those who do only occasional proposal writing do not have the expert skills on staff and must hire consultants. John's failure to recognize and plan for the peaks and valleys of the workload was John's undoing. He neither diversified the services he offered nor did he do any serious marketing throughout those peak months; he was too busy writing proposals and invoicing clients to give even his thoughts, much less his time, to searching for new clients. It was a matter of time before he would be forced to seek a salaried position again.

Note the common mistakes, the most serious of which is the general failure to market until business slows or comes to a halt. But the failure to diversify is also a severe handicap to your new consulting practice, which affects your marketing in several ways: (1) it limits your market prospects to only those who need that single, special service you offer; (2) it limits the size of your projects to that single service; and (3) it handicaps you against competitors who offer a wider diversity of services than you do.

THE BASIC TRADE-OFFS

We make trade-offs throughout our lives, giving up one thing to gain another or otherwise compromising between alternatives, such as the trade-off between what we would really prefer and what we can afford in the houses we buy, the cars we drive, and the clothes we wear. For example, one of my consultant friends, Al R., makes a great deal of money every year but has traded off having a normal home life because he must travel and be away from home more than 300 days a year to earn that money. I sampled that lifestyle for a time, but eventually I refused to make that trade-off, despite the greater income possibilities. On the other hand, a few years ago I did trade off the ego-boosting impact of a luxurious downtown office suite for the convenience, lower cost, and tax benefits of an office in my own home.

Most trade-offs are deliberate decisions. *You* decide what the alternatives are and what compromises you will make. *You* decide what you will pay or sacrifice for the gains you want. And this applies generally to your practice as a consultant—the more highly specialized the expertise and services you offer, the more sharply targeted your marketing and the higher the fees you can charge (theoretically, at least). But this usually means a more limited or restricted market and may mean a more difficult search for clients. Of course, the reverse is true; making your offering a more generalized one (e.g., a range of services, instead of a single, sharply defined and highly specialized service) broadens its appeal and increases the number of prospects. Of course, it also increases the number of direct competitors with whom you must compete for your contracts, and it tends to decrease the size of the fees you can charge, at least in theory.

A somewhat more subtle effect is the psychological one. Broadening your field of claimed expertise tends to lessen your credibility as a consultant because clients tend to equate consulting with specialization and so consider the most highly specialized consultants to be the most highly qualified ones. This is an important consideration because you inevitably must sell to the client's perception, not your own. And that is what makes the image you manage to create a critical one. But the trade-offs you make sometimes affect that image. In my case I can offer clients a special knowledge of government contracting and extensive successful experience in it, and I would love to confine my consulting to thoughtfully stroking my beard as I counsel clients who are in pursuit of government contracts. But in a practical sense much of my consulting work requires me to supply that expert knowledge as actual participation in the writing of proposals, which may mislead prospective clients as to the nature of what I do to help them. In fact, I find it necessary to trade off between that desirable image of the scholarly expert counselor and the marketing generalist, writing, lecturing, presenting seminars, training clients' staffs, doing market research, and several other chores as part of the marketing services I offer. They are all part of consulting, and the refusal to offer a *complete* consulting service has hindered many independent consultants in their efforts to build a successful practice. The question of what to trade off is one you must answer for yourself. However, when it comes to the breadth and diversity of the services you offer, you must be guided principally by what it takes to survive, especially in the early months. Ultimately, you will establish a pattern, as you discover what services are most marketable, most profitable, and most suitable to your own talents, skills, and desires. You will almost surely wind up with a far different set of services than you visualized when you started a career as an independent consultant.

MARKETING

One basic mistake many newcomers to consulting make is offering too narrow a range of services; however, it is equally common to market to too narrow a range of potential clients and, even worse, to fail to understand the role of marketing in the consulting enterprise. Often an individual launches a consulting enterprise on the basis of a single client or two and assumes that the quest for additional clients need not be a concern until the day more clients are needed. It is only after leaving a job, making an investment, often incurring serious debt, and dedicating many months of effort that the new practitioner begins to discover that most clients and contracts do not come as easily as that first one or two did.

Probably the deadliest of all marketing mistakes is the assumption that the right time to market is when business is slow and you have the idle time to devote to marketing. Unfortunately, many people reason that it is a waste of money and valuable time to market when you have lots of business. However, the results of marketing efforts are seldom immediate. In fact there is some lag between the marketing effort and the resulting sales in every enterprise, even in ordinary retail sales, but this is especially true in the field of professional services. The gap can be many months, for a variety of reasons. Even the most effective marketing of consulting services is likely to pay off substantially with contracts only months later, months during which income may be near zero.

THE TEN LAWS OF SURVIVAL

In a sense this entire book is focused on survival, and you will be reading many highly specific items concerning survival as well as success. Unless you are extraordinarily fortunate, you are almost certain to come face to face with many disappointing and sometimes disheartening realities. Some common pitfalls in the consulting business include:

- The deceptively easy first assignment turned out to be a real bear. It almost forced you to give up the idea of being a consultant before you got it under control and completed it.
- That pleasant fellow you accepted as a client without insisting on a written agreement fought you every inch of the way, constantly misrepresenting what you thought was a clear understanding between the two of you and making you fight to get paid.
- That struggling little company that was so unconcerned about the cost of your services proved to be unconcerned because they didn't have any money anyway. You never did get paid or you settled for less than the full fee and had to pay an attorney or collection agency a third of that for helping you collect even that much.
- One of those associates you brought in to help you handle a project that needed three people was incompetent. You had to cover for him and work extra hours so you wouldn't "look bad" to the client. And the other associate you hired had tried to steal the client from you.
- The accountant who set up your books cost you a great deal more than the original estimate; he was full of long-faced and regretful explanations.
- The printer botched your stationery, and you had to have it redone.

- The answering service lost several important messages that probably cost you a client or two.
- Almost everything you bought to furnish and equip your office cost more than you planned.

There are a few laws of survival that may help:

1. The first law of survival is to *expect* everything to go wrong and *plan* for it by having alternatives already planned and ready to be implemented when needed.
2. The second law of survival is to make $50 mistakes, not $500 ones. Mistakes provide you with the education you need, and you should fully expect to make them, but you can learn just as much from the cheaper ones.
3. The third law of survival is to avoid or at least delay every expenditure possible. Take 10, 20, or 30 days to pay your bills. Use the old typewriter a little longer. Type over the old telephone number and type in the new one on your old letterheads. Do your own filing. Get that downtown office next year. Don't be in a big hurry to order the new brochure. Shop around for a better price; printers' prices vary considerably.
4. The fourth law of survival is to never refuse a job you can earn a profit on. Accept that small job that is definitely yours if you want it, and never mind that big job you were promised; it will probably never materialize, anyway, and you will have lost the small one that you can have now. Forget those vague promises; only the bird in the hand counts.
5. The fifth law of survival is to never get so successful that you turn down a job or fail to make time for marketing because you are already too busy or overworked. The failure to market when you are busy is the certain harbinger of ultimate disaster; tomorrow's contract is just as important as the one you are now working on.
6. The sixth law of survival is forget the clock and the calendar too. Forty-hour weeks and two-week vacations are things of the past, as far as you are concerned, at least until you are firmly established. You'll rest and vacation when business is slow, if you put in the overtime when you have the work. Work now and rest later.

7. The seventh law of survival is don't start believing your own press clippings—don't overrate your own importance and become too much the specialist. You are never too "big" or important to earn a dollar doing honest consulting work, even if you think the task it is not as prestigious or upscale as you had envisioned.
8. The eighth law of survival is to remember that you are worth what you cost. Discounting your rates when you are badly in need of the work is not only unprofessional, but it demeans you in the eyes of the client and eventually damages you, as word gets around that clients can bargain with you for your best rate. There are other ways to help the customer economize and win the job without compromising your fees or your professionalism. Don't be misled by clients' promises of lots of business later, recommendations to friends, and so on. Those are bargaining tactics used by some clients, and you should not be misled by them.
9. The ninth law of survival is to be totally businesslike in your dealings. Stick to your fee schedule and unless there is good reason to make exceptions (e.g., a formal purchase order or letter of commitment from a large and well-established company with an A-1 credit rating), ask for a retainer as "earnest money" upon signing an agreement. Always ask clients to sign a simple agreement with you, explaining the commitments of both parties clearly.
10. The tenth law of survival, and in many ways the most important law, is to be totally ethical. That means being completely honest, respecting and keeping confidences, safeguarding clients' proprietary information from unauthorized disclosure, and rendering honest bills for your services.

Experience, Education, and $50 Mistakes

It is probably an apocryphal tale, but more than one executive is credited with having said, "I know that one-half of my advertising budget is wasted, but my problem is that I don't know which half it is." Advertising is one of many areas in which we spend money hopefully, without any reliable means for estimating the outcome to determine whether the expenditure is likely to be a worthwhile investment. It is hardly surprising that many of those expenditures do not pay off adequately, leading us to characterize those investments as mistakes rather than as the price of education, which they are.

You will make many decisions that will not turn out as well as you had hoped. Knowing that you are buying an education, why not take a small advertisement in the yellow pages, rather than a large one, if you insist on trying that medium? If it works, you can always increase it next year. Why buy 1,000 expensive, two-color, embossed or engraved business cards and stationery when you don't even know whether you will soon be changing your address, telephone number, business name, copy, or services offered? You won't lose any clients by ordering 500 plain white cards and stationery, tastefully printed on adequate—not costly—stock. Why buy a $5,000 word processor, when you can start with a $1,500 system or even with a good typewriter?

Consider establishing your office in your own home, if it is a practicable idea. If it is not—and admittedly there are cases where it is not—you do not need to set up offices in the most expensive part of town or in the most recently built (and thus usually the most costly) office building. You can almost always find something a bit more modest and yet thoroughly adequate.

You never need be self-conscious, apologetic, or self-deprecating about running your enterprise on a sound financial footing and economizing wherever you can. On the contrary, many of your clients will be impressed that you are level-headed and practical. That is not a bad image to acquire.

There Are No Small Jobs

In the theatre they say that there are no small parts; only small actors and actresses. In that same vein, there are no small consulting jobs. I don't have a $5,000 or $10,000 proposal-writing job every month. I sometimes paid my office rent by helping a student polish a doctoral dissertation or ghostwriting a marketing brochure for an executive.

I have clients who, although they have adequate staffs to write their proposals, still like to have me come in and help them analyze the request and recommend a strategy. Or they retain me to simply organize and lead their team and possibly write just a key section or two. Some clients ask me back later to review and critique their proposal drafts. But I also have clients who ask me to come in and present one-day or two-day training seminars to their staffs. I consider that a part of my consulting service and enjoy doing it as well.

Jeffrey Lant, the well-known management consultant in Cambridge, Massachusetts, found a large market for the frequent books he writes and publishes to counsel and aid other consultants. He has made this a major activity of his practice, which includes seminars and general consulting services. Gerre Jones, an Albuquerque, New Mexico marketing consultant, undertakes a variety of consulting assignments for professional design firms, but also writes prolifically, publishes some of his own writings, offers workshops, and keeps busy in other ways. Steve Lanning, a marketing consultant specializing in direct mail, publishes the *Consulting Opportunities Journal*. Dave Voracek, whose firm, The Marketing Department, provides a variety of services to clients, also publishes a newsletter and started an adjunct service called The Design Department.

The list could go on and on; however, the message here, is that successful consultants are, in most cases, individuals who are enterprising, versatile, and unafraid to diversify and exploit opportunities. They all agree that the independent consultant is well-advised to be conservative in expenditures, as well as in inflating his or her self-image.

THE CONSULTANT'S IMAGE

By now, I hope, you understand that your own image of what you are is not the critical one; only the client's or prospective client's image of you really matters, in a business sense. It is important that you recognize this, for you must understand the client's perspective: The client often does not perceive the arrangement as one of *buying* a product or service from you, but rather as *hiring* you temporarily. Far too often, unfortunately, the client tends to regard you as an employee, albeit a temporary one, rather than as an independent entrepreneur entitled to function as an equal and independent entrepreneur furnishing a service of value.

This misunderstanding of your role can lead to an unpleasant and unhappy consultant-client relationship. However, in most cases the evolution of this client's perception of you as a temporary employee can be avoided if you practice certain measures to establish and preserve the proper image.

The Self-Image

First and foremost you must settle the relationship firmly in your own mind. You must think of yourself as an independent contractor, and you must also value yourself and your services properly. You are delivering a service of value to your client, making a fair exchange of your services and special abilities for money. You are fully competent to do everything the client requires of you, and you have complete confidence in yourself and in your ability to do that. Unless you firmly believe that, you are unlikely to persuade anyone else to believe it. Inevitably, no matter how brave a front you put up, your convictions about yourself manage to shine through the facade and are perceived by the client and the clients's staff or associates. Most of all, however, bear this in mind: Your true value, what you are being paid for, is not your time. That's a very much mistaken notion that some have. Time is the *measure* by which you charge, but it is not really the commodity you sell. What you sell, or should sell, is *results*, and you need to help your clients understand that too.

Through the Client's Eyes

What has been said here is in no way in opposition to the truth that it is how the client perceives you that is most important in the relationship, much more important than how you see yourself. However, what you think of yourself shows through the relationship and is sensed by the client, coloring his or her impressions.

The client does not have to like you, helpful although that would be; clients do business often with individuals they do not particularly like, when the business relationship is a brief one. However, when you must work closely with a client for a substantial period, amity between you helps a great deal. If that is not possible, at the least you must be a person who is not abrasive in any way. You must see to it that your personality is compatible with the client's own personality.

The Roles You Must and Must Not Play

We all play many roles in life, and most of us play more than one role (e.g., worker, father, mother, friend, confidante, supervisor, etc.). The consultant is a role too, but consultants often play the wrong roles in the client's offices. The following is a list of roles to avoid:

Mr. or Ms. personality. This role is filled by someone full of good cheer and compliments for everyone in sight, memorizing everyone's name, bringing in doughnuts every morning, and otherwise buttering everyone up.

The name dropper. Don't drop those names, not even if you really do know all those prominent and influential citizens.

The militant, male chauvinist, or impassioned libber. These roles are all akin to each other, all impassioned seekers after justice. Save these arguments for another time and place.

The supremely confident know-it-all. Forget how stupid everyone who doesn't agree with you is; be patient with the less fortunate and forgive their ignorance if you want to get along.

The hero. Don't come on too strongly—no braggadacio about your great feats of the past.

The night club comedian. Don't tell racy, off-color stories, make ethnic jokes and slurs, be a back slapper, or try otherwise to be an amateur Bob Hope. It's much harder than it seems, and even if you are a good comedian it doesn't help your image as a serious consultant.

The great polemicist and orator. Don't get into political, religious, or other discussions about which so many people get emotional. Lengthy discussions of sports are often in that same category.

The eager beaver. Don't rush about offering unsolicited help, especially not in matters unrelated to the work you were retained to do. Be responsive if you are asked—you may occasionally be asked for your opinion on some matter not related directly to the effort for which you were retained—but wait to be asked.

The irrepressible marketer. Important although marketing is, don't make the mistake so many make of trying immediately to "fatten your part," as they say in show business, either by trying to expand the contract you have just won or by trying immediately to sell another contract with the same client. This can be related to the eager beaver problem, in which the consultant is involved with everything but the job for which he or she was hired, trying desperately to set up future business. You can wear out your welcome very quickly this way.

On the other hand there is a role you should play as a serious professional.

The total and complete professional. This role requires quiet confidence, a courteous and friendly personality, but a subdued manner, dedication to doing the job as quietly and efficiently as possible, and a willingness to listen intently and actually *hear* what is being said. So many people listen—*apparently listen*, that is—but never actually hear. Learn people's names, acknowledge others pleasantly with a nod, a hello, "Good morning," or whatever is most appropriate, but then go about your business.

THE ART OF LISTENING

A great deal has been made of "the art of listening" in recent years, because so often, when another person is talking, we tend to spend the time thinking about what we are going to say next rather than truly listening and grasping what the other person is saying. "The art of listening" is a catchy phrase, but it doesn't really make the point because so many people interpret listening as being silent while the other person is talking. However, listening means *hearing* what the other person is saying—hearing the words and concentrating on their *meaning*.

President Franklin D. Roosevelt delighted in telling a story that demonstrated how little most people listen. He said he tried sitting in his wheelchair just inside the door at formal receptions at the White House and greeting each visitor or pair of visitors with his typically brilliant smile, a warm handshake, and a murmured, "How do you do. I've just murdered my grandmother." No one ever reacted, he said, because no one was really listening. They simply did not hear what he had said.

Listening to what the other person is saying—really listening and *hearing*—is relatively rare. One highly successful salesman reports that his major secret is listening. Once he gets his prospect going on a favorite topic, whether it is fishing, golf, or manufacturing ball bearings, prolonged listening and *hearing* on his part invariably results in his prospect remarking on what a brilliant conversationalist the salesman is!

This sounds a bit cynical, as though listening is purely a sales maneuver. It is not. It is the means for determining what the prospect really needs or wants, which is the key to making the sale.

We have already established that many prospects cannot tell you what their problem or need is; they can describe symptoms and nothing more. An important part of your function as a consultant is to be an analyst and to determine what the problem is, even before you win the contract. That ability is, in fact, an important part of your marketing skill. It is the key to being able to furnish real help to your client. It can be accomplished by listening to what the prospect has to say.

The successful salesperson is always a consultant in making the sales presentation, no matter what he or she is selling. Fuller Brush salespeople demonstrate how to solve housekeeping problems. Avon and Mary Kay salespeople help prospects find the answers to beauty and makeup problems. Clothing salespeople help prospective customers find the clothes that enhance their appearance. Every successful salesperson performs a service to benefit the prospect. There is no other reason to buy from any salesperson and no other reason for any salesperson to work.

As an independent entrepreneur, regardless of the product or service you sell, you are that salesperson. You will succeed only to the extent that you can help your prospects get what they want. It is only by listening that you can learn (1) what the prospect thinks he or she needs and (2) what the prospect really needs.

DECIDING WHAT BUSINESS YOU ARE IN

It startles and even outrages many listeners to be told that they do not know what businesses they are in, just as it may startle and outrage you to read this accusation. But it is true. Unless you are that rare exception who has been exposed to the right kind of marketing indoctrination, you are almost surely defining your business in terms of what you sell or wish to sell. If you are an office procedures expert, for example, and make a career of advising others on organizing their office procedures or doing it for them, you may define your business as consulting or office management. That seems like a logical way to define your business. What difference does it make, anyway? Isn't it an entirely academic question? The truth is that it is not an academic question; in fact, your success depends largely on how wise you are in deciding or perceiving what business you are in.

The answer to this question is not always a simple one. Before trying to find an answer, let's consider some related ideas.

A Common Denominator of All Businesses

Marketers have made the point that every business is a service business, meaning that every customer buys what the business sells for the benefit to be derived—that is, for what the item being sold will do for him or her. Of course, there are other motivations, and it will be necessary to discuss them later, in a more detailed examination of marketing. But here let's keep it simple, recognizing that everyone buys something, even a manufactured product, to gain some benefit from it. Whatever the actual item we sell, ultimately it is what that item does for the buyer that is the service we really sell.

What Clients Really Buy

Consultants are in the problem-solving business. Probably everyone is in that business, in the final analysis, but many people associate consulting with problem solving, so it is a good place to begin the analysis of your venture. Everyone has problems, and the reason for retaining a consultant is to solve the problem by the most efficient—and usually most rapid—means possible. But even that does not always tell the story. Sometimes the client is an executive who is under great pressure to correct a problem situation. Under these circumstances the consultant is in the rescue business! On the other hand, when the client is an executive who is trying desperately to become established in the organization—that is, to gain recognition—the consultant is in the hero-making business!

Diagnosing what the client *really* wants is the key to discovering what business you are in, at least at the moment or in those particular circumstances.

Obviously you cannot base your appeal on a specific promise to get the client off the hot spot or to make the client a hero or heroine. Your appeal must be far more subtle than that. But you must understand the client's true motive if you are to make the most effective appeal.

In those cases in which the client does not consciously perceive his or her motivation in these terms (although it may be an unconscious desire), you can help the client see one of these possibilities as the chief benefit of your services. It is safe to say that all organizations have problems, and individuals are responsible for solving the problems, so the basic appeal to solving problems is always a sound one. However, most executives, especially young ones who are still working at establishing their images, yearn at least subconsciously to gain special recognition by doing something "heroic" for their organizations. Many successful marketing campaigns are based on arousing the Walter Mitty that lies buried in most of us.

Customers buy love, prestige, ego gratification, security, success, recognition, and many other emotional satisfactions. They need to belong, to be recognized as having worth, to be appreciated, to feel important, to be loved, to be admired, to be successful. Oddly enough, however, people who achieve these things are often unsatisfied because they don't *feel* secure, loved, successful, important, and so forth. Many successful people feel like frauds, achieving success they believe they have not earned and do not deserve (see, *If I'm so Successful, Why do I Feel Like a Fake? The Impostor Phenomenon*, by Joan C. Harvey, Ph.D. with Cynthia Katz, published by St. Martins Press, 1987).

As we've discussed earlier, we must try somehow to see matters from the client's viewpoint, for it is the client's viewpoint that will determine who will get the contract.

Clients Are People!

As far as marketing is concerned, all truth lies in the client's perception. You may be sure that you are delivering a major benefit to the client, the ideal answer to his or her problem, or the means for making him or her a hero or heroine in the organization, but it does not matter if you cannot persuade the client to believe it. The techniques for accomplishing this persuasion will be discussed later, but for now remember that you must be able to see matters from the client's viewpoint and try to find the means for helping the client perceive the benefits you offer.

On the other hand, clients are sensitive, too, and you must take care to avoid giving offense. You must consider the client's own pride. The fact that a client has called on you for help does not mean that he or she necessarily feels less competent than you to do the job. An amazingly large number of clients choose to believe that they are perfectly capable of doing the job themselves but are just too busy to do it or that it is not a wise allocation of their time. This may even be true in many cases, but what difference does it make if it is or is not true? Ordinary diplomacy dictates that you must not flaunt your knowledge.

Even if the client does admit to needing expertise that he or she does not have, it would be risky to appear to be patronizing or condescending. You must exercise a great deal of tact. Many executives and professionals freely admit that they do not write well and are happy to turn the job over to someone else, especially a professional writer. Unfortunately, many others insist that they write as well as anyone, when they have the time, but are usually too busy to do their own writing. However, there are countless cases in which the client has called on a free-lance writer, asking for a quotation to edit or "clean up" a hopelessly inept proposal or manuscript. The client does not wish to admit that the writing is inadequate and that the manuscript should be rewritten. The foolish consultant remonstrates that the manuscript is a mess and needs complete rewriting, a tactic that will probably cost him or her the job. The smart consultant agrees that a heavy edit is needed, furnishes a quotation for the total rewrite, and winds up with the job and a satisfied client. (There is nothing unethical or dishonest in calling the job "editing," when you know it will be "writing," if you are charging a fair price to do what you know must be done and then doing it.)

Most of us want to believe that we are the very best at whatever we do, and we think that the client ought to be able to recognize that obvious fact. The client, however, unless he or she has had a great deal of experience, has no way of knowing that one computer consultant is better than the next computer consultant. All the consultants the client talks to claim total competence in all matters relating to computers, so how is a client to know the difference? In those circumstances, many clients simply call for bids and award the project to the lowest bidder.

Helping the client perceive the difference—that is, "educating" the client—is a major requirement in the successful marketing of consulting services. Even if you are willing to try to be the lowest bidder—generally a self-defeating practice in itself—it would not be the winning strategy in a great many cases. In fact, to win in the marketing of technical and professional services, you must be able to prove that you and/or your plans are superior to those of competitors.

THE TWO BASIC SALES SITUATIONS

There are two basic sales situations in which you will find yourself. In the first situation there is a *felt need*. The client is aware of and accepts the need for consulting services to solve a problem of some sort, whether it is a technical problem that requires some highly specialized expert or a staff shortage that requires a professional temporary or two. In the second situation you must *create* a need for consulting services. The client may or may not be aware of a problem or need, but even if he or she agrees that there is a problem to be solved, the decision to accept outside services has not been made.

These are two entirely different selling problems. In the first case you are selling against competition. You know the contract will be awarded to someone, and it's your task to convince the client that for him or her to realize the greatest benefit the contract should be awarded to you. In the second case you are selling against bias, perhaps, if the client has not yet decided that retaining a consultant is the thing to do. Instead of persuading the client that you and your plan are better than your competitors and their plans, you must somehow try to convince the client that your services are needed and can provide valuable benefits. Of course, there is the hazard here that having succeeded in persuading the client to retain a consultant, the client may yet wish to conduct a competition, rather than making the award directly to you, so that you will have created an opportunity for your competition.

In either case you are likely to be required to do some analysis and propose a specific plan to satisfy the client's need, as well as furnish an estimate of costs (i.e., submit a proposal). It is probably in your own interest to encourage the client to require this. The client will very likely rate you on how well you understand and appraise the problem your services must be designed to solve, as well as on how effective in solving the problem your plan appears to be.

The failure to listen carefully to what the client has to say can be fatal to your marketing effort and even to your entire company, as the following example illustrates. Sam was a former Navy employee, an engineer, and his small company did business almost exclusively with the Navy, as a number of companies in the Washington area do. Unlike other military services, the Navy tends to be its own prime contractor and tends to do most of its major purchasing in the Washington area. The problem was that Sam knew too many people in the Navy and was too familiar with their needs. He was sure that he knew more about what they needed and wanted than they did, and he began to ignore their stated requirements in favor of his own mandates of what they would get from him. He didn't hesitate to tell his clients in the Navy that they need not tell him what they wanted him to do; he knew all he needed to know already. This arrogance began to cost him the contracts he had once been able to gather in almost routinely, and it was not very long before his once prosperous organization was no more. The Navy had no difficulty finding other competent engineering consultants who were more compliant and responsive in listening to their statements and satisfying their needs.

THE INDEPENDENT CONSULTANT: SPECIALIST OR GENERALIST?

It is ironic that the independent consultant must be both very much the specialist, technically and in the perception of the client, and very much the generalist, in practice as a "one-man band,"—that is, doing all or nearly all the technical, managerial, and administrative tasks necessary to the successful operation and survival of a small business. Even the technical functions of a consulting practice are highly diverse. And while even as an independent consultant you may be able to call on outside help or associates to help carry out some of your functions, the burden for all of them falls on you.

On Being Too Much the Specialist

At one extreme is the consultant who is so specialized that he or she has only one or two services or solutions and works overtime trying to force fit the client's problem into one of those services or solutions. Of course it doesn't work. The client will not tailor his or her needs to your specifications. You must tailor your services to the client's need.

This means that consulting is inherently a *custom* service, and you must not lose sight of that. It also means that the more sharply you focus your specialization the less able you are to customize your service. You must be highly flexible, if you are to be able to tailor your services to each client's need, as you should. Oddly enough, although the basis for consulting is generally specialized knowledge and skills in some area, consulting soon proves to be interdisciplinary and forces you to be something of a generalist within your field.

As a proposal consultant, for example, I find it highly useful and even necessary to have an extensive knowledge of the government, procurement regulations, publication processes, writing and editing functions, sales and marketing principles, advertising and copy writing, and management, as well as the skills that are inherently necessary for any consultant. In fact, my clients expect me to be able to advise them in all these matters. Weakness in any of those areas would limit my usefulness—hence my market appeal—and the scope of my services.

Clients themselves often tend to force you into a mold and label you, however, because it is a normal human tendency to sort and classify everything and everybody. For example, because an organization I once managed wrote technical manuals for NASA's Goddard Space Flight Center, we were nearly passed over for a value engineering project that we were well equipped to handle. The client had no idea we had a staff to handle such a job. In the client's eyes we were simply technical writers, rather than an engineering support organization. Only vigilance and aggressive marketing on our part won us the project.

The Independent Consultant as a Technical/Professional Specialist

Of course, the special technical skills that each consultant must have depend on the field in which he or she consults. However, in general the practice of consulting requires the application of several technical/professional skills, and usually the independent consultant must be capable of providing all the skills. Every consulting assignment requires at least some of the following six direct-support functions, and many require all of them:

Listening
Analysis and problem definition
Problem solving
Doing
Public speaking
Writing

Listening and Doing

Listening and doing are functions required for virtually all consulting assignments or projects. You must master and practice the art of listening to—*hearing*—what the client says, as well as to what those whom you interview and/or must work with have to say. You must actually *do* the engineering, computer programming, office procedures design, training development, or whatever tasks constitute the basis of your consulting specialty. It would be rare that a client would not require you to at least lead and guide the "doing" effort.

Analysis, Problem Definition, and Problem Solving

Analysis, problem definition, and problem solving are functions you must carry out in a majority of instances. Even when clients identify their problems quite clearly and dictate the desired or required solution, you should be able to analyze the symptoms and verify the clients' statements or discuss them with the client if you find them at all inaccurate.

Public Speaking and Writing

There is frequent need and always good use for expert speaking and writing. You may be called on to make presentations and/or to train or brief the client's staff, but you will also find speaking before groups valuable as a marketing tool and as the basis for another consulting income center. Writing falls into the same category and is so often necessary that it should be included as a necessary function of consulting. Writing also may be the basis for an important income center in your practice.

The Independent Consultant as a Businessperson

Consulting is a professional calling, but it is also a business; and the successful independent consultant must be a businessperson—that is, a manager and an administrator. The functions and skills required for management and administration of any business include at least these:

Accounting and related recordkeeping
Financial management
Cost analysis
Scheduling and time management
Marketing and sales

There are other skills that are definitely elements of general business management and administration for many kinds of enterprises. But those mentioned here are usually the main functions in managing and administering a consulting practice. The first four elements are the same in principle for all business enterprises. However, for the independent consultant, marketing is a special problem. It is something of a "gray area" of management and administration and is not readily separable from the technical/professional side of consulting. It will be discussed briefly here and in much greater depth and detail later, since help in marketing your consulting services is the single most important objective of this book.

Accounting and Recordkeeping

A great many individuals entering into a small business immediately enlist the help of a certified public accountant to set up a complete accounting system for the enterprise and to handle all bookkeeping and accounting work. A major motivation underlying this is the belief that accounting is a mysterious ritual that most mere mortals cannot hope to even fathom, much less practice. This motivation is reinforced by a dreadful fear of the Internal Revenue Service and the mistaken belief that the chief purpose of keeping books is to comply with the legal statutes and preferences of the IRS.

There is nothing wrong with retaining a professional accountant to handle all your accounting needs. However, there are good arguments for doing it yourself, too, and it is far less difficult than you might imagine. Or you may choose to compromise between the extremes of turning it all over to a professional accountant and doing it all yourself. (I have myself tried both extremes and have for years used a compromise solution quite successfully.) The alternatives include:

The accountant sets up your books and a system for you to follow, so you keep the day-to-day journals, the check stubs, and the invoices. The accountant comes in periodically (e.g., once a week or once a month) and does your formal postings, balancing, reconciling the bank statement, and making up estimated tax returns and other tax papers when necessary.

The accountant sets up the system and instructs you in how to do postings and "keep the books." Periodically, perhaps every quarter or every six months, the accountant examines your books to do all your taxes and prepare the standard reports (e.g., profit and loss statement, balance sheet, and others).

You use one of the standard accounting systems designed especially for very small businesses (you can buy the combination journal/ledger and instructions that constitute such a simplified system in almost any good office supplies store) and get an accountant's help to do your taxes and prepare your standard reports.

In my own case, the accountant does little more than end-of-the-year state and federal corporate and personal income taxes for me. I had tried to have an accountant handle it all for me, and I was dissatisfied with the arrangement for several reasons, the most important of which was that I had to hold my breath for three months to find out how I was doing. I decided that I needed to know immediately when things were going wrong, and I found that the do-it-yourself systems actually gave a *daily* report on our financial progress. Moreover, it's a great deal less expensive and a great deal simpler.

You must be aware that the purpose of accounting is not to make life easier for the IRS, although the law requires you to keep some kind of record. The accounting system's primary purpose is to furnish you with information on which to make sound decisions—on which to *manage* your practice to your own best advantage. Of course you want that information while there is time to make adjustments (e.g., you may discontinue something that is costing you money or renew a marketing effort that is producing good results), not when it is too late to correct a mistake or take advantage of an opportunity. It is quite easy to be entirely unaware of such things if you do not have a good accounting system that automatically alerts you. If it is to be useful, the system must furnish information that satisfies three requirements:

1. It must be accurate information.
2. It must be timely information.
3. It must be the right information for your purposes.

It is not possible for a public accountant to do for you what you can do for yourself in this respect. Moreover, the accountant has an understandable tendency to burden you with a system that often is not only far more complex and sophisticated than you need, but actually tends to conceal the facts from you, rather than highlighting and dramatizing them as it should.

Of course, the large corporation has a comptroller or chief accountant who is an expert at reading the figures and who devotes all his or her time to analyzing these for the corporation. But since you must do it for yourself, you need a system that you can understand and interpret easily.

In addition, remember that the accountant is not familiar with your profession, let alone the circumstances of your individual practice, and cannot possibly anticipate what you need. Those simple systems, however, give you up-to-date information, if you keep them up. In it you can usually identify every cost center you have, what it has cost you this past week or month, and the total cost for the year to date. You have the same figures for all costs and for all income so you can make comparisons as often as you like and spot changes in a trend immediately.

Financial Management and Cost Analysis

Some organizations also use their accountants or comptrollers as financial managers. I believe this to be a mistake. Accountants and comptrollers are concerned normally with day-to-day operations, including the establishing and maintenance of records, creating reports, verifying expenses, and getting the data to the various managers who need the information. On the other hand, financial managers are, or should be, concerned with future projects and overall management of many functions and processes affecting the organization's finances, such as the following:

Cost analyses, to ensure that work is estimated and priced accurately. This is not a simple matter, and it is not at all unknown for organizations to operate at a loss for a long time without realizing it, because they have failed to make a realistic and accurate analysis of all their costs.

Optimizing the organization's cash flow and financial position by ensuring prompt invoicing, taking advantage of all discounts, managing assets to minimize interest payments and maximize return on investment, and other such measures.

Cost control, including the use of available cost reduction and cost avoidance practices.

Funding operations, including equity funding, debt financing, and other available measures.

Scheduling and Time Management

Scheduling and time management are executive functions that as an independent consultant you will normally do for yourself. They can be complex in the large company but are usually quite simple in the small organization. However, if you get into work situations in which you must keep accurate time records, you will have to organize some sort of formal system.

Marketing

Marketing is rarely a simple function. In the case of selling consulting services it usually gets quite complex because such services can rarely be sold through the conventional or traditional marketing methods. Many consultants who have tried such methods (e.g., media advertising, brochures, and personal calls on prospects) have been puzzled and dismayed by the disappointing results. To some degree this reflects a failure to formulate a specific and detailed marketing plan in advance, especially identifying the specific benefits you offer via your services and the specific kinds of prospects to whom you wish to appeal. Many new consultants believe that if enough people are made aware that they (the consultants) are now ready to solve clients' problems for them, the telephone will start ringing. Actually, the opposite is true. Rarely does a client choose a consultant casually as a result of a conventional advertisement or sales call. Clients usually find consultants through indirect means (e.g., recommendations by friends, meeting consultants at business meetings and conventions, hearing consultants speak at such events, reading about consultants in articles, and reading articles and books written by the consultant).

Many of these activities of consultants are marketing functions, and they call for the application of certain skills listed earlier as technical/professional skills. It is partly for this reason that the subject of marketing is handled separately here. However, the importance of marketing to consulting success is itself enough to merit and justify treating the subject separately.

The remainder of this chapter covers how to survive the first year and set the survival and success patterns for succeeding years. For me and for a great many other independent consultants, the secret of that survival and success has been having more than one consulting service and/or related product to sell (i.e., other profit centers) and effective marketing of all the services.

DOS AND DON'TS, ESPECIALLY FOR THE FIRST YEAR

The first year of a new venture is almost surely the most critical one. The sensible main objective of the first year is not success; it is survival. The second and only slightly less important objective of the first year is education—learning what works and what doesn't work for you, what to do and what to avoid doing, and whatever else only experience can really teach you.

General Suggestions for Minimizing Costs

Don't get carried away with the enthusiasm of a new venture. Although enthusiasm is a great asset and will help you considerably in being successful, it should not blind you to the reality of that first year. It is quite possible that you will pay more money out than you will take in, especially if you are not quite careful in what you pay out. Remember that what you spend this first year—and possibly even in succeeding years—is the cost of your education, but the education need not be disastrously expensive. Here are some suggestions for conserving your cash and minimizing your first-year expenses.

Make no long-term advertising commitments, such as yellow pages advertising or an advertising contract with a newspaper.

Set up your first office in your home, if at all possible. If you must have an office outside your home, choose a modestly priced one in the nearest business district, especially where you do not have to pay monthly parking fees.

Rent a single office, not a suite, or sublease an office from someone with a suite and an available office. This can be quite inexpensive and comfortable.

Consider the possibility of desk space in a communal office. These are offices in which you pay a modest sum for your own desk in a large room, with an answering service and access to a conference room, copier, stenographic services, and a mail room. This is a good arrangement if you will not spend much time in your office. It gives you a telephone number, business address, mail address, and place for the occasional conference with clients on your premises. It also saves you the cost of furnishing an office, which minimizes the initial investment.

Be conservative in furnishing your office. Look for a company that rents office furniture and sells leftovers. Such companies often have great bargains in nearly new office furniture. Also watch the classified advertising sections of your newspapers for salvage sales, bankruptcies, and other such special events.

Be modest in ordering your business cards and stationery. Plain white thermographed (raised printing) cards and stationery in black ink on good quality stock is entirely adequate. Expensive cards and stationery will not produce extra income for you.

Shop around. The market is competitive. You can easily spend $5,000 for a personal computer and word processing system, for example, but you can also get an adequate system for $2,000 or less.

A Few Special Cost Avoidance Tips

In the almost unbroken prosperity that we have enjoyed over recent decades "we"—that is, American buyers and sellers, appear to have completely forgotten that ours is a competitive economic system. Fortunately, a few sellers still deal competitively, and a few buyers still seek out the best offers. It is easy to pay too much for things if you fail to be conscious of and take advantage of the competitive system. Shop carefully and explore all the options (e.g., renting versus buying and small vendors versus large corporations).

Cost avoidance tips should also be remembered when you win assignments you can't handle alone. Sometimes you need others with skills similar to your own, and sometimes you need others with complementary or supporting skills. For example, at times I have had to find other proposal consultants to help me handle a proposal task too big for one person; at other times I have needed specialists in logistics or some other discipline in which I am not skilled, or I have had to have drafting or illustrating help to support me. Unless you are trying to build an organization, these are temporary arrangements, usually with other self-employed individuals.

The results of my searches for supporting personnel often have been disappointing and costly. More than once I have paid others and worked late into the night to do their work over because I considered it not up to my own standard. Perhaps the client would have accepted it, but I would not, for reputation is fragile and once damaged almost impossible to repair. I am unwilling to submit work I believe to represent less than my best effort.

I have learned to follow certain principles, expressed as the following dos and don'ts:

Do require references and check them out carefully. An amazingly large number of people take others at face value and fail to verify references.

Don't hire people by the hour. Doing so compels you to pay them for each hour worked, no matter how productive or unproductive they are, no matter how satisfactory or unsatisfactory the result is. Even when the result is satisfactory, why should you be penalized because someone else is a slow worker? Perhaps the hourly rate inspires the other to work slowly!

Do retain the other party as a subcontractor, not as an employee or even as an associate. Reach an agreement on what is to be done, when it is to be done, what the quality standard is to be, and the price. The agreement should be in writing.

Do make it clear that payment will be made when you accept the product as meeting the quality standard agreed upon.

A great many people can be quite convincing about how good they are at what they do and yet can turn out to be rather poor performers. I strongly subscribe to Pareto's Law, also referred to as the "80–20 Rule."

Vilfredo Pareto (1848–1923) was a French-born economist who did his significant work in Italy and is therefore mistakenly referred to as an Italian economist (and even as a Swiss economist sometimes). He discovered that in the Italian economy and in a great many other areas—perhaps in most things—a small proportion of the cause is responsible for a disproportionately large portion of the result.

Pareto's Principle, still another name for the phenomenon he perceived, simply recognizes that there is great disproportion in distributions. For example, 20 percent of any production team normally produces 80 percent of the output; unfortunately, this leaves the other 80 percent of the team producing only 20 percent of the output. Also, 80 percent of the money in a bank is deposited by 20 percent of the depositors, and 20 percent of the workers in a project produce 80 percent of the result. And, as value engineers have discovered, it is often true that 20 percent of the parts in a machine do 80 percent of the work.

This demonstrates a law of inverse ratios, revealing a horrible inefficiency and waste: 80 percent of the cost is incurred to produce 20 percent of the result, and 20 percent of the cost produces the other 80 percent of the result. In sales organizations, for example, it is not at all unusual to find that 20 percent of the salespeople produce 80 percent of the sales, while the remaining 80 percent of the sales force produce only 20 percent of the sales. This has been found to be largely true in all sorts of applications and activities. I find that probably not more than 20 percent of the workers in any field are truly good, and the other 80 percent are scattered along a spectrum ranging from fair to poor.

The real hazard is *semicompetence.* It's easy to recognize the truly competent and truly incompetent, but it is usually difficult to be sure about the semicompetent individual. This person often gets away with substandard work for a long time before you are sure that the work really does not meet your standards. I found it in accountants who had good references and could say all the right things, but whose books never balanced, whose invoices were always being sent back to correct errors, and who could never come up with the right answers to ordinary questions asked by management. I found it in technical writers who diligently put in long hours, but who in the end resigned when the time came to surrender a manuscript, leaving nothing but a large notebook filled with indecipherable notes and in some cases not even that. And I found it in engineers who discussed the work convincingly enough but whose designs and protoypes never met the specifications or matched the reports they wrote. In fact, I was grateful when I found someone whose work I heartily approved of because it assured me that I did have specific standards, when sometimes my disillusioning experiences caused me to wonder whether I was being excessively and unfairly critical.

Many of these semicompetents are experts at creating the appearance of competence and success in what they are doing. Beware of appearances. Judge by results. It's the only way to be sure.

You should also beware of moonlighters. I hesitate to condemn them as a class, but I have had many bad experiences. Many are excellent performers, but be cautious and check their references carefully. Unfortunately, many are unreliable because they have regular, steady jobs and do not depend on their moonlighting. They often get tired and begin fading long before the job is done. They may take time off for a movie or a party at critical junctures, or they balk at doing work over when it is unacceptable. And sometimes they simply disappear and are not heard from again. I have had all these discouraging experiences with moonlighters and prefer to trust subcontracts to full-time, self-employed individuals who depend on the work for their survival. They are almost always more reliable.

Since the odds are not exactly in your favor, you should practice defensive tactics when entrusting some portion of your success to others.

3

Founding the Consulting Practice

Well begun is half done.

—Horace

IF YOU HAD IT TO DO OVER . . .

What were your mistakes or major problems when you started? How did you handle them? What would you do differently today? What advice would you offer beginners? I asked several experienced and successful independent consultants these questions recently in preparation for writing this new edition. I was favored with full and eloquent responses from individuals whose opinions I value greatly. Unfortunately, it is simply impractical to attempt to reproduce all the words of experience and wisdom offered, but a sampling follows.

Some of the advice and opinions you will read here may be in contrast with my own opinions and the counsel I offer you in these pages. That is as it should be; each of us draws our own conclusions from our experience. But none of us has experienced exactly what you will, so none of us can give you advice totally specific to your own individual need. Take from this, then, whatever is relevant and helpful to you.

Gerre Jones is a marketing consultant, a veteran with over 30 years of professional experience, providing services also in public relations and as an editorial consultant. He is president of Gerre Jones Associates, Inc. and Glyph Publishing Company of Albuquerque, New Mexico. He is also editor/publisher of a widely read and often quoted newsletter, *Professional Marketing Report*, read by the design professionals whom he serves in his practice. He has written a number of books published by McGraw-Hill, and his own firm has published a number of his marketing manuals. Working with McGraw-Hill and *Architectural Record*, he developed and led many public workshops in professional design services. Therefore, he speaks about consulting with considerable authority. With his permission, I offer his words here, taken from several of his published works almost exactly as he phrased them, although abridged slightly to suit my needs, for which abridgement I apologize.

Early mistakes and problems:

1. Gaining credibility in your chosen field.
2. Initial capitalization.
3. Coming up with peripheral and related activities to form a logical, productive mix; a mix that sees each element contributing to and promoting the others. (I can and do promote my workshops, consulting services, and newsletter in my books; my books, newsletters, and consulting are promoted in my workshops; and so on.)
4. Establishing sources of referrals.

What I would do differently today:

1. Do more direct mail promotion for my newsletter.
2. Keep my name in front of my major client base.
3. Become fairly selective about which clients I take on. (After a while you decide you don't have a lot to prove anymore, and you really don't *need* some of the challenges represented by some would-be clients.)
4. Pay *passionate* attention to details.

Advice for beginners:

1. Have enough cash in reserve to live on for the first 9 to 12 months. You probably won't need it (I didn't) but it helps to relieve some of the pressure.
2. Train yourself to become a skilled and persuasive writer.

3. Train yourself to become a persuasive, forceful speaker.
4. Maintain an interest in as many areas as possible. I don't believe a consultant can know (or read) too much.
5. Incorporate as a Sub-Chapter S corporation immediately.
6. Find a good accountant.
7. Expand slowly and within a business plan.
8. Have a written marketing plan. Review and update it at least twice a year.
9. Know your competition.
10. Be prepared to spend a lot of time on airplanes and nights in hotels, particularly as you become better known and more in demand.

Howard J. Blumenthal, who conducts his practice in New York City, also serves clients as a marketing consultant, but in an entirely different and probably more widely diversified arena. He is an expert in developing presentation products for entertainment, training, publishing, and related interests. (In fact, he guided the development of an audiocassette package based on the first edition of this book.) Like many other successful consultants, Howard has published a number of books and has graciously given his time to help others seeking success as independent consultants. Here is his advice (based on a personal interview) to those launching new careers as independent consultants; again I have paraphrased somewhat to suit the needs of the reader. (Howard uses many associates in his work, and so speaks in the plural, although he is an independent consultant.)

Early mistakes and problems:

Initially we concentrated on creating marketing communications products in book, audio, and video form. Decisions took too long, and we found ourselves waiting an unusually long time for answers, generally with several revisions of the proposal along the way. As we expanded into our four current areas—audio, video, books, and games—and started to look at helping existing publishing companies to grow into new areas, the clients began to appear on a regular basis.

What I would do differently today:

Nothing. The learning curve was necessary. It allowed me time to really focus on the principal activities of the business and to visit with a broad range of clients who were very helpful in that focusing process because they told me what they needed from the outside.

Advice for beginners:

1. Be prepared for a good three to six months of marketing before you get your first important client. And if you happen to get your first one easily be aware that getting the second one may be far more difficult.
2. Be sure that there is a need for your services in the industry that you have targeted. Find out whether there are already any consultants who are doing what you propose to do. It's a good idea to work on related industries (publishing and entertainment, in my own case) to ensure a greater range of opportunities and to enhance your value. (Those in publishing are impressed by credentials in entertainment and vice versa.)
3. Don't be afraid to charge clients what you are worth.
4. If you are going to represent yourself as an expert, be an expert. Read the trade magazines, keep in touch with knowledgeable people in the industry, and see to it that your opinions are respected. If you attempt to sell what everyone already knows, you will have a difficult time finding success.
5. Select an industry with real growth. Don't be misled by smoke and mirrors.
6. Use a good brochure in addition to your business card. Keep it brief and businesslike, and spare the hype; readers know it's a sales presentation, but don't oversell.

Dr. Jeffrey Lant, who hung out his consulting shingle in Cambridge, Massachusetts after earning his doctorate at Harvard, is a management consultant who provides a variety of services to nonprofit organizations to aid their fund-raising efforts. He is steadily gaining recognition as an author and publisher of his own rapidly growing library of books for consultants, each of which is based on what he has learned during his years in the consulting and general business world. (His books will be listed later as recommended resources.) Here, again, is an abridged version, (based on his published works and our correspondence,) with my apologies for doing so, of Dr. Lant's own words:

> Early mistakes or problems:
>
> I had assumed at the beginning of my practice that clients really wanted to solve their problems, that when I was retained the client had a clear conception of his problem and had made the commitment to solve it. One of the greatest shocks in my consulting career was to find that this isn't always true. Supplying technical assistance to clients isn't nearly enough to succeed as a consultant. One must also be an advocate of what I call *guerrilla theater*—that is, you must be willing to do whatever it takes to make the client sit up, take notice, and move to action. In the literature on consulting I found far too little attention given to the change process, a process I believe the consultant must understand fully and must have his own system for managing.
>
> What I would do differently today:
>
> I would develop what I call the "Problem Solving Process" (described in my book, *Tricks of the Trade*, Cambridge, JLA Associates, 1986). That is, I would follow my own inclinations and not be unduly influenced by the client's views.
>
> Advice for beginners:
>
> Focus, focus, focus. Don't try to be all things to all people.

David Labell is a Washington-area computer applications consultant. He is a man of definite opinions, which he succeeds in expressing quite clearly. He offers his clients services he characterizes as IBM-compatible information management—database design and administration, programming, systems analysis, technical support, and training—in relation to both microcomputers and mainframe systems. His observations are similar to those of Jeffrey Lant, reflecting a degree of disillusionment and disappointment with clients. He laments having been born too early to be as much at home with computers as are many of today's bright teenagers. Based on an interview and conversations, some of his observations follow:

Early mistakes and problems:

My biggest obstacle was learning to use IBM mainframes. I had the good fortune to bungle my first project, not because I did poor work but because I misread my client, an aerospace company. I didn't realize that some clients hire consultants specifically to abuse them. Now that I know that, I handle those clients better.

What I would do differently today:

I would study more computer science, accounting, and foreign languages, such as Russian and German. I would also have studied electronics, mathematics, and physics.

Advice to beginners:

Do not go to a trade school. The best way to learn computer programming is to own a computer. So far, not one newcomer has taken this advice from me.

MESSAGES THAT COME THROUGH

Obviously these experienced consultants have different views as to what their major problems were, what they would do differently today, and what they would advise those contemplating a career in consulting. Perhaps the differences in early problems or what they now consider to be mistakes reflect differences in the nature of the fields in which they consult or in the types of individuals who normally retain them. Perhaps the differences are in the personalities and ideas of the individuals or in some individual characteristic of how they approach their clients and their projects. Or perhaps the differences are the result of purely random events and chance situations and have no significance at all.

Whatever the reason for the differences, the fact that there are such differences illustrates (1) the heterogeneous nature of consulting, (2) that consulting is not itself a profession but a way of practicing a profession, (3) that consulting is a custom enterprise in which each experience is unique and (4) that experience produces common sense conclusions. Perhaps the most sound advice is included in the following messages.

Don't expect instant success in marketing, not even if you have beginner's luck in winning your first client or two. Have no illusions about that.

Try to have some cash reserve to see you through the early period, preferably through the first year. You may or may not need it, but it will enable you to focus more on what you have to do and less on how stressed you are.

Know your field as completely as possible; be a true authority in it to gain the respect you will need to succeed as an independent consultant.

Plan your marketing carefully and be realistic about the validity of the market and the need for your services in it. Do the necessary research to verify your premises, and don't let wishful thinking delude you.

Despite the importance of these messages, they are essentially philosophical ones on subjects we will be discussing at great length. But a consulting practice is a business as well as a way to practice a profession, and there are also a great many other considerations, practical matters, involved in and necessary to getting started in a practice of your own. The rest of this chapter is devoted to discussing those business issues.

LICENSING

Unless your basic profession is one that requires licensing to practice or your local statutes compel you to have a mercantile license of some sort, you probably do not need a license, for consulting is not itself a licensed or regulated enterprise. If you are uncertain about it, you can seek information or guidance from any number of the following sources to determine whether licensing is required and, if so, how to proceed:

A local lawyer
The local chamber of commerce
County, city, town hall

The business editor of the local newspaper

Local business owners

The local U.S. Small Business Administration office

Even where licensing is required there may be special provisions. For instance in Miami I was required to have a mercantile license, but as a war veteran I was entitled to a very much reduced fee. Moreover, the licensing authority was kind enough to give me permission to conduct my business without a license until the beginning of the new license year.

THE MATTER OF A BUSINESS NAME

A government executive, whose work compelled him to review many consultants' proposals, was fond of remarking during such reviews, "The smaller the company, the bigger the name."

He always made this observation with a sigh and a tolerant smile because he applauded all enterprise and truly wanted to award contracts to new, small firms. Still, there was an ambivalence in his reaction because he admired complete honesty. He felt that a grandiose business name such as "International Computer Systems & Information Consultants Ltd." was an effort to impress and deceive him into believing that he was dealing with a truly major organization. That led him to wonder what else in the proposal or sales presentation was window dressing.

There is a certain dignity in simplicity. In fact, many supercorporations became so well known by their acronyms (e.g., IBM, RCA, GE, etc.) that many people do not even know the exact names for which these letters stand. Obviously it is not necessary to adopt a long and elaborate name, and it may be to your disadvantage to do so.

The two most popular practices of consultants for naming their practices is to identify themselves and what they specialize in by (1) their personal name or (2) by adding "and associates" to their name.

Usually the consultant will have another line or two, in addition to an address and telephone number, that further defines the exact nature of the services offered (e.g., marketing plans, direct mail services and/or market surveys).

One immediate advantage of using your personal name in this manner, if you operate as a sole proprietorship, is that you have no legal complications. On the other hand, if you use a trade name (e.g., "International Marketing Consultants"), it may need to be registered. If you incorporate, that business name is registered when you file your documents of incorporation, but if you are a sole proprietorship or partnership you usually must comply with state and local statutes that require you to file fictitious names or dba (doing business as) names so the authorities can always determine the true owners of each name.

This is not an especially costly procedure, normally, and you can do it yourself, if you wish; however, most people retain a lawyer to handle it for them. (A clerk in the Philadelphia City Hall was able to advise me completely on proper procedures for doing this, even to exact wording of the required advertisements, when I registered a business name in that city some years ago.) It normally amounts to filing statements with the state and local governments and placing three consecutive advertisements, in the local daily newspaper or in a special legal periodical, *The Legal Intelligencer*, to advise readers about the enterprise and the proprietors.

Even if you use only part of your own name (rather than your complete name) as part of the fictitious business name (e.g., Honeycutt Marketing Associates), it is likely that you will be required to file that name since it does not really identify you as the proprietor. It is probably best to to consult a lawyer in such a case, since these are general observations based on my personal experience and are definitely not intended to be taken as specific legal advice.

WHAT TYPE OF BUSINESS ORGANIZATION SHOULD YOU USE?

An amazingly large number of fledgling, one-person consulting enterprises spring to life as corporations, often on an accountant's or lawyer's advice but equally often on an entrepreneur's mistaken notion that incorporation is a must for success. There is nothing wrong with incorporating, and it may well turn out to be the best route for you, but first consider the other ways to organize your venture.

Sole Proprietorship

If you own the business and all its assets in your own name, whether you work alone or have help (or even associates), you have a sole proprietorship. That means exactly what it says: you are the sole proprietor. The assets are entirely yours, and you are also solely and entirely responsible for the liabilities.

This is by far the simplest way to operate, but some consultants are increasingly apprehensive about the potential liabilities of being totally responsible in these times of excessive litigation, which many find a persuasive argument for incorporating.

Partnerships

Obviously, a partnership is suggested when you have one or more partners. Proprietorship, in a simple partnership, is vested in all partners, equally or according to whatever agreement exists between or among the partners. The partners share responsibility for all liabilities and ownership of all assets. You should have a detailed agreement drawn up, properly notarized, and witnessed. It is a good idea to have an attorney handle this for you. In fact, it is usually wise for each partner to have an attorney to represent his or her interests. Even if you operate as a sole proprietor, however, there may be advantages to naming your spouse as a partner. It is best to consult an attorney to evaluate the options before making your decision.

Limited Partnership

A limited partnership is like a corporation in some respects, in that although it has the legal and tax characteristics of a simple partnership, the liability of the partners can be limited to the capital invested. However, this arrangement is generally unsuited to the type of venture we are considering here.

Corporations

Corporations are entities, in the legal sense, just as every human is an entity. The U.S. Supreme Court defined a corporation as "an artificial being, invisible, intangible, and existing only in contemplation of law," a definition that has been echoed frequently in other courts and in legal texts.

In many ways, the corporation is treated as though it were a person. That is why it is the corporation, not you personally, that is ordinarily responsible and liable for the obligations of the corporation.

There are a number of types of corporations. Some are public, accepting investors by selling stock in the corporation. Most independent consultants who incorporate, however, form close corporations. You can sell stock privately, to the limits prescribed, in a close corporation, but you cannot offer stock to the general public.

You can incorporate as a nonprofit corporation, but that has more disadvantages for this application than it has advantages. You can draw a salary and expenses, plus normal fringe benefits, and you can treat yourself quite well as an employee, but the corporation cannot accumulate a reserve of profits and you never have an equity position—that is, a business you own personally and can sell.

Some individuals opt for a Sub-Chapter S Corporation, an entity that does not have to pay corporate taxes. To qualify for this you must have no more than 10 stockholders and you must draw income from operations, not investment, an arrangement that may or may not be suitable for you. (You may have noted that one of the consultants quoted earlier, Gerre Jones, believes firmly that this is a must for the independent consultant.)

Generally you will form a close corporation, one held "closely" with limited participation. It is possible, in fact, to hold all the offices yourself! Most who form corporations, however, bring in family members and sometimes close friends to act as other officers and directors of the corporation.

Pros and Cons of Incorporation

In my own experience, accountants and lawyers tend to encourage you to incorporate. Probably those who so advise are sincere in their apparent beliefs that everyone in business ought to be incorporated; the nature of their work almost mandates that conviction. Unfortunately, however, each stands to benefit directly if you incorporate—lawyers charge fees to do the paper work, and accountants get much more work to do when you are incorporated—so there is always the question of whether they are being objective in recommending that step.

There are pros and cons in incorporating, as there are in most things. Aside from the possible (and dubious) benefits of adding prestige to your professional image, incorporation limits your liability. If someone sues your corporation, and even gets a judgment against it, your personal property is normally immune to that judgment. On the other hand, incorporation adds more bookkeeping and accounting tasks and a few extra taxes as well. The disadvantage of this added paperwork burden is balanced by the tax shelter advantage of incorporation. Unless the tax code changes considerably—as it may very well do in these times—the corporation offers some opportunities to manage your affairs so as to lower your overall taxes. However, many individuals believe that if they incorporate their businesses they will immediately and automatically be allowed many more deductions for business expenses and thereby enjoy lower tax rates and other benefits. This is not entirely true. First of all, you will still pay whatever your individual tax rate is on the money you draw from the corporation for your personal use, whether you pay yourself a regular salary or simply draw money from time to time. The lower corporate tax rate—assuming that it is lower, which may or may not be the case for you, depending on certain circumstances—applies only to the money left in the corporation, money that the corporation banks as profit or earned income.

The deductions you take for business expenses are essentially the same, whether you are incorporated or not. Your insurance, other taxes, interest paid, rent, and other expenses are deductible under all kinds of business organizations. However, as a corporation you may be able to give yourself certain benefits that are not taxable as income and are deductible business expenses for the corporation. (Your tax expert should advise you on that.) In general, the tax benefits begin to accrue to you significantly when your earnings are higher, rather than when you are earning only a modest income.

Another reason many incorporate is the mistaken notion that incorporation adds to their prestige and heightens their professional image. That simply is not true, especially since you can incorporate in most states today for about $40! The forms are quite simple (a single page, in Maryland) for an uncomplicated close corporation.

Even obtaining bylaws and other necessary supplies of corporate life does not present a problem. My own local phone directory lists three suppliers of "Corporation Supplies" in one Maryland suburb alone. These suppliers offer corporate seals, stock certificates, printed bylaws, resolution forms, record books, and other such items. In fact, these suppliers are quite expert in the whole matter of incorporation and can usually advise you as to where to go to get the necessary forms and how to go about filling them out and filing your application for incorporation. Such supplies are relatively inexpensive. I paid only between $40 and $50 for my complete corporate kit when I incorporated, and it can't have gone up very much since then.

I have met individuals who believed that they could not incorporate because they worked from their homes. They thought that incorporating would require them to set up offices in commercial locations. Don't be misled. The state really does not care where you conduct your business, as far as a legal address is concerned. Remember too that incorporation does not have to be done immediately. You can incorporate when you wish to.

Where Should You Incorporate?

Delaware has long been the favorite state for companies wishing to incorporate, because Delaware has made incorporation simple. Consequently, it enjoys by far the largest number of corporations, even though few of those corporations maintain headquarters in or even operate in that state! However, they are considered a "foreign" corporation in the state in which they do operate and must register as such; this involves a few penalties, such as taxes. At the same time, they must keep a registered agent in the state of their incorporation.

Today most states have liberalized their requirements for incorporation so that it is usually inexpensive and easy to incorporate in your own state. That eliminates the problems of being forced to register as a foreign corporation and being forced to pay someone to act as your registered agent in the state of your incorporation, since you are your own registered agent when you operate in the state of incorporation.

Consider, then, your own needs, your own problems, your local laws, current federal tax laws (they do change, sometimes significantly with respect to corporations), and whatever else applies to your individual situation, and act accordingly.

DO YOU NEED A LAWYER? IF SO, FOR WHAT?

There are many reasons to retain a lawyer. A good lawyer can help you by:

Doing things for you that require legal expertise and/or familiarity with the system.

Advising you as a legal expert

Advising you as an objective observer

Representing you and your interests

However, you can also do a great many things for yourself and save a great deal of money in the process. Ordinarily you can handle your own incorporation, registration of business name, applications for licenses, drafting simple letter agreements, and similar chores that are feasible as do-it-yourself projects. There are many books available to help you learn how to carry out these tasks (see the listing of references in Chapter 17). These books include sample forms you may use and guidance in how to handle corporate tasks (e.g., writing resolutions, holding directors meetings, and opening corporate bank accounts) and derive maximum benefits from incorporation. Many of these books supply a complete set of bylaws that you may be able to use, perhaps with some minor adaptations, as your own corporate bylaws.

One word of caution—do not ask your lawyer to make your business decisions. Depending on the individual, some lawyers may make it clear that what they offer is their best opinion to help you reach decisions, while others may force their recommended courses of action on you. Even the best lawyer is only an advisor, no matter how sound the advice offered; you must make the decision based on all the advice and your own good judgment. But that good judgment depends on your own complete understanding. Require that your lawyer explain the advice and the rationale for it—and do insist on knowing the rationale—in language that you can understand. Without this knowledge, you do not understand the basis for the advice, and so you cannot possibly make a sound decision, except by pure chance.

DO YOU NEED AN ACCOUNTANT? IF SO, FOR WHAT?

Virtually everything said with regard to your need for and use of a lawyer applies with equal validity to the need for and use of an accountant. Strictly speaking, you do not need an accountant; it is possible to manage without one (especially if you use the simple proprietorship method of doing business), using one of the several alternatives suggested earlier. However, there is a difference in the frequency of accounting services versus legal services. You would probably use a lawyer's services in setting up and organizing your practice, but after that only intermittently, if and as legal problems arose. But you must do accounting regularly, keeping records of every day's events. A list of the kinds of functions that must be performed in all accounting systems follows:

Journalizing. Entering bills, receivables, and other items into the daily journals as they happen. A small system may have only a single day journal for everything, whereas a large system may have a number of day journals, each devoted to a different kind of event.

Posting. Transferring the journal entries to their proper pages and columns in the ledgers. As in the case of day journals, the size and number of ledgers used depends on the size and complexity of the system.

Balancing and auditing. Validating the correctness of the entries posted through verifying various mathematical balances and checking specific items to track down the problems when balances are not achieved.

Calculating overhead. Determining the cost of doing business as a mathematical rate—that is, the percentage of direct labor and/or other costs.

Generating various reports and statements. Preparing such items as the profit and loss statement, the balance sheet, and various monthly, quarterly, semiannual, and annual reports.

Tax work. Making out tax returns for the various government agencies (federal, state, and local) to which taxes must be remitted, along with whatever reports and statements are required.

Scheduling payables. Listing invoices to be paid, with schedules for the payment dates, calculated for maximum cash flow and other financial advantages.

Invoicing receivables. Sending out invoices for money due the client.

Miscellaneous. Follow-up statements and notices urging payment of invoices, preparing special reports, making estimates, calculating and preparing payroll checks, and whatever other tasks arise.

While all accounting systems must perform these tasks, the actual functions and elements of the system may vary widely from one organization to another, depending on several variables, chief of which are the size of the organization, the nature of the organization's activities, and the nature of the accounting system itself.

Fortunately, these tasks are not nearly as formidable as they may appear, at least not for the independent consultant. Except for the tax work, keeping books via one of the simple patented systems, such as *The Dome Simplified Weekly Bookkeeping Record*, is quite easy. The system includes a general day journal (the left-hand page) and a ledger (the right-hand page). You journalize each event (e.g., expenditure, sale made, bill paid, etc.) as it happens, noting the number assigned to the type of item (e.g., 3 for advertising, 21 for repairs, 30 for travel expense, etc.). At the end of the week you total all the number 3 items and post them opposite number 3 on the ledger page, and you do the same for all the other numbers. You keep cumulative totals on everything, including income, so you know where you stand at all times. You can determine at a glance how total expenditures compare with total income, what cost items are your greatest ones, and just about anything else you want to know about the cash flow of your business. The ledger has three columns for all the cost items and the income or sales items: total this week, total end of last week, and total to date.

When I turned to this system, after suffering the frustrations of permitting an accountant to do it all and tell me what he wanted to tell me when he wanted to tell it to me, which meant as much as three months after the fact, I sought out another accountant. I wanted him to do my taxes only, but he wanted to do much more. I spent an hour arguing with him before he came to accept the fact that I was not going to pay him hundreds of dollars to "design" a special system for me. In fact, when he came to the realization that he would have to accept me on my terms or not at all, he finally admitted that my decision to use the simple Dome system was probably a wise decision for me, and we have had no problems since, except that he complains about my giving him too much detail at tax time. But we like the detail; it tells us how we are doing and allows us to take corrective steps in time to solve any potential problems. That's a critical consideration.

Accountants' Special Language

Accountants have their own jargon, just as lawyers, doctors, engineers, and insurance experts do. It can be confusing because words that you and I believe we understand have different meanings when accountants use them. For example, you might take "cost of sales" to mean marketing or selling cost, what it cost you to get the order. That's not what it means in the accountant's office. There it refers to all the costs to fill the order. A sale is not an order there; it's money received. "Cash basis" doesn't mean what you think it means, either; to an accountant it means you post a payment when you make it and a receipt when you get it, whereas in some systems you post a payment when you get the bill and a receipt when you send out the invoice.

I confess that I do not understand most of the jargon, either. I manage to live with it by ignoring it. I am not the least bit afraid to ask "dumb questions." As in the case of dealing with your lawyer, be sure that you understand what your accountant tells you. Ask all the dumb questions you like, without inhibition, and make sure that you *understand* and *agree* with the rationale before you bow to your accountant's recommendation.

In short, use your accountant as a doer of things you can't or don't want to do yourself and as an advisor whose opinions are worthy of serious consideration but not necessarily indicative of the course you will finally pursue. You, then, and no one else, must make the decisions.

What Accounting Is: Its True Purpose

Far too many individuals entering into business subscribe to the naïve notion that the major purpose of accounting is to please the IRS. That is not so. The main purpose of accounting is to support management by furnishing information.

Management is a topic of never-ending fascination in the business world. Hundreds of books are published on the subject every year, and it is taught to thousands of college students. It is offered in thousands of seminars and special training courses. And every few years there comes a new theory or technique of management that promises to offer new insights into effective management styles. We have had Program Planning Budget Systems, Program Evaluation and Review Technique, Management Grid, Cost Effectiveness, Management by Objectives, Theory X, Theory Y, Theory Z, Quality Circles, One-Minute Management, management through people, and others. And still managers look for some essential ingredient, some magic formula that will reduce management to an exact science so that anyone can be equipped with simple tools to effect great management.

These mavens of management are equally fond of creating clever little aphorisms. They are especially addicted to adages that suggest the management is the art of manipulating people. They say such things as "Management is the art of getting other people to do what you want them to do," or "Management is the art of getting people to *want to do* what you want them to do!"

Management is not that mystical or complex, nor is the mastery of it that simple. (Nor, in my opinion, is it that cynical an art.) If I had to reduce this to some brief definition, I would be inclined to say that management is the art of getting maximum desired results from available resources. It may or may not have to do with other people. Even small enterprises in which one person does it all have to be managed!

Management is mostly a matter of objective thinking and sound judgment, qualities that cannot be reduced to mechanical functions nor built into simple tools. Most of all, even given the capacity to reason objectively and arrive at sound judgments, it is a matter of information, for no one can think objectively and make sound judgments without having the essential information. Any decision is not and cannot be any better than the information upon which it is based. Therefore, the information produced by accounting is essential to good management; and producing sound management information is the major objective of and reason for accounting.

THE INFORMATION YOU NEED

To put you in total control of your enterprise, your accounting system must deliver the most critically important items. A list of these items follows:

Overhead costs. Rent, heat, light, telephone, advertising, postage, etc.; what and how much they are and whether they remain relatively constant or fluctuate.

Sales figures. Dollar figures, frequency of sales, types of sales/-clients, trends up or down, if any.

Cost of sales. Total cost of winning and completing every project or assignment.

Markup. How much you are adding to your total estimated cost of each project so that you can meet all expenses and realize a profit.

Profit. Surplus over *all* costs for each job, in total and as an average.

Studying this kind of information regularly will enable you to discover almost immediately any increases in costs, decline in sales, slippage in profitability, and relative profitability of one type of sale or project over another. These are all key factors in the success of your enterprise. It is a fact of business life that even in a small enterprise you can be so busily engaged that you can go on for months losing money without being aware of it. Unfortunately, if enough time elapses and enough money has been lost before you discover that costs have gotten out of hand or that you are marking up your costs insufficiently, it may be too late to recover. Current information is essential to the health of your enterprise.

For example, when my business required a great deal of printing on a regular basis, I kept a close watch over printing costs. If they appeared to be climbing more steeply than they should, I conferred with my printer over it or even changed printers. Sometimes I found that one printer had the best price on one type of work, while another had the best price on another kind of work. And in some cases, where the schedules permitted it, I had the work done out of town, via mail order, which often reduced the cost.

This information also told me clearly what types of activities were most and least profitable. This is certainly indispensable information for planning future action—that is, what types of sales and contracts to pursue and which to avoid.

On the other hand, I was well aware of what were reportedly the typical sales seasons—peaks and valleys of activity and sales volume—and I monitored my own sales accordingly. Surprisingly often I found that my own sales did not follow the reported pattern, but were even the exact opposite, peaking when the conventional wisdom said sales should be in a lull. The conventional wisdom is only opinion; the ledger figures are facts.

SOME COMMON MISTAKES OF BEGINNING CONSULTANTS

Business experts with the U.S. Small Business Administration and Dun & Bradstreet often report and remark on the high rate of failures among small businesses, often as high as 70 percent of new starts. This indicates a success rate of approximately 30 percent. This may seem minuscule, but it is amazing that as many as 30 percent do survive and succeed given that (1) a large majority of these new starts are by beginners with no prior business experience and (2) there is an enormous "opportunity" to make fatal mistakes. Some of those typical mistakes that often prove fatal to the newly launched small business include:

Failing to understand the meaning of *profit*. A great many beginners in business think that everything left after recovering costs is profit, but they fail to assign themselves a salary and count that as one of the costs.

Assuming that successful marketing means being the low bidder. Many beginners underprice everything they bid on and assume that they will somehow manage to muddle through. They do not use a realistic estimating system.

Overpricing everything they bid on. Again, they do not use a sound estimating system.

Failing to charge their enterprises for—that is, count as business costs—items provided from personal possessions (e.g., use of a personal automobile, telephone, office space at home, etc.).

Independent consultants who operate this way do not always fail—many go on for years eking out a living of sorts—but their practices are, nevertheless, failures as business enterprises. Financial success means being able to realize personal income that is at least as much as you could earn on someone else's payroll and yet showing a reasonable profit each year—at least 5 to 10 percent after taxes. It is commonly accepted that a business that is not growing is a failure, and no business can grow without a profit.

SOME BASIC RULES

You must know and charge on your books each and every cost incurred for and in your practice.

Your personal draw or salary is a cost, chargeable to the practice. *It is not part of profit.*

Anything you supply in kind, such as office space in your home or a personal computer you already own, must be evaluated and charged at fair value. You may want to pro rate the cost or "sell" the property to your practice, as appropriate. (The IRS allows charges only for space in your home that is *totally dedicated* to the business.)

All costs must be recovered by the practice, and you must price work so as to recover all costs and show some profit.

Despite all this, you must still be competitive in price. That means you must keep close control over your costs.

BASIC COST CENTERS AND COST DEFINITIONS

It is not the purpose of this book to teach you accounting, nor am I at all qualified to do so. However, it is extremely important to have a thorough understanding of costs if you are to be successful. My experience delivering seminars and consulting services to the owners of small businesses—especially those in consulting enterprises—has demonstrated quite clearly the need for this kind of information.

Were you to take a formal course in accounting you would soon find yourself learning a large number of technical terms. But here we will consider only the most basic concepts concerning costs so that you will not only have a general understanding of this important subject, but you will know enough about it to ask the right questions when you do not understand something. Knowledge of these concepts will also provide you with valuable management information, as discussed earlier.

One concept you must remember is that there are only two kinds of dollars—those you take in and those you pay out. Don't allow any jargon to cloud your view on this. Every dollar discussed or posted in any accounting system falls into one of those two classes—income or outgo—no matter what the accountant calls it. (Dollars invested in plant, inventory, or other centers are not an exception to this; they are neither income nor outgo, but are simply dollars—assets—converted to some other form.)

The concept of "cost centers" is essential to your understanding of accounting procedures. It means, simply, that there are a number of main categories, or "centers," of cost. For example, there are fixed plant costs, which represent the cost to your practice of your physical facility (e.g., heat, light, maintenance, etc.). Payroll, or labor costs, is another cost center, as are marketing and printing, if you have appreciable quantities of these costs.

Each enterprise has its own cost centers, and they vary from one to another. Advertising is a cost center only if you spend a significant portion of your operating budget on advertising and you want to establish it as a cost center. You may want it to be a major consideration in your accounting system, so you set up a special account or even a separate ledger for it. However, that is not as important as recognizing that it represents some significant portion of your total costs and distinguishing it, at least in your mind, as one that merits keeping an eye on it and keeping it under control.

Another way to define or identify costs, again as arbitrary identifiers, is to use functional names. For example, certain costs may be identified as variable costs because they do not remain constant from month to month. Telephone charges, travel expenses, and printing costs may fall into this class. On the other hand, rent is a fixed cost, at least for some extended period, usually a year at a time.

Other common categories are overhead costs, material costs, and G&A, a type of cost similar to that of overhead. Do not let these terms confuse you. Remember that these are functional names, assigned to remind you of the nature of the costs and help you understand where the money is going. For example, advertising may be a fixed cost or a variable cost, and it may also be an overhead cost, depending on where and how you choose to assign it. Nevertheless, it is a cost. Regardless of the name used, these are all costs, and no amount of jargon can change that. One major distinction in type of costs that is essential to make, however, is that of direct and indirect costs.

Direct and Indirect Costs

It is obviously true that it costs money to operate any kind of business venture, large or small. However, the ratio of direct to indirect costs varies widely for different types of enterprises. What is considered a direct cost in one kind of venture may be considered indirect in another enterprise. The difference may be due to the nature of the enterprise, it may be the result of an individual accounting system, or it may simply reflect the owner's personal preferences.

It is critically important to understand these two broad categories of cost. In some circumstances, such as most marketing to governments and their agencies, success in winning the contract depends on this understanding, as reflected in your proposals.

Any cost incurred specifically and exclusively for and assignable totally to a given project, task, assignment, or client is a *direct cost*. Any cost incurred in general and not assignable to or identifiable as having been incurred specifically and exclusively for some project, task, assignment, or client is an *indirect* cost.

Direct Costs

In most cases the chief item of direct cost on your bill is labor, your own labor or that of associates or employees. Consulting is a labor-intensive enterprise, which means it provides services and normally does not require a significant investment in equipment and/or inventory. As an independent consultant you usually bill your client mainly for your services, based on the time you have devoted to the client.

You often have other direct costs, even if they are not significant portions of the entire bill. These costs should be added to the labor charge when billing a client. A list of costs typically incurred in consulting follows:

Travel
Per diem (food and lodging)
Telephone toll charges
Printing/copying (reports, etc.)
Express delivery charges
Mainframe computer time
Online database charges
Messenger services
Secretarial/stenographic support

If your accounting system is such that you have no way of distinguishing which costs were incurred for which client, you obviously cannot bill your client directly for such charges. Still, you must recover those costs if you are to stay in business. In this case you must call those costs indirect and recover them in your overhead rate, as indirect costs.

Considering these costs to be *indirect* may seem convenient because it simplifies your recordkeeping to a small extent; however, treating these costs as *direct* costs wherever possible offers certain distinct advantages. It minimizes your overhead rate and is thus beneficial to your marketing and sales efforts; it also places the costs where they belong. For example, if you make a number of long-distance calls in connection with a specific project, those calls ought to be charged to that project and that client. And to do so you must keep records of and ascertain the costs of those calls.

The same thing applies to printing, messenger service, travel, and other expenses. They are "other direct costs" (other than direct labor, that is) and are normally recorded as such in cost estimates. If you do not take the time to keep track of such other direct costs and to charge them to the proper contract and client, you are inflating your overhead unnecessarily and inflicting those costs on other clients, not to mention adding to your own burdens in marketing your services at the same time.

There is one exception to this. Costs incurred for overhead activities (e.g., marketing) should be recorded and logged so that you can determine the cost of the activity, but the cost is entirely an indirect cost.

Indirect Costs

Most ventures have many indirect costs, a few of which have been cited earlier, and these fall into several broad categories. A list of typical indirect costs includes:

Rent (which may or may not include heat, light, and other utility expenses)
Parking
Insurance (usually several kinds, some required by law, others by prudence)
Taxes (depending on location and local laws)
Licenses (as appropriate, if and as required by local laws)
Depreciation (recovering the cost of major equipment, furniture, and other capital items)
Stationery (business cards, letterheads, and envelopes, at the least)
Advertising (any/all)

Telephone (at least that portion covering the general service, not assignable to specific projects)

Travel (general, including auto expense, unless assignable to specific projects)

Printing and copying (general, that portion not assignable to a specific client)

Contributions to charitable causes, political campaigns, etc. (you can be sure that you will be solicited)

Subscriptions (you should subscribe to several journals)

Memberships (you should belong to a professional association or two)

Entertainment (business lunches, etc.)

Some of these costs or portions of them may appear as "other direct costs" in some projects. It is possible that a project will call for you to travel, to print materials, or to advertise as part of a contracted project. Such expenses become direct costs.

Kinds of Indirect Cost. Many people equate indirect cost with overhead, using the two terms interchangeably. However, *overhead* is really a category of indirect cost.

The cost of *fringe benefits* is another subcategory of indirect costs. Paid time off (holidays and leave), free group insurance, stock options, bonuses, and other such items are accounted for and posted separately from the rest of the normal overhead.

G&A (general and administrative costs) is considered an indirect cost as well. The G&A expense pool includes certain special classes of expenses, typically those costs incurred to support the central corporate core of large organizations. A multidivisional corporation would assign all costs of operating the central headquarters or corporate offices to the G&A pool, for example. However, not everyone keeps a G&A account, although it is essential when doing business with most government agencies.

Overhead is a Rate. Overhead and G&A are dollars, of course, as all costs are. However, for estimating purposes, it is generally necessary to establish an overhead *rate*, the ratio of the overhead dollars to some other factor. In labor-intensive operations such as consulting, the other factor is generally the cost of direct labor. If, for example, you find at the end of a year that your costs for direct labor were $100,000 and your various overhead charges for the year total $65,000, the rate is 65,000/100,000 or 65 percent. That is, for every dollar paid for direct labor you paid 65 cents for overhead expenses, so that your total labor cost—direct plus indirect—was actually $165,000 for the year. To that must be added whatever other direct and indirect costs you may have incurred. If you had another $14,000 worth of such costs, your total cost for the year was $179,000. If you had not separated those other direct costs, your overhead rate would have been 79,000/100,000 or 79 percent ($65,000 overhead plus $14,000 in direct and indirect costs divided by $100,000, the cost of direct labor).

The first year presents something of a problem because you have no previous figures on which to base an overhead rate. Therefore, you must use the best estimate you can. You should be able to accommodate an overhead rate of 65 to 85 percent in a typical independent consultancy if you keep track of all charges that should be recorded as direct costs and thus do not burden your overhead rate unfairly. However, that would be a reasonable expectation for an established consultancy, one in which you were busy a reasonable proportion of your time—say two-thirds—in projects with billable time. Unfortunately, that is not often the case in newly established practices. Time and money spent in marketing efforts is likely to be your chief overhead activity the first year and may well occupy more than one-half your time.

That does not mean that you should shoot for an overhead rate of 100 percent or higher the first year. To do so is likely to make your marketing even more difficult, unless you compensate for the high rate with a modest direct rate for your time. Either way, you will have to be competitive, and you may have to subsidize your operations extensively the first year.

In today's consulting market there are probably few fully capable consultants accepting a daily rate of less than $500, although that may vary somewhat with local conditions and individual policies. For example, $500 works out to $62.50 per hour on the basis of an eight-hour working day, but one consultant does not charge for overtime while another does. Or one may charge a $50 hourly rate, but charge premiums for overtime, weekends, and holidays.

Let's take a hypothetical case in which you decide that you ought to pay yourself $25 an hour (a $52,000 salary), but you estimate that your overhead rate the first year will be about 125 percent. That means that you must charge the client $25 + $31.25 = $56.25 (cost per hour) × 8 + $50 (pretax profit) = $500 a day. That is generally a competitive rate in today's market. If you are doing billable work about one-third of the time, you are billing at the rate of about \$43,300 a year. This will not even cover your own salary much less all the costs, which your estimate will have established as \$52,000 + (1.25 × \$52,000) or \$117,000.

Even if you raise your rate a little to equal \$600 a day you will have increased total income by only about \$26,000. If you succeed in keeping overhead down to, say, 65 percent, while charging \$500 per day and paying yourself a more modest \$15 an hour, the figures would be quite different. Total estimated costs for the year would be: \$31,200 for salary and \$20,280 for overhead, for a total of \$51,480. Total billing (income) would be approximately \$43,300, with a gross profit (loss) of \$8,180.

While still a loss figure, the latter is considerably more tolerable and a great deal closer to the break-even point. A small increase of billable days, about 7 percent, would put your practice on the brink of profit. However, increasing the number of billable days is not the only answer. You should be especially conservative in generating and controlling costs, as well as in minimizing what you draw personally that first year, and you should remember these two important points:

1. You need to market aggressively and continuously. There is probably never a time when it is safe to relax in the quest for new clients.
2. You need to maximize the number and type of potentially profitable activities in your practice, for there are many ways of providing your consulting services to clients.

Both of these are very important aspects of building a successful consulting practice, but by far the most important areas are marketing and sales—that is, finding leads and closing them.

4

Marketing and Sales: Finding Leads and Closing Them

There are several ways to judge the health of an enterprise, and a close study of the sales log is a good place to start.

SUCCESS IN MARKETING IS ALWAYS A TONIC FOR AN AILING BUSINESS

According to such expert sources as the Small Business Administration, a major cause of small-business failure is "undercapitalization,"— not enough money. But not enough money for what? Not enough to make a proper original investment? Not enough to advertise adequately? Not enough to market properly? Not enough to survive many months of "negative cash flow" (another euphemism meaning more money going out than coming in)? These expert observers rarely focus their diagnosis more closely than this. It's difficult to deny that any failed business might well have survived (although perhaps only for a little longer) given more capital to invest in support of the venture.

Other causes cited frequently for the many failures of small businesses every year are the broad generalizations of inadequacies or inexperience in management, accounting, inventory control, purchasing, and other areas.

The one cause of failure rarely cited is inadequate, ineffective marketing. And yet that is almost surely by far the most common cause of business failure. For example, E. J. Korvette, Robert Hall, and W. T. Grant, were all profitable, growing companies that suddenly failed and could not be resurrected.

Many explain such failures to be the result of companies not "keeping up with the times." Others accuse the organizations of poor management, failing to meet competition, and similar shortcomings in their business operations. These are more rationalizations than explanations; they blame but don't explain what is meant by failing to "keep up with the times," "poor management," and other alleged derelictions of business responsibility. For almost all business failures, these and others, ultimately translate into failures in the marketing functions of the organization. Their sales begin to slip, and they continue to slip until they begin to experience that famous "negative cash flow"—losing money—and ultimately they are out of capital and over their heads in debt. Yes, they fail to keep up with competition and "the times" (i.e., changes in the marketplace, changes in popular merchandise, changes in methods of marketing). Perhaps they become complacent and fail to detect the changes and the slippage taking place. Perhaps they smugly assure themselves that they have become household words, have built such secure niches that they simply cannot perish. But even mighty Chrysler would have perished as a result of declining sales had it not been for (1) federal government rescue operations; (2) a new and tough chief executive officer who did something about their lagging sales, as well as almost single-handedly persuading the federal government that the economy of the United States could not afford the failure of Chrysler; and (3) an almost-too-good-to-believe recovery of the automobile market at the right time.

Those failures just referred to were the failures of organizations who no longer felt "hungry" enough to fight for sales, who thought that they could take their customers—former customers, as it turned out—for granted. All the most brilliant management, superb accounting systems, totally efficient inventory control, tough-minded and shrewd purchasing, and other such hallmarks of the well-managed organization will not save the organization that does not make enough sales. Nor will the normal deficiencies in all these important functions of management and administration bring about the collapse of an organization that is demonstrating marketing success—that is, making enough sales. It is actually difficult to fail when your marketing is highly successful and almost impossible to succeed when your marketing success is marginal at best.

It is no exaggeration to say that marketing is by far the single most important function of even the established organization, but far more so of the new venture, for neither survival nor success is possible without successful marketing. Every other problem can be solved or overcome when the sales are producing the income that is the bloodstream of the venture.

WHAT IS MARKETING?

There is a great deal of confusion about marketing, beginning with understanding just what marketing is. A great many people, including many who ought to know better, believe that marketing and sales are synonomous terms with synonomous functions. That is not so, and the difference is more than semantic.

For one thing, marketing is not confined to organizations dedicated to earning profits; every organization must market to survive. Churches and temples seek new members and donations. Military organizations seek recruits. Politicians seek voters and campaign contributors. Political parties seek volunteer workers. The Red Cross seeks blood donors. Even the U.S. Postal Service and the Federal Supply Service have marketing organizations, and all government agencies lobby their legislators seeking supporters for larger budgets every year.

It's all marketing. Marketing is the pursuit of whatever or whoever it is that provides the sustenance for the organization (e.g., customers, clients, members, donors, contributors, volunteers, enlistees, etc.).

That begins to sound very much like sales, and in many ways it is difficult to distinguish the two from each other, especially when we study marketing in terms of independent consulting. In fact, it is fair to consider that the sales function is part of marketing, the final act of marketing, whereas the earlier actions include preparatory and necessary activities and functions. The following steps illustrate this progression:

1. Decide (define/identify) exactly what you want to market—what is to be your service (and/or product, if there is one).
2. Decide (define/identify) what your market is–*who* you are going to sell to—those who are the right prospects for your service.
3. Determine how you will reach those prospects with your presentation.

4. Define your specific *offer.*
5. Design your sales campaign and carry it out.

Decide What You Want To Market

There is a built-in dilemma in deciding exactly what your service is to be. Making the service too narrow limits your market, but making your service too broad dilutes and weakens your image as a consultant, who is by definition a specialist, not a generalist. As we discussed earlier, start with whatever appears to you to be the right answer—a compromise between the two extremes—and use your experience, as you go, to modify your services (and/or product) until you are satisfied you have found what you need and want.

Decide What Your Market Is

As an independent consultant you can't market effectively to the entire world. (Even supercorporations have difficulty trying to do this.) Having decided, at least on a provisional basis, what services you will provide, you must identify the right prospects for those services—those most likely to need or want those services, hence, most likely to become your clients. This is a critical step.

Determine How You Will Reach Those Prospects

Obviously you must be able to reach your prospects with a presentation of what you have to offer if the prospect list is to be of any value to you. In my own case I tried to rent mailing lists of the kinds of prospects I wanted to reach—those who were most likely to need help in writing proposals—and found that I couldn't do so. Despite the enormous variety of mailing lists handled by the list brokers, and despite the many ways in which the list brokers could have their computers manipulate, sort, merge, organize, and reorganize all those lists that made up the mailing list databases, the listbrokers could not produce for me a specialized list of government contractors of the types that I wanted. It was not their fault; none of their names were coded in such a manner as to enable them to do that for me.

I therefore had to build my own mailing lists, which meant also that I had to find or invent the means for doing so. In fact, being able to reach the prospects you have targeted is one of the tests for the validity of your prospect definition. Obviously it is only valid if you can find the means for reaching them and presenting your sales appeal. Otherwise it is only an interesting theory.

Define Your Specific Offer

In defining the specific offer we are much closer to the sales function, to devising a sales *strategy,* in fact. Here, too, is where we get to some rather fine points of definition about what the word *offer* really means. Probably to most people, even to a great many marketing specialists, the offer is simply what they wish to sell. In my case, were I to use that concept, my offer would be services in writing or helping to write proposals or whatever other services I provide to my clients in that connection. But that is not what I mean by the term *offer,* as used here and in the list of marketing functions. For while I do help my clients develop proposals and I do train their staffs in proposal writing, my *offer* is to help them win contracts. That is what my clients really want. Their hope that I can help them achieve that inspires them to retain me and pay me the fees I charge.

Therefore, the offer is what you promise to *do* for the client as a *benefit* resulting from your services, and this must be based on whatever you believe is the client's most ardent wish. The benefit they will receive from your services is the reason for retaining you and paying you for those services. This is true even when the client does not consciously recognize it! To define your offer properly, you must understand the client's mind—you must know what the client hopes to achieve in retaining you.

Design Your Sales Campaign and Carry it Out

Now that you know what you wish to sell, to whom you wish to sell it, how you will reach those prospects to present your offer, and what your offer is to be, you are finally ready to design your sales campaign.

You reach prospective clients in many ways—making direct calls, mailing literature, becoming active in associations, lecturing, writing, getting your name on bidders' lists, and registering with agents or brokers who can help you win assignments. In this phase of marketing you decide what ways you will use, prepare the sales materials you need for this, and plan the methods and schedules. The more carefully you have designed this campaign the more successful it is likely to be. But "design" is based on all those earlier marketing steps, so that the effectiveness of your sales campaign depends largely on how well you have done the earlier marketing work. This is why it is the difficult to separate the two terms. Both refer to winning business—clients, in this case—but while sales is the business of wooing and winning clients, marketing is the business of determining what clients to woo and win and how to go about doing so.

DISCOVERING WHAT CLIENTS WISH TO BUY

Deciding what services to sell cannot be based on what *you* want; they must be based on what clients want. But, you say, how can I know what clients want?

That question can be answered in two words—ask them— although that is admittedly not a satisfying answer, at least not until we determine how to go about asking them and getting useful answers. I do not mean literally to begin approaching strangers who appear to be good prospects and saying, "Hello, what kind of consulting services do you want to buy?" And yet, in effect that's what I do propose you do. For there are several ways to ask the prospective clients what they want and what it will take to persuade them to become clients.

First, let's start with a few generalities we know to be true:

Everyone has problems.

Everyone wants to solve those problems.

Everyone has at least one problem that is more worrisome than the others, for some reason, more urgently in need of solution.

Everyone has desires, things they want to gain.

Everyone has fears, things they want to avoid.

These simple statements are the basis for all advertising and for all marketing and sales. It is through knowing and taking advantage of these truths that all successful sales and marketing are achieved, for these are the motivators, the reasons people say yes to various sales appeals.

Consider how insurance is sold, for example. Probably a few people buy insurance as a means for saving money, but by far the majority of people who buy insurance do so out of fear, the fear of being defenseless in an emergency. They are motivated by the sense of insecurity most of us have, which insurance salespeople fully understand and use in reminding us of the need to have this hedge against disaster.

Basic Motivations

All marketing and sales efforts are necessarily based on some preconceived motivational factor. If fear or the desire to avoid some result is one basic motivation, the desire to gain is the other. Most efforts to sell material items are based on this motivation. Every effective sales appeal can be shown to conform with this. Consider the consulting specialties that follow, and mentally check off the motivational factor, fear or gain, you believe would be most likely to inspire prospects to become clients:

Plant/office/home security measures	☐ Fear	☐ Gain
Engineering	☐ Fear	☐ Gain
Financial advisor	☐ Fear	☐ Gain
Executive search	☐ Fear	☐ Gain
Convention planning	☐ Fear	☐ Gain
Hearing aid	☐ Fear	☐ Gain
Public relations	☐ Fear	☐ Gain
Safety	☐ Fear	☐ Gain
Training	☐ Fear	☐ Gain
Mergers and acquisitions	☐ Fear	☐ Gain
Receptions and party planning	☐ Fear	☐ Gain
Taxes	☐ Fear	☐ Gain
Industrial methods	☐ Fear	☐ Gain

Transportation	☐ Fear	☐ Gain
Office organization	☐ Fear	☐ Gain

Some of these were rather obvious. The first one, services in behalf of physical security, is obviously sold via the fear motivation, for that is dictated by the very nature of the service. On the other hand, anyone wishing to get help in an executive search wishes to gain something.

In most cases the motivation could be either fear or gain. Even in the case of plant security the motive could be gain, under certain circumstances. Suppose, for example, that a company has a person on staff who is responsible for plant security, and that person, for whatever reason, wants help in discharging that obligation. While the reason for having the security function is fear, the motive in retaining a consultant is gain—that is, gaining help in doing the job.

The same consideration applies to some other items and can be applied to marketing them, given certain circumstances or kinds of needs. In our example, the owner of the plant and the individual responsible for making it secure have different motivations. Each might retain a security consultant, but each has a different problem than the other, and that is at the heart of the marketing strategy. You must know what the problem is to make the most effective appeal—that is, to make the right *offer*.

It is identifying the problem to be solved that is the key to developing the strategies of the marketing and sales campaign. It is a cliché of marketing that every salesperson must be a consultant to be effective, in the sense that every salesperson should be offering to solve the prospect's problem in making the sales appeal. Determining what the problem is becomes the next step.

Go back to the list of consulting specialities again and decide which items could be sold via either or both basic motivations and the circumstances or needs under which one or the other appeal would be used. This analysis leads directly to the formulation of the offer because it is based on determining what the prospect's need is—what want must be satisfied. This is the key to the entire appeal. It is the final objective of the entire marketing effort—that is, making the right appeal to the right prospect.

* * *

What I hope you found in scanning the list of consulting specialties is that most, in fact probably all, services listed could conceivably be sold by either or both fear and gain motivation. That is a general truth, although it does not mean that all sales appeals ought to be based on both motivations. In most cases one is far more useful than the other and applicable to far more situations—that is, it is much more likely to be appealing to the majority of prospects than the other. Even in selling life insurance, gain motivation (e.g., gaining peace of mind) might be used with some effect, but the fear motivation is almost invariably far more effective.

Motivation versus Prospect

The matter of who the prospect is may be the determining factor in what the motivation must be. In the security example used earlier, the plant owner and the security manager each had a different problem as a result of his or her different responsibilities. Simply knowing the prospect's identity (in terms of job responsibilities, in this case) furnishes the major clue to proper motivation. Suppose you were a security specialist and had decided that the prospects you would target (and could reach effectively) were all individuals responsible for plant security. But you knew that these prospects were not themselves expert in the field of security; they didn't even have much time to research the subject because they were all general administrators in industrial plants and had many duties to perform. That would dictate your general strategy of offering your help and special expertise, perhaps in an appeal that stressed: "Don't go it alone; special expertise is readily available." But even so you might find a fear motivation workable: "Your plant is not as secure as you think it is; let an expert show you the most modern methods."

In short, it is essential to know who and what your prospect is (and/or to have selected a target audience of prospects most carefully and thoughtfully) when devising your strategies.

It might be helpful to scan that list of consulting specialties and motivations once again, considering the different types of prospects you might target and how each choice would affect the motivator you would use and the general strategies upon which you would base your offer. It will dramatize for you the extreme importance of planning your marketing by identifying the prospects for your services.

Motivational Research Methods

There is an entire field of activity in marketing, especially in the subordinate field of advertising, given to motivational research—that is, to what inspires people generally to buy. But it applies to the general consumer market. In marketing your consulting services, the research you do is far different and depends on how, as well as to whom, you propose to sell your services.

The Most Basic Method

We have been discussing a first method of research, a method based on your own advance knowledge of your field and of the prospect to whom your appeal is addressed, combined with a simple analysis of probabilities. Many marketing campaigns are based on nothing more than that, and that is sufficient in many cases. But there are other research methods available, some of them far more specific and more precisely focused.

Personal Interviews

If your chosen method of marketing includes making personal calls, you have an excellent opportunity to conduct the kind of research that leads to effective sales presentations. Until now we have been discussing common problems, problems stated on a broad and general basis, as they apply to a large number of prospects. However, in personal discussions with prospects you have the opportunity to discover and address the specific problem(s) of the individual prospect, as well as learning (over the course of many such calls and interviews) what are the general problems of your chosen population of prospects.

Identifying problems ought to be the first order of business in such calls. As an example, when I was devoting much of my time to developing training programs for government agencies, I once called on an executive in the Occupational Safety and Health Adminstration (OSHA) training office. I introduced myself briefly and inquired as to the nature of the work in that office. I learned very quickly that the major focus of the moment was the installation of courses to train occupational safety and health technicians, and the immediate problem was developing a junior-college curriculum based on a new training program the office had had developed by a contractor.

The contractor had delivered two manuals, a student manual and an instructor's manual, but not a word suggesting a method of implementation of these into a formal course of instruction. The manuals themselves were complete in their coverage, but the instructor's manual failed to lay out any guidelines for its use.

A simple proposal offering to solve the problem won an immediate purchase order and, subsequently, a great deal more work from that office and others to which my services were later recommended by this satisfied client.

The key is to do far more listening than talking, especially in the early stages of the visit. You should encourage the prospective client to talk; you also should have (and show) a healthy and sincere interest in learning more. There is a pattern for this:

Learn in advance–before the actual visit–as much as you can about the general and immediate organization and the individual upon whom you are calling.

Ask a few general questions, phrasing them so as to make it clear that you have "done your homework" and know something of the organization, but want to learn a little more.

Guide the conversation to learn about the routine, everyday problems of the organization.

Continue this to zero in on the most troublesome problem(s) of the moment (the chief "worry item" or problem the prospect appears most eager to solve).

Discuss possible solution approaches to determine where the prospect's interests lie or what approach appears most acceptable.

Offer your specific services to test general reaction; discover the organization's normal methods for purchasing services, and get clues as to the best followup.

Propose specific followup, such as making a telephone call, submitting a proposal, arranging a presentation, or other measures, as discussion has suggested.

Usually this kind of call and interview is itself a follow-up of a lead gained earlier; it is difficult to arrange this spontaneously in the course of making cold calls. It is an important step, however, for most consulting assignments of any reasonably large size. The purpose of such calls is to make sales, of course, with research being a fallout of the calls, rather than the objective. The research benefit should not be neglected, however, because it is an important factor in making your marketing increasingly effective.

Of course, this entire approach may not be suitable for you. One individual who considers himself to be an independent consultant is a hypnotist who focuses his services on helping people overcome phobias. However, because of the widespread interest in giving up cigarettes he has made special efforts to help individuals quit smoking, and he conducts both individual sessions and group sessions. For him, obviously, the personal call on prospective clients (or are they patients?) is not a viable marketing plan. The same consideration would apply to others who deal in services to individuals or groups and charge by the hour, by the visit, or by the series constituting a program, such as financial advisors, investment counselors, and résumé consultants.

Surveys and Questionnaires

Surveys and questionnaires are a traditional method of gaining information from a large number of people. This may or may not be suitable for your purposes, depending on whether you have or can acquire a suitable mailing list and can devote the time and money to what is usually a rather tedious and expensive program. However, if your practice already includes some form of direct mail (e.g., a newsletter), you are already well-equipped to conduct such a research program.

Generating Leads

Except for those special situations such as the hypnotist and the investment counselor, consulting assignments are normally fairly sizeable, usually running to at least several hundred dollars and more often to several thousand dollars or more. This consideration alone (although there are also others) dictates that the marketing of consulting services is not a "one-call business." You rarely win a contract in a single call or sales appeal to a prospective client; it almost always requires a series of contacts, appeals, and/or presentations to a prospect to acquire a new project or client, and often even to win a new project from an old client.

This means, in practical terms, that making sales of your consulting service normally involves and requires at least two distinct steps:

(1) prospecting for and getting sales leads—people and situations that appear to be good prospects for contacts; and (2) following up the leads to sell and close.

To a large degree, generating the leads is the step that determines the ultimate success of the marketing. If the prospecting is not done well a great many "leads" may result that prove not to be leads at all, given that a legitimate sales lead is a true prospect for a contract.

Using Inquiry Advertising for Motivational Research

Inquiry advertising is advertising designed specifically to generate leads. Distributors of direct mail sometimes run advertisements offering something free or for a nominal cost (e.g., a newsletter, a special report, or a product). This method is designed to elicit responses from only those who would be good prospects for whatever the mailer wishes to sell. The direct mail dealer does this to build a mailing list of good prospects. Automobile dealers, real estate brokers, home improvement firms, and many others who are in enterprises that are not one-call businesses use the same idea; it's just the method that's different. The automobile dealer or real estate broker may offer to buy the respondent's lunch or provide a free floor mat to anyone who calls to see the new models and comes to listen to the sales presentation; the home improvement dealer probably sends a salesperson to call or follows up with a telephone call and an effort to set up an appointment to call on the respondent.

Judicious mailings or advertisements of your own will soon provide you with the clues you need, while they also develop leads for you to follow up on. By experimenting with what you offer as an inducement to respond, you can soon determine what the respondents' chief interests and concerns are. As an example, return to our plant security expert. You want to evoke responses from such individuals to develop leads. You have a mailing list you developed from association directories, advertising, the yellow pages, and other sources, so you decide to make a mailing.

You construct a simple sales letter in which you introduce yourself briefly and advise the readers that if their plant is using security devices and systems that are more than ten years old they are woefully out of date and ineffective. But if the plant security expert will send you a request on a formal letterhead or accompanied by a business card, you will send, free of charge, a special report explaining what it takes to be up to date in plant security today.

You construct a slight variation of that letter too. The second version explains that plant security is not a part-time job; it requires frequent inspections. You'll be happy to send a free report explaining how to make such inspections, if the respondent makes the request on a letterhead and/or with a business card.

A third variation says that there are several common mistakes made in designing plant security systems, as a free report you have explains. Again, you make the free offer.

The report you are going to send is the same in each case, and covers all the points made in each letter. However, you code each of these letters so you can tell which one each request responds to. You can do this by making variations in your name (e.g., J.F. Smith, John F. Smith, J. Frederick Smith) by altering your address (e.g., Dept. 23, Drawer 46, or Security Specialties), or by other such devices.

You print and mail an equal number of these to portions of your mailing list—perhaps 500 or 1,000 each—and wait for results. The response rate will tell you which was the most productive appeal—that is, which produced the largest number of sales leads to follow up.

You could offer to make a free plant inspection to anyone who requests it, but that is likely to produce fewer responses because it will be taken by many as equivalent to "Yes, I am interested. Please send a salesperson to see me." Probably a better time to offer that free security inspection, if you wish to offer it, is in following up the first response, when you are trying to set up a personal call and interview.

Alternatives to Mailing

There are other ways to get your offer to potential prospects if you do not have a mailing list, don't want to run advertisements, or want to supplement either of these. Make your letters into simple brochures and distribute them on literature tables at conventions, conferences, seminars, workshops, association meetings, and other such events and occasions.

You can often manage to run your simple print advertisement, offering your brochure or special report, as an editorial or news item in local newspapers, trade magazines, association journals, and newsletters. You can also make that offer by mailing news releases, which will be discussed in Chapter 5.

"I KNOW IT WHEN I SEE IT"

The preceding discussion was based on the assumption that the client knows what he or she wants—that is, the client recognizes not only the existence of a problem, but knows what the problem is and what is necessary to solve or eliminate it. The client has what is sometimes referred to as a "felt need."

There are also clients who feel a need but have not identified precisely what that need is. Some authors have recently labeled this as the I-know-it-when-I-see-it philosophy. In fact, the client probably observes certain symptoms but has not tried or been able to analyze those symptoms and decide what the problem, or the remedy, is. Often the situation is like the nail in the shoe; it's an annoying condition, but not intolerable, and you are too busy to take care of it right now. You'll get around to it one day, when you have the time. However, if you just happen to be standing in front of a shoe-repair shop while waiting for a bus, you might just stop in and have the nail removed or pounded down, simply because it is now suddenly and by chance convenient to do so. In much the same way many sales are made spontaneously because it has suddenly become convenient for the client to settle that troublesome problem without further delay.

That is the exceptional case. In most cases this condition requires that you offer some aid to the client in perceiving what you offer as what he or she needs. Your presentation should include a description of symptoms to help the client recognize the applicability of your services to his or her needs. Simply listing or describing the benefits in clear terms will accomplish this. For example, some of us who bought personal computers when the CP/M operating system dominated the scene have a substantial investment in software programs for those computers. That has made us reluctant to buy the computers that use the PC/MS-DOS operating systems that dominate the market today but which cannot use the CP/M software. It would require us to scrap all that software. But there are now means for running our older software on the newer computers, and the mere information that this is possible is enough to arouse our interest. We recognize the applicability immediately.

You must help clients who "know it when they see it" make the connection between what you offer and the clients' problems. The mistake is in assuming what clients will perceive. You must operate on the assumption that clients know only what you tell them, and no more.

CREATING NEEDS

There are also prospective clients who are untroubled at the moment; they have no problems, at least as far as they might relate to your services. Or, *they do not know that they have a problem!* Not yet. Not until you help them discover their problem and their need or want.

Some marketers or advertising specialists call this creating a need. Actually, that is a convenient idiom, for you cannot literally create a need, and you cannot persuade anyone to want something they truly do not want, although it may appear sometimes that you have done so. However, for convenience we sometimes speak of creating needs as though we actually can do so, and we will use the term here in that idiomatic usage.

There are two ways to create a need. One is by creating a new service or product. The mere fact of offering your consulting services as something new creates a need, especially if the services you offer are unique in some manner. Anyone who becomes your client thus confesses to a need or a want that did not exist before.

The second way to create a need is by "educating" the client—by *giving* him or her the problem and then the solution. In the CP/M computer example, the owner is not aware that he or she has a problem in owning what is already an obsolete computer, one with a limited memory and capability. But many computer owners are unaware of the benefits they are missing. They need to have it explained to them that they have a problem.

WHO IS REALLY YOUR CLIENT?

Despite all that has been said here already about knowing who you are addressing in your quest for clients, there is often the question: Who is *really* your client? It is not necessarily obvious. Suppose that you are a computer systems consultant and you have been retained by Joe Warshofsky, purchasing agent for Ajax Ball Bearing Works, Inc. to help him automate his purchasing system. You will guide him in the purchase of a desktop computer and suitable software, design the overall system, based on the software, and train him and his administrative assistant in operating the system. Who is your client?

The short and cynical answer you might get from some consultants is "whoever signs my check." And to a degree that is true; it is the company, Ajax, who is the client in the sense that they have obligated themselves to use your services and pay for them. Yet, it is Warshofsky (presumably) who interviewed you, was sold by you, made the decision to retain you, and issued the purchase request leading to the purchase order. It is Warshofsky for whom you are doing the work, whom you must satisfy, and by whose authority you remain on the assignment until it is finished. From almost every viewpoint, then, but especially from the viewpoint of gaining a satisfied client for its future marketing benefits, it is Warshofsky who is truly your client.

Warshofsky may never call you back for another assignment—may never need your services again—but he can recommend you to those in his own company and those in other companies. A satisfied client is always one of your greatest marketing assets.

Recommendations are a special problem for me because I help clients compete with other organizations of their own type; I help them win contracts in competition with other companies. So it is not often that a client will recommend me to another company, a competitor. Still, even in that situation recommendations are possible. In large organizations different executives or staff specialists are assigned responsibility for different proposals, and so one who has been pleased with what I did will recommend me to another executive in the same company. Or I have met others in the company who remember me when they have proposals to write. But people leave companies and join the staffs of other companies, and some of those call on me to help them in their new companies. Therefore, it is important for you to recognize that the *individual* who is responsible for retaining you and for whom you are doing the work is your true client.

A FEW BASIC PRINCIPLES OF SALES AND ADVERTISING

Despite the fact that conventional advertising and sales methods rarely serve much purpose in marketing consulting services, it is still necessary to understand a few basic principles of these activities. And it is especially necessary to demystify the subject by demolishing some of the popular myths and misconceptions that have sprung up over the years.

Emotion versus Reason

If you were to judge by superficial attributes—that is, by external appearance—you might come to believe that buyers generally try to buy whatever they believe to be the superior product and/or best value. The logical corollary of that is that effective advertising and sales techniques consist of sound arguments demonstrating superiority in quality and value. Even some misguided salespeople and advertising copy writers appear to believe that, in fact. The truth is, as much as we try to resist it, that we react more to emotion than to reason. We would like to believe that we are always motivated by reason, but we actually are far more inclined to follow our emotions and *rationalize* our decisions, persuading ourselves that the decision was a sound one, based on logic!

The late Elmer Wheeler, often acclaimed as "America's greatest salesman," expressed this same idea with his widely quoted and now classic, "Sell the sizzle, not the steak. " And he took his own advice. Many stories have been told about his prowess as a seller par excellence. For example, a retailer who was stuck with a large supply of long underwear he had been unable to sell, appealed to Wheeler for help. Wheeler succeeded in selling the entire stock by making a large display accompanied by the sign: THEY DON'T ITCH.

Selling versus Advertising

Selling and advertising are both activities within the broad realm of marketing. Each has some distinguishing features, and yet they have more features and characteristics in common than in contrast. In fact, to do the subject justice I find it necessary to treat advertising as a form of sales effort—written selling, in the cases of print advertising, direct mail, and proposals—but selling in all cases. Therefore, I use the two terms almost interchangeably, and in most cases refer to both, even when I use only one of the terms.

What We Really Buy

One of the common myths is the belief that we buy *things*. We do not. We buy what things *do*. (It is for that reason that sage marketers have observed that we are all in the service business.) One often-quoted observation, for example, is that customers do not buy quarter-inch drills; they buy quarter-inch holes. That is an insightful way of expressing that people are really buying a capability for making quarter-inch holes. Or perhaps they are buying a capability for hanging a drapery traverse rod or for putting up a bookcase.

We could refer to another classic remark that expresses this truth pungently: "If you want to sell lemonade, you have to make the customers thirsty first." That's why the free appetizers in cocktail lounges are usually salty (e.g., pretzels, peanuts, chips, etc.). Advertisers make prospects thirsty through psychological devices, such as showing you people sporting in the hot sun on a beach while they also flourish bottles of some beverage so cold that the outside of the bottle is covered with beads of condensed moisture.

The "White Space" Myth

Those who are still unfamiliar with advertising truths believe that to be successful print advertisements must be brief—scant copy with lots of white space around them. But there are many examples of highly successful full-page advertisements that were or are nothing but solid text. That doesn't surprise marketing professionals. One of their accepted premises is expressed as "The more you tell the more you sell." Long copy, almost invariably, is far more effective than short copy, and this works for all kinds of sales presentations. The trick is to capture and hold the prospect's interest. If you do that, the prospect will read or hear you out patiently, no matter how long the copy or presentation. If you do not succeed in capturing and holding the prospect's interest, short copy will not save the day. In fact, the whole belief in short copy is predicated on the premise that you will not be able to hold the prospect's interest, which is perhaps a self-fulfilling prophecy for many!

The Two Main Elements

The AIDA acronym is used to explain the claimed principles of selling and advertising. The rationale is this:

A for get Attention.
I for arouse Interest.

D for generate Desire.

A for ask for Action.

It is my suspicion that this acronym is just too cute to be a coincidence, that the acronym came first, and the explanations second, a force-fit. Although there is truth in it, it has fatal weaknesses, in my opinion.

One weakness is that if the acronym is taken literally, you may gather the impression that whatever you do to "get attention" need not necessarily have anything to do with the rest of the presentation. Unfortunately, many copywriters and other marketers have gathered that same impression, so that we see many attention-getting devices that are irrelevant to the main message.

Another weakness is that the dividing line between "arousing interest" and "generating desire" is difficult to find. The distinction is unclear, in fact. Are they two separate steps? Or is the third one an evolution of the second one—that is, does aroused interest grow and eventually develop automatically into desire? In fact, a general quarrel I have with the acronym is that it portrays the process as a mechanical one with steps that are represented as being distinct from each other, when they are not truly so. Each step requires definition, as well as explanation, which I believe was done to create a memorable acronym.

The meanings of the third and fourth steps are especially far from being clear. The final step refers to asking for the order. *Order*, however, wouldn't do because AIDA is not the name of a familiar Verdi opera, so the creator of that acronym had to find a euphemism and thus chose *Action* for the role. The idea is right—you should somehow ask for the order—but it is not always appropriate. In many cases you are competing with others for the contract, and the client has already decided to buy—will definitely buy from one of the competing consultants—so you don't have to ask for action.

Having attacked that more-or-less-accepted standard set of principles, I am obligated to suggest something better. But before I do so let me hasten to say that I do not quarrel with how most expert marketers actually organize and construct advertising and sales presentations, but only with how some explain the technique, as in the case of that acronym we have been discussing here. I think that there is a far better, more rational, and more accurate way to explain the process.

I conceive of successful sales and advertising presentations as requiring two major elements: Promise and Proof. The presentation must be based primarily on a promise of some specific benefit or set of benefits, which are essentially an appeal to emotion. Properly done, this achieves the first steps of getting attention and arousing interest, perhaps even generating the desire to buy, although it is extremely difficult to discriminate accurately between interest and the desire to buy, which really comes about when the prospect is convinced that you can and will make good on the promise (if the promise is sufficiently appealing to the prospect). The proof is whatever evidence is necessary to convince the prospect that you can and will make good on the promise—that buying what you are selling will, in fact, produce the results you claim.

Whether you need to ask specifically for the order depends on the situation. Asking is far more applicable to one-call selling, if the sale is to be consummated at all. Asking for the order is likely to become a consideration for you only when and if you diversify into those related consulting profit centers of publishing and speaking, which we will discuss in later chapters. It is usually not even an academic consideration in selling traditional consulting services.

Promise

There is nothing very mysterious about the idea of the promise. It is what you claim you will do for the client—that is, what the purchase of your services and/or product will do for the client. But the promise must meet certain criteria:

It must be clear and specific.
It must have a single, major focus.
It must be an emotional appeal.
It must be sincere.
It must be honest.
It must be believable.

Some of these items may appear to be redundant or even in opposition to each other. The discussion that follows will clarify what each criterion means.

A promise that is clear and specific. A promise, for example, that your solution will be "better" or "state of the art" is not clear or specific. Quite the contrary, it is vague, it is your opinion only, a characterization. Instead, promise some specific result (e.g., 20 percent higher reliability, twice as many leads, 37 new markets). Quantify, if possible. Reduce to the absolute minimum your use of adjectives and adverbs, and stick to the nouns and verbs. TV commercials are good examples. They promise you the easy solution to apparently impossible laundry problems or, probably more effectively, admiration and plaudits of family, friends, and relatives for cleaner, bright clothes or shiny dishes.

A single, major focus. Don't distract the prospect and dilute the impact of your promise by promising too many things, even if you can deliver on all those things. Focus the prospect's attention on one major benefit. If there are others, perhaps a whole class of benefits, and you think that you must mention them, be sure they are subordinate to the major benefit and do not mask or obscure it.

An emotional appeal. The promise always stresses benefits that have emotional appeal—a troublesome problem solved, reduced costs, greater profits, relief of stress, greater happiness, more prestige, greater security, or other such benefits that the prospect can almost taste or feel. TV commercials are good examples of emotional appeals. They appeal to vanity, the need for recognition, the need to solve troublesome personal problems, and other such human needs.

Sincerity. Avoid hype. Somehow, insincerity manages to show through, despite the best effort of silver-tongued salespeople and copywriters. Promise only what you yourself believe in. That is sincerity. Don't turn to TV commercials to find examples of this! They often pay public figures and even ordinary citizens to be "sincere" for them.

Honesty. Honesty is a quality close to sincerity, although not quite the same thing in a presentation. Whereas sincerity is promising what you truly believe you can deliver, honesty is a frank presentation that admits the minor flaws. Honesty enhances a business relationship, especially in the marketing process. (Again, not always found in TV commercials.)

Believability. Again, we must refer to sincerity and honesty in discussing this. Believability refers to the prospect's perceptions, not to yours. Recall the admonition to focus on a single, major benefit, even if you can deliver a dozen major benefits. Focus the prospect's attention, but do not make the prospect skeptical. You may very well have to understate the promise so that it is believable. Don't lose sight of the fact that it is the client's perception that is the truth. (Admittedly, much of commercial advertising is considerably less than believable, although they try hard.)

It is always the client's or prospective client's perception that we must try to shape and direct. In most matters, but especially in marketing, the client's perception determines whether or not we are successful. It is essential that you manage to see the situation from the prospect's viewpoint if you are to reach a true understanding of what it takes to persuade the prospect to retain you.

Proof

Proof is a little trickier than promise. In a court of law there are the so-called rules of evidence, which are statutory controls over what is admissible—what constitutes evidence or proof—and what is not admissible. Obviously, that is not what we mean here. We define proof as whatever the prospect will accept as proof or evidence, and perhaps evidence is a more accurate term. What passes for evidence or proof in marketing would rarely stand up in court, but that is beside the point, for we are dealing again with the prospect's perceptions of truth.

There are varying degrees of proof required in marketing situations, according to the risk or investment required. A prospect might gamble a few dollars to satisfy curiosity, even if he or she is not thoroughly convinced (buying a $5 or $10 report or manual, for example), but investing several hundred or several thousand dollars is quite another matter. It is going to take quite a lot of evidence to convince the prospect that the investment is sound enough to merit that risk.

You must first have a prospect with a serious interest in what you offer and a desire to enjoy the benefit(s) you have promised. It is only such a prospect as that who is even interested in your "proofs" that you can and will deliver on that promise. In fact, if you have done a good job in stirring the prospect's enthusiasm and desire for the benefits you promise, the prospect *wants* you to prove your case and justify his or her purchase. It is, of course, much easier to "prove" something to someone who wants to believe you than to someone who is still skeptical.

In organizing and presenting the evidence you must usually address these three issues:

1. **Plausibility.** Evidence that your proposed services are logically appropriate to solve the problem or accomplish what you have promised.
2. **Capability.** Evidence that you have the skills, experience, and any needed resources to provide and carry out the services.

3. **Reliability.** Evidence that you are a dependable consultant who always carries out your projects faithfully and keeps your promises unfailingly.

There are a number of kinds of evidence commonly used and generally accepted by prospective clients as suitable. Some of the items fit into more than one of the three categories, and so may be cited more than once in the following listing, although you would not repeat the item in making a presentation to a prospect.

Plausibility. The chief evidence of plausibility is simple logic. A logical cause-and-effect narration is generally adequate. It should reveal a true understanding of the prospect's needs and desires—that alone is quite reassuring to the prospect—and should develop the complete logic of your proposed services vis-à-vis the need. As added evidence, if necessary, you can bring in citations of previous projects that successfully applied these services to similar problems or needs, although you normally present this information elsewhere in the progression.

Capability. If this is a task for you alone, the chief capability is you, with your education, experience, and skills. If you require physical facilities (e.g., your own office, a computer, special equipment, etc.) you must explain exactly what you will supply and how the items will be obtained. If you require support (e.g., associate consultants, vendors, or support services of any kind), describe these and relate in detail where they will come from. Be completely specific here.

Reliability. Your "track record"—that is, earlier successful applications of your services and faithful execution of projects—should be related here, again with as much detail as possible. If at all possible, provide names and telephone numbers of former clients who can and will report favorably on you to an inquirer. Include, also, letters of commendation and other testimonials to the qualities of excellence, dependability, and other such virtues of your service. (Be sure to ask satisfied clients for such letters, as you build your practice. They are quite persuasive evidence of your good qualities as a consultant.)

Be careful to avoid the hype and generalities cautioned against earlier. Such tactics may generate skepticism on the part of the prospect, or they may cause you to fail to provide the needed detail, which is absolutely essential. Promising to "provide all necessary facilities and resources" is nearly meaningless. You must be specific and detailed as to precisely what you anticipate will be needed and how it will be obtained.

Generalities and hype are not convincing; anyone can speak in generalities about almost anything. But only the true expert can provide the detailed plan for doing the job. A sales presentation must be credible; it must convince the prospective client that you are as expert as you claim to be. The presentation of a completely detailed plan inspires the client's confidence in you by indicating that you know what is needed and how to achieve the necessary results. There is probably no single quality or factor more important in the consultant-client relationship than confidence of the client in the consultant. It is nearly impossible to win a contract or to work with a client lacking that confidence in you.

It is a mistake to expect clients to accept your personal résumé as a persuasive sales presentation. Unfortunately, many independent consultants prepare brochures that are little more than their personal résumés and expect prospects to hire them on that basis. It rarely happens. It is almost always necessary to present the kind of persuasive presentation described here, formally—in a lengthy and formal proposal—or informally—in a face-to-face presentation or an informal (letter) proposal.

NEEDS: DO THEY CHANGE?

Earlier we discussed the difference between "felt" needs and "created" needs. Simply stated, the appearance of a new service or product creates a new need. There could not have been a felt need for TV before TV existed. Creating TV created the need for it. New products/services achieve different levels of success in the marketplace. Understanding why this happens will lead to a clear understanding of needs or wants, and that understanding is a valuable asset in marketing.

One of the outstanding successes of recent decades was the Xerox copier. It was an almost immediate success because it was fast, automatic, used plain paper, and required absolutely no skill and no special preparation to operate and make copies. The copies were considerably less than perfect in those early machines, but they were better and far easier to make than anything produced by any of the other copying methods. The need was not new; there had always been a need for the most convenient, most rapid, and most economical way to make copies, and each generation of new methods succeeded if it was a better way to satisfy the need.

In short, there are no new needs (or, if there are, they arise quite rarely); there are only better ways to satisfy needs that have existed for a long time. That explains the swift success of radio, TV, VCRs, and many other devices that are better ways to provide home entertainment. It explains why central coal furnaces replaced fireplaces, oil burners replaced coal furnaces, and gas replaced oil as the most popular home-heating methods.

What Does "Better" Mean?

The clue to satisfying needs and motivating prospective clients lies in what the client believes is "better," for it is only the client's opinion that counts in the decision as to who will be favored with the contract. What is better to you, the seller, is not necessarily what is better for the prospect. During the Great Depression, *better* probably meant less expensive, as a reflection of those lean times. But in these times of increasing affluence, *better* tends to mean faster, easier, and more convenient. Convenience has become a major motivator, a factor that accounts for the success of many enterprises that probably could not have succeeded earlier. Never overlook the importance of convenience as a motivator; for many people today that is far more important than cost or any other consideration. For that reason always make it as easy as possible for the client to do business with you. The convenience factor, even such a small matter as having an easier time finding someone else's telephone number or some difficulty in finding yours, might easily tip the scales in favor of a competitor.

Still, this does not mean that cost is never a factor; it often is the critical factor. Reliability or freedom from risk can also be decisive factors. Perhaps the client mistrusts innovative approaches or has some notion as to how the job ought to be done and will resist any effort to do the job any other way. These many motivators will be discussed in detail later in this chapter.

Determining the Client's Position

Although you should make the effort to sell the client whatever you believe to be the best approach, you should first make an effort to determine two things: (1) whether the client already has some prejudice for or against some given approach or method (and if so, what that bias is) and, (2) how the client is likely to respond to your effort to sell him or her on your idea of how the job ought to be handled.

Obviously, that is not an easy job, but neither is it an impossible one. There are ways of persuading the client to help you determine how to maximize the probability of winning the contract.

"Asking" the Client What Is Better

Of course, when I tell you to ask the client what to do to maximize your chances for success I do not mean that literally. And that is not only because it would be disastrous for the consultant-client relationship to ask such a question directly, but because the average client could not answer your questions accurately even if he or she wanted to; usually the biases are not conscious ones. That doesn't make them any less real, of course, but your approach must be indirect and subtle. Here are some ways that usually work.

If you are pursuing a specific contract that you know will be awarded to someone, the "asking" takes place in your conversations with the client. You should be asking judicious questions, getting the client's view of the need or problem and eliciting as much information as possible. Inevitably the client must reveal much of how he or she feels about what must be done, especially if you ask the right questions and make the right leading remarks to gauge the client's reactions to them. For example, when I am in preliminary discussions with a client who is considering using my help, I inquire as to who in the organization will be working on the job with me, what their job titles and responsibilities are, and whatever other information I can get. I make remarks recalling similar cases of the past and suggest ways of approaching different things. All of this usually helps me get quite a lot of data reflecting the client's attitudes and biases, if any, as well as how he or she is likely to react to some of the ideas I might suggest.

In some cases you may have been issued a written description of the problem or need. You should study this closely and get as much as possible out of it in preparation for face-to-face discussion. On the other hand, if you are sending out feelers (e.g., brochures, sales letters, or other material designed to help you develop leads), these can be used to "ask" prospects what it is they would like to have—what would arouse their interest. For example, when I experimented with different sales letters in promoting the sale of my newsletter on marketing to the government, I soon discovered that the promise readers responded to most enthusiastically was that subscribing to and reading my newsletter would help them win government contracts. I found, also, that of all the regular features in the newsletter the monthly two-page column on proposal writing was the most popular. And when I led seminars in marketing and proposal writing, I discovered, to my surprise, that my audiences became greatly interested in learning the basics of cost accounting, although they probably could not have themselves predicted that they would have found the subject an interesting one. It was only when they had listened to some opening discussion of the subject that they decided it was appealing. It was yet another case of "I know it when I see it," and it was only one of many times I encountered that reaction.

Remember it is foolish to try to *guess* what prospects want. You must ask them what they want and then help them discover it.

A FEW MOTIVATORS

There are more than four billion humans on this planet, each of us a unique personality, and no two of us identical. Yet we have many common needs, wants, drives, desires, and other characteristics in common. We all need love, warmth, security, self-esteem, prestige, success, and ego strokes, among our many emotional and physical needs. The differences between and among us relate to the priorities we give each of these things and what represents them to us as individuals. For example, banks are reputed to be far more generous with high-sounding titles than with salaries, and presumably many bank employees are motivated to stay because of the titles and despite the salaries.

An insurance salesman obviously had this sort of stroking in mind when he assured me, "Mr. Holtz, a man in your position cannot afford to be without at least $500,000 in coverage." "Your position" was meant to make me feel quite important and so motivate me to make the purchase. How could I argue that my "position" was not prestigious and important?

I didn't sign the insurance contract; the ploy was a bit too obvious. Moreover, I would not have signed in any case. I could not have afforded the payments, no matter how "important" I was! All the emotional/psychological ploys in the world are not going to sell someone who truly is uninterested in buying what you are trying to sell. It's a lesson some marketers never learn, and they waste a great deal of time and effort trying to compel uninterested prospects to become interested.

If you are offering your services to business organizations you are dealing with employees—executives, usually—who have two kinds of motivators: (1) the motivation to do what is best for their employer and a proper thing to do as part of their job responsibilities, and (2) what is in their personal interest. Of course, the conscientious employee tries to be objective in his or her judgment and decide entirely on the basis of what is right for the organization, but it is inevitable that self-interest must influence judgment. And those influences always fall into these basic motivational categories of fear and gain. However, remember that there are negative motivators—factors that motivate individuals *against* awarding the contract to you or making the purchase at all—as well as positive ones. Here, for example, are just a few examples of the kinds of fears that act as negative motivators, inhibiting the client from making the purchase or from selecting you as the consultant for the job. (These and similar ones are possible fears you must try to anticipate and overcome in your sales presentations.)

> The consultant is a stranger to me and not recommended by anyone I know. How can I be sure that he or she will do a good job?
>
> This is a new idea; I have never heard of it, and it is in a field I know nothing about. How can I gamble on something so new?
>
> The costs will be too high, and I will be blamed for spending too much money.
>
> I may be criticized for choosing this unknown consultant arbitrarily without competition.

On the other hand, fears may be positive motivators, and aid and support your sales presentations:

> This problem is really an intolerable one and must be solved for the company before it becomes any more serious.
>
> I'm not sure I can handle this problem myself, and I can't afford to let it go unsolved for very long.
>
> Someone else in the company may get this before I do, and it will look as though I've been asleep.

The boss may hear of this and wonder why I didn't do something about it before now.

The gain motivators can work for you too:

Hey, here's somebody who knows what to do about this troublesome problem; it's a chance to solve this problem once and for all.

Getting this new system in here is good for the company, and it won't hurt my reputation either!

This could make life a lot easier for me. I would be doing a much better job for the organization.

We really need this service.

There are also gain motivators that can work against you if you are not aware of them when you develop and make your sales presentations:

Hey, who is this guy (woman)? I can get somebody with a bigger name, somebody who will make me look better. (Nobody ever got fired for hiring IBM!)

I like the idea, but I think I can get it done for less money.

I could butter up the boss by asking his opinion on who we ought to retain for this job. Maybe he has a consultant he likes.

I would look better and maybe the company would be better off if we made this a competitive procurement.

There is no doubt that fear is a powerful motivator, quite possibly more powerful than the drive for gain. Perhaps this reflects a basic insecurity that most of us have that the success, prosperity, health, and/or happiness we are enjoying is only temporary and we are always in danger of losing it.

Other needs that motivate us include:

Being "in on things" or "up on things." It almost always helps close sales when you assure prospects that you are offering the *newest*, *latest*, or *most advanced* product or service.

Being "on the inside." Everyone, apparently, wants to be privy to exclusive information and get "inside tips" permitted to only a privileged few. Many successful advertisements promise this. (Presumably, this is an ego booster.)

Emulating success. Testimonials by celebrated public figures, especially those considered to be heroes (e.g., sports and entertainment stars), do more than merely bring conviction. They also set examples for prospects to follow. If it is good enough for the celebrated figure, it must be worth doing or having. To a lesser degree the same psychology works when you advise a prospect that some other, perhaps not at all well known, individuals or organizations have used your services. This is evidence of the validity of your services, and is a model of success that can be emulated; it arouses the desire to do so in many prospects.

THE NEED TO TEST

Since what is negative for one person may be positive for another, there is no certain way to know which motivators will work in any given case, except by testing. Testing can be done by test mailings or test advertisements or by testing in face-to-face presentations, both mentioned earlier as methods for discovering motivators. Remember, however, that you are testing motivators you selected.

THE TWO BASIC MARKETING PROBLEMS

Almost everyone marketing almost anything finds himself or herself selling against competition most of the time. However, whereas most people use the term "selling against competition" to mean competing with another supplier for the sale, in another sense you are always or almost always selling against competition of one sort or another. There are three basic kinds of competition:

1. Another consultant offering to supply the needed services.
2. The client's resistance to doing business with someone new and unfamiliar trying something new and unfamiliar.
3. The client's reluctance to spend the money—that is, competing with the client's desire to buy other items out of the available budget.

You can divide the conflicts into two marketing problems: (1) you are dealing with a client or prospective client who is definitely going to buy the kind of services you offer but has not yet made the final decision as to whom to retain, or (2) you are dealing with a client who has not yet decided whether to buy what you are selling, from you or from anyone else.

These are factors you must consider in devising your marketing strategy, whether you are face to face with your prospect or preparing your marketing materials, which will be discussed in Chapter 5.

5

Releases, Brochures, and Other Marketing Matters

Marketing with a pen.

THE LINK BETWEEN MARKETING AND WRITING

Marketing takes many forms, many of them written ones. The language must be persuasive to carry out its mission successfully, but readers must be induced to read first, and that is itself a marketing job and an increasingly difficult one. In these times, so many media compete for our attention (e.g., radio, TV, newspapers, and magazines). The writer's task of seizing and holding the reader's attention is no minor chore any more.

Getting and holding the subject's interest are the same principles we discussed in the previous chapter as prerequisites of the sales presentation. You can't do much of anything until you have accomplished that. To appreciate this let's consider first the task of developing a publicity release, also known as a news release or press release.

RELEASES AND NEWSWORTHINESS

Editors are well aware that you and all the other millions who send out releases every day are asking for free media space or time to advertise your product, your service, or your operation. But it is not literally free. The editor does not use your release—give you free space or time–without getting something in return. The editor will trade space or time for something *newsworthy*. That is, you can "buy" that space by providing the editor with something the editor's readers/listeners/viewers would find interesting.

Newsworthiness is the key. Actually, I use the term rather loosely here, for the typical publicity release is not newsworthy in a literal sense, not truly news. I use the term here to mean worthy of being printed or aired on radio or TV, and that worthiness is strictly in terms of reader/listener/ viewer interest. For the editor is not concerned at all with what interests him or her personally, but only in what will interest the audience.

The broad lines of those interests are easy to draw. The subscriber to "Jones's Daily Investor's Report" does not expect to see a piece on inventory management, even if that is of personal interest, so don't send that release to Jones; he won't use it. Send it to "Management Daily," "Manager's Monthly," and "Inventory Weekly." It is their readers who will want to read that release.

The physical format of a release may vary over a wide range of options, as Figures 5–1, 5–2, and 5–3 reveal. The minimum requirements are that the piece must identify itself as a release and identify its origin or source—that is, who issued it. But there are other considerations that can make a considerable difference in whether you succeed in getting the publicity you are after. A list of these considerations follows.

Double space the copy. The editor will want to edit your copy in most cases.

Put a date on the piece.

Put a release date on it—"For immediate release," if it is not embargoed, but a specific release date on it if it is embargoed. (Copies of speeches are sent out in advance, but embargoed until the speech has been delivered, for example.)

Provide a contact—someone to call for more details if the editor wants more information.

Indicate where the copy ends with a standard notation, such as "End" or "30," (an old telegrapher's sign-off), or "###."

Type on one side of the paper only.

If you use a headline—and I recommend that you do—don't be cryptic and above all don't get cute or clever. The purpose of the headline is to get attention and summarize the main point of the

For Immediate Release

AVON NEWS

Contact: Fern Edison
212/399-4509

THE **ONE MINUTE** PHENOMENON CONTINUES...

WITH AVON'S SEPTEMBER RELEASE OF "**THE ONE MINUTE SALES PERSON**tm"

"This book **provokes us to think**...analyze... be solution-oriented, and, above all, realize that the fuel for motivation comes from within ourselves."
-- Shelby H. Carter, Jr.
V.P., General Sales Man
The **Xerox** Corporat

mental and importa
want in All

*The first **ONE MINUTE** book ever to appear in mass-market format

he $15 hardcover bests
vailable in a $5
he lowest

n sales. ... ON

(Av... perback; September 1, 1986; $5... 6.95 Canada;) by ...ncer Johnson, M.D. and Larry Wilson presents the simple but key element to successful sales; By helping the other person get what s/he wants, you can get what you want.

Behind the disarmingly basic format of **THE ONE MINUTE SALES PERSON** is thorough, in-the-field research that included a reader review and a survey. The review was done with 185 sales professionals, with the authors present, who input about what worked in their experience, and what didn't. The survey, focusing on what makes a successful salesperson, involved 47 vice presidents and sales

more...

PUBLICITY DEPARTMENT
AVON BOOKS, THE HEARST CORPORATION, 1790 BROADWAY
NEW YORK, N.Y. 10019 (212) 399-4506
Publishers of AVON, BARD, DISCUS CAMELOT & FLARE

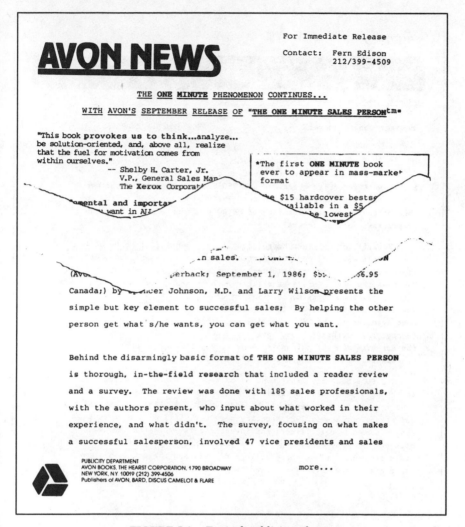

FIGURE 5.1. Typical publicity release.

release so the editor can judge swiftly whether it is of interest. The easier you make it for the editor the more likely you are to "sell" the piece.

Don't get "literary." Use the simplest language and the most straightforward explanations possible. That is the best kind of writing.

METRO

News Release

P.O. Box 61429, Houston, Texas 77208-1429. 713/225-1151

CONTACT: Janet Redeker

FOR IMMEDIATE RELEASE
January 27, 1982

The MTA Board of Directors voted today to authorize the Executive Director to establish a METRO Transit Security Department with expanded security enforcement. The Board took this action to enhance the safety and security of METRO's patrons, employees, and properties, and the general public.

Today's action gives Metro security personnel full peace officer status in a well defined jurisdiction which includes any land, easement, right of way, rolling stock(buses) or other property owned or controlled by the Authority. This is the first such program ever created in Texas, although 14 such departments exist in other transit systems such as New York, Washington, D.C., Los Angeles, and Atlanta. Other law enforcement agencies in the METRO service area such as Houston, Bellaire, Harris County, and Southside Place have expressed their positive support of the establishment of a Transit Security Department and mutual aid agreements with other agencies will be sought.

METRO's Security Department is currently staffed by 26 persons, including supervisory, operations, investigations and clerical personnel. Nine more patrol officers will be added by May 1, 1982, as part of the budgeted increase in 1982 security services. All of the current supervisors, patrol officers and investigators are certified peace officers and have an average of 7.4 years experience. Of the seventeen field personnel, eleven have college degrees and the other six have associate degrees or college credits.

-more-

FIGURE 5.2. First page of news release.

If your release purports to be news (e.g., a new product or service offered an eager public or a startling new discovery in your field), do try to use the journalist's style of summarizing all the key points—who, what, when, where, and why—in the first sentence. If it is a feature piece, try for a novelty type of attention getter in the headline and follow it up immediately in the first sentence.

News Release

GSA #8328

December 11, 1981

GSA Chief to Close Seven Laboratories in Economy Move

Administrator Gerald P. Carmen said today he will close seven testing laboratories that have supported the General Services Administration's governmentwide supply system. He said the action will save $3.3 million annually.

Seventy-six employees will be affected by the closures. However, attempts will be made to reassign them into other elements of the Federal Supply Service in the same commuting area.

"Our Federal Supply Service is turning more and more toward procurement of off-the-shelf commercial items," Carmen said, "so there is less need for research and development to establish specifications for products or to develop government-unique testing methods. We will rely more on testing and quality assurance by reliable vendors and use of warranties and performance bonds to protect the government's interest. GSA will concentrate quality assurance efforts on warranty enforcement and audits of material."

Carmen said the change is in line with the Administration efforts to streamline and make government operations more efficient and to rely more heavily on the private sector.

The Research and Development Laboratory in Washington, D.C. will be closed December 31; Laboratories in New York, Chicago, Fort Worth and Auburn, Wash., will be closed by March, and those in Kansas City and San Francisco by August 1. This schedule will allow for an orderly transition to ensure that adequate contractual safeguards, such as extended warranties, are in place.

(MORE)

U.S. General Services Administration, Washington,DC 20405 (202) 566-1231

FIGURE 5.3. A federal agency news release.

It is always possible to find interesting items for releases, although it is not necessarily easy to do so. But it is worth the effort, for by far the vast majority of releases are dull, self-serving, poorly written, and are never published. When I was trying to find such items for my own releases to publicize my government-marketing and proposal-writing services, I found opportunities among the government's procurements, so I could come up with such headlines as these:

The government paid me to answer their mail.

Government contract issued for go-go dancing.

Federal agency rents mules and handlers.

Of course, you won't always find such material for headlines, nor should you use such headlines unless they are truly appropriate and accurate leads for your items. The most clever headline won't help if it has nothing to do with the content of the release. Fortunately, it is not necessary to always have a blockbuster of a headline because you are usually addressing readers with special interests. Any appeal to those interests—to what is new and potentially profitable or otherwise useful in some way—will do the job *provided that the editor understands that appeal*.

The headline may or may not be one the editor will like and use—editors tend to have their own ideas about what their readers want to read and how to best command their readers' attention—but that is not important at the moment. The more important point is to create a headline that tells the editor why he or she ought to use your story. Don't use a headline filled with technical jargon unless the release is going to a specialized trade periodical, because the editor will probably not understand it. For example, editors of *Personal Computing* would probably have no difficulty understanding the significance of TECHNOCOMP CORPORATION ANNOUNCES 5.2 MHZ RAM, but the lay person or the editor of the *Millersville Times* would have some difficulty judging the newsworthiness (much less the attention-getting power) of that headline. You would do far better to use something such as NEW, SUPERFAST (5.2 MHZ) COMPUTER CHIP ANNOUNCED BY TECHNOCOMP. That enables any editor to grasp the idea that this is a new and newsworthy development, whether he or she knows anything about computers. The body of the release will go on to provide the details and clarify further the significance of the headline announcement.

Typical Items for Releases

Straight news in a release is rarely of the front-page variety, of course. It is usually information of interest to a special group, such as a given industry or profession. These items are rarely of interest to the general public, although many might be suitable for specialized sections of a general-interest periodical, such as the financial pages or food section of a newspaper. Examples of the kinds of news items found in releases include the following:

Information about people within the industry or sphere of interest, including notices of newcomers, retirees, promotions, and obituaries, particularly of those figures most prominent in the industry.

Announcements or advance notices of mergers, new starts, contract awards, divestitures, stock offerings, new constructions, expansions, and other such stories.

Stories behind the story—inside or little-known information about such developments as mergers, divestitures, sell-offs, new products, and cutbacks.

Technical details of new products, stock offerings, mergers, financial manipulations, or other developments of interest.

Government activities affecting the readers, such as new legislation, regulations, and reports.

Announcements of relevant new books.

Notices and/or reviews of new products and services.

Announcements of special events, such as conventions, association meetings, and trade shows.

Copies of speeches by individuals at special events.

Statements by individuals prominent in the field of interest.

What Is "Interesting?"

You can almost always capture someone's attention and sustain his or her interest when you get into the subject of his or her *self-interest* (e.g., health, success, happiness). But even this varies to some extent. Everyone has the need to feel secure, for example, but security has different meanings for different individuals. To some a job that appears to be steady and pays a decent wage represents security, but others require far more, such as substantial savings, a retirement account of their own, and perhaps a great deal of insurance. However, there are two basic drives that motivate us, and appealing to them will often arouse interest. The two drives are (1) the desire to avoid the undesirable and (2) the desire to gain the desirable, sometimes referred to as fear and greed. For example, fear drove thousands of people into debt to build and equip elaborate and costly individual bomb shelters in the 1950s. And, of course, insurance, security devices, and many other kinds of goods and services are sold principally through fear motivation.

The desire for gain also commands attention and interest. There is no apparent end to the appeal and the supply of books and newsletters purporting to guide people to success in the stock market and in other kinds of investments. The late Joe Karbo reportedly sold some 600,000 copies (at $10 each) of his little paperback book titled *The Lazy Man's Way to Riches*.

The following list represents other appeals that many find interesting, all of which have stood the test of time.

Inside information or tips. Most of us have a desire to gain access to the information that is denied to most, is even, perhaps, a little illicit!

FREE! That word endures as a lure!

SALE or BARGAIN. Like FREE, these words endure forever. There are successful businesses who have everything on special sale every day of the year, and most shoppers appear to have no trouble with this idea.

How it works. Few people can resist the desire to solve the mystery of how things work, whether you are talking about satellites or legislative decision making. Make such subjects easy to understand and you have an audience.

Humor helps to spark interest, but the ability to be humorous, especially in writing, is rare. Everyone likes a laugh, but humor that doesn't succeed is a deadly bore. It is best to simply report the facts without editorializing or trying to *make* the item a humorous one. No one will condemn or criticize you for straight reporting, as long as you report accurately.

You can find something interesting to report about any and every subject imaginable. Use the public library and do some research.

Linkages: Keeping Your Eye on the Ball

Too often copywriters get carried away with the challenge of writing effective copy and forget what they set out to do—in this case, to generate leads for future contracts. An excellent release that is widely published is a success as a release, but it is not a success as a marketing effort if it fails to generate sales leads for you.

To be that success, your release must do two things beyond getting published: (1) it must do something to induce or provoke readers into responding directly to you in some manner, and (2) it must be selective so that those who respond to you are *qualified* leads—that is, individuals who are good prospects for consulting work.

The release must somehow make it clear that you are a consultant, while it defines at least the general area of your consulting expertise and services. That definition must provide the reader with a clue of what your services do for your clients—that is, what kind of problems you solve and/or what benefits clients can expect from your services.

Probably the easiest and most direct way to establish the correct linkage is to have your specialty incorporated into your business name or subtitle, such as in the following examples:

Accurate Real Estate Appraisers
Government Marketing Consultants
Convention Planners, Inc.
Editorial Experts, Inc.
Office Systems Designers, Ltd.

If you link that with the content of the release—if the connection is obvious—most readers will at least perceive where, how, and why your services can and should be of interest. Given that much, if your release is widely circulated, it will probably produce at least a few leads, in time. But you can improve the odds by doing something to stimulate the response.

One thing that is often effective is the how-to success story, especially when it is "the inside story." Promise to tell readers how so-and-so (e.g., "the president of a prominent metalworking company") increased productivity 18 percent through a simple method available to everyone. This approach almost always commands attention. Even better, promise to show readers how *you* helped that individual get those spectacular results.

Of course, you can offer a set of several such reports and get even greater impact, especially if those reports show how your services can deliver the same benefits to different kinds of industries or clients. That means offering to provide some kind of brochure or report to any reader who requests it, which is exactly what you want—requests from those interested in learning how to increase productivity. You send them your report, which need not be elaborate (a report typed on regular paper and reproduced by some inexpensive means is perfectly suitable), and your sales literature, and follow up with telephone calls.

Powerful although this kind of "response device," or inducement to respond, is, it is by no means the only kind. If you study the junk mail you receive instead of casting it away immediately, you will discover a great many ideas for response devices (e.g., free appraisals, free estimates, samples, free newsletters, etc.). In fact, later in this chapter we will discuss newsletters, seminars, and other such profit maker marketing tools.

BROCHURES AS MARKETING TOOLS

Of all the many written instruments used for marketing, brochures are probably the most widely used. Brochures are the basic marketing tool for many, if not most, consultants and can be found in every possible size, color, format, quality, and application. The cost to produce brochures varies greatly. Many brochures are a single 8 1/2-by-11-inch sheet folded to fit into an ordinary business envelope, while others are dozens of pages long, formally bound, and require a large envelope for their mailing.

There are situations in which such elaborate brochures are justified. However, in most cases it is totally unnecessary to go to such extremes. Even a brochure printed on a single sheet and folded to fit into a business envelope is adequate if properly typeset and printed on a reasonably good grade of paper. The brochure is not intended to land a contract; even one of those excessively elaborate and costly ones couldn't do that. Brochures are intended to help you generate marketing leads for follow-up. That is all they can do.

A 3-by-9-inch brochure offers many advantages. It not only fits into a standard business size envelope, but it is also convenient to carry in an inside pocket, a purse, or a briefcase of any kind, which enables you to carry a supply with you at all times.

That convenience extends to anyone to whom you hand such a brochure. The recipient also may slip it into a pocket or purse easily. In fact, a brochure of this size is often even more useful than a business card, not only because it is a convenient size but because it carries a message far beyond that possible for a little card.

You can use your brochure exactly as you might a release, offering the same inducements to respond and using quite similar copy. But the resemblance tends to end there. One major difference between the brochure and the release is that you have total control over distribution of your brochures. It's a trade-off, of course. You have complete control over the distribution of your brochures, but that distribution is up to you primarily. The alternatives are to do the actual physical distribution yourself via direct mail or by attending conventions, conferences, trade shows, and other such gatherings; or you can have mailers and other marketing support specialists do it for you.

It is wasteful to mail brochures alone; if you are going to go to the expense and labor of a direct mail program, you should make up a complete package, which includes such items as a sales letter, a brochure, and a return envelope, as a minimum.

This does not rule out having a more elaborate brochure, but that kind of brochure should be reserved for follow-up contacts and should be in addition to, not in place of, the smaller brochure.

A FEW OTHER SALES MATERIALS

There are many marketing applications for writing, and if you develop these properly they are likely to be among your most productive and fruitful marketing activities. There is the sales letter, a marketing tool used almost as widely as the brochure, although it is not quite as versatile, bids and proposals, advertising copy, newsletters, books, and articles for periodicals.

Sales Letters

The typical sales letter, is of the high-pressure type, with bold type, capital letters, two-color and even three-color inks, circles, exclamation marks, handwritten notations, and other such high-excitement symbols. This type of sales letter is as inappropriate for selling consulting services as is huckstering on the streets. If a sales letter is to be of any use at all to you, it must be quiet and dignified, while still observing all the valid principles of selling effectively. Figure 5–4 is an example of such a sales letter.

Bids and Proposals

The writing and submittal of bids and proposals is such an important matter that Chapter 8 is devoted exclusively to it. Along with bids and proposals is the important subject of something generally referred to as "capability brochures." This subject is much more closely related to proposals than to brochures and so will be covered in Chapter 8 as well.

Newsletters

Newsletters are or should be as important to you as are bids and proposals and so will also be the subject of later, detailed coverage.

Articles

Articles published under your byline in suitable periodicals can be an important marketing tool, and you should make every effort to write such articles and have them published. They do a great deal for your professional image. Potential clients tend to be impressed by them, and they certify your authority in your special field. Reprints of your published articles are most useful as inserts in your mailing packages and in appendices or exhibits of your proposals. Q & A (question and answer) columns are excellent, if you can persuade some editor to allow you to do this on a more or less regular basis. The idea is to prove your capability and the worth of your services by offering a few samples through such devices, but being published is itself an impressive credential to many people.

Following that same philosophy, when you speak publicly to groups, invite questions and even comments from or open discussion by the audience. That not only gives you a chance to show your

Consulting Opportunities Journal

P.O. Box 17674, Washington, DC 20041

$500 and more per day consulting, or grossing up to $10,000 and more in a single day working a favorite profit center, today's consultants are cashing in on growing demands for their knowledge. The age of the consultant-entrepreneur is here!

Dear Colleague,

You are sitting in a great position to turn your knowledge into "gold" in the months and years just ahead. And it doesn't matter if you're just starting out or an "old pro" in consulting, or whether you are part or full time in your practice.

The months and years ahead will bring unprecedented consulting opportunities to those men and women, in all fields, who are prepared for them.

Consulting Opportunities Journal (COJ) was founded to bring you information on those opportunities. We also report on trends, tips and techniques on how to most efficiently market yourself in today's potential-laden environment.

The response to COJ has been great. Being founded and written by consultants for consultants, the COJ has earned the reputation of a no-nonsense, straight-from-the-shoulder 'How-To' publication. No "ivory tower" stuff here.

Its writers earn their living from consulting in their various fields. So you can be assured that COJ's writers cannot afford (and neither can you) the luxury of writing about theory versus how it actually is "on the street." Each one of our consultant-writers, now and in the future, has faced and overcome the marketing problems, difficult client relationships, proposal-writing struggles and outright loneliness and more that we've all faced at one time or another.

Consulting is as much a leadership business as it is a people business. The COJ covers the people giving advice to the leaders of our society. The COJ is the only publication of its kind in the world. We are dedicated to your success in consulting, now, more than ever before.

It is to this end, to maintain our place of leadership in the consulting profession, that we are making you, what I believe, the most generous offer you have seen--from any national publisher in any field. First, let me tell you what subscribers are seeing in the COJ:

* How and Where to Get Consulting Leads (Self-Marketing Strategies that Can Be Used in Any Field)
* How to Set Fees (Also, What Others are Charging)
* How to Write Winning Proposals & Reports
* What Goes Into Launching a Successful Seminar or Newsletter (Information that can save you plenty!)
* IRS Proposals and Tax Considerations Affecting the Independent Consultant
* How and Where to Find Writing and Speaking Opportunities

(continued)

FIGURE 5.4a. Sample of a typical sales letter.

* Consultant Networks, Consultant Brokerages: What They Are, How They Work and How to Work with Them (Are They the Ultimate Income Source?)
* How to Discover, Develop and Market Information Products and Other Profit Centers of Your Own
* Data Banks, Research Centers, Make Them Work For You or Your Client, Telephone Marketing and much, much more!

Along with covering scores of publications to bring you the happenings in the booming consulting industry, we have just acquired Consultant's Digest and merged it into COJ--at no extra cost to subscribers. There's even a Q & A column where you can get specific answers from specific questions from COJ's own consultant to consultant editor, Herman Holtz.

When you come right down to it, the COJ could be broken up into several newsletters--each with the same or higher subscription rates. There could be one on Self-Marketing Strategies, Consulting Contracts/Fee Negotiation, Direct Mail Marketing/Advertising Strategies for Consultants, Developing and Marketing Seminar and Newsletter Properties and others. But these are all included in your COJ subscription.

A year's subscription to COJ is only $24 for six full issues. And it's totally tax-deductible along with a money-back guarantee. Plus, there's no extra charge if we increase our publishing schedule during your subscription term. (Saves $6.00 over single copy)

Those watching the mushrooming consulting industry tell us that, within two short years, a weekly publishing schedule will be needed to touch all the bases. We don't know about weekly, but from the looks of things now, a monthly publishing schedule is not far off!

A 2-year subscription is just $39 (a savings of $21.00 off the single-copy price), and a 3-year term is only $57, a big $33.00 savings over single-copy!

Now, let's get back to my "most generous" offer I mentioned earlier. We've just made a special purchase of 7 top-selling titles of consulting guidebooks from The Consultant's Library, the nation's leading consulting book publisher (See the attached list).

As if all the foregoing benefits of a COJ subscription weren't enough, now you can get up to 3 (THREE) books FREE--up to an $80 value with your paid subscription! You simply select one book FREE for each year of your chosen subscription term.

This is a limited-time offer and may be withdrawn soon. To ensure your selections, order today on the special order form enclosed. Use the handy postage-paid envelope for additional speed and savings.

Isn't it time you discovered all the benefits to you and your family from your own consulting practice?

Yours for a successful consultancy,

J. Stephen Lanning

J. Stephen Lanning
Publisher

FIGURE 5.4b.

expertise, but it helps you understand prospective clients' views, attitudes, problems, needs, biases, and other characteristics that should be enormous aids in your marketing. Learn as much as you can about how your prospects think, for in marketing the only view that counts is the client's view. Your main goal in every contact, especially those face-to-face contacts, should be to learn about the prospective client. Do more listening than talking—much more.

Books

Even more than articles in periodicals, books published under your byline help establish and confirm your technical or professional authority and lend you a great deal of prestige. Many successful consultants are the authors of books. Gerre Jones, who was quoted earlier, is the author of several books in his professional field, published commercially. Jeffrey Lant, also cited earlier as a well-known figure in the field, achieved much of that recognition through publishing his own successful and widely circulated books about consulting.

Oddly enough, in some ways it is easier to get a book published than to get an article accepted for publication. Admittedly, you may not earn a great deal of money from your books, unless you publish and market them yourself, as Lant does, but you will reap benefits for marketing your services as a consultant.

Advertising Copy and Writing Sales Materials Generally

We tend to think of advertising as the printed notices in periodicals, written largely by professional copywriters in the advertising industry. However, all those items we have been discussing are advertising copy, and the following principles apply to all of them.

The mark of the amateur writer and the kiss of death in advertising copy is overwriting, especially extravagant use of laudatory adjectives and adverbs, superlatives, and other hyperbolic excesses. The novice copywriter apparently reasons that readers will accept any claim that is outrageous enough and repeated often enough. Consequently we find brochures peppered with such words and terms as these:

expert/expertise	adept	renowned	worldwide
highest standards	leading	tremendous	unique
remarkable	superb	sensational	outstanding
national authority	peerless	unmatched	incredible

Not one of these terms is objective. Without exception they clearly mirror opinions, claims, bias. They reflect self-appraisal, blatant "Madison Avenue copy." Perhaps such words were effective once, in a less-sophisticated time, but they are an assault on the senses and the intelligence today. Such words are, in fact, virtually invisible to readers, the result of overuse and straining readers' tolerance for hot air.

FACE TO FACE: CLOSING

Ultimately, in most sales situations, you must come face to face with the client (figuratively, perhaps, in some cases, but literally in most) to close. To many the word *close* means getting the order, as in "closing the sale." To the professional sales expert the word has a second meaning—that is, it refers to closing the sales presentation by *asking* for the order. In the traditional sales situation, especially when a big-tag item such as an automobile or a large contract is involved, it is an accepted premise that the salesperson must close—ask for the order—many times before getting the desired signature on the order form. So at some point you must close your presentation and try to close the sale.

Even on more modestly priced items this is often true. How many times did you get a solicitation for *Time* magazine or some other item sold via mail before you finally caved in and ordered it, if you did? The seller would be quite surprised if you responded to the first solicitation with an order, although a few prospects do. It is accepted in marketing that far more sales are closed on second, third, or even fourth closes than on first ones. Perseverance and patience are keys to success here, as they are in so many things.

Of course, selling consulting services may not appear to work quite that way. But it does, albeit on a more indirect and less obvious, and usually even more protracted, basis. You send out many brochures and letters, speak at numerous gatherings, chat with dozens of people at conventions, follow up with innumerable telephone calls and perhaps lunches, submit more than a few written bids and proposals, make frequent presentations, and ultimately you wind up with a few signed contracts or purchase orders from some of those activities. In most cases you have made many closes before you won the prize. Even after you have won good leads you have had to make several closes to most of those leads before you won a contract.

Of course, there are exceptions. Once in a while you get lucky and get the lead, make the sale, and close the order all on one occasion. If you get that lucky on your first try—and that has happened, unfortunately, to some beginners—don't let it destroy your good judgment and cloud your vision. Such a stroke of fortune is a fluke that will probably happen only rarely, if ever again, and you can destroy yourself with disappointment and frustration at your inability to make it happen again.

Marketing is playing percentages. You do everything possible to stack the odds in your favor by trying to generate the best possible leads and by every other means available, but in the end your success is controlled by numbers, by probability statistics. You cannot close every lead, only a percentage of the leads. Normally, the more leads you generate the higher the percentage of sales you will make. This means you must do something to reduce the time wasted on prospects you are most unlikely to sell—that is, determine who the poor prospects are before you spend too much time on them.

There are some zealots among the many sales experts who will assure you that you should be able to close each and every lead. But there are some leads you cannot close for any of many possible reasons. You will sometimes run into a prospect, especially in a large organization, who has nothing better to do than to chat with you, but who has no authority or perhaps no sincere desire to do business with you. You may run into a prospect who is simply picking your brains so he or she can become a big hero/heroine in the organization, using the information and ideas stolen from you. Or perhaps there is no budget available and the prospect is probing possibilities for a future project that is not likely to materialize.

Because these kinds of things do happen, it is wise to practice a defensive measure known as "qualifying"the prospect.

Qualifying Prospects

Qualifying a prospect is a simple proposition that all salespeople must learn. It means simply taking some measures to assure yourself that the individual you are spending your time with is indeed a true prospect, one who *can* retain you and is serious about retaining a consultant.

The prospect must have the following qualifications to be truly a prospect for you:

A need appropriate to your specialty—one that you can satisfy.
The money necessary to retain you.
The authority to retain you.
The sincere intention of doing business with someone.

There is first that matter of making sure that you are not wasting your time discussing some vague need that may very well turn out to be well outside your field. The only practical way you can address this is to probe until you are satisfied that you know what the client will require. Be aware, however, that frequently the client really does not know what the need or problem is, but can describe and list only symptoms or complaints and may very well be rather vague about those too. You will have to probe until you gather enough information to make an analysis and reach at least a preliminary conclusion. However, keep that conclusion to yourself, for now. You have not yet been retained nor paid for your time; disclosure here would be premature and might result in your analysis being passed on to other consultants as a definition of need.

The question of money to retain you has different practical interpretations. In some cases the question might be literally whether the individual has the cash in hand. In others, as when dealing with organizations rather than individuals, it is a question of whether the individual has both budget and authority or has access to and influence with someone else who has the spending authority. The latter is an important consideration. In many cases someone in an organization can recommend and help sell you to the right individual in the organization, although lacking personally the authority to retain you.

Finally, you must try to determine whether you are discussing a realistic project or wasting time on an imaginary project.

A suitable euphemism for asking about money tactfully is, "Are funds currently available for this project?" Another way to put it is, "Is this project budgeted yet?" Or, "Has this been funded yet?" Any question along these lines, delivered quietly and matter-of-factly, will usually be accepted as an objective, businesslike query, asked strictly for information and not as a challenge or intimation of mistrust.

All the questions you ask in qualifying a prospect must be tactfully phrased and asked in that same quiet, matter-of-fact tone. That's especially true when determining whether the individual you are talking to has the authority to make a decision. Among the questions you might ask to determine this are:

Who will have to sign off on this?

What's the decision-making (or approval) process on this?

Will somebody besides you have to okay this?

If you find that you need to probe the matter of the client's intent, you may have to ask some rather direct questions. The leading questions that follow should steer the discussion in the right direction for you to make a sound judgment.

Has an official decision been made yet to go ahead with this project?

Is this exploratory, or is there definite commitment already to the project we are discussing here?

How soon do you expect this project to begin?

When would you need me to start on this?

Has this project been budgeted yet?

From the answers you get to these questions you can generally judge whether you are discussing a planned project or wasting your time on a project that is likely never to materialize, or whether you are being used cynically, for that happens occasionally too.

6

Marketing to the Public Sector: Federal, State, and Local Government

American governments are not only the biggest buyers in the world; they are also the biggest buyers of consulting services.

A BRIEF GLIMPSE AT THE GOVERNMENT MARKETS

The most recent official report on federal procurement covers the third quarter of fiscal 1987. It reports 15,026,804 purchases, totaling $131,837,784,000. That is somewhat less than three-quarters the probable total of annual procurement because government purchasing tends to get heavier in later quarters. Also there are certain federal agencies exempted from reporting their purchases (e.g., the Postal Service, which employs over 700,000 people and alone spends over $20 billion for salaries, goods, and services every year). So federal procurement today is well in excess of $200 billion annually.

The federal government consists of 13 departments, 60 "independent agencies," and several dozen assorted bureaus, commissions, and other organizations, each of which is divided into subordinate agencies, so that the total approaches 2,000 such federal entities. Moreover, most of these have a chain of offices throughout the United States, the majority of which do a great deal of independent buying.

But these figures are small compared to the total number of state and local government agencies. The U.S. Census Bureau, which refers to these entities as "governmental units," offers the following data for state and local governments in the latest census (1980).

State governments	50
Counties	3,042
Municipalities	18,862
Townships	16,822
Local school districts	15,174
Special districts	25,962

Each of these government entities also has a complement of bureaus, agencies, and institutions. It is easy to understand why the state and local government agencies spend more than twice as much as the federal government. Well over $600 billion is spent annually for government purchases, a significant portion of that for consulting services.

WHAT GOVERNMENTS BUY

The nature of government purchasing has changed a great deal over the past few decades. Whereas governments once contracted primarily for public works (e.g., the construction of streets, highways, bridges, dams, and public buildings), today there are few goods or services the governments do not buy. In some cases the governments—especially the federal agencies—are the only customers for certain items. Who else will rent mules and handlers today or issue contracts for the supply of baggers in military supermarkets?

Perhaps an even better indication of the scope of this market is the fact that the federal government alone employs approximately 130,000 people in full-time procurement activities alone. It requires a great many people to manage to spend nearly $1,000,000,000 every day!

It should come as no surprise that the bulk of federal purchasing is for the support of the military, but aside from that the procurement practices of state and local governments do not differ much from those of the federal government. Typical government procurements at all levels include:

R&D projects
Insect and disease control
Crime prevention and control
Communications
Education
Housing
Health services
Social services
ADP services
Program evaluation
Studies and surveys
Technology transfer
Operations research
Public relations
Training

Government agencies may experience a need for consultants for almost any kind of work, including work of the type that most organizations carry out with their regular employees. However, governments are motivated by political considerations more than by considerations of efficiency and so do not function in the same philosophical environment as do other organizations. Examples of work assigned to consultants, despite that it is ordinarily handled by regular employees, include:

Public information/public relations services, including, in some cases, running the entire public information office.
Developing work statements and other elements of requests for proposals.
Reviewing, evaluating, and scoring proposals received.
Answering government mail and telephones.
Managing and administering government correspondence-course programs.
Operating government facilities, such as computer systems and laboratories.

THE PROCUREMENT SYSTEM

One excess in our federal government's procurement system is an overabundance of supply categories. There are approximately 100 general categories in the federal system and many subcategories. As a result, the total government procurement of consulting services is obscured by the fact that by far the majority of such services are not called "consulting." If you study the *Commerce Business Daily*, the federal government's special publication through which the agencies announce their needs and list the solicitation packages available, you discover that consulting services are solicited under a number of categories. These include:

Experimental, developmental, test, and research work
Expert and consultant services
Technical representative services
Architect-engineer services
Photographic, mapping, printing, and publication services
Training services
Miscellaneous

Many of the needs listed under other categories also require consulting services to carry them out. You are likely to find opportunities for government consulting contracts listed under the following categories as well:

Maintenance and repair of equipment
Modification, alteration, and rebuilding of equipment
Operation and maintenance of government-owned facility
Installation of equipment
Funeral and chaplain services
Salvage services
Medical services
Training aids and devices
General-purpose automated data processing (ADP) equipment, software, supplies, and support equipment

Basic Procurement Philosophy

The basic philosophy of all government purchasing is selection by competition. This is at least theoretically the fairest way to afford everyone an equal opportunity to win a share of government business, while keeping suppliers honest and assuring the government of the best possible prices and quality. Although the system is not perfect, it is, on the whole, a "clean" system that achieves its main objectives reasonably well. Whatever government procurement scandals do exist are almost entirely problems of bureaucratic inefficiency and stupidity; they rarely involve bribery or corruption.

Ideally, procurement officials would like to award contracts to the lowest bidders in all cases. However, this is not always possible. Price is only one consideration in these times of increasingly complex and sophisticated systems, and it is of secondary importance when other important factors are considered, such as safety, quality, performance, durability, reliability, practicality or viability of plan, and ability to perform. This "ability to perform" qualification is especially important. Too often, even with all the safeguards in place, government agencies have found their contractors unable to perform satisfactorily, and therefore they scrutinize proposals most carefully for evidence of the ability to perform, making this evidence a most important element in your proposals and sometimes the key to success. The concern over these technical/quality factors applies to the procurement of services as well as to that of goods—perhaps even more to buying services than to buying goods, in fact.

Specifications

When it comes to most negotiated procurements, a lack of specifications is often the problem. In fact, it is precisely because the government cannot furnish detailed specifications that the contract must be negotiated. The government needs your recommendation and asks you to furnish the specifications in proposing a project to satisfy the need. In fact, if the government could furnish detailed specifications it would probably be less costly and more efficient all around to invite sealed bids rather than request proposals.

Sometimes this inability to furnish specifications is inherent in the nature of the requirement (e.g., when research is the project itself) or the client may lack the specialized knowledge or skills to detail the specifications. In some cases the client may be purposefully vague in order to elicit as many new and innovative ideas as possible before deciding which is the best one.

This results in two kinds of competition in government procurement: (1) typical price competition, which means making a choice based on sealed *bids* and (2) quality or technical competition, which means making a choice based on a technical evaluation of all *proposals*.

As more procurements require studies and recommendations by those contending for contracts, it is even more important for consultants to obtain the skills necessary to write successful proposals (see Chapter 8 for a full discussion of proposal writing). More organizations in the private sector are also adopting proposal requirements as a means for finding and selecting consultants for assignments.

Special Cases

There are some special cases (e.g., small purchases of up to $25,000 each in the federal system, somewhat less at state and local levels) for which there are simplified procedures. There are also provisions made for emergencies, when the agency's need is urgent and there is simply not enough time for the agency to follow normal procedures. In addition, there are some cases in which only small businesses (as defined by the Small Business Administration) are permitted to propose or bid. These and many other matters concerning public purchasing are covered by regulations.

Procurement Regulations

The typical excesses of government extend to the statutes and regulations governing procurement. Until recently there were three distinct sets of procurement regulations: (1) the original Armed Services Procurement Regulations (ASPR), which later became the Defense Acquisition Regulations (DAR); (2) the Federal Procurement Regulations (FPR); and (3) the NASA Procurement Regulations (NASPR). There were also literally thousands of bulletins and memoranda that had the effect of regulations. These have been combined, merged, revised, and reduced to a single set of regulations, the Federal Acquisition Regulations (FAR), which have already been modified to some extent by more recent procurement legislation (e.g., the Competition in Contracting Act). There are a few basic principles embodied in these federal regulations that are generally reflected also in the procurement regulations of state and local governments. The principle provisions of regulations covering sealed bids (also known as "advertised" or "formally advertised" procurements) include:

Bids must be delivered to the place specified by the time specified. Late bids must be rejected.

Sealed bids are opened publicly. Anyone may attend and witness the bids being opened and read aloud.

Awards are made to the lowest qualified bidder in each case. Compare this with the rules governing procurement by "competitive proposals," formerly referred to as "negotiated" procurement:

Proposals must be delivered as specified by the time specified. Late proposals are to be rejected.

Cost information must be provided in a separate proposal and may not be given in the main (technical) proposal.

Technical evaluation must be according to some objective rating scheme, and the scheme must be described to the proposers, along with the significance of cost figures in evaluation, as part of the original information in the solicitation package.

The government is free to negotiate with proposers after proposal evaluation and to require supplements, presentations, or other additional inputs before reaching a decision.

Government representatives may opt to visit the proposer's premises to verify that the proposer has the facilities to perform. This can also be extended to include a preaward audit to confirm the acceptability of the proposer's accounting system and/or financial stability. (This is not often done for small contracts, however.)

Appeals and Protests

You are always free to appeal or protest an award decision. It is usually of little use to do so in the case of a sealed-bid procurement, since the rules are so simple and clear. However, protests of award decisions based on competitive proposals are quite common and are sometimes successful.

The appeal procedure is quite simple because it is an administrative appeal not an action at law. It requires simply a letter to the contracting official or, in the case of the federal government, to the comptroller general of the United States, who is also head of the

General Accounting Office (GAO). The letter may be informal and should set forth the basis of your complaint. This action, regardless of its outcome, in no way compromises you or your further actions. You can even go ahead and sue in the courts, if you wish to, as some large organizations have done.

It is not necessary to become a lawyer to do business with the governments; however, you should know (1) the general policies and procedures and (2) that there are voluminous regulations that you can search out, if necessary.

Types of Contracts

There are two basic types of government contracts: (1) fixed price and (2) cost reimbursement. Just as contracting officials would prefer sealed-bid purchasing whenever possible, they also usually prefer fixed-price contracts. However, that is not always possible because of the many variants and uncertainties, such as the following:

Indefinite quantities. The government often does not know how many or how much of something will be needed. This is especially the case when someone is awarded an annual supply contract for goods or services. The contract fixes the rate(s) and the period for which they are to apply but leaves the total open.

Research and development. R&D is almost impossible to predict or estimate with any certainty.

Surveys and studies. The rationale is the same as for R&D.

Phased projects. Each phase is evaluated before deciding on the next one.

Cost-reimbursement contracts take into consideration the many indefinite quantities and require reimbursement for such costs.

The government also uses purchase orders, which are a specialized form of contract used for small purchases. Technically, a purchase order is a contract too and is a far simpler way of handling the paperwork of contracting. Purchase orders may be used to contract for individual tasks, under the Small Purchases Act and the procurement regulations that apply to small purchases, but they may also be used to authorize each individual task under an annual contract with a consultant.

MARKET RESEARCH

Although the government procurement market is highly competitive in general, there is often little or no competition when the purchase is a small one and when the requirement has not been *advertised*—that is no formal solicitations have been made or mailed to prospective bidders. Therefore, to win these smaller contracts, you must find and bid/negotiate contracts that have not been and won't be formally advertised, or before they are advertised. Within the limitations of small-purchase regulations, it is possible to do a substantial amount of government contracting this way.

There are also provisions in the regulations for noncompetitive procurement when the need is such that the normal time requirement for awarding a contact competitively cannot be tolerated or when what is required is so unique that it can be obtained from only one source.

Making a Start: Studying the Federal Marketplace

The best way to begin your study of the federal market is to read the *Commerce Business Daily (CBD).* If you study the announcements (synopses of current requirements and opportunities) listed in the *CBD*, you will begin to become familiar with what and where the federal agencies are and what they buy. You should send for many of the solicitation packages and study them. Examine the awards section as well; it reports which contracts were awarded to which organizations, which is also valuable market information.

You can order a copy of the *CBD* from the Government Printing Office (GPO) or from the Department of Commerce. Although it is mailed daily, it may be three days to week before it arrives in your mail. Fortunately, the *CBD* is now available in an online edition, called "CBD Online." If you have a personal computer and a modem, you can arrange to get this edition easily.

Once you decide which agencies are likely to be the best prospects for you, you can begin to file copies of Standard Form 129, Application for Bidders List. You need to file a copy of this form with the contracting office of each agency with whom you wish to do business. This form tells the contracting officer what solicitations are likely to be of interest to and bring responses from you. You will then be listed on each agency's bidders list and receive many solicitations (i.e., invitations to bid or propose) without asking specifically for them.

You can also visit contracting offices periodically and ask about current requirements. You will be given the opportunity to examine file copies of current solicitations. In fact, the larger procurement offices often have a separate room, a bid room, with copies of current solicitations posted on a bulletin board.

Two other sources can help you become more familiar with the federal procurement system. Contact your nearest Small Business Administration office or visit one of the 13 Business Service Centers operated by the General Services Administration. These centers were established and are operated expressly to aid business people learn how to do business with the federal government.

With all these facilities and resources available there is little reason to neglect the huge federal market for consulting services.

Following up in State and Local Markets

State and local government markets, taken together, are about twice the size of the federal government market. Individually, however, each is relatively small; and therefore, their systems do not provide prospective suppliers with as much assistance in learning how to participate. Still, most do emulate the federal system and the parallels are there.

State Governments

Each state government has a central purchasing and supply office. This may be an independent entity in the state government hierarchy, or it may be an office within an organization (e.g., the state's finance office or administrative agency). Although the location of the office may be different from state to state, nearly all state purchasing and supply offices have the following in common:

All urge prospective suppliers to visit their offices personally and become acquainted with the several buyers, the requirements, and the procedures.

All have some form of required registration or bidders list application, which prospective suppliers are urged to complete and submit.

Many supply lists of all purchasing office personnel, including buyers and what each buys.

Many have technical specialists (as the federal government does) for the approval or negotiation of contracts for computer equipment, supplies, and services.

All award annual supply contracts for items that are commodities—that is, goods and services they buy regularly throughout the year.

Most delegate to the various other agencies throughout the state the purchasing authority that is peculiar to the other agencies' needs (e.g., consulting services).

Most permit local governments to utilize state supply contracts to buy goods or services that the local government needs.

All have some kind of provision for small purchases and noncompetitive purchases, as established by statute.

Most will supply you by mail, upon request, a brochure of some kind, explaining their system and governing statutes, often accompanied by a thick document that identifies their supply groups (often closely resembling and sometimes identical to the federal listings) and names of various commodities. They will also supply forms for you to complete to get on the state's bidders lists and qualify as approved suppliers.

Some will supply a lengthy list of state agencies (e.g., hospitals, mental institutions, prisons, museums, departments, administrations, commissions, etc.), often with the names of administrators who do independent purchasing for those organizations.

Most advertise their requirements and bid opportunities in a local newspaper, generally in the classified columns under the heading "Bids and Proposals." For major procurements they sometimes use display advertising in the financial pages of the newspaper (see Figure 6–1).

Special Considerations

In some states, preferential treatment is given to in-state bidders, which may give you an edge when competing with out-of-state bidders, but it may be to your disadvantage when competing outside your own state. Many states also emulate the federal government by offering loan and loan-guarantee programs, setaside procurements for small businesses and for minority-owned firms, and counseling for small businesses.

NOTICE OF REQUEST FOR PROPOSAL

NOTICE OF REQUEST FOR PROPOSALS

The Parking Violations Bureau of the New York City Department of Transportation is soliciting proposals for the operation and maintenance of a new data processing system (the "STAR" System).

A copy of the Request for Proposals can be purchased for $25.00 (cash or certified check) from the Contract Purchase Section of the New York City Department of Transportation, Room 1017, 40 Worth Street, New York, New York 10013, Monday to Friday, between 9:00 a.m. and 3:00 p.m.

Proposer's Conferences are scheduled at the Parking Violations Bureau, 770 Broadway (at East 9th Street), 15th floor, New York, New York at 11:00 a.m. on Tuesday, August 19, 1986, Tuesday, August 26, 1986 and Tuesday, September 2, 1986.

Proposals are scheduled to be submitted to the Contract Purchase Section of the New York City Department of Transportation, Room 1017, 40 Worth Street, New York, New York 10013, on September 22, 1986, no later than 11:00 a.m.

FIGURE 6.1.

Local Governments

Visit the local seat of government to study the organizational structure and the procurement procedures. The larger local governments often have purchasing organizations, descriptive literature, lists of supply groups, and procedures that rival those of the federal government and larger state governments. Local governments, and the contracting possibilities they represent, are far more extensive than you may have realized. The many agencies and institutions of local governments are most likely to become your clients. The agencies most likely to need your consulting services include:

- Hospitals
- Transit authorities
- Port authorities
- Consumer protection agencies
- Boards of education
- Departments of housing
- Economic development administrations
- Public roads bureaus
- Prisons
- Halfway houses
- Equal opportunity offices
- Offices of human rights
- Environmental control offices
- Library systems
- Child protective services
- Health services
- Tax collection offices
- Special commissions

Even though purchasing authority may be delegated to these other agencies, you must be registered with the government's central purchasing organization because the central organization often does the actual contracting. In such cases you must market to those other agencies but still handle all administrative and contracting matters with the central purchasing office.

SUBCONTRACTING AND OTHER SPECIAL MARKETING APPROACHES

None of the contracting organizations, not even the supercorporations, do everything themselves. Most, especially the larger organizations, find it necessary to subcontract a great deal of the work. For example, when RCA won a $1 billion contract for the Ballistic Missile Early Warning System, RCA awarded over 300 subcontracts, representing about two-thirds of the entire budget! Subcontracting to the winners of government contracts alone represents a great deal of opportunity for you. Watch the CBD awards section for a listing of these opportunities.

Occasionally the winner of a large prime contract will ask for and get permission from the government to advertise a need for subcontractors in the pages of the CBD. You should therefore be alert for such notices in the relevant categories.

Often the primary contractor, who is seeking subcontractors, will invite bids and request proposals, just as the government does. In fact, the terms of major contracts often clearly imply a requirement to do so when letting subcontracts. Therefore, it is a good idea to prepare and circulate capability brochures (see Chapter 8 for a detailed discussion of these brochures) to all organizations that appear likely to let subcontracts for services such as you offer.

On the other hand, you may wish to offer your services to contenders for contracts *before* awards are made—that is, as soon as you learn of the request for proposals (or even earlier than that). Many organizations want to pursue contracts for which they are not fully staffed. They have a need, therefore, to include in their proposals the résumés and promised services of experts who will act as consultants to support the program. Thus, you can be assured of a subcontract if the organization manages to win. (Execute a written agreement with the other organization to that effect, since you do not have the leverage of being the primary contractor.) You may wish to permit more than one contender for a given contract to include your résumé and promise of availability to support the program. This is not unethical if all parties are aware that your résumé will appear in competing proposals and do not object to it.

Another alternative is co-bidding, whereby you bid with someone else, making the two of you a far stronger contender for the contract than either of you alone. Usually this is still a primary contractor and subcontractor presentation, but in this case you both participate in writing the proposal. You should decide these roles solely on the basis of which makes you the stronger contender.

FORMS

There are two federal forms you should recognize. Standard Form 33 is the form used for both sealed-bid invitations and proposal requests (see Figure 6–2), and the other is Standard Form 129 mentioned earlier (see Figure 6–3).

STANDARD FORM 33, NOV. 1969 GENERAL SERVICES ADMINISTRATION FED. PROC. REG. (41 CFR) 1-16.101	SOLICITATION, OFFER, AND AWARD	3. CERTIFIED FOR NATIONAL DEFENSE UNDER BDSA REG. 2 AND/OR DMS REG. 1. RATING:	4. PAGE 1 OF
1. CONTRACT (Proc. Inst. Ident.) NO.	2. SOLICITATION NO. RFP-SBA-7(i)-MA-78-1 ☐ ADVERTISED (IFB) ☒ NEGOTIATED (RFP)	5. DATE ISSUED 11/14/77	6. REQUISITION/PURCHASE REQUEST NO.
7. ISSUED BY CODE Small Business Administration 1441 L Street, N. W. Washington, D. C. 20416		8. ADDRESS OFFER TO (If other than Block 7) Contracting Officer, c/o Program Manager Small Business Administration, Room 610 1441 L Street, N. W. Washington, D. C. 20416	

SOLICITATION

9 Sealed offers in original and 6 copies for furnishing the supplies or services described in the Schedule will be received at the place specified in block 8, OR IF HAND-CARRIED, IN THE DEPOSITARY LOCATED IN Rm. 610, 1441 L St., N.W., Wash., D.C. until 5:00pm EST (local time), FRI, DEC 16, 1977 (Time, Zone, and Date). If this is an advertised solicitation, offers will be publicly opened at that time. CAUTION—LATE OFFERS. See par. 8 of Solicitation Instructions and Conditions.

All offers are subject to the following:
1. The attached Solicitation Instructions and Conditions, SF 33-A.
2. The General Provisions, SF 32 ______ edition, which is attached or incorporated herein by reference.
3. The Schedule included below and/or attached hereto.
4. Such other provisions, representations, certifications, and specifications as are attached or incorporated herein by reference. (Attachments are listed in the Schedule.)

FOR INFORMATION CALL (Name and Telephone No.) (No collect calls):
Lillian Harris, Program Assistant, AC 202/653-6894

SCHEDULE

10. ITEM NO.	11. SUPPLIES/SERVICES	12. QUANTITY	13. UNIT	14. UNIT PRICE	15. AMOUNT
	Provide technical and management assistance as specified in Parts I thru IV of the Schedule to individuals or enterprises eligible for assistance under Sections 7(i) and 7(j) of the Small Business Act, as amended. This solicitation is a 100% small business set-aside.				

OFFER (NOTE: Reverse Must Also Be Fully Completed By Offeror)

In compliance with the above, the undersigned offers and agrees, if this offer is accepted within ____ calendar days (60 calendar days unless a different period is inserted by the offeror) from the date for receipt of offers specified above, to furnish any or all items upon which prices are offered, at the price set opposite each item, delivered at the designated point(s), within the time specified in the Schedule.

16. DISCOUNT FOR PROMPT PAYMENT (See Par. 9 on SF 33-A)
N/A % 10 CALENDAR DAYS; N/A % 20 CALENDAR DAYS; N/A % 30 CALENDAR DAYS; N/A % N/A CALENDAR DAYS.

17. OFFEROR NAME & ADDRESS (Street, city, county, state, & ZIP Code) CODE FACILITY CODE Area Code and Telephone No.: ☐ Check If Remittance Address Is Different From Above - Enter Such Address In Schedule.	18. NAME AND TITLE OF PERSON AUTHORIZED TO SIGN OFFER (Type or Print) 19. SIGNATURE	20. OFFER DATE

AWARD (To Be Completed By Government)

21. ACCEPTED AS TO ITEMS NUMBERED	22. AMOUNT	23. ACCOUNTING AND APPROPRIATION DATA	
24. SUBMIT INVOICES (4 copies unless otherwise specified) TO ADDRESS SHOWN IN BLOCK ____		25. NEGOTIATED PURSUANT TO ☐ 10 U.S.C. 2304(a)( ) ☐ 41 U.S.C. 252(c)( )	
26. ADMINISTERED BY (If other than block 7) CODE Small Business Administration Office of Management Assistance 1441 L Street, N.W. Washington, D. C. 20416		27. PAYMENT WILL BE MADE BY CODE Small Business Administration Budget and Finance Office, Room 405 1441 L Street, N.W. Washington, D. C. 20416	
28. NAME OF CONTRACTING OFFICER (Type or Print)		29. UNITED STATES OF AMERICA BY: ____ (Signature of Contracting Officer)	30. AWARD DATE

33-128 *Award will be made on this form, or on Standard Form 26, or by other official written notice.*

FIGURE 6.2. Standard Form 33, for solicitations.

BIDDER'S MAILING LIST APPLICATION

INITIAL APPLICATION
REVISION

FORM APPROVED OMB NO. 29–R0069

Fill in all spaces. Insert "NA" in blocks not applicable. Type or print all entries. See reverse for instructions.

TO (*Enter name and address of Federal agency to which form is submitted. Include ZIP Code*)	DATE

1. APPLICANT'S NAME AND ADDRESS (*Include county and ZIP Code*)	2. ADDRESS (*Include county and ZIP Code*) TO WHICH SOLICITATIONS ARE TO BE MAILED (*If different from item 1*)

3. TYPE OF ORGANIZATION (*Check one*)

INDIVIDUAL		PARTNERSHIP		NON-PROFIT ORGANIZATION
CORPORATION, INCORPORATED UNDER THE LAWS OF THE STATE OF				

4. HOW LONG IN PRESENT BUSINESS

5. NAMES OF OFFICERS, OWNERS, OR PARTNERS

PRESIDENT	VICE PRESIDENT	SECRETARY
TREASURER	OWNERS OR PARTNERS	

6. AFFILIATES OF APPLICANT (*Names, locations and nature of affiliation. See definition on reverse*)

7. PERSONS AUTHORIZED TO SIGN BIDS, OFFERS, AND CONTRACTS IN YOUR NAME (*Indicate if agent*)

NAME	OFFICIAL CAPACITY	TEL. NO. (*Incl. area code*)

8. IDENTIFY EQUIPMENT, SUPPLIES, MATERIALS, AND/OR SERVICES ON WHICH YOU DESIRE TO BID (*See attached Federal agency's supplemental listing and instructions, if any*)

9. TYPE OF OWNERSHIP (*See definitions on reverse*)

MINORITY BUSINESS ENTERPRISE		OTHER THAN MINORITY BUSINESS ENTERPRISE

10. TYPE OF BUSINESS (*See definitions on reverse*)

MANUFACTURER OR PRODUCER		REGULAR DEALER (*Type 1*)		REGULAR DEALER (*Type 2*)
SERVICE ESTABLISHMENT		CONSTRUCTION CONCERN		RESEARCH AND DEVELOPMENT FIRM

☐ SURPLUS DEALER (*Check this box if you are also a dealer in surplus goods*)

11. SIZE OF BUSINESS (*See definitions on reverse*)

SMALL BUSINESS CONCERN*		OTHER THAN SMALL BUSINESS CONCERN
**If you are a small business concern, fill in (a) and (b):*	(a) AVERAGE NUMBER OF EMPLOYEES (*Including affiliates*) FOR FOUR PRECEDING CALENDAR QUARTERS	(b) AVERAGE ANNUAL SALES OR RECEIPTS FOR PRECEDING THREE FISCAL YEARS

12. FLOOR SPACE (*Square feet*)		13. NET WORTH	
MANUFACTURING	WAREHOUSE	DATE	AMOUNT

14. SECURITY CLEARANCE (*If applicable, check highest clearance authorized*)

FOR	TOP SECRET	SECRET	CONFIDENTIAL	NAMES OF AGENCIES WHICH GRANTED SECURITY CLEARANCES (*Include dates*)
KEY PERSONNEL				
PLANT ONLY				

THIS SPACE FOR USE BY THE GOVERNMENT	CERTIFICATION
	I certify that information supplied herein (*Including all pages attached*) is correct and that neither the applicant nor any person (*Or concern*) in any connection with the applicant as a principal or officer, so far as is known, is now debarred or otherwise declared ineligible by any agency of the Federal Government from bidding for furnishing materials, supplies, or services to the Government or any agency thereof.
	SIGNATURE
	NAME AND TITLE OF PERSON AUTHORIZED TO SIGN (*Type or print*)

129–105

STANDARD FORM 129 (REV. 2–77)
Prescribed by GSA, FPR (41 CFR) 1–16.802

FIGURE 6.3a. Standard Form 129, Bidders List Application.

INFORMATION AND INSTRUCTIONS

Persons or concerns wishing to be added to a particular agency's bidder's mailing list for supplies or services shall file this properly completed and certified Bidder's Mailing List Application, together with such other lists as may be attached to this application form, with each procurement office of the Federal agency with which they desire to do business. If a Federal agency has attached a Supplemental Commodity List with instructions, complete the application as instructed. Otherwise, identify in item 8 the equipment, supplies and/or services on which you desire to bid. The application shall be submitted and signed by the principal as distinguished from an agent, however constituted.

After placement on the bidder's mailing list of an agency, a supplier's failure to respond (*submission of bid, or notice in writing, that you are unable to bid on that particular transaction but wish to remain on the active bidder's mailing list for that particular item*) to Invitations for Bids will be understood by the agency to indicate lack of interest and concurrence in the removal of the supplier's name from the purchasing activity's bidder's mailing list for the items concerned.

DEFINITION RELATING TO TYPE OF OWNERSHIP
(See item 9)

Minority business enterprise. A minority business enterprise is defined as a "business, at least 50 percent of which is owned by minority group members or, in case of publicly owned businesses, at least 51 percent of the stock of which is owned by minority group members." For the purpose of this definition, minority group members are Negroes, Spanish-speaking American persons, American-Orientals, American-Indians, American-Eskimos, and American-Aleuts.

TYPE OF BUSINESS DEFINITIONS
(See item 10)

a. Manufacturer or producer—means a person (or concern) owning, operating, or maintaining a store, warehouse, or other establishment that produces, on the premises, the materials, supplies, articles, or equipment of the general character of those listed in item 8, or in the Federal Agency's Supplemental Commodity List, if attached.

b. Regular dealer (Type 1)—means a person (or concern) who owns, operates, or maintains a store, warehouse, or other establishment in which the materials, supplies, articles, or equipment of the general character listed in item 8 or in the Federal Agency's Supplemental Commodity List, if attached, are bought, kept in stock, and sold to the public in the usual course of business.

c. Regular dealer (Type 2)—in the case of supplies of particular kinds (*at present, petroleum, lumber and timber products, machine tools, raw cotton, green coffee, hay, grain, feed, or straw, agricultural liming materials, tea, raw or unmanufactured cotton linters*). **Regular dealer**—means a person (or concern) satisfying the requirements of the regulations (Code of Federal Regulations, Title 41, 50–201.101(b)) as amended from time to time, prescribed by the Secretary of Labor under the Walsh-Healey Public Contracts Act (Title 41 U.S. Code 35–45). For coal dealers see Code of Federal Regulations, Title 41, 50–201.604(a).

d. Service establishment—means a concern (or person) which owns, operates, or maintains any type of business which is principally engaged in the furnishing of nonpersonal services, such as (*but not limited to*) repairing, cleaning, redecorating, or rental of personal property, including the furnishing of necessary repair parts or other supplies as part of the services performed.

e. Construction concern—means a concern (or person) engaged in construction, alteration or repair (including dredging, excavating, and painting) of buildings, structures and other real property.

DEFINITIONS RELATING TO SIZE OF BUSINESS
(See item 11)

a. Small business concern—A small business concern for the purpose of Government procurement is a concern, including its affiliates, which is independently owned and operated, is not dominant in the field of operation in which it is bidding on Government contracts and can further qualify under the criteria concerning number of employees, average annual receipts, or other criteria, as prescribed by the Small Business Administration. (See Code of Federal Regulations, Title 13, Part 121, as amended, which contains detailed industry definitions and related procedures.)

b. Affiliates—Business concerns are affiliates of each other when either directly or indirectly (i) one concern controls or has the power to control the other, or (ii) a third party controls or has the power to control both. In determining whether concerns are independently owned and operated and whether or not affiliation exists, consideration is given to all appropriate factors including common ownership, common management, and contractural relationship. (*See items 6 and 11.*)

c. Number of employees—In connection with the determination of small business status, "number of employees" means the average employment of any concern, including the employees of its domestic and foreign affiliates, based on the number of persons employed on a full-time, part-time, temporary, or other basis during each of the pay periods of the preceding 12 months. If a concern has not been in existence for 12 months, "number of employees" means the average employment of such concern and its affiliates during the period that such concern has been in existence based on the number of persons employed during each of the pay periods of the period that such concern has been in business. (*See item 11.*)

- **COMMERCE BUSINESS DAILY**—The Commerce Business Daily, published by the Department of Commerce, contains information concerning proposed procurements, sales, and contract awards. For further information concerning this publication, contact your local Commerce Field Office.

129–105

STANDARD FORM 129 BACK (REV. 2–77)
☆U.S. Government Printing Office: 1977—261-047/3836

FIGURE 6.3b.

7

The Initial Meeting with the New Client or New Prospect

The key to successful consulting is understanding the problem, and that means learning how to listen. But you must also be businesslike, while still being professional.

RULE NUMBER 1: HAVE A CLEAR UNDERSTANDING FROM THE BEGINNING

There are many circumstances under which your first meeting with a new client or prospective client might take place. The first meeting, however, is not a mere casual introduction or handshake at some routine business function, with the polite exchange of trivial chitchat. It means a face-to-face contact during which you have a serious discussion with the new client or prospect, one in which you have the opportunity to ask questions and appraise each other's needs and talents.

Before this initial meeting, you must determine whether the other party is a client, and therefore will be paying for your time during this first meeting, or a prospective client, the contact with whom you must write off as a marketing activity chargeable only to your overhead account. There are no easy answers to this question of who is paying for your time in this initial session. You must judge each case individually. However, be cautious of those who offer you lunch as a way of obtaining free professional advice. Many people think lunch is an ample fee, and some consultants believe such contacts can lead to eventual assignments. Although such assignments can occur from the "free lunch" for the most part they are not a profitable venture for a consultant.

Occasionally a prospect who invites you to lunch will make it clear that he or she is not trying to get something for nothing, but is willing to pay for your time having lunch and offering information and/or advice. If this does not happen, it is up to you to establish from the beginning a clear understanding regarding chargeable fees in order to avoid differences later. To do this, you must assess the gamble. You can't afford to offer much free consulting but are the possibilities of work resulting from the meeting substantial enough to warrant some free information? Is the prospect a substantial organization with many needs that match the services you offer, or is the prospect someone who is unlikely to be able to offer anything but a small commitment? Estimate the possible reward in deciding how much to gamble.

You may have the fear that if you insist on being paid for your time, despite the invitation to lunch, you will lose the potential contract. That is a false fear. Anyone who is offended by this is almost certainly a rather poor prospect for business, and you will almost surely lose nothing by turning such prospects away. Assuming a businesslike position and requiring your clients to be equally businesslike, inspires the prospect's trust and and establishes a sound business relationship. You must require respect for yourself as a businessperson as well as a professional expert and consultant if you are to place your practice on a sound footing.

RULE NUMBER 2: BE A DIGNIFIED PROFESSIONAL—ALWAYS

In your first meeting it is important to remember that you are selling more than your expertise, your ability to solve a client's problem, or your time. What you are selling is your image as a highly competent and expert advisor, a total *professional*. A professional image inspires clients to trust you. And it is the client's perception of you that determines your success or failure as a consultant.

Despite the difficulties in defining the professional image and the impossibility of prescribing a formula for creating it, it is possible to offer a few guidelines to help in achieving it.

Dress conservatively. One consultant I knew in the past was referred to jeeringly by his associates and contemporaries as "Gypsy Jim," more for his green jacket, yellow slacks, and red shoes than for his itinerant working style. As a result he was not taken very seriously by even his associates, let alone by his clients. You need not go to the extreme of what was once the traditional "IBM uniform"—that is dark suit, dark tie, black shoes, and white shirt—but do dress quietly and in good taste.

Don't try to be Bob Hope. If you must be a humorist, do not relate ethnic, chauvinistic, or racy jokes. But do be amiable, smile easily and frequently, and be witty only at your own expense.

Keep your mind open. If you are dogmatic by nature, work at overcoming that characteristic; it is essential that you manage to have an open mind, demonstrating that while you are knowledgeable, you are also always ready to consider dissenting views.

Keep calm and modulate your voice. Don't carry on a conversation in a loud voice, get highly excited, appear anxious, brag, or show signs of temper. On the other hand, don't be excessively self-deprecating or excessively modest; you must manage to give yourself credit for what you are and can do—for the real *quality* of what you offer—but without the obvious "hype."

RULE NUMBER 3: SELL WITHOUT HYPE

Marketing is, in my opinion, the most important thing you do, for without marketing success you won't have a practice. And selling—that is, actually getting the contract—is the final act of marketing. For successful selling, remember the following rules:

Don't use hyperbole such as "millions" of cases, when you really are referring to several dozen or even to several hundred cases, "unprecedented," when that is not literally true, or "magnificent". Most people will lose faith in everything you say, even allowing for rhetorical excess, once you have uttered obvious and gross exaggerations.

Don't use superlatives such as most, greatest, largest, or latest. Like hyperbole, they are dismissed by most people.

Don't rely on adjectives and adverbs. Bertrand Russell remarked that faith is what we turn to when we have no evidence, and extravagant modifiers and hype are what we turn to when we have no facts.

Do stick to nouns and verbs as much as possible.

Do make *reports*, rather than *claims*. Using nouns and verbs forces you to do this.

Do quantify as much as possible, especially when you have some impressive numbers to offer. (I refer to these as "startling statistics," when I find some I can use in a proposal or other marketing presentation.)

The Difference Between Bragging and Reporting

The following examples illustrate the differences between a claim and a report.

> "When I design your systems and write your programs, Mrs. Murray, you can be sure that they will be many, many times more efficient than anything you now have, and they will save you lots of time and money."

> "Mrs. Murray, Charley Sugrue, the comptroller of Western Lumber Products, said that I reduced the run time of their accounting and inventory programs by more than 12 percent and saved them over $32,000 last year in computer time alone. I have his letter saying this, if you would like to see it."

The first example is a claim or a promise, but there is no evidence offered. Anyone can make such a statement, but the prospect is not likely to believe it without supporting proof.

The second example is also a claim, in a sense, but it does not appear to be bragging because it names a client, furnishes what appear to be facts, even to naming the individual, and offers to present the absolute proof. The prospect can call Charley Sugrue for verification, of course, but almost surely will not because she knows that you would not make that claim and name the individual if you could not back it up.

A report has no need for hype because it has the strength that results from being able to simply report the facts. And in marketing, the facts are whatever the client accepts as facts. You supplied figures and did not round them off. Had you said "almost 15 percent" or "over $30,000," the numbers would have sounded less authentic and would have been less convincing.

In the final analysis, it is a report because the client will accept it as a factual report. For practical purposes that is all that is necessary.

To make credible sales presentations you must have the facts and you must cite them in such a way that their factuality—truth—appears indisputable. However, even the truth is not automatically accepted if it is not sold or presented in such a manner that it is perceived as and so accepted as truth. Unfortunately, just as truth can be rejected when presented poorly, lies are often accepted as truth when they are presented so as to appear to be true.

SELLING IS CONSULTING

Successful salespeople focus not on making a sale but on helping prospects solve their problems. Show the prospect how to solve the problem through what you sell, and you have a sale. The following example illustrates how this worked for Warner Electric Clutch and Brake Company of Beloit, Wisconsin.

Some years ago it became my duty to develop a special sales training program for Warner. The program was to be turned over to the approximately 500 dealers of the company to train the dealers' sales representatives. Significantly, Warner was completely unconcerned about touting the name Warner in the program. They didn't insist on more than the merest mention of their name, in fact, despite the thousands of dollars the program was costing them, for they were so dominant in their field that they would be the chief beneficiaries of any increase in the sale of the types of products they manufactured.

The sales problem Warner addressed was a simple one. Their products could be used effectively to update and modernize many old industrial plants, which would be a far less costly way of achieving the modernization than replacing old machinery. But most of their dealers' sales representatives lacked the technical knowledge to act as consultants to prospects. The program was to train sales representatives in such applications of their products so that the sales representatives could show prospects what to buy to solve their problems of outdated equipment. And so the training program focused on basic orientation in modern systems, especially automation machinery and systems, familiarization with the typical older systems and machines in widespread use in the United States and elsewhere, basic functions and applications of the various items in their product line, how older machines could be modernized through the product line they sold, and relevant consulting techniques, such as analysis and synthesis, with indoctrination in the need for and benefits of being a consultant to prospects.

The Significant Difference

The difference between consulting in the sales function and consulting for a fee is simply that in the sales function you analyze the prospect's problem to demonstrate how your services will solve that problem, whereas in the paid consulting role you actually solve the problem. For example, when a company solicits my help to train their people in proposal writing, I research the kind of work the company does, the kinds of people (their skills and jobs in the company) who are to be trained, what the company's experience in proposal writing has been, and what, if any, are their perceived needs. Only after I have mastered this do I prepare or offer, a sales presentation, such as an outline of proposed coverage and other details, with my rationales for what I propose as a direct and effective solution to their problem.

The Notion of Selling Benefits

You can't study selling very long before you discover the conventional wisdom of selling benefits. For the benefits approach to be truly effective, you must describe these benefits in the direct context of the prospect's individual need, showing the linkage.

Many people have the notion, for example, that my knowledge of government marketing generally and proposal writing especially can be applied as a standard presentation to any audience interested in learning the subject. That is true only as long as I teach the subject primarily in the abstract, even with examples of specific applications. Unfortunately, that is not an appealing prospect for many potential clients. They want a program that is focused on and slanted to their specific needs. It did not take long for me to discover the need to make my proposal specific in this sense. Thus I learned to practice my consulting skills in selling my services—that is, to determine my prospect's individual and unique needs and tailor my program correspondingly.

The Consulting Steps in Selling

Obviously you cannot afford to make the exhaustive and detailed analysis in this free consultation that you would in a consultation for which you were being paid your normal fees. However, even though the consulting effort is different, the objectives are the same:

Identify the prospect's overall goal/desires, perception of problem(s), and apparent symptoms.

Make a reasoned analysis of these factors to define the problem properly.

Synthesize an approach to solution through services you offer.

Formulate a sales presentation to implement your solution and explain it—sell it—to the prospective client.

Do sufficient analysis to enable you to synthesize a highly specific presentation, as opposed to a vague and general one, for it is only detailed and specific presentations that are truly persuasive. How much detail to provide is the difficult question.

A proper and sensible answer is, "Just enough to close the sale." Determining that is equally difficult. Some clients/prospects need only the mere suggestion of an approach from you, and they can take it from there. Others can be led to the very brink of solution and still not be able to handle the problem. Therefore, you must size the prospect up, as he or she is sizing you up, to decide how much is necessary to sell the job without "giving the store away." Generally, it is far better to err on the side of giving a bit more than necessary than of giving too little to win the contract.

In my activities helping clients develop proposals I may be asked to help analyze the requirement and suggest a basic strategy, participate in writing the proposal, lead the client's proposal team, or even write the entire proposal myself. I have done all of these. But in the discussion with the prospective client, before I am actually hired, the client may be probing my thoughts on time I am paying for to get my ideas on proper strategy. To avoid giving away that which I have to sell, while still keeping the prospective client interested, I might find it necessary to say something like this:

> It appears to me that the customer here is greatly concerned with costs, yet fearful that the contractor might sacrifice quality for costs. I believe that we can work out a strategy to keep costs low while ensuring that quality will not suffer. I believe that I would need (some estimate of hours or days, as appropriate) to develop this for you.

If the prospect tries to push me beyond this observation— which might itself be an indication that this prospect is trying to use me and get something for nothing—I would be deliberately vague and general, pleading that I need more time to work out the answers. I thus make it clear to the prospect, as tactfully as I can, that I will offer nothing more unless I am retained. In the meantime I concentrate on closing the sale.

If your own services are more highly specialized than mine are (e.g., if you are a specialist in some exotic computer field), you may be able to give away quite a bit more that will still be of little value to the prospect without your specific services. Only you can make that judgment.

PRICING PROBLEMS

It is inevitable that at some point the subject of price is likely to arise. And more often than not pricing or, in many cases, the way the question of price is handled becomes the most critical problem in the sales presentation. Too often it becomes the pivotal point, unless you take special steps to prevent that from happening. But there are many indications of what is happening and what the prospect is thinking that are revealed in connection with pricing. Consider the following:

> Don't volunteer the price when making a sales presentation. Wait until the prospect asks what the price is. In addition to the psychological advantage, this also indicates the prospect's serious

interest. Presumably the prospect has now found you and what you propose technically acceptable and so is ready to move on to the subject of price.

Don't quote a price, even when the prospect asks for it, unless you are ready to quote. A premature quote or an evasion not handled properly here can easily be the death knell of the sale.

Some prospects ask price almost immediately, even before more than the briefest discussion of their needs and what you can do to satisfy them. Such prospects are, of course, generally price shopping. This means that they have a clear idea of what is needed (or think they know exactly what they need) and are simply seeking the lowest cost. Or it may mean that that the prospect has a tight budget and does not want to spend time in serious discussion before learning if you are affordable. Sometimes these are prospects who cannot afford consulting services but are desperately seeking someone who might want the job enough to work for a microscopic fee.

Some prospects are not seriously interested in the details of what you propose or they may have lost interest somewhere along the way but are tolerating you and your presentation out of courtesy. You are probably wasting your time here unless you can find a way to strike a nerve.

Serious prospects hear you out, ask pointed questions about what you propose, and then ask the price. That is the indication of serious interest and is often the point at which you win or lose the contract.

The Significance of the Pricing Problem

The problem of the salesperson who talks too much is well known; there are many stories of sellers who unsold prospects after they had sold them because they didn't know when to stop talking. The seller did not sense that the prospect was now ready to become the customer; it was time to stop selling and close.

It is not always easy to sense that moment to close. Probably some of the greatest salespeople have an instinct for sensing that moment or perhaps they have simply trained themselves to estimate it almost unconsciously. However, it is possible to sense that moment by relying on specific indicators that the prospect is about ready to accept your offer. One of those indicators is the query as to price. Only a seriously interested prospect is going to ask you how much, and when this happens you are at a critical juncture. However, when a prospect asks you to quote a price, you need to ask yourself if you are ready to quote the price yet. If it is too soon, how do you delay quoting a price without offending the prospect by avoiding an answer?

When is "Too Soon" in Quoting Price?

You should not close until you have completed your basic sales presentation, explaining your promise and presenting the necessary evidence to back it up and/or until you have some sound reason to believe that the prospect is about ready to agree to the contract you propose. There are occasional exceptions to this, admittedly, such as when a prospect is presold on you by virtue of earlier experience or personal recommendation or otherwise gives good evidence of a readiness to "sign up" with you without further discussion. The signs are usually obvious in such cases. Far more common is the case of the prospect asking the price before you have finished your presentation and before you are ready to close.

In the normal face-to-face situation your presentation is not a lengthy monologue. It is a question-and-answer session between you and the prospect. This format furnishes the best basis for tactfully avoiding a premature response to the question of how much without alienating the prospect in so doing. The following are dialogues that suggest some tactful methods used successfully by many consultants for fielding the question of how much:

Prospect: Tell me, how much will all this cost me?

You: Frankly, I don't know yet, and it would be unfair to you for me to make a guess at this point. I need to discuss this with you just a bit more before I can make a reliable estimate. But I will give you that estimate as soon as possible.

Alternative #1: I can make a rough guess now, if you want me to, but it would probably be on the high side because I need to gather some more information. If we can postpone that for a few minutes I can give you a more accurate answer to your question.

Alternative #2: There are several options possible, and we need to discuss these before I can give you a accurate estimate.

Alternative #3: I can price this on a total, fixed-price basis or on an open-ended, daily or hourly rate. If I can put off answering your question for a little while longer I'll be able to suggest the pricing base most favorable to you.

Prospect: Well, can you tell me what your rates are?

You: Certainly. When I give you that estimate, I will also explain the rates and how I arrive at the estimate.

Alternative #1: Because my assignments and contracts vary so much, my accountant has set up a whole rate structure for me, with different day rates for short-term or casual assignments than for long-term contracts and, for the same reason, both a daily rate and an hourly rate and a base for estimating assignments on a fixed-price basis. I don't mind quoting and explaining these to you now, but I don't think that will be very helpful here because I don't know yet which would be suitable in this case.

Alternative #2: Sure, here are my basic rates (quoting them), but that doesn't really tell you anything because it is the final cost, not the rates, that matters.

Alternative #3: Sure. My rate is $XX a day. But you should know that I don't count the hours in a day, and the rate is the same for 12-hour days as it is for 8-hour days. It also applies to weekends and holidays, when it is necessary to work on weekends and holidays. My accountant calculated the rate to cover all that without charging premiums and doing a lot of extra record keeping. In the long run I cost you less because I don't have all that extra bookkeeping of hourly time records, and you don't have to worry about overtime and other premium time. And, anyway, in the end it isn't the rate that counts but the total cost.

There are other options possible. Some consultants believe, for example, that the quotation of an hourly rate (e.g., $62.50 an hour) is more palatable to most prospects than quoting a daily rate (e.g., $500 a day). Others prefer to charge a relatively low hourly rate, but charge substantial premiums for overtime, weekend, and holiday effort. Some consultants prefer not to quote verbally at all; instead they promise a follow-up written proposal and quotation. This may be dictated by an actual need for more time and research to double-check the facts and figures, but many consultants follow this practice for psychological reasons. It dramatizes the importance of the proposed program by asking for time to study the program carefully before committing yourself to a firm estimate. Also it is businesslike and displays a willingness to put your offer and commitment in writing.

There are several advantages to putting your offer in writing even if it is a brief and informal proposal, and you should seek and welcome every opportunity to do so—even create such opportunities (see chapter 8 for more information on this topic).

There are some consultants who have sliding scales or who invent rates, even varying overhead rates arbitrarily, for each prospective contract, as they think suitable or necessary to capture the contract. While I think this an unwise practice generally, I myself once offered special, lower rates to minority-owned enterprises that were struggling to get established. Eventually I decided that this was an unsound practice that caused me too many problems, and so I abandoned it.

WHERE TO CONDUCT INITIAL MEETINGS

Although your first contact with a new prospect may be a most casual one, the first meeting, one at which you will make a presentation and try to make a sale, must be planned. Assume that you will call on the prospect and plan to do so unless the prospect suggests some other arrangement. Such a suggestion often results when the prospect is from out of town and expects to be in your city on some near date.

If your office is in your home and you find it impractical to conduct business meetings there, for whatever reason, there are alternatives. Perhaps the most obvious of these is to meet for lunch. Many business relationships begin with a lunch.

Two questions arise in this situation: (1) Is it proper to have a drink and/or smoke at lunch with a new prospective client whose standards you do not know? and (2) Who should pay for lunch?

Use common sense to resolve both of these questions. If your client does not drink, it is best for you to refrain also. If the client requests a non-smoking section, honor that request. Take your cue from the prospective client to avoid offending him or her.

The question of who pays for lunch is also quite clear. The individual issuing the invitation for lunch normally expects to pay for it, regardless of the business relationship between the two of you. Remember also that it is unwise to put up a lengthy struggle for the check, regardless of who issued the invitation. You should know how to accept the situation gracefully and with courteous thanks.

THINGS TO SETTLE AT THE INITIAL MEETING

One thing that causes much trouble later, after a contract has been signed and the project is underway, is the failure to have achieved a complete and specific understanding with your prospect and soon-to-be new client. Consultants often undertake assignments with only a vague understanding of what they are to achieve (sometimes they are not even clear on what the price is to be), confident that they will somehow muddle through successfully.

Clients are equally guilty in agreeing to projects with out a clear understanding of the agreement made. A written contract or letter of agreement is of little help if it does not include a clear specification or statement of work. The client has difficulty defining the problem clearly, while the consultant, eager for the contract, is reluctant to press the client too hard for details of what must be done. Although this is a problem when formal proposals must be drawn up and submitted, it is even more commonly a problem when the agreement and negotiations leading to a contract are informal and based entirely on verbal understandings and agreements.

Follow-Up

Some first meetings wind up in commitments or agreements, but many others turn out to be exploratory and inconclusive. Unless you do something specific and positive to prevent that dead end, you will have simply wasted your time and energy. The first meeting should never be permitted to end without preparation and planning of the next step. That step may be a written proposal, a firm commitment to and date set for lunch, a formal presentation, or other definite commitment calculated to move toward a sale. But it is up to you to plan and prepare for a follow-up. Otherwise it is almost foregone that nothing will result from the first meeting.

8

Proposal Writing: A Vital Art

It has become an article of faith that it is the best proposal writers who win the contracts because they are apparently the most qualified contenders.

THE EVOLUTION OF MODERN PROPOSAL PRACTICE

Until a few years ago the typical proposal was little more than a price quotation; it contained only a sketchy description of what would be supplied or done. In many cases printed brochures were enclosed to provide this description. Even when a relatively large or long-term contract was involved, a standard form or two was used to specify the terms. However, as technology advanced and government projects became larger, it became increasingly necessary to make the competition one of technical and management capabilities even more than one of cost. Also, since many government projects involve research and development, it is important to choose a contractor with attractive and promising ideas. A proposal that does little more than quote a price no longer provides enough information on which to base these increasingly complicated and technical decisions.

The modern proposal is the instrument for implementing this idea of choosing the best qualified contractor and/or the qualified contractor with the most attractive and most persuasive ideas for the project. It is the principal means by which we present our credentials and ideas, and by which the client evaluates those credentials and ideas and makes a choice.

What is offered in this chapter as a general guideline in writing proposals is generally applicable and appropriate for responding to requests for proposals (RFPs) issued by federal, state, and local governments, by private organizations, and by foreign governments and foreign privately held organizations.

WHY PROPOSALS ARE REQUESTED

RFPs are calls for help. They are used when the client does not know how to solve the problem (in many cases cannot even identify it), needs additional resources, or wants to study and evaluate different ideas and approaches before selecting one. (And in the case of governments, there is the additional reason that the law requires competitive proposals.) The proposals that are submitted based on these RFPs provide the client with something on which to base an evaluation of the contenders for the contract and judge the suitability of each. To submit a successful proposal, you must read the RFP carefully and respond to many of the expressed but unwritten messages it contains.

> Here is our definition of the problem and its symptoms. This is all we know. We want help in solving it. What would you suggest?
>
> Here is a concept that has appeared in the literature. Is it a practical idea? Can it be developed into a useful and practical methodology? How would you proceed to develop this? What kind of results would you foresee and project?
>
> Here is an idea that has been put forth for a new kind of weapon. How would you develop this concept into a working prototype?
>
> Here is a new need (to counter a new threat, new weapon by the Soviets, new hazard of our own modern equipment, etc). Give us your best ideas for developing a solution.

THE INGREDIENTS OF THE RFP

The typical RFP has four major elements:

1. A letter explaining who is the issuer of the RFP, when proposals are due and where they are to be delivered or sent, who to call if there are questions, what kind of contract is contemplat-

ed, and any other pertinent matters (e.g., an announcement of a preproposal conference).

2. Proposal instructions, which may include information about what is to be in the proposal (e.g., the required information), how proposals are to be evaluated (in the case of government this will include information of an actual rating scheme, along with some criteria), a dictated proposal format, cost estimate forms, or other such material.
3. Standard information about the requesting organization, purchasing policies and regulations, contract terms, invoicing, and other administrative data.
4. A statement of work, describing the client's problem or need, symptoms, objectives, and other such information. Theoretically, this is a specification, a complete and detailed description; however, in fact, it is often incomplete. But it is what your proposal must address, nonetheless.

KINDS OF INFORMATION ASKED FOR IN AN RFP

To determine which consultant has the best ideas and best qualifications, most RFPs ask you to provide in your proposal these kinds of information:

An analysis and discussion of the requirement, as stated in the RFP, to demonstrate a full and complete understanding of the requirement, as described, and a capability for designing an appropriate program.

A preliminary program design or approach, with sufficient explanation to demonstrate the suitability of the design or approach proposed.

A specific proposed program, with adequate details of staffing, organization, schedules, end products, interim products, procedures, management, quality control, and whatever else you deem important enough to merit special discussion in the proposal. Cost estimates must often be presented in great detail.

Your qualifications to carry out the proposed program successfully. This includes knowledge, skills, facilities, and any resources normally required for the program you describe and propose.

The record of your verifiable relevant experience in similar projects for other clients, naming those clients. This serves as evidence of your skills and your dependability as a contractor.

WHAT IS A PROPOSAL?

From the preceding discussion, you know the definition of *proposal* from the client's viewpoint. But how does the consultant define it, and what does proposal writing require of him or her?

First there are considerations of the physical format of the proposals and the amount of effort required to produce them. Many consultants choose not to pursue government business because they consider the proposal requirements too onerous to make the rewards worthwhile. Whether they are or are not depends on your personal view, especially on how you feel about writing and how badly you need sales.

Small projects suitable for the independent consultant, which in today's economy are probably roughly in the range of $2,000 to $15,000, usually require only simple, informal proposals, actually letters of several pages in which the proposal is embodied. In fact, these are often called letter proposals. But even when formal proposals are required, they tend to be fairly small (unless you are in pursuit of the larger projects of perhaps $100,000 or more). Typically, for small to medium-sized projects such as an independent consultant is likely to pursue, a formal proposal will be between 25 and 50 pages.

Remember these points when evaluating an RFP and writing a proposal:

With only an occasional exception, there is just one winner in a proposal competition for a contract. Winning second place is only slightly better than being in last place, although there are sometimes useful advantages to being "close," even if you do not win.

It is not enough to demonstrate that you can do a good job or as good a job as anyone else. You must somehow prove yourself and your plan better than all the others.

Clients are most unlikely to perceive for themselves that your approach, your plan, and your qualifications are superior to all the rest. They are unlikely to make the effort to do so, even if they have all the technical knowledge to do so. You must explain why and how your plans are superior.

From your viewpoint then, a proposal is a **sales presentation**. It cannot succeed unless it sells.

PROPOSAL SCENARIOS

Many different circumstances cause the issuance of an RFP and inspire the writing of proposals. The most common situation is probably the one in which the client has identified a need of some sort and has decided to seek help from an outside specialist, for whatever reason. Presumably an award will go to the writer of the best proposal. However, if the need is not too pressing and none of the proposals submitted is very attractive, the procurement may be cancelled. So it is not always possible to win by being the best of a bad lot.

Some RFPs are inspired by consultants working with the client, usually unintentionally. That is, the consultant intends to promote more work for himself or herself, not to create opportunities for competitors. But the client sometimes decides to solicit competitive proposals despite the fact that the original idea was yours, an unfortunate consequence of aggressive marketing.

Fortunately there are many cases where it is possible for you to suggest something to a client or prospective client that elicits an invitation to submit a sole-source proposal, one for which there are to be no competitive proposals. This may come about because the client has complete faith in you and does not wish to consider anyone else, or it may be the consequence of your offering a proprietary and unique idea or product (e.g., a special computer program or some special and unique knowledge).

Finally, you may offer an unsolicited proposal as a result of some knowledge of a client's needs or as a normal follow-up of a sales lead.

WHO MUST YOU SELL?

It is often necessary to sell more than one person in the client's organization. You may have convinced the individual with whom you have had direct contact, but that individual may be required (or may prefer) to review the matter with others and get approval. In many cases the individual may want to retain you or to select you from among a group of potential contractors, but actually needs your help in selling the idea in his or her own organization.

You must always operate on the assumption that there are others who must be sold, especially when you are submitting a proposal. More often than not, a number of people will review proposals, whether sole-source or competitive, and judge them; and those judgments will have an influence on the buying decision.

Written proposals are your most effective sales tools. Although verbal presentations may be successful in some selling situations, they must always be followed by a written presentation, one that is a permanent record for clients to review, study, discuss, evaluate, and consider at length. Writing a proposal also offers you the opportunity to develop it at length, with careful study and consideration. You allow yourself time to plan, draft, reconsider, edit, rewrite, and polish until you are satisfied that the presentation is everything you want it to be.

When writing your proposal, remember not only who you are trying to sell but also who you are selling against. Is your competition the rival consultants or the client's reluctance? This reluctance is often a difficult obstacle to overcome. It takes many forms, including:

Reluctance to turn to outside sources for help.

Reluctance to do something differently.

Reluctance to do something about an old problem that has been tolerated for a long time.

Reluctance to battle internal resistance to "contracting out."

Reluctance to admit (even to themselves) that there is a problem.

Reluctance to spend the money.

SELLING YOURSELF

Too often a consultant wastes his or her time and energy selling something the client has already decided to buy—that is, the basic service or assistance—and neglects to sell what the client has not yet decided on—that is, *you.* When writing your proposal—your sales presentation—remember to sell yourself, to detail how your services are superior to those of your competitors.

PROPOSALS FOR THE PRIVATE SECTOR VERSUS THE PUBLIC SECTOR

Probably the most significant difference between procurement in the public and private sectors (and, hence, the respective proposal requirements and strategic considerations) is that clients in the private sector have more latitude in decision making than those in the public sector, who must follow certain public statutes governing purchasing.

This distinction may affect your proposal writing. For example, when you respond to a government RFP you can take advantage of your knowledge of the statutes that apply to such purchases.

Another quite important difference is that in the private sector you are more likely to be accepted as a competent professional. The assumption is that since you are in the pertinent line of business and competing for the contract, you must be capable in that field. Government clients, on the other hand, generally require that you provide information to prove your competence, and therefore your qualifications, to bid on and to be considered for the contract. This is at least partially a consequence of the legal requirement to evaluate each proposal objectively; but it also reflects some experiences the government has had with incompetent contractors whose work had to be redone or whose work affected highly critical and important matters (e.g. safety or performance of critical military systems). You should expect that RFPs issued by government agencies will require you to furnish evidence of your qualifications and capabilities, technical and otherwise, for carrying out the work successfully. There is a growing tendency in the private sector to emulate government proposal practices in all respects, including this, but it is a good idea to furnish such evidence whether it is asked for or not.

Still another important difference is that governments tend to demand a complete cost/price analysis in all but small contracts, and that analysis requires you to reveal all your cost factors, direct and indirect. Reluctance to reveal such proprietary and confidential information to anyone, including government agencies, is one reason some consultants decline to pursue government contracts.

The relative risk in revealing your program strategy is another difference. It is not unprecedented for unscrupulous individuals in the private sector to appropriate the plans and confidential information you reveal in your proposal and use this information for their own ends, thus victimizing you by what amounts to simple theft. This is a serious problem, and the risk so represented should be taken into account when proposing to any organization, particularly one in the private sector. It is possible for this to happen when proposing to a government agency, but is relatively rare there, so the risk is far smaller.

THE EVALUATION SYSTEM

Federal procurement regulations require an objective rating system to be used to evaluate and assign to each technical proposal a figure of merit representing its respective technical quality. (Costs must usually be supplied in a separate proposal, withheld from those evaluating the proposals until they have completed their evaluations.)

The resulting evaluation schemes vary widely from one agency to another and even from one procurement to another. Sometimes the RFP reveals and explains the evaluation scheme and criteria in relatively elaborate detail, while in other cases the explanation is rather sketchy. The examples that follow illustrate two rather common approaches.

Example 1

The following are the criteria on which technical proposals will be evaluated. Item (1) has twice the value of item (2), which has one-half the value of item (3).

Item (1): Understanding and approach.
Item (2): Qualifications of proposed staff.
Item (3): Qualifications of the organization.

Award will be made to that proposer whose proposal is deemed to be in the best interests of the government, costs and other factors considered.

Example 2

Evaluation criteria are as follows:

1. Understanding of the problem:	0 to 5 points
2. Practicality of approach:	0 to 10 points
3. Evidence of realistic anticipation of problems and planning for contingencies:	0 to 10 points
4. Proposed management and organization:	0 to 10 points
5. Qualifications of proposed staff:	0 to 25 points
6. Qualifications of organization:	0 to 25 points
7. Resources offered:	0 to 15 points
Maximum possible score:	100 points

In those cases in which greater detail is provided the several criteria listed (as in the second example) are further detailed by subordinate items reflecting the analysis of each.

The Cost Criterion

Note that little mention is made of costs in these examples, except that it will be "considered." This defeats the purpose of the evaluation requirement because it leaves final decision entirely to the judgment of the officials making the procurement (although there is an appeal or "protest" process prescribed for seeking a remedy against unfair or illegal procurement practices, a subject that merits a separate discussion).

There are, however, other ways in which the cost factor is taken into account. In many cases costs are simply included in the list of criterion items as a specific, weighted factor added to the technical score. Presumably the proposer with the lowest cost is awarded the maximum number of points allowed, while the one with the highest cost earns zero points. But, as proposers we are not entitled to know exactly how the evaluation is made.

There is also a method that links cost with technical considerations, dividing the dollars by the technical points to arrive at a cost per technical point. Presumably this results in the contract being awarded to the proposer with the greatest value to offer—that is, the lowest price per technical point. Of course, for this to be viable the client must first screen all proposals and eliminate those technically unacceptable, regardless of price. Such an elimination of unacceptable proposals, regardless of other considerations, is a common practice, although there are a few exceptions (e.g., contracting officers who believe that every proposer is entitled to a chance to revise his or her proposal and make it acceptable.)

The Inevitability of Comparative Evaluation

The listing of evaluation criteria with specific weights suggests that the proposals are to be measured against absolute standards set for each criterion; however, this is virtually impossible to achieve. Take, for example, the 0 to 25 points listed for qualifications of the staff proposed. Would that mean that the perfect staff would merit an award of 25 points? Would the client attempt to judge how near to or far from perfect each proposed staff is? Or does it mean that the proposal with the staff judged to be best qualified earns the most points, perhaps the full 25?

Of course, such methods mean that the evaluation must be comparative. Your staff and all your other qualifications will go through two evaluations: (1) to screen it for general acceptability and (2) to rank it on each criterion. No evaluation scheme can be entirely objective; human judgment is inevitably involved. Therefore, you must do whatever you can to influence that judgment in your favor by employing every element of sales and marketing strategy available to you.

THE PROTEST PROCESS

Protests may be lodged with either the contacting official responsible for the procurement contract in question or with the comptroller general of the United States, who is in charge of the General Accounting Office (GAO), a branch of Congress. A substantial staff of lawyers and others work there, devoting their full time to resolving protests. But you do not require a lawyer to register a protest; a simple letter, setting forth the facts as you see them, is sufficient.

The protest is an administrative appeal, not a legal action, and so in no way substitutes for a lawsuit or compromises a future lawsuit. That is, you are not legally bound by the protest and its decision should you choose to sue the government, something major corporations and others have been known to do fairly often.

Probably most people who are not truly familiar with the process view the protest as a measure one pursues after learning that the contract was awarded to someone else. Consequently, most protests are made after the award has been made. Unfortunately, that is the worst possible time to lodge the protest. You may win the protest, but most likely you will not win the contract for the following reasons:

The project is already well under way and the decision is that even if the award was improper, it would cost the government too much money to cancel the contact and reaward it.

The decision is that the award was defective, but you have not demonstrated that it was you who should have won, and it would be prohibitive to recompete the contract.

The agency decides to cancel the procurement entirely, possibly to recompete it at some future time.

In fact you may protest any element of and at any time in the procurement process if you believe that there is something improper. For example, a client of my own protested successfully that the requirement did not permit enough time to write a proper proposal, forcing the agency to extend the closing date. Another protested successfully that the evaluation scheme had built-in anomalies so that the award violated the scheme specified, forcing cancellation. And another, in quite a large procurement, protested successfully that the winning proposal had been delivered and accepted some minutes after the deadline and managed to have the contract awarded to him, much to the embarrassment of the agency.

Of course, there are a great many protests that do not succeed. Many of them fail because they offer irrelevant arguments and should not have been made at all. A common argument is that the protester offered a lower price, which is rarely a valid argument. One protester who used that argument had submitted a proposal that had been rejected as technically unacceptable, and so could not have won anything in any case. Another complained that the winner's price was too low and that the winner would lose money on the contract. The contracting official advised him that it was not against the law to lose money.

It is legitimate to protest just about anything you believe improper or unfair about a government procurement. The apparent impropriety or unfairness may prove to be a simple mistake, or it may be an illegal effort to "wire" the procurement for some favored consultant, which is probably not quite as prevalent a practice as many think it to be. However, if you feel you are being denied a fair opportunity to pursue government business, you have the right to challenge the decision.

Signs to Watch For

There are several ways in which a procurement can be rigged to give a favored consultant an advantage. Be alert for the following indicators:

The closing date is so close as to virtually preclude anyone not *already prepared to respond* to be able to get a decent proposal together in time.

The specification of what is required as qualifying characteristics is tailored unreasonably.

The specification of what is to be done is excessively vague and thus is extremely difficult to respond to with any assurance that your proposal will be responsive—that is, it makes it ridiculously easy to declare your proposal nonresponsive and thus to disqualify it.

The statement of work or specification of what is required is so excessively and unnecessarily tailored that it restricts free and open competition.

None of this is intended to suggest that such practices are commonplace or that the system is not basically fair and honest; it is. But circumstances lead to these situations, no matter how innocently, and you are entitled to relief from them. That is the purpose of the protest process.

SOLE-SOURCE PROCUREMENT

Procurement regulations provide for sole-source procurement, generally under one of three conditions:

1. The need is urgent and for one reason or another (e.g. the typically late enactment of an appropriation bill by Congress or an unanticipated emergency) there is simply no time for the typical three-to-six month procurement process.
2. The requirement is for a proprietary product, service, or experience of some sort that is unique and unavailable elsewhere.
3. The procurement implements a contract resulting from an unsolicited proposal.

Unfortunately, not all sole-source procurements are so justified. Many are announced in the *CBD* (claiming that the announcement is for information purposes only, whatever that may mean), with the alleged justification that the favored consultant has some special qualification. This is alleged then to offer the government the benefits of a more efficient program than would be possible with another contractor. To add insult to injury, that special, unique experience was often acquired in a current or recently concluded contract with that same agency!

Again, this may be legitimately so, but there is ample evidence, often cited by the GAO in their studies and reports, that many agencies abuse their privileges and make sole-source procurements that are not truly justified, often simply to speed up the process. In fact, the sheer number of such noncompetitive procurements announced daily in the *CBD* appears excessive.

In any case you may use the protest process to challenge such procurement intentions and demand the right to compete if you believe that you can do the work as efficiently as anyone else.

What Happens Next

In general your protest results in a request by GAO for copies of whatever documents are involved—the RFP, the winning proposal, and your proposal, if it is a challenge of an award, for example—along with a statement from the contracting official, responding to your complaint. While GAO studies these you have the opportunity to respond to the contracting official's statement and he or she has an opportunity to respond to your statement. Theoretically, GAO may then issue its decision. In most cases that is the end of the process. However, you still have the right to sue in a federal court, if you choose to.

PROPOSAL FORMATS AND RATIONALES

Some RFPs mandate a specific format for the proposals requested, even to mandating a format for staff résumés. Most list, describe, discuss, and even specify the information required, often in great detail, but do not specify a format, leaving that to you. A recommended four-section general format that has proved to be highly satisfactory and readily adaptable to most proposal requirements is offered here.

The recommended proposal format is based on the general premises that (1) the client is asking for help with a problem, (2) it is a sales presentation and must use sound sales tactics, and (3) it must have a single, major strategy. The third consideration is all important because it allows you to show how your plan is superior to other proposals in some decisive manner.

The following general format is one that has been successful in winning millions of dollars worth of contracts. It offers information in a logical flow, while it still implements the promise-and-proof sales strategy described earlier. It is presented here as the format for a formal, bound proposal, but the format is easily adapted to informal letter proposals, incorporating the same philosophy.

The four main sections and ancillary elements (when needed) are these:

Front matter
Chapter 1: Introduction
Chapter 2: Discussion
Chapter 3: Proposed program
Chapter 4: Experience and qualifications
Appendices and exhibits

These chapter titles are generic. More imaginative titles specific to the individual client's needs, are recommended. This will make it clear that the proposal was custom written for the client.

Chapter 1: Introduction

The first chapter is divided into two sections: (1) About the Offeror, which is an introduction to who and what you are, with a very brief summary of your interest and qualifications, noting details to be offered later; and (2) About the Requirement, which is a preliminary analysis, validating your understanding of the requirement and laying the foundation for your strategy.

Chapter 2: Discussion

Here you explore the client's problem in depth. In this chapter you should demonstrate conclusively that you fully understand the requirement and all that it implies (possibly even better than the client does); show that you have the necessary technical experience, knowledge, skill, and creative imagination; show that you have analyzed the problem thoroughly and have identified all alternatives and possibilities; and present the optimum approach along with the rationale.

It is in this chapter that you must make your technical sales arguments, implementing the strategy you have decided on. Here you may have to "educate" the client, explaining in detail your analyses, your reasoning, your conclusions, and your plans for delivering to the client all the benefits, especially those around which you have built your main strategy. Here you must explain how you will meet the impossible schedule, reduce the costs, maximize the probability of success and eliminate the possibilities of failure, and implement your promise. Here you must parade the benefits to be derived from your plan—especially the unique benefits that would not result from others' plans. This chapter must end in a clear presentation of your approach, laying the groundwork for the next chapter.

Chapter 3: Proposed Program

Chapter 2 was the promise. This chapter is the proof—*the* proposal—the specifics of what, when, where, how, and how much you propose. Everything before has been prologue, everything after, epilogue. Here you must show exactly how you will implement the strategy and approach you promised in Chapter 2.

Charts will enhance your presentation. Use an organizational chart if there will be associates working with you. A functional flow chart showing phases of work and major functions and a chart matching these major phases and functions with labor hours required for them will also be effective. And you may also choose to use a milestone chart to illustrate the schedule.

Chapter 4: Experience and Qualifications

It is my usual practice to include the staff résumés in chapter 3, as those résumés provide evidence of the qualifications of the individuals proposed to staff the project. This chapter, however, provides evidence of the overall organization's qualifications.

This can be tricky when you are operating as a one-person enterprise. In many cases, especially when responding to a formal RFP with a formal proposal, it is necessary to comply and respond as though you were a larger organization. You can offer your résumé as an individual, covering formal education and all relevant experience, wherever it was gained in the history of your career, but you must also offer your résumé, with accounts of your projects, as an independent consultant—that is, experience gained in providing services to your own clients, rather than to an employer's clients. In fact, much of the information will be the same in each application, but the orientation will be different in each case.

This chapter should also include an account of all facilities and resources that relate in some way to your consulting enterprise generally and/or with respect to the proposed program (e.g. computers, copying and reproduction machines, photographic equipment, laboratory facilities, a library, photo files, or access to any relevant resources.

Front Matter

Formal proposals include front matter—a title page, a table of contents, and an executive summary, or abstract, which is used by most proposal writers to highlight the major selling points of the proposal. However, an informal, letter proposal would not usually include the front matter. The effect of an abstract can be easily achieved in a letter format through sensible organization (e.g. the "inverted pyramid" of journalism, in which the entire story is summarized in the lead and details follow).

A typical title page is shown in Figure 8–1. Figure 8–2 illustrates a typical table of contents and Figure 8–3 demonstrates how a brief letter proposal might be organized according to the principles advocated here.

A PROPOSAL

to the *AMERICAN SOY BEAN COMPANY*

to train 500 Bean Counters in Quality Control Procedures

Prepared by

JCI Associates, Ltd

Consultantsville, California

January 22, 1999

Copyright 1999 by JCI Associates, Ltd.

FIGURE 8.1. Title page of formal proposal.

Back Matter

You should include an appendix when you have material to include that you believe will be of interest to some readers, but not to all, (e.g. the complete text of a document or a drawing you refer to in your proposal). An exhibit, on the other hand, is often included when

TABLE OF CONTENTS

CHAPTER NO.	TITLE & CONTENTS	PAGE NO.

LIST OF FIGURES

FIGURE NO.	TITLE	PAGE NO.

LIST OF TABLES

TABLE NO.	TITLE	PAGE NO.

FIGURE 8.2. Format for table of contents.

several copies of the proposal are called for, but only one copy of some supporting item—a set of slides or a sample of the product of some earlier project, for example—is available. When using such an exhibit it is wise to advise all readers that such an exhibit exists, although not an integral part of the proposal itself, so they are alerted to seek it out.

HRH COMMUNICATIONS, INC.
P.O. Box 1731
Wheaton, MD 20902
(301) 649-2499

September 23, 1989

John W. Herr
Vice-President
American Soy Bean Company
99881 Process Avenue
Soy Mash, Pa 17765 Ref: QC Training Proposal

Dear Mr. Herr:

It gives me great pleasure to offer my assistance in helping you to reduce the number of rejects on your production lines while increasing customer satisfaction with your products. The research I have carried out since our recent meeting and discussion at the convention in New York City bears out the correctness of your judgment: I agree completely that training in quality-control procedures is the proper avenue to improvement.

I visited your plant, as you suggested, and interviewed several of your employees, using a structured interview that I developed some years ago in carrying out a preliminary task analysis for a similar program for the Acme Paintbrush Corporation. That program, I am proud to report, produced a 14-percent increase in net production through reducing line rejects by 11 percent. And subsequent reports by the company reflected a 27-percent drop in returns by customers.

I am sure that we can do at least as well for you. Of course, while I will use the general approach that proved so effective in the Acme Paintbrush case, I will develop a program designed especially for your company.

In summary, the program will be drafted in 60 days, tried out, revised and validated over the next 60 days, so that you will have a fully tested and ready-to-go program within 120 days. Full details are offered in the following pages for study by your staff and yourself.

(over please)

FIGURE 8.3. First page of an informal, letter proposal.

THE NECESSARY IMPACT

As must any sales presentation, a proposal must have great impact, if it is to do its job well. To provide that necessary impact, the following qualities must be apparent to the client:

Total competence. The client must sense your power as a consultant who brings complete technical and professional competence to the job.

Dependability. The client must feel that you are completely reliable and will never fail to carry the job through to a successful conclusion.

Accuracy. The proposal must convey the sense that you are careful to be absolutely precise and accurate in every action and in every step you take.

The keys to accomplishing this effect have already been provided, but a brief review is in order.

Specificity and detail. Anyone can generalize about almost any subject, so generalizations have little impact. A presentation that cites specific facts and details, particularly quantified data, is much more likely to impress a reader and be credible.

Startling statistics. Study your facts to see what impressive numbers you can develop (e.g. total person-hours of directly relevant experience, number of pages of training material you have written, total dollar amount of contracts resulting from similar proposals.) If numbers are startling enough, see if you can work them into the introduction.

Clear and unambiguous language. Avoid euphemisms; you are not in the diplomatic corps. Be direct; leave no doubt as to your meaning.

Quiet confidence. Hype sounds defensive, as though you are trying to compensate for weakness. Avoid adjectives and superlatives that convey this weakness; instead use a quiet, confident tone that conveys strength.

Taking charge. Most clients want a consultant who will relieve them of worry and tedious, time-consuming involvement. Make it clear that you know exactly what to do—present highly detailed plans—and be sure that your explanations, descriptions, and rationales reflect confidence in what you propose to do. However, remember to also make it clear that you will remain under the client's control.

Be thorough. Don't make any assumptions. Thoroughly investigate and document all your points. Carelessness and lack of attention to detail can lose you the contract.

STRATEGY AND ITS EVOLUTION

Successful proposals are most often those based on specific, well-thought-out strategies. Repeatedly I have seen proposers, who neither the client nor the competitors had ever heard of before, win a contract because the dark horse presented an effective strategy that was implemented well.

Since proposals are usually custom projects with only a single buyer they must be based on a specific strategy. There are no percentages to play here, as there are in mass marketing. It's all or nothing in most cases; multiple-award programs are the exception. And even then the number of awards is usually severely limited; you must still have submitted a first-class proposal to have won anything.

Read the Client As Well As the RFP

Repeatedly I have heard neophytes at proposal writing mutter to themselves as they read an RFP, "I wonder what they really want." They believe that some kind of guessing game is involved. They have trouble grasping that the client is often not at all sure of what is needed and wants help in identifying the problem, as well as in solving it.

To devise effective strategies, you must first determine the client's frame of mind, which is usually one of the following:

The client has a good and probably accurate understanding/definition of the problem/need.

The client all but concedes that what is described are probably only symptoms, and the consultant will have to decide what the true problem or need is and respond to it.

The client claims or professes to know what the problem or requirement is, but is probably mistaken; you must discriminate between what the client thinks is the problem and what it really is.

Understand What a "Problem" Really Is

Not every RFP calls for services to solve a problem that the client lacks the knowledge to solve. In many cases the client knows exactly how to solve the problem, but lacks the wherewithal to solve it in-house. In such a case, the preliminary analysis necessary to develop a sensible and specific strategy should consider these factors:

What appears to be the best (i.e., fastest, most efficient, most dependable, least expensive, most risk-free) way to do the job?

What prejudices/special concerns/worries does the client appear to have, if any, about how to best do the job?

What appears to be most important to the client? Cost? Schedule? Technical approach? Qualifications of staff? Qualifications of organization? Working relationship?

Do these factors relate to each other? If so, how? Are the incompatible? Can they be resolved? How? Or are they mutually supportive? Do they lend each other strength? If so, how?

Developing Strategy: The Key Questions

The choice of factors on which to base your strategy is not a random one. It should be based on several considerations, the first and most important of which is usually the client's own perception of the problem, which you may or may not agree with. But that must be tempered by related considerations, represented by these questions among others:

Is the client correct in his or her assumptions of problems and/or needs–that is, do you agree with the client's definition of the problem?

Do you have some firm conviction about how to define the real problem or is it merely a suspicion that the client does not truly understand his or her problem—that is, will some work be required to determine first what the problem is before a reliable approach to its solution can be formulated?

Has the client mandated in the RFP some defined set of services and method of operation to which he or she appears to be bound?

If the client all but mandates (i.e., "strongly recommends" or even "suggests") a method/service/approach that is workable, is it the best one (i.e., most appropriate, most efficient, most likely to achieve the stated goals, etc.)?

Is the client's definition so far off that it is impossible? Would it be risky to proceed without (1) an initial problem definition phase or (2) redefining the problem as you see necessary?

How firmly does the client appear to cling to his or her notion? Would it be risky (to sales success) to confront the client directly about this in your proposal?

Are there other problems the client fails to foresee? Are there special problems of meeting requirements that are extraordinarily difficult, such as an impossible schedule?

Does the client appear to be conscious of and/or especially concerned with some aspect of the problem (e.g., meeting a schedule date, getting the job done at lowest possible cost, probability of eventual success, etc.)?

Strategies and Diplomacy

Some of the answers to these questions may pose a difficult sales problem for you, for it is nearly impossible to win an argument with a customer. Still, it is essential that you recognize this common problem for two important reasons. First, your professional integrity should not be compromised; you should feel honor bound to be honest with the client. Second, you may easily paint yourself into a corner if you go along with a false premise and thereby win the contract.

This does not mean there is no solution; in fact these problems actually create new opportunities for you to develop challenging strategies. But you will have to judge which is the right strategy for the occasion. There are clients who do not mind you saying plainly to them, "The approach you suggest is not the best one possible and will add unnecessary cost," or "The approach described is somewhat out of date today and is less efficient than the modern method." But even with those clients, it is far better to say, "There is an approach possible that will reduce the costs," or "A recently developed method promises greater efficiency." That is normal diplomacy, differing with the client without challenging or appearing to attack.

Another strategic maneuver is to find "the worry item" (i.e., whatever appears to be of greatest concern to the client) and focus the proposal on that item.

For example, if an extraordinarily rapid turnaround time is required, you must focus on the schedule and how you propose to meet it without fail. That is, the promise is that you will meet it unfailingly—the client is assured of that—and the proof is your planned program and all the rationale you can develop to show why your plan must and most assuredly will produce the result you promise.

Build your program plan around a method for accommodating the client's chief worry item, and be sure that the proposal dramatizes that suitably.

Finding the Worry Item

It is not always easy to identify the client's worry item. The client may be reluctant to admit to any special concerns or may indeed have no special concerns! In that case, your course is clear. You must decide what ought to be a major worry item—an item you believe the client will agree on once it is pointed out—and go on as though you had detected that concern. In other words, you must *help* the client acquire a worry item!

Other Strategies

Usually the proposed program design is the critical area around which the strategy should be built. However, there are other strategic areas and supporting strategies to be considered too.

Cost Strategy

In discussing costs, you should talk *value* and be clear about value offered. If possible, quantify and pro rate what you offer to do across the total budget to demonstrate the value. Provide as much detail as possible in describing what you propose to deliver. This makes you appear far more honest than competitors who are relatively vague about what they will deliver for the dollars and thus makes the costs you quote far more palatable. It also subtly suggests to the client the possibility of negotiation and prepares the way for discussing all the items that might be negotiable.

If you come across an RFP that is so vague that it appears to be impossible to price the proposal, fight the tendency to go back to the client and ask for clarification. Many clients think they have given you ample information, no matter how unclear their RFPs actually are and resent being asked to clarify what they consider to be a clear request. Instead, use this situation as an opportunity to steer things your way, to develop a winning strategy, in fact! Decide what is probably necessary to get the job done and meet the goals, and draw up your own specifications—that is, the quantification as well as the qualification, of what you propose. Determine your pricing based on these specifications.

This gives you several advantages, in addition to solving the problem. First, it lends credibility to your presentation because you are supplying the specifications–you are the true expert. Second, it shows you are in control. You are telling the client just what ought to be done. This also puts you in control of costs to a large degree. And there is no special risk as long as you quantify everything carefully. Third, it allows you to offer the client options, inasmuch as the client has not offered a clear specification, and that is often a most powerful strategy.

Competitive Strategy

Don't refer to competitors directly at any time. However, it is perfectly legitimate and in good taste when you know that you are in a competitive situation to address this problem indirectly. One way is to include a discussion of what is needed to do this job effectively. List whatever is appropriate—experience, physical facilities, access to other specialists, willingness to burn the midnight oil, and other factors. The mere fact of your pointing these things out—and especially of competitors failing to (they usually do not think to do so)—is often highly effective.

Stress anything you can offer that is unique or unusual. This sets you apart from your competitors in the client's mind.

Presentation Strategy

Prepare your proposal carefully, even if it is an informal, letter proposal, to reflect your professionalism. The following guidelines will help you make a good impression:

Have your proposal typed neatly and cleanly on standard–sized white bond paper or any other that is of a light, near–white shade. You can use your regular letterhead if it is white or light cream color. Don't use dark papers; they are too hard on the eyes.

Use black ink. Colored inks may get momentary special attention, but it's only momentary, and many people find colored type distracting. Be distinctive, but not bizarre.

Use 12-point type and leave generous margins to make your proposal easy to read. Many people like to double space copy, on the theory that it is easier to read, but there is no clear evidence that this is so.

Use a simple report cover. They are inexpensive, and they add to the impact.

Use illustrations. Simple line drawings, possibly photographs in some rare cases, will add to your presentation.

Carefully check spelling, grammar, and other such details. Professionals should not be careless with the language.

If you have a word processor and good printer you can add a few flourishes, such as oversize captions and headlines. You may also find your desktop computer convenient for generating a few simple graphic illustrations to lend impact to your proposal. Use your resources to make your presentation distinctive but not overdone.

Don't ask questions. Despite the fact that many RFPs are sketchy and inspire more questions than answers, it is risky to ask the client to clarify or elaborate on a proposal request. The client may choose to send out additional information to your competitors or may withdraw the request entirely and cancel the procurement. It is usually far better to decide for yourself what the answers should be and bid on that basis (e.g., proposing the specifications), observing the precautions counseled earlier.

Don't be vague. Some consultants believe that if the RFP was vague their proposals may be correspondingly vague. The result is disaster. Be highly specific, following the guides provided here. In fact, many veteran proposal writers far prefer the vague RFP because it usually affords you a much better chance of winning for several reasons: (1) it reduces the competition (many would-be proposers will drop out when the RFP is vague and thus difficult to respond to); (2) it gives you the opportunity to outshine your competitors by being clear and specific, where they are vague and rambling uncertainly; and (3) it allows you to propose a project on your own terms.

Don't start writing too soon. The rush to start writing before reaching a complete understanding of the client's need and, especially, before clearly formulating an approach and a strategy is a common mistake that leads to poor proposals.

Do rewrite as much as possible. Although tight schedules usually make it impossible to do a complete rewrite, you should at the least do a thorough edit to ensure correct spelling and correct usage and to polish the presentation as much as possible.

FUNCTIONAL FLOW CHARTS

People outside the technological fields appear to have difficulty with functional flow charts. Yet, they are among the simplest ways to present and understand a process in which successive steps are required.

Such a chart, at least one depicting a relatively simple process, may be considered a graphic version of a written procedure. Consider, for example, a cook book explanation of how to make a plain omelet. The instructions might be written thus:

1. Heat butter in pan.
2. Beat two eggs in a bowl.
3. Pour eggs into pan.
4. Brown and fold omelet.
5. Remove when done and serve.

As a simple and straightforward flow chart, the process would be as in Figure 8–4.

The instructions might have directed the reader to beat the eggs while the butter was warming in the pan. That would be shown in Figure 8–5. That presentation shows a *phase* or time relationship between the first two component functions, to point out that they

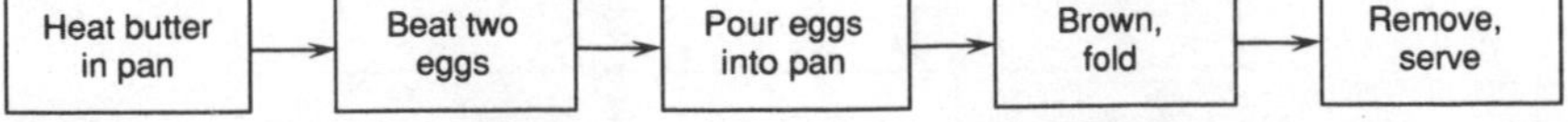

FIGURE 8.4. Simple flow charts.

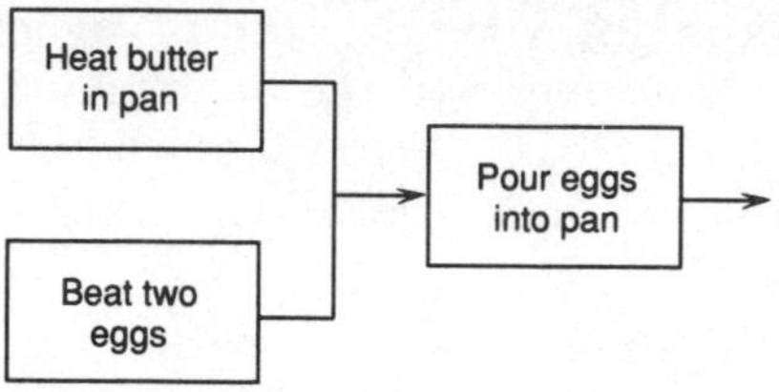

FIGURE 8.5. Flow chart showing phase relationships.

are or can be concurrent, which is often important in demonstrating how you plan to conduct the project and, especially, how you might organize the project to meet a difficult schedule. As processes become more complex it becomes increasingly difficult to explain them in words alone, and graphic aids grow more and more useful. It is sometimes more expedient to show only the major steps, when the intervening steps are obvious. (See Figure 8–6.) But you must be the judge of the right level at which to present and explain your plan.

The processes are rarely simple and straightforward. In fact, the processes are often iterative, as shown in Figure 8–7. This figure illustrates a most useful idea in proposal writing—that is, developing a functional flow chart that is based entirely on the RFP and refining it before you begin to write. This is an idea and methodology I have personally found to be effective in developing successful proposals for rather large projects. If you do a thorough and accurate job of translating the RFP into a flow chart you have accomplished the following objectives:

1. You have your project design before you in a graphic form, one that enables you to study it effectively, perceive interrelationships among the functions, uncover anomalies, and perceive potential problems.
2. You have an almost ideal presentation tool; clients value graphic presentations because it is much easier to grasp the logic of the project in a flow chart. Moreover, less text is required, another boon to busy executives.

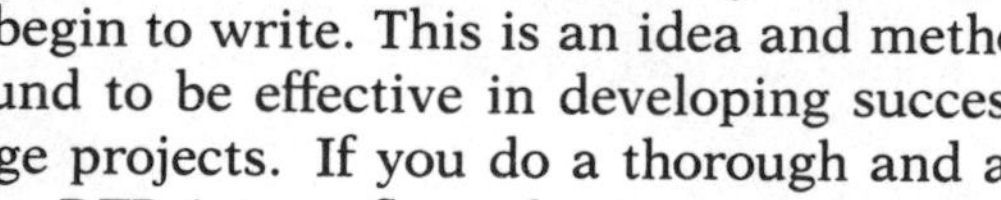

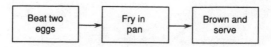

FIGURE 8.6. Simplified flow chart.

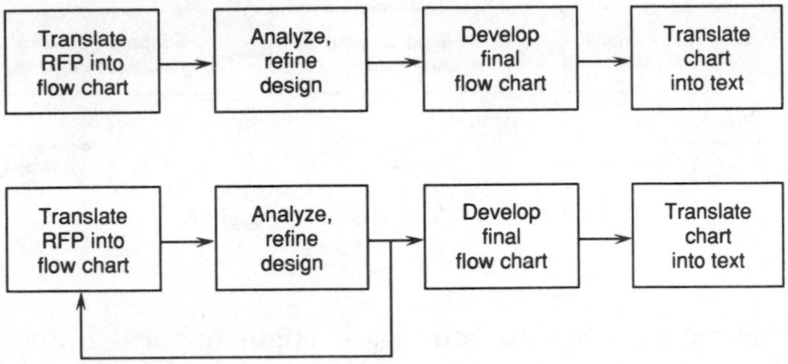

FIGURE 8.7. Proposal process showing iteration.

3. The ability to envision the project in this manner says a great deal about your ability to handle the project. It demonstrates your understanding quite effectively, while it helps the reader to understand your logic. The milestone chart (see Figure 8–8) is another aid to this.
4. Many of your writing problems are solved, since you now write to the flow chart. It's your road map, and it greatly reduces the volume of words you need.

The Logic of the Flow Chart

The logic of flow charts is itself one of the keys to creating them. Figure 8–9 illustrates this logic. If you ask *why* to the notations in

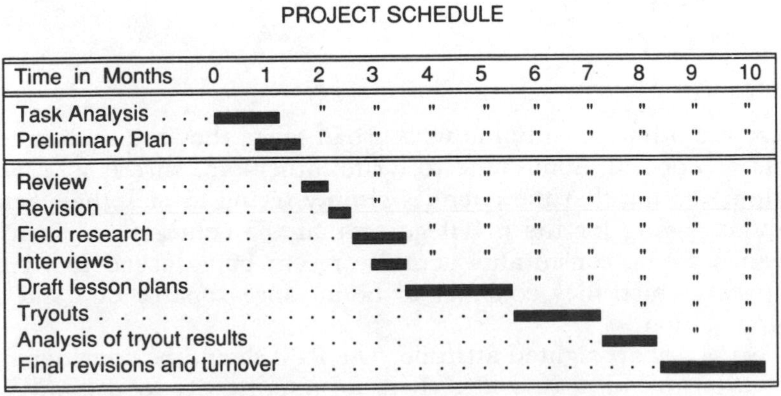

FIGURE 8.8. Example of milestone chart.

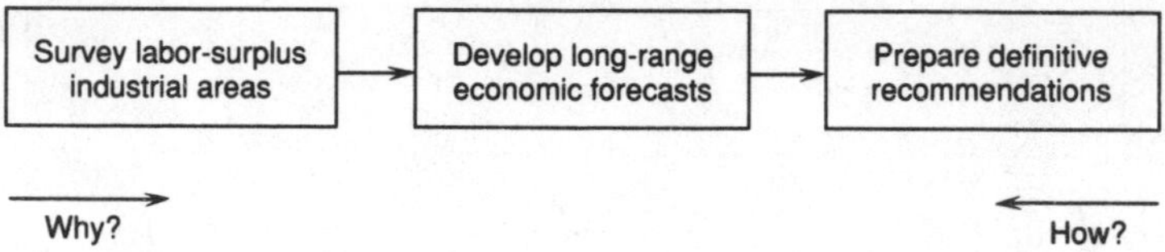

FIGURE 8.9. Logic of the flow chart.

each box, the next box to your right ought to furnish an answer. Going in the opposite direction, the box to the left should answer *how*. In the illustration, you survey labor-surplus industrial areas to develop long-range economic forecasts, and you do that to prepare definitive recommendations, the objective of the project.

This not only enables you to check the validity of your flow chart, it helps you develop the chart in the first place. Although it is sometimes possible to simply translate the client's statement of work in the RFP directly into a chart, most often the RFP is simply not that definitive. You may have little to go on other than the required result. If, as hypothesized in Figure 8–9, the RFP asks you to develop a set of economic recommendations regarding the unemployment problem in labor-surplus industrial areas but gives you hardly a clue as to how you are to proceed, you might ask yourself *how*. That is, you might inscribe "prepare definitive recommendations" in the right-hand box and work to the left. That is the beginning of the process in many cases, and it is where you outshine your competitors.

SUMMARY

There are a few consultants who groan when they are requested to write a proposal. Some hate to write; others are sure it is a waste of time, fearing that the client is simply trying to pick their brains without paying for the privilege or that the contract is "fixed" in advance. Some consultants actually resent being asked to write a proposal, which they consider to be an unreasonable demand and an imposition.

This is a short-sighted attitude. The RFP should be considered an invitation to bid, a privilege. It is an opportunity to present your ideas, rather than your personality. It is wise to grasp every opportunity possible to submit proposals, even when they are not requested. Always put your offer on paper. Give the prospect something to study and digest, something to remember you by even if you don't close this one. In the end it will pay off.

9

Negotiations, Fees, and Contracts

Consulting is a business as well as a profession, and you must never lose sight of that if you are to survive in the profession. And if being businesslike ever costs you a client or a contract, it is almost certain that the client or contract was not worth winning.

FEES, COSTS, AND PROFITS

Should you ever have occasion to fill out one of the federal government's forms for estimating costs you may be puzzled by the next-to-last line that says *fee or profit*. Obviously the government considers the two terms interchangeable. However, in consulting *fee* and *profit* are not synonymous. The fee is what you charge, usually by the hour or day, for your services, from which you *hope* to realize a profit. Fees represent your total income from consulting. Your salary and all other expenses must be paid for out of this total income before you can enjoy a profit. Therefore, although you charge and collect fees for your services, you do not always enjoy a profit.

Charging an hourly or daily fee is the conventional practice in consulting. But there are many exceptions because consulting work often is not labeled "consulting." So many programs are exploratory, awarded and undertaken with no clear idea of how much effort or time will be required, that in some cases the client feels the need to make special contractual arrangements.

In the case of the federal government agencies, who undertake many studies, surveys, R&D projects, and other such open-ended programs, the inclination is to devise cost–reimbursement contracts that permit the government to audit the contractor's books, if the contract is a large one. At the least, except for small contracts, the government requires an analysis of estimated costs that will reveal all elements of direct and indirect costs. Some consultants do not wish to do business with the government because of this auditing requirement.

This is not to say that the government never pays consultants on a fee basis. In fact, the government hires many consultants and is a major or even sole source of income for many consultants. Unfortunately, however, most agencies have an archaic and unrealistic view of what a competent consultant is worth today because they try to equate hourly or daily consulting rates with hourly or daily earnings of government employees, an unrealistic scale against which to measure. One of my own experiences of a number of years ago illustrates the logical absurdities in some bureaucratic thinking.

In 1978 the Region III office of what was at that time the Commerce Department's Office of Minority Business Enterprise (OMBE) hired me to conduct a half-day seminar for their contractors in Wilmington, Delaware. My letter proposal quoted $300 plus expenses. The agency agreed; I conducted the seminar and was paid.

Some three months later the headquarters office of OMBE asked me to present a similar half-day seminar to their staff in Washington. Again I wrote a letter proposal describing the seminar and quoting $300. (No expenses involved this time, since my offices were then in Washington.) This office balked, objecting that their maximum daily rate for consulting was $150. (However, in their generosity, they offered to pay me that full daily rate for my half-day presentation!)

I amended my proposal to accommodate their problem, making a rather minor change to the proposal.

Preparation for seminar presentation:	$150
Presentation of seminar:	150
Total cost:	$300

The agency had no problem at all with this. They accepted it immediately and I presented the seminar.

This suggests that how you present a proposition may be more important than what you propose, and that is true in some circumstances. It is important to understand the other person's problem. In the case of the OMBE office the problem was an internal policy, not the cost of my services. When I solved their problem I solved my own.

In fact, when selling to the government or to any large, bureaucratic organization, remember that the rules are not as inflexible as they may seem. Most often, the individuals are fearful of deviating from usual practice, making exceptions, or asking someone in higher authority to approve an exceptional procedure.

STANDARD RATES

There are no standard rates for consultants. The very nature of consulting mandates that each consultant has a unique worth, determined by a number of factors. But there are typical rates.

When I maintained a suite in downtwon Washington, D.C., a stranger, who had gotten my name from some publicity about my work, dropped into my office unannounced one afternoon and introduced himself. He represented a rather prominent company and was visiting Washington from Atlanta, where his company was headquartered. He was seeking a consultant to help his company in their pursuit of a government contract. He had barely finished his brief introduction and accepted my invitation to have a seat when he demanded to know what my daily rate was.

Of course this was an immediate tipoff. When a prospect wants to know the price before discussing his or her need or your credentials, you are almost surely wasting your time in further conversation. Experience shows that you can do business with such a client only by lowering your rates to less than breakeven, and that such clients almost always are impossible to deal with.

Well aware of this as a result of many earlier experiences, I was more than willing to end the interview immediately and get back to work. I quietly quoted him $500 per day plus expenses, if required. His response was prompt: "You fellows must have a union. Everybody charges $500 a day in this town."

It wouldn't have mattered if I had quoted $300 or $5,000. I did not expect or want to hear from this man again, nor did I. There is no profit and certainly no future in being the cheapest guy in town. The point, however, is that he did encounter a number of consultants, evidently, who all charged $500 a day. And, in fact, most able consultants at that time, according to a poll reported by Howard L. Shenson, a trainer of consultants, reported charging daily fees close to that figure. Today, the average daily rate is about $750 to $1,000 per day, although there are still many consultants charging fees on the more modest scale of approximately $500 per day. That is probably a bottom figure, however, for an able and well-established consultant.

Unless your circumstances are rather unusual or you are now only starting your practice and want to get yourself established by charging modest rates in the beginning, you will probably be well advised to make $500 per day your minimum. The following figures illustrate why this is a realistic bottom rate.

As a specialized expert in your field, you are probably entitled, in today's economy, to earn at least $50,000 a year, and that is probably a most modest figure for these times. That works out to about $4,167 a month, $962 a week, $192 a day, or $24 an hour. That's a first expense, a direct cost. But you are an employee of your business, even if you are the only employee. That means that the $192-a-day cost goes on every day, whether you are working on a project or not. When you are working on a project you can bill that $192 (plus other costs) to the client. Those are *direct costs* because they are incurred for a given, identifiable contract and should be defrayed by the income from that contract. But when you are marketing or planning, you must go on paying that $192 every day. That is *indirect cost* that must be absorbed somehow.

Other indirect costs include rent, heat, advertising, travel expense, entertainment, printing, secretarial services, telephone calls, taxes, insurance, and miscellaneous expenses of many kinds that are not included directly in billings to clients. These costs cannot be attributed to or identified as incurred by any specific contract or project. They must be recovered from clients indirectly as overhead, general and administrative costs, or fringe benefits costs.

This is usually done by levying a kind of tax on all clients and projects. If for every dollar you paid out to employees working on billable time you had to spend another dollar and one quarter for all those indirect costs, you have a burden rate of 125 percent. (To keep the explanation simple we'll speak of a single burden rate, although the burden is generally made up of two or more separate rates.) That means that you must charge the client $192 plus $240 burden rate or $432 to break even. Add a modest 15-percent profit, and you now have a daily billing rate of $496.50.

CALCULATING OVERHEAD

Unless you are your own accountant you need not calculate your overhead or other burden rates. However, it is essential that you understand what these are, what they mean, and where they come from.

In consulting and other labor-intensive enterprises, overhead is calculated as a percentage of direct labor. If at the end of a year you find that you have paid out $50,000 in direct labor and $25,000 in all indirect costs, your overhead rate has been 50 percent (25,000/50,000 × 100). That means that you must charge a client $1.50 for every $1.00 of direct labor to recover your costs. But that does not include profit, and every enterprise must turn a profit to establish some kind of reserve and to grow. The following example takes these factors into consideration.

Direct labor: 10 days @ $200/day	2,000.00
Overhead: 0.50 x 2,000	1,000.00
Other direct costs:	
Printing	275.00
Travel	546.50
Express charges	65.00
Total of other direct costs	886.50
Total costs	3,886.50
Profit: 15%	582.98
Total price	$4,469.48

Even that does not take into account an indirect expense pool for general and administrative expenses that are not normally included as overhead costs. (These are normally incurred in larger, multidivisional organizations, rather than in independent practices.) It does illustrate, however, why you must charge $500 a day approximately, as a minimum, to pay yourself a $50,000 salary.

WHAT SHOULD YOUR OVERHEAD RATE BE?

You can see from the previous example that although you might pay yourself only $2,000 in salary for a given project, the client must pay your consulting practice more than twice that amount. And that is at the modest overhead rate of 50 percent, which is almost surely a lower overhead rate than you will actually experience. Your real overhead rate is likely to be 75 percent if you are careful and manage your practice well, and can easily soar to 150 percent if you get a bit careless in exercising control and restraint. An overhead rate of 75 percent increases the total to $5,044.48, while an overhead rate of 150 percent would increase it to $6,769.48. You would thus have to persuade the client to pay you $677 a day to cover all your costs and provide a profit. It is obvious that overhead expenses must be controlled if you are to be competitive in price and yet profitable.

High overhead is a serious problem when dealing with government agencies too, especially when you are required to supply detailed cost analyses, such as that required in the federal Standard Form 60 (see Figure 9–1). Because government agencies buy so much from the private sector, government procurement officials are usually well aware of typical overhead rates in various industries and are quite sensitive to any they consider to be unduly high. They often consider a high overhead rate to indicate an inefficient contractor.

Provisional Overhead

The explanation of how to derive an overhead rate was based on the premise that you or your accountant had a full year's figures to study in determining what overhead rate you had actually experienced in your practice. This is often referred to as *historical* overhead.

If you may not yet have a full year's experience and records to review or you have a good reason to believe that your current and future overhead will be substantially different than your historical rate, you must resort to an estimated overhead rate, often referred to as a *provisional* overhead rate. "Provisional" means that while you may bill the client on the basis of that estimated overhead rate, after the contract is over you may have to make an adjustment on the basis of the true overhead rate as determined by a postcontract audit. For government contracts, a postcontract audit would rarely take place on contracts of less than $100,000, unless there is reason to believe that a substantial adjustment is necessary. It is also possible that a government client may request a preaward audit to examine the basis for your provisional overhead estimate, as well as some other details.

CONTRACT PRICING PROPOSAL *(RESEARCH AND DEVELOPMENT)*		Office of Management and Budget Approval No. 29-RO184	
This form is for use when *(i)* submission of cost or pricing data (see FPR 1-3.807-3) is required and *(ii)* substitution for the Optional Form 59 is authorized by the contracting officer.		PAGE NO.	NO. OF PAGES
NAME OF OFFEROR	SUPPLIES AND/OR SERVICES TO BE FURNISHED		
HOME OFFICE ADDRESS			
DIVISION(S) AND LOCATION(S) WHERE WORK IS TO BE PERFORMED	TOTAL AMOUNT OF PROPOSAL $	GOV'T SOLICITATION NO.	

DETAIL DESCRIPTION OF COST ELEMENTS

1. DIRECT MATERIAL *(Itemize on Exhibit A)*			EST COST ($)	TOTAL EST COST[1]	REFERENCE[2]
a. PURCHASED PARTS					
b. SUBCONTRACTED ITEMS					
c. OTHER—*(1)* RAW MATERIAL					
(2) YOUR STANDARD COMMERCIAL ITEMS					
(3) INTERDIVISIONAL TRANSFERS *(At other than cost)*					
TOTAL DIRECT MATERIAL					
2. MATERIAL OVERHEAD[3] *(Rate %X$ base=)*					
3. DIRECT LABOR *(Specify)*	ESTIMATED HOURS	RATE/ HOUR	EST COST ($)		
TOTAL DIRECT LABOR					
4. LABOR OVERHEAD *(Specify Department or Cost Center)*[3]	O.H. RATE	X BASE =	EST COST ($)		
TOTAL LABOR OVERHEAD					
5. SPECIAL TESTING *(Including field work at Government installations)*			EST COST ($)		
TOTAL SPECIAL TESTING					
6. SPECIAL EQUIPMENT *(If direct charge) (Itemize on Exhibit A)*					
7. TRAVEL *(If direct charge) (Give details on attached Schedule)*			EST COST ($)		
a. TRANSPORTATION					
b. PER DIEM OR SUBSISTENCE					
TOTAL TRAVEL					
8. CONSULTANTS *(Identify—purpose—rate)*			EST COST ($)		
TOTAL CONSULTANTS					
9. OTHER DIRECT COSTS *(Itemize on Exhibit A)*					
10. *TOTAL DIRECT COST AND OVERHEAD*					
11. GENERAL AND ADMINISTRATIVE EXPENSE *(Rate % of cost element Nos.)*[3]					
12. ROYALTIES[4]					
13. *TOTAL ESTIMATED COST*					
14. FEE OR PROFIT					
15. *TOTAL ESTIMATED COST AND FEE OR PROFIT*					

FIGURE 9.1a. Standard Form, 60 government cost form.

This proposal is submitted for use in connection with and in response to *(Describe RFP, etc.)*

and reflects our best estimates as of this date, in accordance with the Instructions to Offerors and the Footnotes which follow.

TYPED NAME AND TITLE | SIGNATURE

NAME OF FIRM | DATE OF SUBMISSION

EXHIBIT A—SUPPORTING SCHEDULE *(Specify. If more space is needed, use reverse)*

COST EL NO.	ITEM DESCRIPTION *(See footnote 5)*	EST COST *($)*

I. HAS ANY EXECUTIVE AGENCY OF THE UNITED STATES GOVERNMENT PERFORMED ANY REVIEW OF YOUR ACCOUNTS OR RECORDS IN CONNECTION WITH ANY OTHER GOVERNMENT PRIME CONTRACT OR SUBCONTRACT WITHIN THE PAST TWELVE MONTHS?

☐ YES ☐ NO *(If yes, identify below.)*

NAME AND ADDRESS OF REVIEWING OFFICE AND INDIVIDUAL | TELEPHONE NUMBER/EXTENSION

II. WILL YOU REQUIRE THE USE OF ANY GOVERNMENT PROPERTY IN THE PERFORMANCE OF THIS PROPOSED CONTRACT?

☐ YES ☐ NO *(If yes, identify on reverse or separate page)*

III. DO YOU REQUIRE GOVERNMENT CONTRACT FINANCING TO PERFORM THIS PROPOSED CONTRACT?

☐ YES ☐ NO *(If yes, identify.)*: ☐ ADVANCE PAYMENTS ☐ PROGRESS PAYMENTS OR ☐ GUARANTEED LOANS

IV. DO YOU NOW HOLD ANY CONTRACT *(Or, do you have any independently financed (IR&D) projects)* FOR THE SAME OR SIMILAR WORK CALLED FOR BY THIS PROPOSED CONTRACT?

☐ YES ☐ NO *(If yes, identify.)*:

V. DOES THIS COST SUMMARY CONFORM WITH THE COST PRINCIPLES SET FORTH IN AGENCY REGULATIONS?

☐ YES ☐ NO *(If no, explain on reverse or separate page)*

FIGURE 9.1b.

PARALLELS IN THE PRIVATE SECTOR

That huge market (over $600 billion annually) represented by the federal, state, and local government purchases of goods and services has had a profound effect on the economy generally and even on the purchasing practices of private business. For one thing, almost all substantial government contracts result in subcontracts. Subcontracts have become so important a source of income for small business that the federal government has established special offices to aid small business in winning subcontracts.

The procurement practices of the federal government also have shaped procurement methods of private corporations; the private sector is emulating the government procurement practices. This is not entirely a matter of choice. Since prime contractors will have to subcontract portions of the work and since by government requirement subcontracts must be awarded on the basis of competition, the private sector imitates the government systems as the simplest way to comply with such contractual requirements. Therefore, even if you never pursue government business, either directly as a prime contractor or indirectly as a subcontractor, you may eventually find yourself facing quite similar requirements in bidding or proposing. Regardless of the requirements, the ability to develop a good written proposal is important in working with private industry or government.

GOVERNMENT CONTRACT NEGOTIATION

The federal Standard Form 33 (see Figure 6–2) is itself a contract when signed by the two parties, although it usually includes other documents (e.g., work statements, item descriptions, bids, and/or proposals). In the case of small contracts, based on sealed bids, there are no negotiations because the award is made to the lowest bidder.

Of course, there are exceptions to simple acceptance and award. In some cases, even when the contract is a relatively small one, the contracting officer will call or write, inviting you to submit a "best and final offer." This is an effort to elicit a best price from you, and presumably (but not necessarily) it is asked of each proposer deemed equally qualified to be awarded the contract. The contract is subsequently awarded, presumably (but again not necessarily) to the lowest bidder among those invited to submit a best and final offer.

For small contracts this is usually the extent of the negotiation, if it is done at all. But in the case of larger contracts the request for best and final offers is almost automatic, and even that is not necessarily the extent of the negotiation. There may be further discussions regarding technical details of performance and programs as well as costs.

CONTRACT FORMS IN THE PRIVATE SECTOR

Many small contracts have been lost because of lengthy, complex, and excessively legalistic contract forms that alarm clients and often make them suspicious. In my own case it was a $26,000 contract with the American Red Cross that was scuttled by the introduction of excessive legalese. After submitting a proposal, discussing it with the client's training director (it was a training development program that was to be contracted for), and reaching technical agreement and agreement on cost, we were invited to meet and negotiate the contract. Our marketing director, for reasons that were a mystery to the rest of us, decided that he had to have our corporate attorney present. The client became alarmed immediately that we were so distrustful as to feel a need for legal representation to conclude what were to be little more than formalities to agree on a relatively small contract, and terminated our relationship at once. Nevertheless, failing to learn from this experience, our marketing director proceeded to draw up a statement of standard contract terms that would be boilerplate copy for all contracts. These were so legalistic as to scuttle many other contract negotiations and present us with a problem in negotiating all future contracts.

Hubert Bermont, a successful independent consultant of many years experience and publisher of The Consultant's Library series of books for consultants, believes that asking any client to sign a formal contract for a small consulting assignment is risky because it usually alarms the client. Today most of us sign nothing without reading it carefully. We are also somewhat suspicious and mistrustful of the mysterious and often arcane phraseology of lawyers and legal forms. Even when we do read a contract with great care we are usually unsure of what it actually says! So it is not surprising that clients become alarmed by lengthy, Latin-laden contracts for small and simple programs.

This does not mean that there should not be a distinct understanding between you and your client, or that the understanding should not be recorded in some manner. It does mean that they should not be recorded as those thick documents with blue binders and numerous signatures. They should be simple letter agreements, at most, or, as most of my own assignments are, verbal contracts, reached after informal and friendly discussion, which has often followed an exchange of letters inquiring into my services and availability and my response, listing my offer and simple terms, and a handshake. (Such correspondence becomes an important part of the documentation and should be filed as such.)

Perhaps that is because I do my utmost to keep the set of terms as straightforward and as simple as possible. I make it clear that I charge a substantial daily rate, but I do not charge overtime or premium time rates. I recommend what I believe to be the best courses of action, but I do whatever my client decides to have me do. I cannot guarantee any particular outcome, of course; I can guarantee only my best efforts. Therefore, the only things to reach specific agreement on are costs—my fees and expenses—and length of commitment or estimate of time required to achieve the desired result. In some cases I may furnish a not-to-exceed estimate or guarantee completion within some specific time frame. In such a case, that information must be in the agreement too.

Obviously, your own terms and stipulations are likely to be different than mine are, and they should be whatever you believe to be fair and proper for you and your own clients. However, whatever they are, draw them up as standard terms, simply and clearly stated, and include them in any agreement you sign with a client or in a response to a request for quotation. At most you will normally require only a simple letter of agreement—probably a single page—and in many cases you will not require even that.

What Is a Contract?

A contract is nothing more than an agreement. It need not be written; verbal contracts are binding, although it is obviously more difficult to establish the specific terms of a verbal contract when disagreements arise. The sole purpose of a written contract is to minimize any possible difficulties in defining what the specific terms of agreement were should there be a disagreement between the contracting parties.

The reason for committing the contract to writing is not to compel the other party to live up to the agreement. Quite the contrary, if you think you will have to compel the other party to honor the agreement, it would be foolish to enter into it at all; no written language ever makes a contract foolproof or ensures that the other party will live up to the contract. The only good contract is one in which the two parties are sincere in their agreement, and the written instrument is simply to ensure that neither need rely later on faulty memory.

The written contract therefore need document only those items that are or can be stipulated and need not be trusted to memory, such as fees, other costs, schedules, and definitions of product or service. For small consulting assignments little documentation is required. Most of them are based on daily or hourly rates for ongoing services and so are usually easy to terminate or extend on short notice and without complications.

FEES AND COLLECTIONS

Except in the case of established or former clients and large, well known organizations, it is wise to require a substantial retainer. This guarantees some substantial part of my fee and serves as earnest money. I generally ask for approximately one-third the total estimated fee prior to beginning work, one third at the estimated midpoint, and the remaining on completion. Although my insistence on this arrangement has resulted in my not accepting certain assignments, it has also resulted in a complete cessation of legal actions on my part to collect fees owed me. I enthusiastically recommend such a practice for any consultant who undertakes assignments for clients of uncertain or undetermined sincerity and ability to pay for services rendered. Perhaps you will lose an occasional assignment, but usually that would be an assignment you would later have regretted accepting. Most clients worth having do not object to any businesslike request properly presented

COLLECTING FROM GOVERNMENT CLIENTS

A common complaint about doing business with government agencies is that the government takes too long to pay its bills. That complaint has finally resulted in legislation designed to compel federal agencies to pay more promptly. I am skeptical that this so-called "Prompt Payment Act" will solve the problem, for the delays in payment are almost always the result of typical bureaucracy—any bureaucracy.

The best way to receive prompt payment is to take direct action when payment has not been made within a reasonable period—that is, 20 to 30 days. Make a follow-up phone call and insist on learning where your invoice is and why it has not been processed for payment. A little outrage, sometimes a duplicate invoice sent directly to some individual, or other action usually produces payment.

Most payment problems can be avoided if you ask what the payment procedure is before you begin work—who is in the chain of approval, what are the several steps before the check is cut, what information must be included in the invoice, how many copies of your invoice are required, how long should the process take normally? Go back to the individuals in that chain if you do not get your check within that "normal" processing time and start asking blunt questions. This procedure usually produces results. It has for me, almost without exception. And in those two exceptional cases I still managed to get paid within several weeks. Once, in fact, I was required to submit two additional copies of my invoice, and the government insisted on then paying me three times! In the other case I had to finally write a letter of complaint to the agency head, whereupon I was finally paid. One of the advantages of dealing with government agencies is the objectivity typical of the government as a client. You can be very blunt, indeed, when pursuing something such as overdue payment and not offend anyone. (Unfortunately, this is not always the case with private sector clients.) The government client recognizes your right to be paid with reasonable promptness and is likely to be quite apologetic about the delay.

As a small business, you enjoy statutory protection when dealing with the government. By law you are, as a small business, entitled to receive progress payments, whereas a large company might be expected to wait until the project is completed before submitting a bill. Submit your invoices each month; in most cases contracting officers will accept and process invoices from small businesses as frequently as every other week.

ANNUAL RETAINERS

Some clients who use consulting services frequently but irregularly ensure that their chosen consultants will be available to them when needed by placing their consultants on a retainer—that is, paying in advance for guaranteed availability and services if and as needed. This is usually an annual agreement in which the client pays the consultant some fixed monthly sum. If services are not used in any given month, the payments accrue as a credit until the client does call for services, whereupon the client may use the equivalent in services, at regular rates, with normal billing for any services beyond the amount standing to the client's credit. If there is any credit left at the end of the year, it is wiped out and the agreement renewed with a fresh start. That is, if the client has paid the consultant $200 a month and used $3,500 worth of services, the client pays the additional $1,100. On the other hand, if the client has used only $1,000 during the year, the consultant keeps the $1,400 difference.

Obviously, it is in your interest, should you enter into such an arrangement, to key the monthly figure to whatever amount of time you expect the client to require of you each year. But you must also carefully consider what it is worth to you to guarantee your availability to a given client no matter when he or she calls on you.

NEGOTIATING TIPS, TACTICS, AND GAMBITS

In any negotiation, each party tries to read the other's intent, willingness to yield on certain matters, and "bottom lines." You want to determine the maximum price and/or other benefits you can win, while the client wants to know what is the best deal that can be struck with you.

As the seller you probably believe that the other party, as the buyer, has a great advantage in the bargaining session. You are forced to compete with others, and it's all or nothing for you—you win or you lose. But the client can't lose because he or she has the capability of buying from someone else if your terms are not acceptable. And, presumably, the client already knows everybody's asking price, while you are playing a guessing game.

But you may be entirely wrong in that pessimistic assessment. The thing you need most here is information. It's easy to be a brilliant negotiator if you know that you are the low bidder or that the client is not seriously considering anyone else for the project. So you are asking questions and making conversational gambits in the hope that the client will let some precious gems of information slip out to help you judge how close you are to the goal and how you compare in costs and quality with your competitors. You want to know how hard you can press and how stubbornly you can hold out for what you want without losing the contract.

Successful negotiation cannot be a guessing game. It must be based on reliable information, and the most reliable source of information on how the client feels and thinks about all the relevant matters is the client. I am constantly surprised at how many people resort to all sorts of devious means for getting information rather than trying the obvious method of asking direct questions. For instance, in trying to determine how the client really feels about the price or what importance he or she attaches to reducing the price, such questions as the following have often produced the information I needed:

> "I know that the project plan I have proposed is fairly elaborate and sophisticated, possibly beyond what you believe you need. Are there provisions in my plan that you feel you do not need so that we can cut them back and reduce costs or beef up other areas?"

Even an evasive response to this question can be quite helpful, and sometimes the frankness with which the client answers tells you everything you need to know—that is, how highly the client rates you and your plan, whether you need to find a way to reduce costs, or other valuable input. Moreover, the client who truly favors you as the prospective consultant will actually try to hand you the information you need to win the contract.

If you have used the strategy of pricing a basic model and offering several options, the situation is tailor-made for inviting the client quite openly to discuss the various options or to ask you questions about them. An alternative approach is to invite the client to review the major features of your proposed plan with you and ask questions as you go.

I have known cases in which the client has said something such as, "I think your plan is fine and your personal reputation is excellent, but frankly I find your costs far too high." The proper response to this is not an argument, but a question: "May I ask you on what basis you find my price high?" The answer you get here is not as important as the discussion it generates for it gives you reliable information for the person most qualified to offer it—the client. You may find, as I have so often, that in the end the client does not want to give up anything offered in your plan and convinces himself or herself that your plan is the right one and your price is right for that plan. It is truly amazing how often asking the right questions forces the client to do your final selling and closing for you.

On the other hand, if you do find it necessary to reduce your price, it is unwise in my opinion to do so arbitrarily, since that suggests that you either priced the program higher than necessary in the first place or that you are desperate for the contract. It is more credible to negotiate any price cuts by asking the client to give up something, no matter how small the sacrifice might be. Perhaps the client will chuckle inwardly at his or her shrewd bargaining powers in getting a significant price reduction in exchange for a minor sacrifice. That's fine; the client ought to be satisfied with the bargain he or she managed to achieve. What you employed here is a legitimate bargaining tactic; it not only solves a problem, but it encourages the client to believe he or she is making strides toward a favorable contract with you.

Once when negotiating a contract for services to a small company, the client offered me, as payment, a subcontract of the contract I would help the client win. I politely but firmly made it clear that I do not work on speculation or contingency. The client was evidently prepared for that response because he almost immediately proposed that I accept part of my fee in cash and part as a subcontract. I took time to appear to consider it, and then agreed reluctantly and proceeded to negotiate the cash payment and the size and nature of the subcontract. But I insisted on a cash payment that would satisfy my normal fee requirements. Of course, the client was pleased with his competent negotiating strategy, and we concluded the agreement. I never got the subcontract, and I did not expect it. But we were both satisfied, so it was a fair bargain.

You should recognize that a successful negotiation is one in which each party is satisfied, one in which both parties believe they got what they wanted. No contract and no negotiation is of any value if either party emerges feeling victimized.

The enemies of successful negotiation are greed, the intention to outwit and take advantage of the other party, and believing yourself to be far more clever than the other party. The way to win at the negotiating table is to try earnestly to make a fair bargain for both parties and to respect the other's intelligence. But this does not mean that you should not employ sound bargaining and negotiating tactics or that you should reveal your own hand. You may plant throwaway items in your technical proposal and/or proposed budget, items that you are prepared to bargain away. That's a common negotiating tactic, and you may expect the client to make some early demands that he or she is prepared to yield on eventually, as you approach agreement. Remember, however, that you probably are bargaining against what your competitors have proposed, rather than against the client's notion of what the program should contain or cost. Using throwaway items is such a common practice, however, that it is effective only if you follow certain principles and practices in using them:

Do not employ obviously useless or meaningless costs as your gambits. That is underestimating your client, even showing contempt for his or her judgment.

Design your program full scale, the way you would prefer to see it done. Then study it to determine what could be cut out, if required, while still achieving the main objective.

Determine the costs of those items to see how much you can reduce costs overall by eliminating them.

When you feel that you must cut costs to win the job, use this information and negotiating strategy. Don't wait for the client to insist on cuts. Explain how costs can be cut with some predetermined sacrifices, admitting frankly that you analyzed and designed the program especially so that you could, finally, tailor it to the client's wishes, if cost-cutting became necessary. This frank admission and the explanation of your farsightedness alone will help you greatly at the negotiating table. Be sure that the client understands that you pledge three conditions:

1. A specific cost reduction.
2. Achievement of the main objective.
3. A sacrifice of some sort.

10

Consulting Processes and Procedures

In this chapter you will find three essential rules for success in building and conducting your independent practice. These are probably the most important ideas in this book.

THE ART OF LISTENING

Listening appears to be a lost art if we are to judge by the many training programs offered to teach us how to listen. We appear to hear less and less of what others are saying, perhaps because we are so besieged by sound.

These aural assaults have forced us into learning how to shut them out and reject the distraction. We have learned how to "strain" the unwanted out, to quote Isaac Asimov on the subject. Unfortunately, the "unwanted" is often not the unimportant or unnecessary; quite the opposite is often the case. So ingrained and automatic is this reflex in many of us today that we truly fail to hear what others are saying, even when it is very much in our interest to hear clearly.

The pressure to accomplish many things simultaneously and the pressure of competitors for our attention also interfere with our ability to listen. We often try to speed things up, trying to skim what others are saying, as we might skim a report or magazine article. And so we often miss important details, in our efforts to "speed listen," as others speed read, and so leap to conclusions, usually wrong.

And finally, especially when we are trying to close a sale or win an argument, we spend our listening time thinking about what we want to say next, and so we miss almost entirely what the other person is saying.

THE ART OF HEARING

Many of us believe that we are listening, and perhaps we are usually, but too often we are not *hearing* what is said. We must retrain ourselves to hear as well as to listen.

Hearing Is Not a Passive Function

To truly hear what others are saying, especially in most consulting situations, you must assume an active role, prompting, asking questions, signifying understanding, indicating a need to repeat or elaborate on some word or phrase, and otherwise responding. Of course, your initial part in the exchange is quiet listening and hearing, but you can hardly expect the client to be able to judge what you need to know; you must guide the client with occasional questions and prompting.

HEARING AS A SALESPERSON

As a consultant, you must be a salesperson. The irony in this is that it is agreed among sales professionals that the most successful salesperson is one who is in effect a consultant to his or her prospect—who counsels and guides the prospect by showing how the product or service offered will solve the prospect's problem and provide valuable benefits. Therefore selling ought to "come naturally" to professional consultants; you need only apply the consulting technique to the sales situation!

So hearing as a salesperson *is* hearing as a consultant, but as a consultant interested primarily at the moment in making a sale. To be successful as a "hearing" consultant, you must understand the following rules.

One of the most self-defeating actions of some salespeople is that of talking too long, talking when they ought to be writing—the order, that is. They fail to sense the prospect's readiness to buy and go on talking until they *unsell* the prospect.

Other salespeople talk when they should be listening. Not only does this offend and even alienate prospects, it often blocks out information from the prospect, information you need to close the sale. Always yield to a prospect who wants to say something. Ask the right questions, respond as necessary, but be brief and encourage the prospect to talk, for the prospect will tell you how to win the contract if you listen carefully.

Encourage the prospect to discuss the following:

The essential problem or need in as much detail as possible.

The prospect's own notions, if any, about how to approach the problem or need to affect a solution.

Whether the client truly needs special problem-solving skills—that is, painstaking analysis of symptoms to synthesize a solution—or simply needs professional services for specialized, yet routine, work.

Any specific constraints or related requirements, such as limitations of cost, time, or other factors.

The intention and commitment to retaining a consultant.

Whether funds are available.

Whether the individual to whom you are speaking has the authority to retain you or, if not, whose approval is needed, and what the process is. Learn what you can about approval and award requirements.

It is on the basis of answers to these and related questions that you can determine whether you have a serious opportunity to win a contract or are wasting your time in idle conversation. Some of these items–those designed to determine whether there is a serious prospect of winning a contract—are known also by sales professionals as "qualifying" the prospect. Let's explore some of these qualifying items in greater depth.

The Essential Problem or Need

There are consultants who offer solutions for which there are no known problems. They work energetically and enthusiastically trying to force-fit every prospective client's problems to one of their off-the-shelf solutions. But there are prospective clients who are no less biased and shortsighted in identifying and describing their own needs. Some attempt their own diagnoses, despite having called you in as a consultant expert, and all but demand that you confirm it. They appear to be embarrassed by being forced to call on a specialist for help. Often they will assure you that the only reason they called you in is because they simply don't have the time to solve the simple problem themselves, although they could easily enough.

It is best to go along with this prospect's ploy (to embarrass him or her is to almost surely lose the sale) while trying to determine the real need. For example, a government General Services Administration client who was responsible for preparing public information to document changes in the forms and procedures to procure A&E (architect and engineer) services had written the necessary brochure and manual. All he wanted me to do was edit them. I agreed to do the job, but asked to see the manuscripts before I rendered an estimate. As I feared, they needed extensive rewriting and reorganization, not editing. However, rather than risk embarrassing—and thus offending—this executive, I observed that the manuscripts really needed a rather heavy edit to be made into truly first-class products, and I assumed that he wanted nothing less than first-class products as reflections of his work. Of course, there was no way he could object to that argument! I priced the job for rewriting, although the purchase order called for "editing," and we were both satisfied.

Another problem you may run into in identifying or defining the need is the tendency of some clients to surround the simple statement of the basic need with gratuitous remarks and speculations. This can be due to the client's true misunderstanding of the problem, but often it is a case of the client trying to enhance his or her own importance. The result is that it is difficult to distinguish the real problem from other secondary and trivial problems and tactfully respond in a way that satisfies the client and wins the contract.

The Prospect's Own Notions

Even when the client openly admits the need to bring in a specialist as a consultant he or she may have very definite ideas about what needs doing and how it ought to be done. Some clients describe the requirements in such detail, even furnishing outlines and block diagrams, as to furnish a virtual blueprint. This is a direct contradiction of the logical concept under which competitive proposals are requested—that is, it should be a quest for the best ideas, and proposers ought to be encouraged to offer their best ideas. Such preestablished notions deny the client access to those best ideas and handicap proposers in two ways: (1) it misleads you by directing your attention to the client's biased notions and diagnoses instead of to providing objective information and encouraging creative thinking; and (2) it forces you to agree with what may very well be a totally wrong concept and approach.

You must approach this with great caution. A confrontation with the client certainly will not help. But you can't agree to utilize a plan that will probably not produce the desired results or, at best, would be far less than the most effective or most efficient way to do the job.

First, determine whether you have all the information you need to make a qualified judgment about the requirement. You must review critically the information supplied and make at least a preliminary judgment about that to judge the need for asking questions and probing for more details.

Next, determine whether the client is truly biased or is merely trying to be helpful. Is the client open-minded and willing to consider other approaches?

After you have made these determinations, the best approach is to suggest a *possible* difference of opinion in a nonthreatening way, while carefully structuring the situation so as to avoid any necessity for immediate decision or immediate resolution. Give the client time to adjust to the idea of possible change without the stress of direct confrontation.

Avoid the appearance of attacking the client's plan. One way is to drop the merest hint that you have not yet "bought" the client's plan but are still open-minded by some ploy as this:

"Well, that seems to me to be an excellent way to go at this, but since we are in an early talking stage and I haven't yet had time to become familiar with the details, why don't we discuss the specific approach later?"

Even if the client wishes to pursue the matter at once, you can employ this philosophy by objective discussion, rational and unemotional arguments, and reactions conditioned to those of the client. That is, if the client appears to feel a need to defend his or her original position, your objective is still to avoid confrontation and give the client ample time to think about and adjust to your ideas. Surprisingly often, the most determined opposition to your arguments or, for that matter, to any change, melts away when the other party is given time to adjust to new ideas and allowed to save face in the process. It is almost always a grave mistake to press for immediate decision when you and the client differ on important matters.

On the other hand, if this is a formal, written proposal situation, you will usually be compelled to respond directly to a written request and statement of work. However, you can always submit questions asking about the acceptability of exceptions and alternatives to the work statement or specifications. When properly posed, this question often leads to a written modification of the original statement of work or even to a preproposal conference during which the entire proposed program can be discussed freely.

Expressed Need versus True Need

As much as we would like to believe that the main function of a consultant is to use his or her knowledge, skills, and wisdom to troubleshoot, analyze, and solve difficult problems, the fact is that by far the majority of consulting assignments require the solving of routine problems. For the most part the services required are the appropriate skills and knowledge to conduct a survey, design a system, perform a study, write a report, plan a project, evaluate data, determine a need, make a presentation, develop a program, and/or otherwise supply services to carry out tasks that are usually routine for the consultant, even when they are by nature creative services of some kind.

The client's perceptions of the qualifications necessary to accomplish the task vary considerably. In some cases, clients grossly overestimate the difficulty of the task and the qualifications—that is, the knowledge skills, experience, and/or other resources—needed to get the job done, while in others they fail completely to understand the true difficulties or the qualifications necessary for the assignment. Partly because of this but also because they sometimes are unable to draw the proper conclusions from the symptoms and other indications, clients often fail to describe the true problem. For example, when the U.S. Postal Service found it necessary to update the rate data manual used by those who were responsible for using common carrier services in transporting the mail, they discovered that the resident expert who had always done this work had retired and was not willing to come out of retirement even as a consultant to update the manual. They therefore went in quest of an outside consultant to handle this task.

It turned out to be far less a problem than both the client and the consultant had originally anticipated. Both expected a relatively extensive overhaul and rewriting of the original manual to be necessary, but research demonstrated rather quickly that rates had changed little since publication of the prior edition, and only a few pages would require updating. Learning this, the consultant was able to assess the need accurately and submit an appropriate bid for the task.

Generally, it requires some analysis to determine whether the stated problem is likely to be the true problem; and in most cases it is essential that you make that determination before committing yourself. However, there is one exception to this. When contracting with government agencies, if your proposal and contract make it abundantly clear that the detailed specifications to which you agree and commit yourself are those listed by the client in the proposal request and its statement of work, you are protected contractually. If it becomes necessary to make changes later because the original specifications or description of the requirement prove faulty, you can then make and support a claim for a change in scope or specifications and contract amendment to the price. It is exceedingly important for this reason alone that you make this clear in any written proposal or other documentation affecting your contractual obligations.

Specific Restraints and/or Related Requirements

You must determine whether there are any special constraints or requirements that have been established in advance. Be alert for cost ceilings and other such constraints, including:

Review requirements. Must the contract and work be reviewed and approved by higher authority, a list of individuals, or—even worse—a committee? Review committees, especially when they are large ones, can be endless trouble unless they are under the firm control of a decisive leader. But a lengthy list of individual reviewers can be equally troublesome. **Recommendation: Find out about this in advance, ask whether approval must be unanimous, ask what the procedure is when there is serious disagreement or deadlock, and what is your protection against arbitrariness.**

Progress reports. These can slow you down considerably, especially when the requirement calls for formal review and approval of these reports, which often leads to special meetings, with the attendant demands on your time. **Recommendation: Try to get as much information about this as possible in advance. If formal progress reports are required, factor estimated time for these into your schedule and price.**

Government cost analyses, cost revelations, and preaward and postaward audit requirements. Many people object to making such disclosures and therefore don't do much business with government agencies or major government contractors who impose such requirements. (These are not usually imposed on small contracts—those under $25,000—but you must check and make sure.) **Recommendation: If you feel this way, now is the time to find out if there are such requirements.**

Turnkey requirements. These require you to install the system you design, get it running smoothly, and then train the client's staff to run it before "turning over the key." Sometimes clients forget to mention that this is expected. **Recommendation: Be absolutely sure that you know exactly what you are to deliver and protect yourself by documenting it accurately.**

The Prospect's Intent

Qualify your prospects. Is the prospect committed to retaining a consultant, only considering hiring one, or merely searching for free information with no intention of retaining a consultant? Does the prospect have the funding or the authority to negotiate and make a deal for your services? Save your time by investigating this as early in the game as possible by asking whether funds are currently available, whether the program has been budgeted yet, and who must sign off on the program. Ask questions that do not appear to challenge the authority or the integrity of the prospect but yet elicit the information you need. If the prospect is evasive or declines to respond at all, you may easily judge the proper answer from that!

This does not mean you should abandon a prospect who does not have the authority to contract or even to negotiate with you. Such a prospect may easily be a rich source of information on the organization, its needs, its hierarchy, and other intelligence valuable for marketing purposes. Such a prospect may also introduce you to someone who does have the authority to buy and can be persuaded to do business with you. And, in some cases, even the prospect who does not have buying authority can sell your ideas if you provide the proper help, such as a powerful unsolicited proposal or a presentation to the organization's upper management, which the prospect sets up for you.

LISTENING AS A HIRED CONSULTANT

Now that you have listened carefully and heard all you needed to hear to close the sale and win the contract it is time to begin listening as a consultant. Now you are not listening for the information you need to win the contract, but for the information you need to carry it out as efficiently as possible. Just as you must discriminate, in the marketing phase, between the problem/need defined and the true problem/need (when the two are not identical, that is), you must now discriminate between the correct solution to the problem and the client's desired solution when again these are not the same.

One problem you encounter all too often in both listening and hearing situations is that clients cannot discriminate between problems and their symptoms. Those who are not trained problem solvers tend often to confuse the two. One of my own clients told me that his problem was that he was not winning enough government contracts. I agreed that this was a serious problem for someone whose business was government contracting; but, I felt compelled to tell him, the lack of success in winning contracts was the "problem" only from his managerial perspective. From my perspective, that was a symptom of some problem. But what problem?

Poor proposal writing?
Poor estimating?
Addressing the wrong market segments?
Failing to keep in touch with requirements?

Overreaching for markets in which he did not qualify?
Poor track record or past performance?
Poor past contract administration?
Overpricing?

Even this analysis is only a first step, for the initial "problem" identification itself yields to a similar analysis in which the "problem" must be regarded as a symptom to be analyzed. For example, suppose the first analysis results in a judgment that the "problem" is "poor proposal writing." What are the true possible causes or problems?

Poor program design?
Weak or poorly written staff résumés?
Weak or poorly written organization credentials?
Unpersuasive, unconvincing writing?
Unimpressive/unimaginative presentations?
Poor or insufficient graphics?
Poor or insufficient strategies?

Each of these may be analyzed in similar fashion. Is poor program design, for example, due to:

Unorganized proposal efforts?
Inexperienced staff used to write?
Poor technical (design) capabilities of staff?
Cursory and imperfect analysis of client wants?
Hasty and casual design efforts?

Each of the series consists of identifying the symptoms, some of which are obvious and others of which must be identified by troubleshooting methods, testing each as a hypothesis to decide whether it is a valid symptom or an irrelevant factor, and deciding for each symptom remaining as a relevant factor whether it is a cause or an effect. Each of the series becomes more sharply focused on possible solutions. In fact, the series of analyses should continue until final solutions are suggested. The final step is to select that solution which is best suited to your own situation. Most problems have more than one solution; you must decide which is most appropriate for your own case.

In our example the next stage of analysis will be the critical one. All the possibilities listed begin to point to these choices:

Create a proposal department or at least hire a proposal manager.

Retain consultants to lead proposal efforts.

Send someone (the marketing manager?) to proposal-writing training seminars.

Of course, the client will have to decide which of the alternative solutions is appropriate, but you might be asked to make recommendations. In such case you must conduct still another analysis to determine which is most efficient, most effective, most practical, and/or most acceptable to the client. And in this case there is a special problem. How could a consultant recommend the hiring of consultants as a solution? It would be necessary here to develop a complete set of pro and con facts for each alternative and ask the client to make the decision.

A BASIC APPROACH TO ALL ANALYSIS: FUNCTION

Qualitative analysis is the separation of something into its constituent parts to determine what it is made of, how it is made, and how it all functions together. Quantitative analysis determines the amounts of the various components and other data of size and proportion. Although it is possible that we might have occasion to perform quantitative analysis, we are concerned primarily with qualitative analysis. To put this another way and in a more relevant perspective, we use qualitative analysis to uncover *causes*, so that we truly understand the problem, and lead us to *synthesis*, which we pursue as a means to create a remedy or solution.

The key to analysis is function. This functional analysis separates all the component functions of the item, whatever it is, and then sorts them into their various classes, describing the contribution of each to the main function, which must also be identified as a first order of business in the analysis. This is the basis for *value management* (also known as value analysis and value engineering) and describes generally that which has come to be known also as *systems analysis*. The basic methods of functional analysis can be a most valuable asset to you in both your role as a marketer and as a practicing consultant. That's because it is an orderly and systematic way of analyzing things, whether you are analyzing a client's requirements in the preparation of a proposal and development of a capture strategy for it or whether you are analyzing systems, problems, needs, and even jobs as a consultant. (Analyzing positions or position titles in an organization, using the value methods, it quite enlightening and can be particularly valuable to you as a consultant. Try it and see if you still think a secretary ought to file, type and make coffee.)

This is not intended to be and does not purport to be a definitive course in value anaysis. But it does borrow from that basic discipline and adapts what it borrows to your needs and interests as an independent consultant.

What It Does versus What It Is

To accurately determine the worth and essential nature of anything, you must consider not only what it is—and consider even that primarily for purposes of identification only—but what it *does*—its function. That is the essential item in value analysis, the item from which all else stems and all benefits become possible.

For example, what is a wrist watch? What does it do? The answer you get too often to this question is that it "tells time." But a watch does not "tell" time at all; people do that. A watch *indicates* time. You can see already that the name does not even suggest what a watch does. The conventional watch has a pair of "hands" that indicate the time. Many modern watches now use digital readouts as indicators and are called "digital" watches. So both types of watches indicate the time, but the digital watch has many advantages over the old style. For one thing, even the cheapest digital watches tend to be more accurate and far less prone to a need for service because they are entirely electronic and thus have no moving parts.

So, if they are superior in some ways, why do people spend much more for dial watches in preference to digital watches? They do so because a wrist watch is more than a device to indicate the time of day. That is its *main function,* but it also has a second function. For some people a watch is also a piece of jewelry. These people often choose the dial watch.

The value analyst would consider the primary function of a watch to be the practical one, defined as "indicates time," while its secondary function (if it is a watch that is also regarded as jewelry) is defined perhaps as "gives pleasure."

A value analyst would approach the initial analysis in an organized fashion to get answers to several questions:

1. What is it?
2. What does it do?
3. What else would do that?
4. What else does it do?
5. What else would do that?
6. What does it cost?

To ensure objectivity, clarity, and commitment, answers must be rigidly disciplined to appear only as verb and noun; modifiers of all kinds are banned (e.g., "indicates time," "gives pleasure," etc.). "What else does it do?" forces you to look at secondary functions that may be

Supportive of and necessary to accomplish the primary or main function.
Supportive of but not necessary to the main function.
Additional to and a valuable or desirable function.
Additional to but not a particularly useful or valuable function.

I carry a tiny clasp knife on my key ring to open packages and serve other such chores. It has also a screwdriver, nail file, and bottle opener attachment. I have no use for those extra gadgets; they add undesired weight, bulk, and cost to the item, and I would have preferred a small knife without these items, but I had no choice; it was the only such knife I could find. Inevitably the worth of secondary functions that are not essential to the primary function becomes a matter of subjective judgment, varying with individual interests.

Determining what something does is sometimes rather difficult. For example, what does my pocket knife do? I am tempted to respond "opens packages," but that is wrong. I open the packages, the knife does not. Moreover, someone else may use it for far different tasks than opening packages. We need to offer a simple but universally true definition, probably one that uses "cuts" as the verb—"cuts software," perhaps, since certainly it would not cut anything very hard. Of course, some people may use the knife for other things than cutting, but the definition ought to address the intended purpose of the item.

Identify function(s) *objectively*. It is by this means that you can determine not only how well anything performs its function(s), but also how well the functions contribute to the overall need.

For example, the main function of a paper clip is to temporarily bind papers. A secondary function was added to some paper clips in the form of serrations to add gripping power, but the idea has not really caught on because it adds nothing very significant to the function; by far the majority of paper clips are plain, as they have been since the beginning.

Any fool can find a complicated solution to any problem; genius lies in finding the simple solutions. It appears to be almost a natural law that unnecessarily complicated systems die early deaths, replaced by simpler systems that achieve the same results. Too often we are tempted to burden our products and systems with unnecessary additions that do not contribute to the main mission and even detract from its accomplishment. Early radios, for example, had several dials that had to be manipulated to tune each receiving circuit to the frequency of the desired station. Edwin H. Armstrong ended that complication and difficulty with his invention, the superheterodyne, which simplified tuning by converting all desired signals to a single frequency for which all but the basic tuning circuit were tuned in advance. Nor has anyone improved on the superheterodyne since; it is still the basic design of all radio and TV receiving equipment. That is another hallmark of the right design or solution—it is usually extremely difficult to improve upon.

Functional analysis is an organized, procedural discipline that follows two specific rules: (1) use only nouns and verbs, and (2) reach agreement on the need.

Rule Number 1: Verb-Noun Rule

Use a single verb and noun to define a function; no modifiers are permitted, although sometimes a compound noun is necessary. This forces clear and unequivocal thinking. You must decide, without the hedging of adverbs and adjectives, what the function, intended functions, and/or needs or purposes are.

You must learn to ask "what" and "why" and settle only for clear and unequivocal answers. If you fail to define the problem clearly you are not likely to reach a solution, and you can't define the problem without having a good understanding of the need.

For example, in one consulting organization the manager was plagued by the frequent return of his invoices by his customers, who asked that the invoices be corrected. Analyzing the accounting system, in search of the problem—not the solution, for the problem was not yet identified—the manager found a system in which raw figures were collected on a worksheet, from which they were transferred to the invoice. The manager asked the accountant what the function of the worksheet was. He was told that labor charges from employee time cards and other charges from suppliers' invoices were collected and posted on the worksheet before being transferred to the invoice.

"Why?" asked the manager.

"That's a standard system for this kind of operation," replied the accountant.

"What do you do with the figures on the worksheet?" asked the manager.

"Transfer them to the invoice," replied the accountant.

"But why do you need the worksheet?" asked the manager. "Why can't you post the numbers directly on the invoice, since this is a cost-plus contract that requires us to show all the costs and burdens in detail?" (He had already discovered that the mistakes were being made in the final transfer of figures from the worksheet to the invoices.)

The accountant shrugged, while he also looked somewhat incredulous at the question. "It's a standard system," he protested. "Everybody does it this way."

The manager eliminated the problem by eliminating the worksheet, which was clearly unnecessary in this case, since there was no processing or reorganization of the figures, but only a simple transfer. The worksheet had no useful function, in fact, it allowed a greater opportunity to make mistakes. The devotion to a traditional practice was a burden and source of problems.

To be able to define function accurately with a single verb and noun, you must identify the need or purpose first, again in uncompromising demand for objective information. Take the case of analyzing the job and proper employment of a secretary, for example. What is the need, the reason for using a secretary? The correct verb-noun definition of what a secretary *should do* is "save time"—the executive's time, that is. Even a relatively junior executive probably costs the organization from at least $25 per hour to many times that amount, while a secretary costs far less, but yet too much for filing and making coffee. Secretaries should open mail and answer telephones to save their bosses' time, field routine matters, manage their bosses' schedule, fend off and redirect those who ought to be guided to someone else, and generally enable their bosses to maximize the time they have available to concentrate on important matters that require their attention.

Robert Townsend, former head of Avis, reported in his book *Up the Organization!* (Alfred A. Knopf, New York, 1970) that he refused to have a secretary, instead calling someone from the typing pool when he had filing or typing to do. This approach indicates some consciousness of the waste represented by the way secretaries are employed today, but it also reflects a complete lack of logical analysis. Why should the head of a large firm such as Avis spend his time making his own travel arrangements, keeping his appointment book, answering routine mail, and otherwise doing five-to-ten-dollar-per-hour work? All of us, regardless of rank, authority, wealth, birth, or privilege of any kind have the same allotment of time every day, but our time is valued differently, at least in terms of what it costs the organization.

The same philosophy of analyzing needs and functions can be applied to many other things as well as to equipment and people—to forms, to systems, to procedures, and even to rules. The example of the error-ridden invoices and the unneeded worksheet is not an exception; it is typical. In another case a small print shop doing work for the Government Printing Office was having a similar problem. The work required furnishing rates for each element of each job—camera work to make negatives, plate making, collating pages, stapling, cutting, trimming, packing, and shipping, among others. The print shop listed all these costs on an estimating sheet when bidding the job, used a similar form to record the actual count of pages, staples, and other information and sent that latter form to the accounting department to be transferred to an invoice in all its detail, as required by contract. This double transfer of figures furnished excellent opportunities for mistakes. The cure was similar to our worksheet example. The original estimating form was modified to provide a column for actual quantities alongside the column of estimated quantities, and a copy of the form was attached to the invoice, which listed only the total figure. The Government Printing Office found this quite acceptable.

Modifying the form not only eliminated the problem, it made a more efficient use of labor, which alone justifies the changes. And note again the simplicity of the solutions. Remember as you study problems that elements performing secondary functions that *appear* to be supportive of and necessary to the primary function are often really not only unnecessary but are actually harmful. So the questions: "What is it?" and "What does it do?" often lead to "Do we need it?" and "Does it contribute?"

The opposite is also sometimes true. An engineering services firm employing thousands of people nationally in over 40 small offices ran the weekly payroll for all on a large IBM mainframe computer in its New York City headquarters. Yet, when summer vacation time rolled around the home office had to ask each branch office manager to determine how much earned vacation time each employee had. They had failed to arrange for the computer to keep track of this most basic element of a master payroll record. Certainly someone failed to analyze the necessity of this simple function to the overall efficiency of the system.

These and many other irrational acts in organizations result from the failure to do reasoned analysis, especially the failure to identify the need and primary function required and to do so in that simple and objective verb-noun discipline that forces commitment.

Rule Number 2: Agree On the Need

Sometimes we hear someone blame a dispute or failure of some kind on "a breakdown in communications." That's a partial truth in many cases two people didn't understand each other. But in a great many cases: the "misunderstanding" is really a failure to reach agreement. This failure to reach agreement with a client on defining the true need means that you are pursuing a goal that may be the right goal in your opinion, but it is probably the wrong goal in the client's opinion.

There are many reasons for such failures to reach agreement with a client on just what the need is, including:

The reluctance to dispute the client for fear of losing the contract; you hope you can muddle through somehow without having to confront the problem of a client who is grossly misguided as to what his or her true need is.

A client who is less than clear in explaining his or her own ideas and thoughts so that you are not even aware that you are in disagreement.

A client who has been totally noncommittal and unresponsive to your proposal, leading you to believe that you have persuaded the client to your view and that you are now in agreement (but this is not so).

Your own failure to make your thoughts clear so that you mistakenly believe that the client understands and agrees with your diagnosis and proposed project.

Your failure to analyze and express the need in that simple verb-noun definition.

It is not necessary to provoke a direct confrontation to reach agreement and to ensure that you do understand each other. If you find yourself in disagreement with the client or, at least, have not yet reached agreement, working through the first few steps of the value analysis will often help persuade the client to your view. (If it does not, avoid confrontation and pursue the negotiating tactic advocated earlier of expressing arguments and proposing to shelve further discussion for a few days.)

The formal process in value analysis is to pose and seek answers to this series of questions:

What is it? (Descriptive, functional name)

What does it do? (Main function)

What else does it do? (Secondary functions)

What does it cost?

What else would do it? (The same main function with at least equal quality, reliability, and efficiency)

What would that cost?

This series of questions compels you to organize your analysis and synthesis along unemotional, logical lines. (The same series of questions may be proposed for each element or component performing a secondary function of some kind.) This kind of analysis has led to many design and manufacturing simplifications that not only reduce costs but in many cases produce a better product at the same time.

Saving money is not its sole purpose, however. The method may be used to conserve energy, time, materials, or other resources. The questions are modified to direct the analysis properly. What would that cost? may become How long would that take? For example, when the Environmental Protection Agency found itself in difficulties getting its program to improve water treatment facilities completed within the time schedule mandated by Congress when it authorized the program, the agency called on value engineering consultants to work on the problem. (Specifically, the agency was to award $10 billion in grants to communities, but it was taking up to two years to approve applications by the communities.) The team of three consultants tracked the problem down through the analysis of each element required to process each application and found that the problem was in the communities' slowness in writing final engineering reports that were required by law to qualify for the grants. More precisely, the problem was that the engineers waited until their engineering studies were completely and totally finished before even contemplating the writing of their reports, which could have been more than half completed by the time the engineering studies were finished. Guidance in this solved the problem.

Value engineers have developed their own special block diagramming method to assist in the analysis and presentation of functional analyses. A simple example of this is presented in Figure 10–1, which illustrates the logic of an ordinary mouse trap.

In this presentation the overall goal or need is expressed as "eliminate mice," whereas the main function is "kill mice." The distinction and the reason for it is an important one. The need is to get rid of mice, not necessarily by killing them, however. The *device* used and analyzed here is designed to kill mice. If another kind of device had been studied the main function might have been defined as "trap mice," but the need would have remained the same because the need has nothing to do with the method, while the main function has everything to do with the method. The *How?* defines the relationship:

How to eliminate mice? By killing mice.

In this case there are secondary functions that are necessary to accomplish the main function, but there is one that is only supplementary—that is, "ring bell"—and not necessary to accomplish the main function.

Brainstorming

I have found brainstorming a useful way to reach agreement with clients in many cases, especially when my assignment requires me to work with, and often to lead, the client's own in-house experts. This is almost invariably a disparate ad hoc group who often do not even

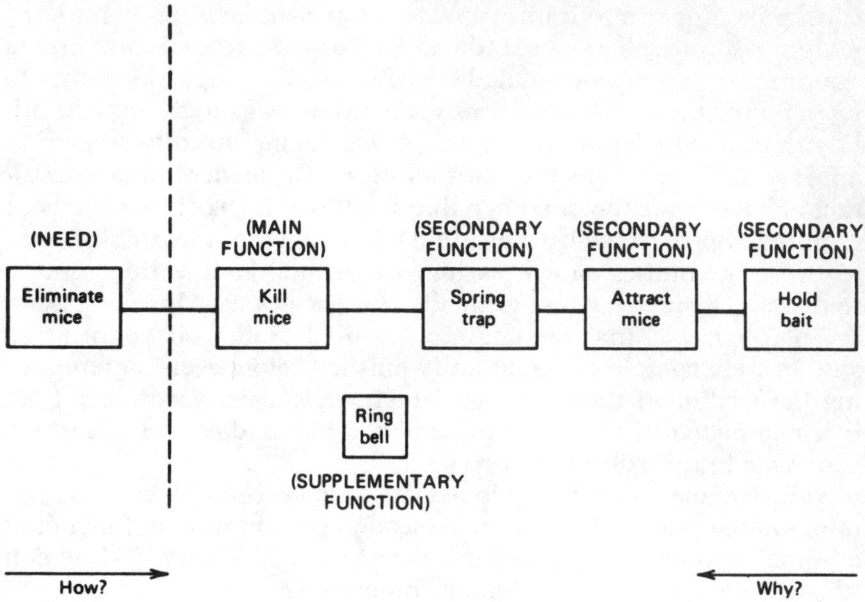

FIGURE 10.1

know each other very well. They require firm and positive leadership, and brainstorming fills the bill quite nicely in a great many cases.

The method was invented by advertising executive Alex Osborne, and the overall objective is to inspire a synergy of fresh, creative ideas through free association.

A brainstorming session is conducted in three major phases:

1. The group is assembled, with a leader, who lays out the rules. These rules may include throw any and all ideas on the table, spin off on others' ideas, offer twists on your own ideas, and be entirely uninhibited but no ridiculing others and their ideas. All ideas are to be recorded and considered. The leader then throws out the basic question to be answered or the problem for which solutions are sought, encourages everyone to participate, and enforces the rules. Ideas are recorded on a blackboard or poster board where everyone can see them.
2. When the group runs out of fresh ideas the next phase starts. Here ideas are evaluated and thrown out, retained, modified, or combined with others.
3. Final evaluations and choices are made.

This is intended to be a group activity. Value engineering teams use the discipline, as do many other teams. However, it is possible to do this on a solo basis too. The creative process involves three stages also:

1. **Concentration.** Thinking intensively about the matter, seeking ideas consciously.
2. **Incubation.** Putting the matter out of your (conscious) mind, after you have exhausted all approaches consciously, and going on to other things (i.e., turning it over to your subconscious mind).
3. **Illumination or inspiration.** Your subconscious mind provides an answer, as when you wake up one morning with the answer to something that has defied conscious solution or when a word or name that has eluded you suddenly pops into your head.

Whatever the means, you must somehow manage to reach a clear and mutually understood agreement with the client.

Rule Number 3: Written Agreements Must Be Specific

You must never sign an agreement that is not absolutely specific in what you agree to do, when you agree to do it or have it completed, what you agree to deliver and how much of it, how much you are to be paid, when you are to be paid, and all other such important details. The agreement must be quantitative as well as qualitative. The failure to be specific is a major reason for problems. Remember that when you write a proposal you are in effect proposing a contract, for your proposal will probably become the key part of the contract, incorporated in it by reference. You thus have time to think things out and decide exactly what you wish to have in the contract as you write your proposal.

It is rare that some kind of deliverable item is not involved in a project, even a project calling for services. At the least, there is usually a requirement for a final report and often for a series of reports. That is the only physical evidence that the client can show for the money spent, so it often assumes a correspondingly large importance to the client.

In many cases the client has no firm idea of how to specify requirements for the report(s), and so it is not a good idea to press the client for specifications. Instead, you should offer your own, making your own best estimates.

A 100-page report, typed double-spaced, as many clients prefer, will run to approximately 25,000 words, which is a considerable amount of writing. Ordinarily, you will want to include some charts or graphs. A few decades ago you would probably have had to rely on a commercial illustrator to do these for you. Today, if you are equipped with a modern personal computer, you can probably create all the charts and graphs you need by computer. However, if you do not have a computer, you can get much of what you need in the form of excellent do-it-yourself art materials from local supply houses.

What Should Be Spelled Out

There are no hard and fast rules as to what must be specified. In custom work, each case is unique. But do specify everything that is going to cost you time or money, for you must be paid for your time and reimbursed for your expenses. Since you can't know in advance just what all those will amount to, you must cover these in two ways: (1) plan all the chores and functions and estimate the time and money you will have to spend on them (e.g., travel, toll calls, printing, writing, research, interviews, etc.), and (2) write in general provisions specifying that you will be reimbursed in full for time and out-of-pocket costs for these items, being sure to list all the types of expenses you expect to incur.

The estimated costs are a must for the fixed-price contract, for the client is obligated for only a specific total of dollars. Therefore, it is important that you estimate carefully, but it is also important that you fix limits. If you estimate a 100-page final report on a fixed-price contract you are obligated for that only. But if you had not specified the number of pages the client would feel justified in demanding 300 pages, and you would have no grounds for refuting the demand. On the other hand, had the client accepted your proposed 100 pages and later decided to demand 300 pages you have the basis for renegotiating and amending the contract.

Cases of this type are not rare or unusual. Once, having prepared and delivered a training film and 50 copies of a manual, as required by contract, I was confronted with a demand for an additional 150 copies of the manual at no charge. Oddly enough, the demand did not come to me from the client, but from our own marketing vice president, who was relaying the client's request and who evidently shrank from telling the client quietly that we would be glad to supply more copies but would have to charge for them. When I explained that I was not willing to have my department stand the loss, he indignantly demanded that I tell that to the client.

I did so. I had no difficulty explaining calmly to the client that while we would be happy to supply a few extra copies—we had a few on hand—we would be forced to charge for as many as 150 copies. We did, in fact, have to go back to the printer to produce another 150 copies, but there was no problem. (There rarely is when you are calm and businesslike.) The client was quite willing to pay for what he wanted. In fact, I rather doubt that the client had ever expected us to provide additional copies free of charge; almost certainly our own man had presumed that the client was seeking extra copies at our expense. Most clients respect your right to be as businesslike as they are, and they are astonished if you are not. This is not to say that I never found a client unwilling to take advantage of me if I permitted it—it has happened to me at the hands of individuals in supercorporations on two occasions—but those have been the exceptional cases. (I am rather sure that the two individuals were not reflecting their companies' policies, but acting in what they thought to be their personal best interests.)

Verbal Understandings Are Important Too

Good relationships are formed when you are open and honest from the beginning with your clients, while still trying to be diplomatic and tactful.

I have not found many clients willing to retain me on a completely open basis—that is, sign a blank check for me by retaining me at a daily rate on an indefinite basis. Although such arrangements are made occasionally, as when an organization retains you as a technical/professional temporary, they are the exceptions. In most cases the client wants some idea of what the entire commitment is likely to be. Therefore, I make it a practice to try to get enough detailed information about the requirement to enable me to arrive at a reasonable estimate of the cost and offer the client a not-to-exceed figure on that basis. I then try earnestly to live with my estimate. If the job runs slightly over, I absorb the difference normally, assuming that I underestimated the time required. If the job runs over due to the client adding work or due to an inaccurate estimate based on inaccurate input from the client, I discuss amending our contract. I have rarely had a problem with this; most clients are reasonable about it if you have been careful to arrive at a clear understanding from the beginning. I work at making sure that the client understands exactly the basis for my not-to-exceed estimate. I do something to create that basis in writing—in a formal contract or puchase order, if we have one between us, or in a letter of understanding otherwise. However, it is equally important—perhaps even more important—that the client has been helped to understand that clearly in the beginning. The paper in the files is not helpful if the client is not conscious of what it says and if he or she feels, somehow, victimized when you ask for an amendment to your agreement and more money.

In a recent case, for example, a client retained me to help them prepare a proposal that was due only a week later. Obviously, I could not spend more than seven days on that task, and I agreed to do my level best to prepare a first-class proposal despite the time constraint. Near the end of the period, my client's customer allowed an extension of several days for the proposal, and we raised our sights a bit on the task, so that I spent two additional days on it. My client agreed that this was a change and issued me a second purchase order to pay me for the extra two days. It took a little conversation and several days to reach agreement, but there was never a question about my right to be paid for the extra days.

Specifying Rates

The daily (or hourly) rate you charge includes the salary you pay yourself, the overhead, and a profit margin. Although there are some exceptions, for most of us the overhead is a major element of cost in our daily rate, often as much as 50 percent of that rate. And a major overhead item is our unbilled time, especially that time we spend in marketing.

That means that when we draw a long-term assignment, our overhead costs plunge sharply during that period. Should we then favor the client who retains us for an extended period with a significantly lower rate reflecting that reduced overhead?

You are likely to encounter clients who will expect to be able to bargain with you about your rates, especially when they can offer long-term assignments or promise a great deal of work for the future. Should you agree to negotiate your basic rates in such circumstances?

There are some consultants who will not vary their rates under any circumstances. There are some who will bargain and negotiate, given special circumstances. And there are those who will negotiate whenever things are slow and they feel a need to win an assignment, even at a reduced rate.

You must make your own decision on this issue. But if you do negotiate special rates with a client, be sure to have a clear understanding of what the rates are and for what duration they are effective. It's a good idea to document the special rates in a written agreement or contract, since it is a special case.

There are hazards in this arrangement. Suppose you agree to charge a special, reduced rate on the basis of a promise that you will be working a minimum of so many days per week or so many total days over the next three months. And suppose that most of the promised work does not materialize, and you are employed only sporadically for a day here and day there. You must protect yourself against this with written guarantees—guarantees that you will be employed for some minimum number of days over the specified time period or paid your full rate if the promised volume of work fails to materialize. If the client refuses to enter into such an agreement, the refusal speaks for itself.

11

Final Reports, Presentations, and Other Products

Reports and other products are sometimes the most important aspect of the consulting project. In any case, they are always a reflection of you, the consultant—how well you perform and how effective your services are. But they tend also to become permanent records and leave permanent impressions.

WRITTEN REPORTS: PRODUCTS OF THE CONSULTING PROJECT

Most consulting projects require the development and delivery of some physical product(s). In almost all but the most brief and informal projects, at least one written report is required, whether or not there are other products such as computer tapes, slides, manuals, procedural lists, or management plans. If the project is relatively large and/or long term, and especially if the client is a large organization with multiple levels of management, you will almost surely be required to submit progress reports, usually on a monthly basis, with a final report at the end of the project. The monthly progress reports, often required in as many as ten copies, permit various executives and technical specialists to monitor the project and judge how satisfactorily it is progressing and to learn of special problems if any exist. They may be an ad hoc oversight committee and/or may want to offer suggestions, as well as criticisms and general comments. And, of course, the individual executive who authorized or even inspired the project–and who may in that sense be the true client, despite the fact that your contract is with the organization–has an absolute need, as well as a desire, to maintain a constant awareness of the entire project in most of its details. He or she is responsible for the program and may have to report on it and answer questions about it regularly at staff meetings. (You may also have to arm you true client with informal memoranda and notes in preparation for those boardroom inquisitions! Even if you are invited to visit the boardroom periodically to make a presentation of and discuss the status and progress of you project, at least one of the staff is expected to be able to answer all questions and provide all information called for about the project.)

General Nature and Content of Progress Reports

Progress reports must report accomplishment, problems, plans, and projections, and they must provide suitable transitions from the prior report and to the succeeding one. They must be precise, logical, informative, complete, and accurate. As in the case of proposals and similar writing (see Chapter 8), they also must be factual in tone and style. That is, they must be objective, scrupulously avoiding extravagant superlatives. While the tone should be definitely upbeat, reflecting confidence in the outcome of the project, reports must always present the facts and refrain from exaggerating them.

Progress reports are usually written in a narrative format, reporting events in chronological order, generally in the sequence in which they occurred. (It is possible that occasionally, under special circumstances, a reverse chronology or even a totally different format may be necessary.) Since the progress report is one of a continuing series it should first present a link with the prior month's report, refreshing the reader's memory on the project status of that time as a baseline for the current report and as a way of measuring progress. The single most important consideration is progress or the lack of it and the causes thereof. In the latter case, the report must identify the specific problems encountered, what is being done to cope with them, and what the plans are for the month to come, especially with regard to the problems requiring solution.

A Common Mistake

Only significant facts affecting progress belong in the progress report. Don't confuse effort with accomplishment. Effort that is fruitless because a problem is encountered might be mentioned in passing, but it is the problem and its solution or plans for its eventual solution that should be described and discussed, as appropriate. Suppose that only by extraordinary effort and clever improvisation you acquired difficult-to-get information that proved, unfortunately, to be worthless for your purposes. You have that understandable passion to tell the world about it. Don't. No matter how heroic or brilliant your effort was, no matter how hard you worked, the unfortunate fact is that only success or impediments to success in achieving progress toward the main goal are significant and should be reported.

Organization and Formats

Information can be organized in a large variety of ways, and each type of report or other presentation should be matched to the most appropriate kind of organization. Information can be organized in many ways, including:

Chronological—order of occurrence

Historical—similar to chronological, but not necessarily in strict order of occurrence

Reverse chronological—tracing events back to origins or first causes

Order of importance—least to most important or vice versa

General to particular—least to most specific or vice versa

Syllogistic—beginning with premises and developing logical arguments

Deductive—stating principles and analyzing facts, relating them logically with principles listed

Inductive—examining facts and organizing them analytically for logical inference of governing principles

Although chronological order is the most often used format for project reports, reports of any substantial size are generally divided into a number of sections; each section has its own organization, according to need. On the other hand, some clients have their own standard formats, and you may be required to follow those. If the client does not have a standard or preferred format, it is a good policy to describe the format you propose and ask for approval of it. The following is a detailed explanation of a recommended six-part format:

1. **Background information.** If this is a final report or the only report to be submitted, this first section is likely to be a recapitulation of the overall objective of the entire project, the general strategy and principal functions, and other data that would brief the reader on the project's status. But if this is merely one of a series of progress reports, the introduction need merely furnish a brief transition from the prior progress report and introduce the general objective of the last reporting period's effort.
2. **A chronological narrative.** This narrative recounts all events of the reporting period or total project (as appropriate). If necessary, linkages to or transitions from the prior report may be included in introducing the various elements of the reporting period's efforts.
3. **Problems encountered.** This should include complete accounts of the problems encountered and how they were overcome or solved (or plans for solving them in the next month). It usually includes a follow-up report on projections made in any prior report.
4. **Examination of results.** In some types of projects, such as studies and surveys, the data collected must be presented in full detail, discussed at length, and analyzed. This is generally syllogistic, may involve mathematical presentations, must show methodology of analysis and rationale for using methodology chosen, and should present results such as logical conclusions to be drawn or premises established for future investigation (next reporting period, perhaps).
5. **Plans for next month.** If this is a progress report, you should report potential problems and how they will be handled, and you should project next month's achievements as targeted goals. Be specific about next month's goals.

6. **Examination of total project.** If this is a final report rather than a progress report, this section will extend the examination of results from section 4 to the on the total project and will extend conclusions drawn in section 4 to final recommendations.

Obviously the nature and objectives of each section dictate to a large extent how the information in it must be organized and presented. Raw data, for example, may be presented in a chronological narrative, but when data are to be examined and analyzed they must be arrayed, grouped, and processed to facilitate manipulations and the detection of correlations and other relationships. Hence the data may themselves dictate the organization necessary to achieve the goals of the report. In fact, it may very well be necessary to try several different organizations and reorganizations of the data to achieve this.

Syllogistic presentations are inescapable. The client wishes to know how you reached conclusions and on what basis you offer your recommendations. Where you must explain a premise or principle upon which you base some of your work, it may be necessary to make an explanatory excursion, using a from-the-general-to-the-particular presentation or even reverse chronology.

Factual Reporting and Your Reputation

Project reports have sections that should be confined strictly to factual reporting, while in other sections you may speculate on the meaning of the facts presented earlier. Even here it is necessary to be entirely objective in tone and method and to offer no conclusions, recommendations, or even general opinions for which you cannot or do not demonstrate a logical chain of reasoning supported by demonstrated facts. That is absolutely vital to the overall credibility of your report, and it is essential that you preserve that credibility with scrupulous care. Errors of fact or method bring into question your professional consulting skills and jeopardize your professional reputation. Once lost, credibility is difficult to regain.

One common error often made by consultants is the assumption that their professional image and reputation are so impressive that clients must accept anything they say on "authority" alone. It may be true that some clients will accept your pronouncements as fact or even wisdom, but it is most hazardous to depend on this. You can never be sure that any given client is trusting enough to accept all your counsel without question or that your counsel will always prove wise. An inflated self-image can be detrimental.

It is quite easy to avoid risking your reputation by always qualifying your advice, especially when it is called for and delivered spontaneously under conditions of urgency (e.g., when a client calls in obvious distress, demanding an immediate judgment). And always explain your rationale.

A client called me to ask my help with the Postal Service, which had denied him a second-class mailing permit for his newsletter and invited him to appeal. I probed the problem with questions for a bit and then ventured an opinion, but asked him to do nothing until I had time to do some checking to verify my spontaneous opinion. I was rather sure I knew what the problem was, but I wanted to play it safe by doing some checking. I spoke to a Postal Service official, after reviewing relevant regulations, and then offered my client final advice on how to get his permit. Had he acted on my early advice—he would probably have accepted my judgment without question, had I offered him assurances that my counsel was absolutely accurate and would do the job—and failed to get his permit, I would have lost him as a client, of course. Nothing was lost by asking him to wait a few days while I validated my spontaneous opinion, and I reduced the risk of looking foolish and incompetent.

To preserve your reputation make it a practice to think logically whenever you are speaking or writing "for the record" or in formal counsel to a client. Remember that few things are entirely predictable and no one is infallible. For example, if a client asks me whether federal contracting officials will always bow to pressure from the General Accounting Office to allow protesters enough time to write a formal proposal, I can only answer that they should do so and that I have succeeded in persuading them to do so in the past, but I cannot guarantee that they will always do so. I *must* qualify my answer because I truly cannot guarantee that others will always do what they are supposed to do. If you and your client run into an exception to the rule—e. g. , the contracting official defies the General Accounting Office—your credibility is undamaged because you were not dogmatic or cryptic about your advice.

Imparting such information and qualifying answers runs counter to the principles and practices of some consultants who believe that they must withhold information. They fear that if they are open the client will learn too much and not be dependent on them in the future. They see this policy as one of self-preservation. And it is for that reason, also, that many professionals develop a jargon all their own that is almost indecipherable to anyone outside the profession.

Is this not clearly evident in the use of Latin in medicine and law, for example, and in the distortion of word meanings to make jargon of them? Why does the insurance industry use the word premium to mean payment? Why do accountants say you are on a cash basis when you bill clients and expect to wait 30 or more days to get paid? And why does cost of sales mean total cost of production to an accountant, rather than cost of getting the order? Why do psychologists say behavior when they mean skills or knowledge and not deportment?

Consultants are no less guilty, even when we use mystical jargon in all innocence. I thoroughly befuddled one correspondent by using the term sign off to mean approve. My client, thinking of radio broadcast jargon, interpreted the term to mean say good night and was justifiably confused and somewhat irate with me for confusing him.

For this reason it is wise to consciously and deliberately avoid the use of jargon when communicating with anyone outside your industry—client or only prospective client—unless you take the trouble to explain or interpret the jargon carefully.

I am one of those who rejects the idea that it is necessary to inhibit my clients from learning what I know and/or how I achieve my results so that they must become dependent on me. I am eager to reveal what I know to my clients and so am entirely open with them. In fact, I actually turn this to my advantage by conducting many training seminars in government marketing and proposal writing, earning highly satisfactory fees for doing so!

Aside from that practical consideration, however, there is an ethical question: Isn't the client, who is paying you the fees you ask, entitled to know exactly what you are doing and how you are doing it? Isn't the client entitled to complete disclosure? The basic fear that you may be giving away too much has little basis. Clients may be interested in learning something of your methodology and the rationale for it, but few want to do the work themselves. Quite the contrary, most want to call you back again if your work proves effective—they regard you as a valuable resource.

You may also risk losing your relationship with the client if you are not open. Clients may interpret your evasions and other efforts to avoid disclosure as mistrust on your part, which in turn leads the client to become mistrustful of you.

Editing

Not only must your reports be written carefully and clearly, they also should be edited. If you are a one-person enterprise, you will not have an editor to review and edit what you have written. That job will be yours. You must review your first draft, edit it, and rewrite it. Examine everything you have written in your first draft as a devil's advocate, studying your draft for possible ambiguities. Can anything you've said be reasonably interpreted to mean anything other than what you intended to convey? Are any of the words you used special terms or jargon? If so, and if for any reason you believe it necessary to use those terms, have you somehow provided their definitions? Your writing must be clear. Do not use words the average person is unlikely to be familiar with. For example, I once created a serious problem in communication by using the word epitome in the draft of a manual. To my surprise, almost everyone involved in a dispute that arose concerning my use of this word insisted that they understood the word and that I had misused it, and there were many red faces when we were forced to turn to the dictionary to resolve the matter. Worse, I had to discard this word, not because it was the wrong word to use—it was exactly right, in fact—but because readers would probably misunderstand what I had written, as so many fellow writers and editors had!

Level of Detail

Unless the client has mandated some detailed specification, the level of detail to be included in your reports is primarily one of your own judgment. You should consider these factors in your determination of detail level:

Objective of the project. If the project has as its primary objective the achievement of some end product, such as a manual, computer program, or inventory system, it is usually not necessary to go into painstaking detail. You should merely report progress, problems, and whatever else is necessary to define the amount of progress achieved, account for time and money spent, and otherwise keep the client informed. If, however, the project is aimed at making a study, carrying out a survey, or devising some new methodology that the client is to use, it is likely that the client will feel a need to have a great deal of detail formally documented.

The client's technical level. If the client is a technical or professional specialist in your field, he or she will probably want technical data, but will usually not require painstaking explanations and interpretations of the data. You can use the special idiom and shorthand that the jargon of your field affords you. Be sure, however, that you can use such jargon and still communicate effectively with the client. In many fields practitioners get so specialized that they develop an ultra-special jargon peculiar to their ultra-special niche. An electronics engineer specializing in communications equipment may use technical jargon that is cryptic to an electronics engineer specializing in test equipment or missile guidance systems. Different users of a given technical or jargon term may have different definitions or referents for the term and therefore mean different things by it. Too, jargon tends to evolve and change. Use jargon sparingly and with care.

Objective of the report itself. Some reports are almost pure routine requirements and are hardly glanced at, except to verify that they have been rendered and to see if there is anything unusual or special about them. But some reports are themselves the objective of the project and constitute the end products. For example, I was once awarded a government contract to carry out a swift study and survey for an official who needed the report to support and validate his budget request. In another case the report incorporated a model for a training program evaluation, and that model was the objective of and justification for the entire project. It was the model itself that the client wanted; the rest of the report was unimportant to her.

The Report as an Opportunity

Many reports represent great potential for generating additional business. For example, when I was the general manager of a technical services organization, a government executive with whom I was acquainted approached me about an idea he had. He was sure that one of the major operations carried out by his agency could be done far less expensively by contracting the work out to a private firm such as the one that employed me. His idea was to have me write an unsolicited proposal, which he believed he could get approved as the basis for a contract award.

I found the notion appealing, inasmuch as such a contract would have been for a national network supplying some $15 million worth of auto parts annually to the agency's many vehicle maintenance facilities, and we spent a day together visiting some of those facilities and getting some first-hand information. I then returned to my own office to study the matter at greater length.

I soon realized, as I explored the proposition, that the proposal would require extensive research and thus involve a large effort and be quite costly to write with no guarantees that a contract would actually result.

I found this prospect totally unacceptable and suggested a reasonable alternative. If the official awarded us a small study contract, the resulting report would furnish him all the data he needed to publish a comprehensive statement of work and invite proposals from everyone, including my own firm. I was quite willing to bid competitively and preferred that to the risk.

This is quite proper, although a contractor who does such a study for a fee—that is, under contract—may be disqualified completely from bidding. It is not unprecedented, either, for many clients, especially government agencies, find it necessary to retain consultants to assist them in soliciting proposals and even in evaluating proposals and selecting awardees.

Although this kind of consulting opportunity for new, expanded, or follow-on business may arise from or at the initiative of clients, it arises far more often from the initiative of the enterprising consultant who is always alert for opportunities. Writing a report and reviewing the situation overall, is an ideal situation for searching out opportunities for follow-on contracts, for by this time you have had the opportunity to become thoroughly familiar with the client's situation—the needs and problems of the organization.

Therefore, report writing should be regarded far more as an opportunity than as a chore. In the case of a final report there is frequent opportunity to make recommendations; there is also the perfect opportunity to seek additional work from the client. You should have been alert from the beginning to opportunities—been *seeking* opportunities for follow-on contracts—and the final element in your report is the place to begin selling it. (At the same time, when carrying out a project for a department or division in a large organization, don't miss the opportunity to get acquainted with other potential clients in other departments or divisions of the organizations. These are among your best leads.)

VERBAL REPORTS AND PRESENTATIONS

In the course of many consulting contracts you will make frequent, informal verbal reports, reports that are actually dialogues, in which the client asks questions and makes observations. This is often a crucially important element in achieving client satisfaction. It is also common for clients to request that formal verbal reports and presentations be given to an assembled group. Here, too, it is likely that you will be asked questions and be expected to engage in dialogue after you have first made a formal presentation.

These questions asked by listeners may be sincere inquiries, efforts to gain greater understanding or to make contributions to the project. But they may also be ploys by individuals—especially those who are relatively low-level staff—to gain attention and demonstrate their alertness and intelligence to the senior executives in attendance. There may also be those present who simply resent the introduction of consultants for one reason or another (some infer that the use of consultants impugns their own competence and credentials as in-house experts) and intend to bring you down, if possible. Such individuals may pose deliberately antagonistic questions, by which they hope to discredit you, while enhancing their own images.

You must therefore expect an audience that may be friendly and sympathetic, but also may be antagonistic and predatory. Be prepared to keep your sense of humor and pretend that you do not perceive the all-too-apparent barbs in some of the questions. You can deflect those barbs quite easily with a show of good humor and sometimes even a sense of humor.

I once undertook to develop for the Postal Service Training and Development Institute a model evaluation system that was to make a direct measure of training transfer—that qualitative and quantitative measure of actual improvements in job performance resulting directly from training programs. This was a pioneering effort; no one had made a serious attempt to do this before. Moreover, I had been cautioned by those professionals reputed to be experts in the field that it was an impossible task. (Training and education professionals in my own organization had actually used such dogmatic assertions as arguments to dissuade me from even attempting the project. But those are "fighting words" to me; I think that the word "impossible" should be banished from the language! In any case, I persisted and produced what I thought to be a reasonably respectable first effort at such an evaluation system.

One thing I did not know was that there had been internal dissension about this project in the organization. The person assigned to monitor our contract had opposed the effort because she happened to agree that it was impossible to make such measures.

Most of the people in the large group—about 20 professionals who were various kinds of specialists in training and education—that my staff and I faced were not all hostile, although several obviously were, but most of them were at least skeptical. They believed it would be difficult to actually measure training transfer and attacked the model. We knew that as a first effort the model had to be based largely on arbitrary premises, and so was quite vulnerable to assaults. Yet our admission that a great deal of improvement had yet to be developed and that such improvement was not even possible until extensive testing and field tryouts had taken place disarmed the critics. They had been prepared for battle, not for our complete understanding of their skepticism. We could offer quite respectable foundations for our premises and projections, while we were also able to make them understand that our own accomplishment represented to all of us only the first step of a long journey. We made it abundantly clear that we had no illusions about this.

Interestingly enough, the driving force behind the project was the head of the agency, but it would not have been right for him to have subdued critics by sheer authority of his position. It seemed rather obvious to me that he had asked for the unprecedented large-scale presentation to give all of us–the consultant-developer and the staff critics–our "day in court." I felt rather certain that he had his fingers crossed in hope that we could defend our work adequately and silence the critics.

That raises an important point. As a consultant you owe allegiance to the organization overall, in one sense, but you owe special allegiance to the individual who has been responsible for retaining you and who is, in a very real sense your true client. In making reports and presentations, you are often really representing that individual and his or her own interests.

"Yes, but–" is as effective an "argument" (because it is not an argument or, at least, not a challenge to the other) in such situations as these as it is in selling generally. The conditions are similar: You cannot "win" arguments with clients because to win arguments is to lose sales—to lose clients, that is. Moreover, the more energetically the other party defends an opinion or position, the more bitterly he or she will resent any effort to rebut or discredit that position. Logic is never effective against passion. If it is necessary to resist a client's will—and only absolute necessity should lead to such resistance—you must offer only passive resistance and as much agreement on major issues as possible.

On one occasion an interviewer asked me if I could "write a number" in Boolean algebra. To have guffawed at this or even to have said some such thing as "Boolean algebra deals with logic, not with numbers," would have embarrassed the other. Instead, playing dumb and saying "I'm afraid I don't know how to do that, but I can write you the Boolean equation for any logic circuit," saved the day. He knew immediately that he had made a gross error—he obviously had not more than a vague idea of what Boolean algebra is—but since I gave no hint that I recognized his faux pas he was not distressed. He merely shrugged, and we went on.

Preparation

Some people are fortunate enough to be able to speak well spontaneously, but even they must prepare to make a presentation. Smoothly professional presentations are rarely as spontaneous as they appear to be. But while the appearance of spontaneity is a quite desirable trait in a presentation, it really results from careful preparation. This does not mean, however, that you should memorize a speech, for only a polished and experienced actor can make a memorized speech appear to be spontaneous. Instead, prepare to speak by knowing your subject thoroughly, planning an organized sequence of information, and arming yourself with a guide in the form of an outline or set of notes. (My own preference is for an outline, in classic outline format on one or more sheets of paper, but many prefer an outline or set of notes on a numbered series of cards.)

The Importance of Visual Aids

Visual aids are enormously helpful in even brief presentations for several reasons: (1) they help your audience grasp the information quickly; (2) they provide a change of pace and add interest for the audience; and (3) they lessen the reliance on your words alone and transfer attention from you to the visuals, which relieves you of much of the stress and pressure of an oral presentation.

Visual aids include chalkboards, flip charts, posters, transparencies, slides, videocassettes, filmstrips, and movies, in ascending order of cost and complexity of use. You are not likely to go to great expense in preparing visual aids such as movies or even sets of slides. However, in some cases you may be able to use off-the-shelf films, videotapes, and slides; there are many large libraries of such materials, and it is often possible to rent such visuals or even borrow them without charge. On the other hand, chalkboards, flip charts, and posters are usually quite acceptable for all but the most formal presentations. But there is another resource quite appropriate to this need—that is, the personal computer.

Computer Graphics and Desktop Publishing Programs

Desktop publishing is the newest area of special interest in the personal computer industry. The great popularity and rapid proliferation of personal computers with internal memory capacities as high as 768K (786,432 characters) have made such capabilities available to owners of even the more modestly priced personal computers. In fact, in the current market, with the retail prices of personal computers at all-time lows, almost all offer 640K (655,360 characters) memories, more than enough for fairly elaborate and sophisticated programs. Moreover, even a modestly priced dot matrix printer can turn out good-quality graphics—banners, posters, and line illustrations of many kinds—when driven by these new programs. These can then be used directly, made into transparencies or slides, or pasted up to make large posters and charts.

Handouts

Printed handouts are still another aid in presentations. Some presenters like to hand out such material piece by piece, throughout the presentation, while others hand out the entire package at the beginning. The personal computer and especially the special new graphics and desktop publishing programs are useful for generating this material.

In many cases you can use handouts in addition to or in place of such visuals as posters and flip charts. However, when the information is too voluminous for a poster or chalkboard presentation the handout is the best solution.

Handouts also have the advantage of allowing attendees to take your presentation with them rather than relying on memory and notes. The use of handouts also plants seeds for possible future business. Be sure that you and what you do are clearly identified somehow in your handouts and that the handouts are designed to be worth keeping for future reference!

OTHER PRODUCTS

Many consulting projects require the delivery of products other than reports and presentations. These may include manuals of various kinds, instructional materials, audiovisuals, program tapes, designs, drawings, specifications, administrative guidelines, or even other final products.

The common hazard such requirements invoke is that of disputes resulting from the failure to have a clear understanding and agreement between you and your client when entering into the project. This is not a new topic—it has been mentioned before, especially with regard to proposal preparation—but it is such a common and serious hazard that it is well worth stressing once again. It not only causes problems for the immediate project but also sours relationships and compromises both the possibility of future business with this client and, sometimes, your own professional reputation.

To prevent this problem, you should anticipate the probable need for an end product and come to specific agreement on just what that end product is to be—and that means *quantitative* as well as qualitative definition. For example, if you agree on a need for a manual as an end product, you must agree on estimates of its size, format, number and type of illustrations, content, physical specifications, and number of copies. Anything left undefined leaves the door open to future disagreement.

Phraseology also leads to disputes. Using such meaningless phrases as "best commercial practice" or "good commercial quality," when trying to set standards leaves much room for interpretation and miscommunication.

For example, when we contracted to produce a multimedia training system we stipulated each item to be delivered. We specified that we would deliver "camera-ready copy," a common enough phrase that I naïvely believed was well understood by all, including our client.

The client was greatly upset when he inspected the end product, the camera-ready copy. He objected loudly and unremittingly to the paste-ups and spliced corrections, totally rejecting our protestations that these were all standard practices that met even the exacting standards of the military organizations. He was unmoved until we persuaded him to call on any printers he chose and have them inspect our camera-ready copy. Only when several printers assured him that the copy was completely acceptable and would produce clean printed pages did he finally yield.

Perhaps this is an unusual case; admittedly, few clients are that difficult or that reluctant to learn what they ought to know. But it is not only clients who can be unreasonable. In one case, where the consulting firm was to conduct training operations on the client's premises, the consultant was authorized to sell to his own on-site project—billing the client ultimately, that is—up to $75,000 worth of his own training manuals at prices "not to exceed those charged [his] most favored customer." The consultant organized a $75,000 project to develop and have manufactured such manuals, to be delivered to the on-site project for use, and then billed the client for the $75,000 worth of related costs for producing those manuals.

The client refused to pay the bill, ruling it nonallowable under the terms of the contract. The contractor haggled and haggled, but the client was immovable on the subject.

Finally the consultant brought in an expert to help. The expert, a consultant himself, spent only a few minutes studying the relevant clause in the contract.

"Here is the problem," the expert told his client. "You are billing your client for R&D—the labor and materials to develop this set of manuals. But the client authorized sale of off-the-shelf, proprietary manuals at the best prices you offer anyone. He did not authorize the *development* of new, special manuals and won't pay for your R&D."

The resolution was to set a retail price on the manuals, discount them properly, deliver them, and invoice the client for the books, less the discount. The client then paid the $75,000 bill without a murmur!

Interestingly enough, the outside expert who came in and solved the problem did so entirely on the basis of interpreting the language of the relevant clause. He realized that the phrase identifying the maximum price to be charged could logically be applied only to proprietary manuals and so could not be interpreted to authorize

R&D of special materials. The consultant and client had opposing interpretations of the contract's terms.

You can also win Pyrrhic victories, victories in which you emerge a moral victor but lose far more than you win. One consulting firm that did so charged a federal agency approximately $50,000 to develop two manuals, a student manual and an instructor's manual, for a training program. However, they failed to provide administrative guidance in organizing a program to use these manuals, and when the agency protested that the manuals were of little use without such guidance, the consultant pointed out that the contract did not require such material. The agency had to bring in another consultant to develop a plan to use the two manuals effectively. The first consultant won the argument but lost the good will of the client, of course. Ironically, the original consultant could have easily negotiated a follow-on contract or amendment to the original contract, while retaining the client's good will, but failed to perceive the opportunity to do so.

THE HAZARD OF COMPLETION-PERCENTAGE REPORTS

Some accountants call for a particularly treacherous progress-reporting device by advocating the use of monthly estimates of the percentage of completion for each project. Theoretically, if all goes as it should, the percentage of completion should correlate with the percentage of dollars spent. Serious deviations from that—spending proceeding at a faster pace than completion, that is—is an obvious danger signal. For example, if a given project is scheduled for six months and $30,000, every percentage point of progress (completion) should reflect approximately $300 of the budget expended.

Unfortunately, this rarely works out well. Typically, the consultant is likely to report on a six-month contract along the following lines:

Month Number	Percentage Completed (%)	Remaining Effort (%)
1	10	90
2	25	75
3	45	55
4	65	35
5	70	30

The trend is simply this: The consultant tends to equate time and/or labor hours–percentage of *effort,* that is—with percentage of completion. But the accountant finds the two, money spent and progress made, proceeding along these lines:

Month Number	Completion Reported (%)	Budget Spent ($ and %)
1	10	$4,500 (15%)
2	25	9,500 (32%)
3	45	17,000 (57%)
4	65	25,750 (89%)
5	70	28,000 (93%)

The consultant begins to perceive that early estimates of progress were somewhat optimistic. As the scheduled delivery date grows closer, the consultant begins to see just how optimistic those early estimates were. In the meantime the accountant begins to see a fiscal disaster approaching. In the early months this does not appear to be a problem because the substantial budget expenditures are apparently balanced, at least roughly, by progress. But when the progress proves to be an illusion, it is too late to save the day.

The system should balance the budget against the progress, but it works only if progress is *measured,* not estimated, and measured by some objective means.

FINDING A MEASURING STICK

It is not easy to find an objective set of measures for most consulting projects. There are methods that do work, however, and in principle, the way to set up an objective measuring system is to follow these steps.

1. Break the entire project down into as many distinct, observable, or verifiable steps as possible, trying to make them at least roughly equivalent to each other in effort or size. Let us assume, for example, that you can identify a minimum of 50 such steps or elements.
2. Assign each a prorated percentage value. In this case completion of one of the 50 steps represents two percent progress.

3. Monitor each step or element continuously (e.g., once a week).
4. Score progress each month by assigning values to each step or element and adding them up, along this scale:
   a. Step not begun is zero percentage.
   b. Step begun but not completed is one percent.
   c. Step completed is two percent.

These arbitrary measures—zero, one, or two percent—will average each other out, very much along the lines of a series of approximations. The more elements you have the greater the accuracy will be. But even if the accuracy is less than perfect, it is far, far better than the almost pure guesswork that those typical percentage-completion methods involve, for it is based on measurement, not estimating.

12

Fees and Collections

We all pay for our education, especially the practical one. Here are a few ways to avoid that special consultant's hazard of being tricked or duped into working for nothing.

THINGS ARE RARELY WHAT THEY SEEM

One of my common practices is to require one-third of my total estimated fee upon agreeing to an assignment, another one-third at some identified and agreed-upon midpoint, and the final one-third upon final delivery and acceptance. This has served me well in two respects: (1) it has greatly helped my cash flow, and (2) it serves as "earnest money"—an indicator of the client's sincere intentions to retain you and the ability to pay your fees. It is quite surprising—and expensive—to discover that many people, even some who appear to be in sound financial condition, will undertake an obligation they cannot honor later or perhaps do not intend to honor. Whichever the case, it costs too much to learn this lesson the hard way. At the same time, this is a consideration primarily when dealing with clients who are small and unknown. If you do business with large, well-known corporations such as IBM, General Motors, and Bloomingdales, this may be an impractical demand (although, in my experience, it is not always impossible to achieve even in these cases).

If you do business with federal government agencies, as I have often done, this may be an impossible demand. However, for other cases it is a prudent measure.

The cash flow problem affects even large organizations and is especially painful for independent entrepreneurs. Moreover, if you are charging your expenses to clients at your actual out-of-pocket costs—without markup—you are allowing them the cost-free use of your money, something you can hardly afford to do. To further complicate the situation for you, if you try to overcome the problem by "discounting your paper"—that is, borrowing from the bank with your contracts and/or invoices as collateral or even by assigning your receivables to the bank—you will probably find that banks are reluctant to lend assistance to service businesses in general because service businesses usually have few tangible assets to seize in case of default.

As an independent consultant, you must recognize and avoid clients who manipulate you. There are those who appear to be serious prospects who will unhesitatingly waste huge quantities of your time in preliminary discussions during which they are busily milking you for information, if you permit it, but never retain you. They are manipulating you into free consultation. An even more dangerous manipulative scenario follows.

You are invited to visit the client, who is well situated in a well-furnished office suite in some modern office building. You are favorably impressed with the businesslike atmosphere of what appears to be a successful company.

The well-dressed, affable client greets you cordially, invites you to sit in a comfortable chair, while he offers you coffee and takes an adjoining chair. He smiles, calls you by your first name tentatively, "George—may I call you George?—we have lots of work here, and I can send a lot of business your way." And he is off on a discourse of what marvelous things await you as a result of the good fortune of meeting him.

Once you have reviewed the requirement, you can estimate the probable size of the fee you will require, and you mention it as tactfully as you can, although the new client has not asked you about the cost. (This is itself an omen of possible trouble.)

You are encouraged but because you've been warned you ask, somewhat reluctantly—you don't want to offend this new client—about a retainer. "Sure thing," you're assured, "No problem. Take a few days for the paper work, of course. But in the meanwhile we have to get started on this right away."

Maybe you will get that promised retainer; and maybe you will not. Maybe you will get evasions, excuses, and stalls until it dawns on you that you really have absolutely no assurance that this client can or will pay the bill after you have done the work. In fact, it may be that the client owns absolutely nothing in the office except his briefcase. If you sued and won a judgment you couldn't collect your money. You might make the unpleasant discovery that it is much easier to win in court than to collect what you supposedly won.

WARNING FLAGS

Trouble overtakes the unwary. But how can you be wary unless you know what to be wary of? In the sincere hope that this will help you to avoid having to gain all your practical business education the hard way, here are some signs that should alert you to possible trouble ahead.

Client Indifference to Cost

It is unnatural for any buyer under any circumstances, except possibly the most desperate ones, to be indifferent to cost. The client who asks you what your services are going to cost is revealing a serious interest in and probable contemplation of retaining you. Even if the client is asking your price to compare the cost with that of competitors, it still reflects acceptance of you technically and as a prospective consultant worthy of serious consideration. Most clients do not waste time discussing costs with a consultant who is unacceptable.

If you run into a client who shows definite desire to retain you but is uninterested in the costs, something is probably very wrong. I would be alarmed by that. Clients who agree too readily to my terms and do not even attempt to negotiate alarm me. Perhaps they do not worry about my charges because they have no intention of paying me!

One prospective client called me from California to discuss his need. I suggested he send me some of his material so I could discuss his need more intelligently. He did so, I studied it, and we talked again. He displayed great eagerness to get on with the job, and I waited with a growing sense of unease for him to raise the question of cost. When he did not, I raised it, and he assured me that cost was not an object; he would pay whatever was necessary. That convinced me that we would not do business. But I played out the hand; I stipulated a retainer I would require before going further. I never heard from the gentleman again, which did not surprise me at all.

Beware of the client who professes no interest in cost. Be sure to demand a substantial retainer before proceeding with such a client.

Handshake Contracts

A written contract is not a guarantee of anything, nor is the purpose of a written contract to guarantee anything. Contracts are disputed in courts every day, a certain indicator that they guarantee nothing. Rather, the sole reason for a contract is to submit the agreement to writing in the hope that this will help you to avoid disputes later as to the intent of the two parties—what you and your client actually agreed to. In other words, if either you or your client is not acting in good faith—does not mean to live up to what you agreed on verbally—no written contract is worth signing, and you should not be doing business together.

That does not mean that you should not have a written agreement with your client. However, a lengthy, legal contract is likely to alarm a client and destroy your chances of doing business together. The best approach is to use a simple letter agreement. It commits your agreement to writing and so relieves you of relying on your memory if there are disputes later.

The actual signing of such a simple letter agreement is less important than is the willingness of the client to sign. Beware of a client who balks at signing a simple letter agreement; insist on a substantial advance payment if you decide to continue in the relationship at all.

Handshake contracts can be treacherous. I am suspicious of prospective clients who assure me that their word is their bond and that all we need between us is a handshake to seal our agreement. I am immediately put on guard by the prospect who says, "Trust me." Those are two words that signal danger. When I have allowed clients to overcome my fears and persuade me to vary my policies I have usually come to regret it.

There are times, however, when a handshake agreement is entirely acceptable, but I generally ask the client whether he or she will issue me a purchase order or prefers a letter of agreement. Many large organizations routinely issue purchase orders or letters of confirmation. It is usually the smaller organizations with whom you have to raise the point specifically. Just raising the issue of a written agreement may give you all the information you need.

For example, when you find a client who shows no interest in the cost side of the problem, raising the question of a written agreement helps you tactfully introduce the question of advance payment as a retainer, midpoint payments, and other matters. Perhaps the individual with whom you are talking is not truly authorized to commit the organization. Asking for a purchase order or letter resolves that matter quickly.

Choosing a Midpoint

If you choose to emulate my practice and try to arrange a one-third advance retainer and one-third midpoint payment, you must find some means for defining or identifying a nominal midpoint. That is not always easy to do. I try to set it at the point when I have completed the rough draft of a proposal and have the client's agreement that it is a good draft.

That leaves me with some leverage. The client still needs my services to complete the job properly and has too much invested in me to try to finish the job without my services. The midpoint should be a point at which you have reached a significant milestone and yet a point at which the client still needs you and your services to get the job finished properly. If you succeed in doing this, you are protected for at least two-thirds of your total fee.

If you have difficulty deciding on a midpoint, you may get some help by identifying a series of milestones or objectives for the assignment overall. Then try to select one that comes as close as possible to meeting these criteria:

It occurs well after the beginning and before the end of the project in time. (It is a "midpoint" in a general, not literal sense.)

It represents a major step toward final achievement of the main goal of the assignment.

It leaves you with adequate leverage—the client still needs you and would not be able to finish the project easily without you.

Overtime

Some consultants charge a flat rate by the day and do not count the hours. Others count the hours and charge overtime when they work more than eight hours or on weekends and holidays. Whichever you do, you should have a clear understanding with the client about it, and any written agreement between you should note this carefully.

Progress Payments

For some types of assignments the division of the payments into thirds is not practicable. This is the case, for example, when you are retained on a long-term basis of indefinite duration, such as when you are virtually a contract employee working on the client's premises.

That is not the only such situation. There are others in which the assignment is of indefinite duration—some run into many months, and I have known more than a few to run into several years. Of course it is impossible to estimate the total cost or to fix a midpoint in these cases, and you could hardly wait for many months to collect your fees. In such a situation you must arrange to be given progress payments regularly, at least every month, although weekly or biweekly payments are more usual in such cases.

COLLECTIONS

If it is your good fortune to do business always with clients blessed with AAA credit ratings you may never have a collection problem, although even those with AAA credit ratings can cause you much grief by being agonizingly slow in paying their bills. I have been the victim of well-known large corporations whose bill-paying habits make even the federal government appear to be a fast payer. Fortunately, there are a few things you can do that usually help speed the process.

You must understand that large organizations become somewhat musclebound for a variety of reasons, only one of which is ponderous paperwork and archaic procedures. Those procedures, which in a large organization tend to become enormously detailed, grow up over many layers of management, and violation of these procedures may have serious repercussions. But that is not the entire problem either. One of the greatest problems is the indifference of workers who tend to become bureaucratic in any large organization. And the essence of bureaucracy is that the means is all-important, and the end must be sacrificed to the means when the two conflict. In short, if it is not by the book it simply does not happen. Another typically bureaucratic problem is that only at the highest levels may anyone exercise initiative. (But at the higher levels it is not necessary to exercise initiative!) For example, if the procedure requires three copies of your invoice, but you have supplied only two, the invoice may never move from the in-basket to a payment schedule. Don't expect the clerk to make a copy or to call you; such things happen only rarely. (I once waited eight months for a bill to be paid because of such a problem, unaware that it had not been paid. It would probably have never been paid had I not suddenly discovered the unpaid invoice in our suspense files.)

If you are doing business with a large organization, ask in advance exactly what you must do to get paid and follow the procedure. If at all possible—and it usually is—personally hand your invoice over to your contact. By knowing how the system works you can track down problems of nonpayment much more rapidly.

Payment collection follows a series of steps:

1. Normal billing or submittal of your regular invoice.
2. Statement of money due issued at regular intervals, usually the first or fifteenth day of the month.
3. Courteous form collection letter requesting payment.
4. More insistent, less diplomatic letter.
5. Telephone inquiry, courteous but firm.
6. Severe letter, stipulating firm action, such as legal measures or collection agency, if bill is not paid soon.
7. Matter turned over to collection agency or lawyer.

Of course, you don't want to come to these latter situations, although if the client is resistant to paying you've nothing to lose—you don't want to do business again with such a client. My experience has been that there are few such problems when you discuss payment procedures up front. Still, you can never tell what will happen, even then.

For example, a client came to my office and retained me to prepare a special sales brochure for him. We agreed on a price of $600, and he paid me $300 in advance as a retainer. I prepared several roughs, as I do in such assignments, and we reviewed them together, coming to agreement on which should be developed to its final stage. Shortly after that the client called me and advised me that he had sold his business and wanted to abort the brochure effort. I agreed reluctantly to settle for the money already paid, although I had already done about three-quarters of the work. But the client demanded a refund of the advance retainer! When I refused, he sued me in small claims court. The case lasted about 10 minutes, the judge advising the gentleman that he was lucky to get off for one-half the total fee, under the circumstances. (He, not I, had breached the contract.) Still, the whole affair cost me most of a day sitting in the courtroom waiting for my case to be called, so I was a loser in the whole affair after all, despite being the victor in the case.

It is a good general rule to avoid all litigation, and even all legal expedients, if at all possible. If you turn the matter over to a collection agency or retain a lawyer and sue, it is going to cost you one-third or more of whatever is collected for you. And in civil court the court cannot and will not try to collect for you, even when you win. The court awards you a judgment, which is a hunting license.

Judgments

When you sue and a judge or jury finds for you—that is, enters a judgment for you against the defendant—it does not mean that the defendant will then pay you. You have won a legal battle, but that does not mean that you have won the war for your money. Probably a well-established firm will pay at that point, but you may be up against a defendant who will refuse to pay willingly even then, thinking that he or she is "judgment proof." That means that the defendant thinks he or she has the assets so well hidden or protected by legal dodges that you will not be able to use that judgment to seize the funds and/or property. I have reluctantly allowed some legal debts to go uncollected because I knew that I could win a judgment but would be most unlikely to be able to satisfy it, and in some cases I settled for far less than the total amount for the same reason. It is certainly far better to take any steps possible to minimize the probability of having collection problems.

Credit Ratings

You can subscribe to a credit rating service, of course, and get a rating on any client with whom you wish to do business. However, there are two problems with that: (1) you are likely to find that some of your clients or prospective clients have no ratings established, or (2) you may find that a client who enjoys a good credit rating is a slow or reluctant payer of bills or contests every bill, bullying vendors into settling for less than the full amount. Again, the advantage of getting a retainer in advance is a far better credit rating than any agency or bureau report.

Mechanic's Lien

The law provides that a mechanic (i.e., a professional, a craftsman) may hold your property that he or she has repaired pending payment of your bill. If you fail or refuse to pay, the mechanic may take measures leading to selling your property to satisfy the bill.

As consultant, you could conceivably be in the position of the mechanic, with the client's property (e.g., a computer program you have been working on) in your possession. This does not give you the right to seize a client's property, however, or to reclaim property that you have returned to the client. You must consult a lawyer in the specific case.

SUMMARY

My experience has been that there is a great deal of consulting work available for any consultant who wants to work for nothing or is willing to allow himself or herself to be so used. Perhaps it is inevitable that many of us must learn the hard way that honest clients will never object seriously to your being businesslike in an objective way; those who do object to sound business practices are almost surely clients you are much better off without. I am convinced that I never lost a worthwhile client or anything else worth having by being courteously and impersonally, but firmly, businesslike. It was when I failed to be businesslike that I lost time and money I could not afford to lose.

13

Consultant Skills You Need and How To Develop Them

The inherent anomaly of consulting is that clients want your services as a specialist, and yet, as an independent practitioner, you must rely on yourself for all the ancillary skills and functions, which then requires you to be a generalist!

CONSULTING: BUSINESS OR PROFESSION?

The question of whether consulting is a business or a profession may have more than a bit of significance academically and may, in fact, ultimately have a decisive effect on the consultant's standing, influence, and even income. But those of us who are actively engaged in consulting on an independent basis must face the realities. Consultants are engaged in both a profession and a business. While we provide a number of highly specialized services of a professional nature to our clients, we must also provide business services to our clients and for ourselves—marketing, accounting, invoicing, and the general services of management and administration. Nor is even that the whole story. The complexities of independent consulting go well beyond that.

THE SETS OF SKILLS

Successful consultants must not only possess strong technical and managerial/administrative skills, they must be skillful as an entrepreneur. In some respects the entrepreneurial skills are even more significant than are the others referred to, for it is an entrepreneurial adventure that you embark upon when you set out to establish yourself as an independent consultant, and your entrepreneurship is going to be the principal influence—probably by far the deciding factor—in the future of your consulting venture.

You must be the master of all three sets of services. Your survival as an independent consultant depends on it. You must have the managerial/administrative skills to not only deliver your basic consulting services, but also those necessary for success in conceiving, organizing, and operating those ancillary functions that broaden your income base adequately. For example, I consider writing and public speaking to be essential skills in delivering your basic consulting services, but they are also at least as important in adding profit centers—income producers—to your practice. Repeatedly, in delivering your basic consulting services, enterprising independent consultants have done this with great success, not only building successful practices but often expanding them into even larger and more ambitious ventures. Here are just a few examples of such entrepreneurial successes.

J. Stephen Lanning, a Maryland marketing consultant, launched the popular newsletter Consulting Opportunities Journal and has since made it the centerpiece of his activities, which include other publications and services for consultants.

Dr. Jeffrey Lant, a Cambridge, Massachusetts consultant, has written and published so many volumes on the how-to of consulting and its related activities as to make it difficult to believe that he has much time left for consulting itself, although he is still quite active as a speaker and in other related activities. (He is his own publisher, as JLA Publications.)

Hubert Bermont, a Florida book-publishing consultant spends most of his time attending to the publishing company, the Consultant's Library, that he established a few years ago after the success of his own books on the art and business of consulting.

Howard Shenson, a California consultant, spent more and more time on traveling the country delivering seminars on the how-to of independent consulting, during which sessions he sold many of the books published by The Consultant's Library (some of which he had written himself), and now we see others delivering seminars originally developed by Shenson and presumably now licensed to others by him.

Audrey Wyatt, a Virginia consultant, founded a consultants' association, the American Consultants League, the management of which dominates her busy schedule.

In my own case my consulting service expanded rapidly into seminars and writing, especially the latter, which now occupy much of my time as natural extensions of and integral components in my consulting service. I have, in fact, been compelled recently to go to a much larger computer and peripheral hardware and software system to support my steadily expanding writing activites.

PUBLIC SPEAKING

A great many people fear public speaking. Even the most experienced and most highly respected executives, professionals, and other successful individuals are often terror-stricken at the thought of facing even a small audience, let alone a large one. For that matter, even professional speakers and performers often confess to experiencing fear and nervousness every time they must mount the platform, and they must somehow drive themselves each time to the task of once again facing an audience. So you may or may not "get used to it," to be perfectly honest about it–at least, you may or may not get completely over your fears of facing a large room full of strangers, all of them intent on your words, your gestures, and your facial expressions. On the other hand, most speakers do eventually overcome their fears, if, indeed, they ever had them, for there are, indeed, some fortunate people who have never had any serious trepidations about appearing as the center of attention.

THE NOTION OF "BORN SPEAKERS"

You may have had the notion that there are "born speakers," as there are "born salespeople," and "born artists." If there are any such, they are in exceedingly rare supply; for all practical purposes even the most gifted speakers are those who have worked hard to learn to speak well and appear to be completely at ease. Probably the notion of the "born speaker" arises from the fact that some individuals are blessed with naturally "good" voices for public speaking—strong, resonant, clear, and pleasant-sounding voices.

Yet some quite successful public speakers have voices that are not at all inherently well-suited to speaking. One prominent broadcaster (Barbara Walters) who is probably best known for her ability to persuade public figures to allow her to interview them, has a reedy, shrill voice that some find rather unpleasant, and a pronounced lisp. Dave Yoho, a successful professional speaker with a marvelous speaking voice, relates his struggles to overcome his speech defects as a youngster, while stuttering has not prevented singer/comedian Mel Tillis from becoming successful in public appearances.

Anyone can learn to speak well, and even natural handicaps cannot prevent the determined individual from becoming successful on the platform.

Actually, the key to overcoming fear of public speaking is identifying and facing the basis of the fear. If you fear appearing foolish, take steps to ensure that you cannot appear foolish by being sure that you have something to say and that you are well prepared to say it. But don't memorize your speech, for that is the most difficult thing to deliver without anaesthetizing your audience. Instead, use an outline that lists your main objectives and key points, arranged in some logical order that leads to your main point. You will almost always do far better speaking extemporaneously with such aids than you would reading a written speech or reciting one from memory.

Be enthusiastic and don't be afraid to show that enthusiasm; it's contagious, and it compensates for many things that might be lacking, such as the professional polish that comes only with years of experience on the dais. Avoid any subject about which you are unable to be enthusiastic.

Make sure that you are dressed properly, and the best insurance here is to be conservative; you can never go wrong that way. Wear conventional clothes, with a minimum of flashy jewelry. Attendees may notice your wardrobe before they notice your message.

Don't try to be a comedian. You must be yourself if you are to get your message across successfully.

Have a proper feeling for and attitude toward your audience. They are not your enemies. Quite the contrary; they want you to succeed.

Don't be afraid to gesture freely, smile, scowl, pause, shout, whisper, and otherwise act out your material, as necessary. That, together with enthusiasm, is the real secret of being a smash hit on the platform. You are a performer, or you should be, and your audience wants to be diverted as much as they want to be informed. Even not having a great deal to say that is worth hearing will be forgiven if you are a sufficiently forceful or entertaining speaker.

Planning the Presentation

Presentations must be well prepared. It doesn't matter whether you write out your presentation in full text, memorize it, use notes, carry an outline, or use a set of cue cards, it is the act of preparation that ensures against disaster.

I find in my own case that I do not use the same method for each situation. That is partly because I do not always deliver the same material, and quite naturally I need more planning, preparation, and guidance material for a presentation that I have not delivered before or, at least, not as often as those others for which I require very little advance preparation. In the latter case I need only the sketchiest of notes and those primarily to ensure that I do not, in my enthusiasm, forget to make key points. On the other hand, I have sometimes prepared a full lecture guide for myself when I am breaking in an entirely new presentation.

Of course, you must use the method that is right for you. If you are new to public speaking, it might be best to prepare a full lecture guide. If you get so nervous that you forget everything, you can at least read your presentation. That's better than stumbling along aimlessly. Many public speakers use this method successfully, but they have usually invested time in rehearsing carefully. Some even make notations on paper of where and when to pause, make gestures, whisper, shout, smile, and otherwise supplement and dramatize the material. But if you are truly highly enthusiastic about your subject you will probably not need such cues. True enthusiasm causes you to forget about your anxieties, and you make all the stagy gestures and inflections unconsciously. That is by far the most effective way to make any presentation, but planning is still necessary.

Goals and Objectives

Presentations, written or oral, fall into certain broad categories, defined by a general goal or theme, such as one of the following:

How to solve a problem of some sort
How something works
How something came about (history, causes, origins, etc.)
New developments in a given field of interest
How to do something
Arguments for or against something
Reporting on a project, new developments, new views, etc.
Organizing a group or an effort
Leading a discussion
Offering a demonstration
Introducing another speaker
Presenting an award
Warming up an audience

Aside from these general goals, which reflect only broad categories, you need to have a specific objective or set of objectives when you are planning a presentation. When I offer a seminar on marketing to the federal government, for example, my general goal is to teach my audience both the basic philosophy of marketing successfully to government agencies and the art of preparing bids and proposals, the two key instruments for winning government contracts. But I also have many specific objectives outlined, each of them a milestone marking progress along the road leading to the achievement of the broad goals.

The Beginning

You must let your audience know what your goal is and how you will approach the subject generally, and you should do so as early in the presentation as possible. The introduction should make that clear.

For example, when I present a seminar on proposal writing I start by defining what a proposal is in such a way as to make the general philosophy and theme of the seminar plainly apparent. I make it clear that a proposal is a sales presentation and that we will keep that definition clearly and unequivocally in mind as our standard. I make it clear that the chief ingredient of success in a proposal is sales strategy, and that excellent writing skills help greatly, but only if effective sales strategies and techniques are present. I make it abundantly clear that we are going to talk about winning and whatever is required for that. From the beginning my listeners know the general goals and themes of my discussion.

An Opening

An oral presentation benefits from an opening attention-getter just as a written presentation does. Many performers and professional speakers therefore open with something humorous or novel. This not only gets attention, it also assures your listeners that you are not going to be dull and so creates a receptive mood, which is a decided asset to you as a speaker.

You do not have to tell jokes to get attention and set the mood. There are other ways to get attention at once and be interesting.

Ask a key question, one that addresses the very heart of your presentation. It can be a rhetorical question, one that you are going to answer yourself, such as "What is a proposal? Let's think about that for a few minutes." On the other hand, it can be a question that you do wish attendees to respond to with their ideas. You may have to smile reassuringly and urge them a bit, but inducing their responses can be an effective way of arousing interest immediately and setting the stage for your presentation.

Start your presentation with an amusing or novel anecdote. Do a little advance research and try to come up with an appropriate story.

Use "startling statistics." Did you know, for example, that there are 79,913 governments in the United States, according to the U.S. Census Bureau? Or that nearly one-third of all our citizens receive some form of federal assistance?

Use the unexpected. Did you know, for example, that in many cases making sales to the government is the easy part; the hard part is finding the right doors, behind which government officials are waiting eagerly to buy your goods and services?

Reveal or promise to reveal insider information about your subject, especially information that has been deliberately kept secret.

Reveal or promise to reveal the very latest information on the subject; information too recent to have reached conventional channels.

Open with an apparent anomaly, such as this: Charles Kettering knew as well as other engineers that the self-starter for automobiles was an impossibility. But when Ransome Olds, original builder of the Oldsmobile, hired him to invent one, Kettering knew that he was going to find a way to do the impossible.

Use a gimmick. It can be quite effective when used properly; but be careful, it can backfire. If you place a wrapped package or an apparently strange object on a table with what is quite deliberate and great care before you begin to speak and then carefully ignore it during the early stages of your presentation, you'll arouse a great deal of curiosity. But you must not wait too long to reveal what it is, for it is a distraction that can weaken your presentation if it goes on too long. It must also be related directly to your presentation or your audience will feel that they have been tricked, and they will not like that.

Of course, the opener must lead smoothly into your theme, to which you now proceed. The introduction gives your listeners a road map, telling them in unmistakable terms what it is that you promise to do or reveal with some idea of your overall theme.

The Middle

Now it is time to deliver on the promise made in your introduction. The level of detail varies according to what you are trying to accomplish, the amount of time you have, and the scope of the subject. In my own case I would focus on bids and federal supply schedules, rather than on proposals if I were addressing a group of suppliers who would rarely be required to write proposals in competing for government business. I would focus on special programs for minority-owned ventures if addressing a group of minority businesspeople. It is important to use information relating to the special interests of your audience. Make a point to learn as much as possible about the audience when preparing your presentation. Ask questions of whomever is arranging your appearance, and collect annual reports, brochures, and other literature about the organization. It is both far more useful and far more interesting to your audience to talk to them in terms of their direct and immediate interests than in the abstract. If listeners must translate your generalized examples into their own needs and applications, you may lose a large part of your audience. Regardless of the type of presentation you are making, do what is necessary to learn what the direct interests of your audience are and try to relate your presentation to those interests as much as possible.

Ending

In some respects, closing your presentation is similar to your opening. The conventional close summarizes and reinforces your key points. However, a great deal depends on what kind of presentation you have been making. A logical argument for or against something is generally ended by summing up the facts presented and offering the logical conclusion. An emotional argument is ended by an emotional exhortation that iterates the primary pro or con positions. A how-to is often ended by inviting questions from the audience. However, whatever the case, it is proper form to thank your audience for their attention and patience, and if they choose to applaud, thank them again when the applause subsides.

A FEW PRESENTATION PRINCIPLES

Language is a first consideration in all presentations, whether written or oral. Unless you are understood clearly—unless the message received is the same as the message sent—your presentation cannot be a complete success.

Fortunately, with today's communications (e.g. telephone, radio, and TV for both voice and data) and today's travel—we travel freely, quickly, and often all over the country—regional differences in our

American versions of English are fewer than they once were. If you are a native of Philadelphia, as I am, you must try to remember that in Chicago you must ask for a "sweet roll" when you want what you learned to call a "coffee cake" and what is called in some other places a "Danish." A "soda" becomes a "pop" in New York and a "phosphate" in Chicago. And if you are in some place where hardly anyone is a native, such as Miami, the complications in such matters multiply considerably.

But these are minor difficulties compared with the general uses and misuses of English in America. A remarkably rich language, at least partly due to extensive borrowing from more than a few other languages, there are probably about one million words in the language, divided into two roughly equal halves, one of general words and the other of technical terms.

On the other hand, the size of the average individual's vocabulary ranges roughly between 12,000 and 15,000 words, with 20,000 words considered to be quite a large vocabulary. (However, it is not at all unusual for individuals to have vocabularies of less than 10,000 words.) Some scholars, writers, and others have vocabularies ranging to 40,000 words or above. These are unusually large vocabularies, and quite obviously, considering these few statistics, the latter individuals must avoid more than one-half their vocabularies in writing and speaking if they want to be understood completely by the average reader or listener.

Most of us have two vocabularies, our speaking/hearing vocabulary and our reading vocabulary. Our reading vocabulary is normally larger than our speaking vocabulary, however, and you should keep that in mind and be even more careful when preparing an oral presentation than when writing.

This is not to say that the possession of an unusually large vocabulary is a disadvantage or handicap—unless you permit it to be one. A large vocabulary is a marvelous tool for reasoning and for organizing information to be presented. You should prepare the draft of your presentation with whatever words come to mind as most appropriate, most definitive, and most suitable generally, without regard to your prospective reader's or listener's vocabulary. When you edit and revise your draft into the final document you can eliminate all those "big words"–the terms that are more likely to prevent communication than to further it. Remember that most people can handle more words in reading than in listening because of the greater size of their reading vocabulary and because they can reread written material to infer meanings from context. During editing and revision processes, try to find and use the simplest possible words and terms, and try to eliminate all the pompous and unnecessary phrases. Here are just a few examples; the original words or terms are in the left-hand column, and suggested replacements are in the right-hand column:

in order to	to
comprise	contain, include
epitome	essence, representative
mendacious	lying, untruthful
luminous	glowing
for the purpose of	to, for
utilize	use

Avoid also those awful cliches, words, and phrases that are redundant or grammatically incorrect or that have been so overused that they are stale. These include:

bottom line	point in time
along these lines	cutting edge
fallout	few and far between
goes without saying	in-depth
richly rewarding	matter of course
safe to say	all in all
state of the art	spin-off
mind over matter	be that as it may

Use words correctly. Just a little carelessness can produce ludicrous and embarrassing results. One technical writer, for example, referred to the "duplicity" of the circuits when he meant "duplication" or redundancy, and "assignation" when he meant "assignment." Use a dictionary whenever you are not absolutely sure that the word you are using is the right one, and use a grammar text when you are not absolutely sure about your constructions. Even better, use a professional editor if at all possible. It will save your time and help you produce a thoroughly professional result.

Communication Is Really Persuasion

Understanding stems from an acceptance of or *belief* in the premises. Belief must come first. If we wish to communicate clearly, we must understand the art of convincing others—that is, inspiring their confidence and persuading them to *believe* as we *believe*. In short, to communicate effectively you must be persuasive first and logical second. Yes, most people want logical explanations—rationales—to support what they wish to believe, but they will reject logic that is contrary to that which they wish passionately to believe. Only persuasive techniques stand any chance of overcoming bias.

Most people are strongly biased about only a few things, and even those are often predictable. It is predictable, for example, that many factory workers will be biased in favor of labor unions because their personal interests are at stake; it is in their interests—or at least they perceive it to be in their interests—to be so biased. But they may not be strongly biased about other things and will be willing to listen or read and be *persuaded*.

The basis of all persuasion is to make the other party perceive it as in his or her interest to believe you. Many people will believe the most extravagant promises if you furnish enough supporting data that they find acceptable as evidence or proof and if your presentation is attractive enough—that is, if they want to believe you.

Your ability to persuade an audience is also affected by how you are perceived. If an audience finds you offensive in any way—and that applies to your written presentations as well as to those you deliver personally—they tend to reject what you say. I have witnessed quite excellent speakers with good material strike out with audiences because they somehow managed to come across as arrogant, sneering, boorish, or otherwise offensive. One man overdid his use of the first person, for example, which made him appear boastful and vain. Another came across as smug and condescending. Even if you do not appear offensive, failing to gain their respect has the same devastating effect.

This is one reason why efforts to be a comedian are so dangerous. Any humor that denigrates a class or type of person is dangerous. Even expert comedians are on dangerous ground when the laugh is at the expense of any identifiable group or kind of person—ethnic, religious, political, or other. Even a humorous anecdote about your mother can bring down on your head the wrath of those who think you are insulting mothers generally. If you must try for laughs, make yourself the butt of your jokes. I do occasionally relate humorous stories, but the joke is always on me. I'm the expert who got to be that way by making all the stupid mistakes, and I gleefully relate a few of my most humorous blunders. I often tell audiences about how contracts are sometimes "wired" for favored bidders, but to demonstrate that this is not foolproof I sheepishly admit that I managed to lose a contract that was wired for me and explain how.

A story of this type has a positive effect. It tends to make you likable because you admit your human weaknesses and you are not ashamed to laugh at yourself.

Techniques

When you are facing an audience, remember the following techniques:

Don't display nervous habits such as fidgeting, pulling an ear lobe, playing with keys, drumming your fingers on the lectern, or other such little habits. Aside from what they can do to your image generally, they can become both distracting and quite irritating to an audience who must hear and watch you for several hours.

Don't slouch, lean against the wall, or show other signs of boredom or weariness.

Don't try to explain with words alone. Make use of a blackboard, posters, slides, transparencies, models, handouts, or whatever other aids are suitable and available. They are a change of pace for your audience and a stress reliever for you.

When the presentation is to last for hours and the choice is yours, make your audience more comfortable by using a classroom style (i.e., chairs at tables) instead of theatre style (i.e., rows of chairs). Remember to give breaks, too.

Meet people's eyes as you speak, but do not focus on any one in particular. This might make that individual uneasy and might offend others.

Don't try to speak in public as you do in private. Most of us speak disjointedly in casual conversation, often with such interjections as "Y'know," "uhhhh," "uh-huh," and sentence fragments. These are taboo in public speaking.

Remember to leave the comedy to the professional comedians.

Show your respect and affection for your audience. They want you to succeed in being a good speaker. Relax, smile, and enjoy talking with a roomful of friendly people.

Learn how to stop when you are finished. Stick to your schedule. Don't allow the one-hour lecture to become two hours. Let the audience know that you have finished, ask for questions if appropriate, and thank them.

You will be pleasantly surprised at how soon you will begin to feel comfortable and actually enjoy talking to those who came to hear what you have to say.

Making Slides and Transparencies

With today's 35mm cameras almost anyone can shoot high quality slides at a reasonable cost. Unless you have quite special needs, you can usually make up your own set of slides to use in presentations from the platform.

However, you may find transparencies even more convenient to use than slides. Transparencies can be made on most office copiers, and even if you do not have a copier of your own you can generally arrange to have a nearby copy shop do this for you. The personal computer can also generate the copy you need for transparencies. Today's computers, with their large memories and sophisticated software have an abundance of typefaces, headlines, banners, forms, and clip art for designing transparencies, and can even print out the actual transparencies as well.

WRITING SKILLS FOR THE CONSULTANT

The previous discussion on public speaking also applies to or has its counterpart in writing. You may be able to avoid or at least to minimize making formal presentations from the speaker's platform, but you will have to write a great deal in pursuing your consulting career. In fact, hardly anyone in the business world today can avoid the necessity for writing frequently. The frequently cited "information explosion" and "paper explosion" are not something that happened to someone else; they happened to you and me, and they continue to happen to have have pronounced effects and influence on what we do. And we must not underestimate the enduring role of paper as the principal medium either computers have an enormous impact on our world and make a great difference in how we do things. Still, despite the enormous proliferation of computers and the vast archives of information stored in computer media, storing data in paper archives continues to grow. (In fact, the technological advances and growth that have put computers on desks in almost every office today is itself at least partially responsible for the swelling in paper.) Our knowledge is advancing exponentially in every field—even the meaning of "well educated" has grown dramatically—and it is all transcribed somewhere on paper.

Consider that about 85 percent of all scientists who ever walked this planet are alive today. This is true in many other professions as well—medicine, psychology, sociology, economics, and others. The sheer volume of the new information generated by these professionals inspires and demands the generation of more paper documents. The steadily growing complexity of our knowledge and, for that matter, of our systems demand more and more documentation. Millions of word processors alone are spewing out reports, manuals, proposals, specifications, books, texts, seminar programs, lecture guides, and countless other records and manuscripts written to record, to report, to inform, to document, to educate, and to train. If anything, the availability of computers and word processors have accelerated the growth of information on paper.

Efficiency of the Written Word

An oral presentation reaches a limited audience, even if repeated a number of times. (Tape recordings of oral presentations are sometimes made to preserve the presentations, but they lack the visual elements of the original session.) However, written presentations can be reviewed and studied repeatedly and indefinitely. There is no limit to the number of people who can be reached by a written presentation.

Even the information archives that exist on computer disks and tapes are useless for practical purposes of transmitting information to people until projected on screens or printed out on paper, both severe limitations in their utility. The written word is still the most efficient way to disseminate information, as well as to record it, study it, and use it.

Details and Precision

Written accounts must be as accurate as possible, even more so than formal oral presentations. The written account is a permanent and unchanging record. Misstatements and inaccuracies in a written account will return to haunt you, whereas they are forgiven and often even unnoticed in an oral presentation. This is especially true of a formal written record, such as a technical manual, progress report, or textbook. Readers expect to find gross inaccuracies in newspaper accounts, for example, given the nature of newspaper data gathering and writing, and they forgive these. They are far less forgiving of errors or lack of precision when something much more important than idle curiosity depends on their reading of the document.

Since writing is an integral part of the consulting service, precision and attention to detail in your writing affects the quality and effectiveness of that service. It also reflects on your professional image, which affects the probability that clients will recommend you to others. To quite a large degree your client will judge your professionalism and competence as much or almost as much by what and how you write, as by what you say and how you handle yourself in face-to-face exchanges and the actual results of your work.

Usage

You do not have to be an accomplished master of polished and elegant phrases to be a successful consultant, but you must be able to construct well-organized writing to produce documents that accomplish your purposes accurately and efficiently—documents that are thoroughly professional, that is.

This requires that you master at least the basics of usage and, even more important that you know how to organize a written presentation of each type. If you are in doubt about correct usage, unabridged dictionaries and other references serve as excellent resources. Or you may turn to a skilled editor for assistance. Editing can rather easily correct weaknesses in spelling, grammar, punctuation, and rhetoric; however, it cannot help serious defects in basic planning and execution (i.e., concepts, organization, and construction). That requires rewriting, not editing. Not even "heavy" editing will salvage poorly planned or poorly executed writing.

Therefore the emphasis for the remainder of this chapter will be on those latter subjects, rather than on the basic verities of English-language usage. And, incidentally, it is not absolutely necessary for most purposes to keep a separate text on usage at hand. Many good dictionaries include excellent front matter and back matter on usage and other important subjects, features that are adequate, usually, to help you find the answers to questions of usage. *The American College Dictionary* (Random House) Includes such material, for example, as do *Webster's Seventh New College Dictionary* (G. & C. Merriam Company), *WEBSTER'S NEW WORLD DICTIONARY* (Simon and Schuster), and the *New Comprehensive International Dictionary* (Funk & Wagnalls). I keep these volumes in my own office, and they have been valuable for much more than defining words and their correct spelling. Disputes over which is the best dictionary seem to rage constantly (whatever "best" means in this case), which is one reason I keep more than one dictionary at hand and often consult more than one when I am in doubt. It is an excellent idea to have an unabridged dictionary in your office, as well.

Conception and Initial Planning

Every activity has a purpose, whether we call it a *purpose*, *goal*, or an *objective*. However, we sometimes undertake activities without knowing what that purpose is. In short, we sometimes do not know ourselves why we are doing something!

If you are required to write a report but you do not know precisely the uses to which such a report will be put, you will be unable to plan that report well. Even if you do know the purpose of the report, planning that report means remembering who your client is.

Clients and Patrons or *True* Clients

The nominal client is the organization itself, of course. However, if you had a patron in the organization—that is, someone who helped you to win the contract—you should regard that person as the true client. You must consider the interests and concerns of that individual when you set goals and objectives and submit strategies for the client's organization not only out of loyalty to your true client but as a way of protecting your own interests. You must do everything you can not only to prove that you are not a threat to any individual on the staff but to prove that you actually enhance that individual's image in his or her own organization.

Perhaps it has never occurred to you that a great many employees of organizations actually have a fear of consultants. Or perhaps you have experienced or sensed some hostility from employees when working on the client's premises alongside employees, but you never realized that the hostility is the result of fear—the fear that management feels staff employees are not competent in some area. This is a serious marketing problem for consultants.

The sales manager feels threatened by a sales consultant who can help train a sales force for higher productivity. The comptroller is not fond of the idea of retaining a consultant in financial management, nor is the production manager happy about "an outsider" coming in to help organize or improve inventory control. So many executives and others are almost automatically hostile to the idea of hiring consultants, insisting stubbornly that the consultants cannot supply anything that they, the employees, do not already provide the organization.

Enhancing your patron's image is one way to show you are not a threat to staff employees. For example, there is always the temptation when writing a report as an outside consultant to maximize the importance of your own role, as well as the magnitude of your achievements as a consultant to the organization. But you will be a far more judicious consultant if you are self-effacing and maximize the importance of your patron in preparing reports and other documents for your consulting project.

When the head of marketing in one company retained me to help with a proposal, he was my patron and my client. My job was to be virtually his alter ego, doing a job that would reflect credit on him. When an engineer in that same firm was assigned to develop a proposal later and arranged to have a purchase order issued to me for services, he became my client, and I worked at giving him the best proposal and making sure that he saw, reviewed, and approved all copy before it went to management for review and approval. (Interestingly enough, that engineer was one involved in the earlier proposal and gave me the greatest amount of difficulty in that project, but apparently was impressed enough with the earlier work to bring me back to help with the proposal assigned to him. He was much easier to work with the second time.)

When planning your writing consider both the nominal purpose of the document and how that may affect your client and your relationship with your client. Even a client on whom your services have been imposed against his or her wishes can be won over if you are wise enough in your writing, as well as in your face-to-face relationships, to do everything possible to further your client's interests.

Nature of the Deliverable Item

Every consulting project has a deliverable item of some sort. In some cases the goal of the project is a tangible deliverable item (e.g., a training manual, a computer program, etc.). In other cases the goal of the project is intangible (e.g., a service), but its delivery is accompanied by a tangible item that represents the service delivered (e.g., a written report documenting the service).

In most of my own consulting projects, there is a definite tangible, physical product required, which is itself the purpose of the project—that is, a proposal. On the other hand I am also called on to deliver training seminars, and it is the presentation of that seminar—my lecturing on the subject—that is the deliverable item. But the client requires something tangible too, something that justifies the cost. In the case of my custom seminars the tangible item is the substantial seminar manual I provide. Computer consultants may be asked to produce and deliver a specific program. In this case the two tangible deliverable items will be: (1) the program itself, probably as a tape, and (2) the documentation, probably in both tape or disk and hard copy printout.

In many other cases, such as one in which I assisted an EPA contractor in value engineering EPA's municipal water-treatment grants program, the value engineering assistance was the deliverable service, but the client required a written report as a tangible item to document and justify the project.

Most consulting projects thus require some document as representative of the final deliverable item. In cases of long-term projects, interim documents are required, most commonly progress reports or drafts of final reports.

The Writing Cycle

Writers and others engaged full-time and professionally in all the relevant editorial functions have their own sets of platitudes reflecting the conventional wisdom of the profession. Several of those platitudes reflect the philosophy that good writing is invariably rewriting—that is, a really good first draft is by far the rare exception.

That is the basis for one of the distinguishing features of the truly professional writer or, at least, the professional attitude toward writing. Professional writers accept and operate on the premise that everything they write must undergo the draft/edit/rewrite phases for at least one complete cycle (and many writers are not satisfied with only one cycle of editing and rewriting, but go through several or even many such cycles). The belief that one can write well in a first draft is usually the hallmark of the novice and, unfortunately, a novice who does not write really well. Although there are occasional rare exceptions, it would be foolish to expect to be one of those exceptions!

Editing, as used here, refers to editing by a person other than the writer, preferably a fully qualified and experienced professional editor. Careful writers do a great deal of rewriting before the editor sees the first draft, but it is difficult to be as objective about your own copy as another can be. So although self-editing should be done by every writer, it does not take the place of full-scale, formal editing by another.

Good editing almost invariably reduces the bulk of the draft manuscript by about one-third. Most writers overwrite in their first drafts, and one of the functions of a good editor is to tighten up the manuscript by filtering out the unnecessary redundancies, unneeded and irrelevant details, and other excesses.

In actuality, overwriting is a good practice and is often encouraged, although it *must* be followed by conscientious editing. It is a good practice because it permits both writer and editor to study the material and decide, in a second look, what to keep and what to discard. That is, writers are often encouraged to get it all down on paper and decide later what is most important, most useful, and most effective in meeting the goals and objectives.

There are many writers who do write tight first drafts because they have done scrupulous self-editing, a process that is greatly facilitated by word processing capabilities. What computers and word processors (which are software programs, not hardware) do in automating certain repetitive and tedious chores is insignificant when compared with the reorganization and many revision capabilities it allows. The widespread practice of using typists to enter handwritten or typed manuscript is almost tragic. Writers must work at the keyboard to gain the true benefits of word processing, which improve the very *quality* of writing when used properly. Nor is the common excuse of some that they are not trained typists a valid one. I and many others turn out a stream of books and other manuscripts with two fingers!

Good writers understand that "writing" is not confined to words alone, but includes all relevant aids to communicating the information to the reader. That is, necessary illustrations are the writer's responsibility, for a good writer does not illustrate his or her words, but uses whatever is the most effective and/or most efficient medium for conveying the message (e.g., photographs, line drawings, renderings, charts, graphs, tables, etc.). The writer must decide where illustrations are necessary—where words alone cannot do the job or, at least, cannot do it nearly as well as an illustration of some sort can do—and conceive or find suitable illustrations, make sketches, or otherwise define the need to a specialist, such as a photographer or artist.

Good illustrations should not supplement extensive and tedious text passages; they should replace them. If an illustration cannot "displace its own weight" in words, it is not a good illustration; it does not do the job. The best illustrations require little supporting text. You should use that as a yardstick in evaluating or appraising illustrations.

Writing, then, is an all-inclusive word that involves far more than writing per se. In fact, writing itself is probably not more than one-third of the total effort and is, in many cases, a far lesser portion of the total than even that. There is also planning, research, illustrating, editing, and, in most of the situations we are contemplating, production to be considered. Moreover, much of it is iterative. Even with a well-devised and detailed plan, initial research may turn up information that compels you to revise your plan, or you may have to do research before you can even begin to do any serious planning.

Steps in Development

The development of any written instrument follows a logical progression, beginning with need or purpose. What do you wish the written instrument to be or do? That can be any of a wide variety of things, including (but not restricted to) the following:

Log the project chronologically and logically
Justify the effort and its cost
Guide future researchers
Provide useful information
Report specific advances
Provide how-to guidance
Provide reference data
Inform stockholders
Inform the public
Provide input for a prospectus
Study a problem

This is a first step in defining what you must do. You must actually progress through the development of an entire hierarchy of definitions before you can do very much actual work on the development of a manuscript. You must also identify clearly both your overall goal (e.g., train, advise, argue, document, etc.) and product (e.g., manual, proposal, report, etc.). That done, you must develop a working plan, preferably in formal outline format, to include the following main items:

Set of objectives
Content outline
Format
Illustrations
Schedule

The schedule should include projected times or dates for at least the following items:

Start
Draft completion
Review of first draft
Revision, rewrites
Second review

Final reviews
Production and delivery

Execution

Writing itself can be relatively easy or it can be quite difficult, depending primarily on how thorough and detailed both the basic research and the planning have been. The more thorough the planning—especially the research—the easier it is to piece all the information together coherently. On the other hand, if you have not planned thoroughly, and especially if you have not researched you subject thoroughly, you may expect to be forced to do a great deal of improvising. This is likely to affect the continuity of the final product and make it difficult to produce an acceptable product without extensive editing and revision. Time spent in thorough planning and preparation saves time and helps you produce a better product. The true difficulty in writing and almost certainly the most common cause of bad writing is the lack of preparation. Thinking the matter through thoroughly covers the planning and preparation stages in this case. Even a short, informal document—perhaps a proposal of only a few pages—for which there is no need of extensive formal research and planning, requires mental preparation. Thinking the matter through thoroughly covers the planning and preparation stages in this case. Preparation is not only important for writers detailing subjects about which they have little expertise; it is also important for someone writing on a subject in which he or she is already expert—that is, developing a manuscript for which the writer requires little or no research. Too often the writer is overconfident in his or her expert knowledge and neglects to think the project through. Again and again in leading writing groups, I have found that "bad" writing was not due to any basic inability of the writer to use the language effectively, but was due to the failure to know just what he or she wanted to say; the writer had simply neglected to really *think* about the subject and identify a goal and a set of objectives. It is quite easy to deceive yourself into believing that you know the subject so well that you do not have to "waste" time in research or planning.

Sometimes we even lure ourselves into believing that the ability to memorize and recite certain facts or to use certain jargon demonstrates understanding and mastery of the subject. The training field, for example, tends to be dominated by behaviorists, who insist that training programs must be based on *behavioral objectives*, which are defined as statements of what the trainee must be able to do as a result of the training. Yet, when a section of a training plan offered a list of things the trainee would be able to do as a result of the training, a professional educational technologist complained about the lack of behavioral objectives because he did not see those words used. That indicated that he was dealing in jargon and not in ideas.

A reasonable test or proof of understanding is the ability to explain the concept to someone else, someone who is totally unfamiliar with the subject. Perhaps it is necessary to use the jargon (especially in technical fields) to demonstrate that you are a professional and an expert, but be sure that the use of the jargon is incidental and not central in the manuscript, especially that knowledge of the jargon is not an essential for understanding the document. In fact, another test of true understanding is the ability to translate that jargon accurately into everyday English and into concepts that anyone can understand. That is the job of the writer and the main goal of the document, in many cases.

Don't be misled by the frequently heard advice to use short sentences and short words either, for many short words are uncommon words, and being short does not help anyone understand them. For example, if you tell the average individual that the earth is an oblate spheroid, it is not likely that you will paint an accurate image in many minds, for not many people know just what those words mean. If you tell them that the earth is a globe, but slightly flattened at the poles, something like an orange, they will "get the picture" quite easily.

Use the ability to translate jargon and concepts this way as a yardstick by which to measure your own readiness to begin writing. If you are unable to make the translation easily, do a little more basic research into the subject. You are quite likely to discover that you did not know the subject quite as well as you thought you did! I am quite skeptical when I hear someone say, "I understand it, but I can't explain it," or, "You wouldn't be able to understand this."

Many professional writers do their "thinking on paper." That is, they start writing down the various ideas, notions, and bits of knowledge almost at random, thinking the organization of the product out en route and often in the process discovering gaps that need to be researched and filled. Ultimately, they reorganize and rewrite all the material. In fact, the writer who works this way is developing an introduction, while organizing and planning the rest of the work.

That introduction is known as a *lead*, and the process is *working from a lead*. It is a perfectly legitimate way of working, although it is effective for only relatively short pieces. Even with detailed outlines prepared in advance and guiding me in starting a new book, I have written leads of as much as 50 pages and then discarded them completely because I decided I was on the wrong track. That's not easy to do. In fact, it is quite painful. But it is the kind of discipline you must have if you are going to turn out quality writing.

I work from a lead, doing the planning and outlining primarily in my head, when writing short pieces. However, I plan a book by developing a formal outline and planning the content, chapter by chapter and subject by subject, along with at least some general ideas for illustrations. I work from a lead to develop each chapter, although I am guided generally by the original outline. This method is probably most appropriate for the professional writer because it usually means a great deal of self-editing and rewriting. If writing is a difficult chore for you, the painstaking formal planning and preparation method will surely minimize the amount of writing and rewriting you must do later.

Reading Level

It may surprise you to learn that relatively few people read with great facility above the eighth-grade level, the writing style of which is well represented by the popular and enormously successful *Reader's Digest* magazine. If you succeed in emulating that style and reading level faithfully, you need not worry about your reader's general reading level; you can hardly go wrong in that respect.

On the other hand, as a consultant you are probably working in some rather specialized or highly technical area, and so cannot avoid the use of jargon entirely. The important thing is to know to whom you are writing and to judge accurately your reader's probable knowledge of the jargon.

For example, if you are writing to individuals who are knowledgeable in electronics technology, you can probably use such terms as positive feedback, resonance, and impedance without explanation, but it would probably be wise to provide good clues to meaning when you use such special terms as Chebyshev effect or Butterworth filter. If you are writing to lay people even the three common electronic terms must be explained, if it is, indeed, necessary to use them at all.

It is not the reader's responsibility to understand what you write; it is your responsibility to see that you can be easily understood. In fact, one wise editor of my early experience went further than this. He said that it is not enough to write so that you can be understood; you must write so that you cannot be *misunderstood*.

Along the lines of this philosophy I try to follow a practice of reviewing my own copy while asking myself whether what I have written can be interpreted ambiguously—whether it can be reasonably interpreted to have more than one meaning. If so, it must be changed to minimize that possibility. I do not knowingly permit my writing to be even marginally ambiguous.

Outlining

References to many kinds of outlines may be found, but I know of only two kinds that have any true significance: (1) an outline of what you intend to write *about* and (2) an outline of what you intend to *write*. The following examples will illustrate the distinctions between these outline types. The subject is a symptom diagnosis of a malfunctioning TV receiver.

Outline 1: What you will write about:

1. Visual and aural inspection of picture and sound
   - **a.** Video symptoms
   - **b.** Audio symptoms
   - **c.** Raster
   - **d.** White noise
2. Functional checks
   - **a.** Front panel controls
   - **b.** Rear panel controls

Outline 2: What you will write

1. Visual and aural inspection of picture and sound
   - **a.** Raster present? Video information present?
   - **b.** Audio present? If not, white noise present?
   - **c.** Conclusion as to probable trouble indicated by symptoms—high-voltage problems, loss of video, loss of sync pulses, loss of input RF, other

2. Functional checks
   a. Rotate brightness control: Response? Significance?
   b. Rotate contrast control: Response? Significance?
   c. Rotate volume control: Response? Significance?
   d. Rotate automatic gain control (agc): Response? Significance?
   e. Conclusions from above (probable cause) and/or logical next trouble-check

Note: Use one or more logic trees to illustrate trouble-shooting rationale and analyses.

The difference between these two outlines should be apparent. The first outline may serve in an early stage of planning, but you are not ready to proceed to writing a first draft until you have developed an outline of at least the second level of detail. In fact, the second outline could be even more detailed and often is.

You may have to do some fairly extensive research to be able to produce an outline equal in level of detail to the second model here. But that is a positive effect. It indicates that you were not ready to begin writing before that research.

It is therefore a good idea to develop that first outline, as long as you recognize that it is a *preliminary* step, an exploratory planning step.

Identifying the Readers

Identifying your readers is a necessary step if you are to create a useful document. You need to know who and what your readers are (e.g., students, lay people, technicians, etc.), how little or how much they know about the subject before beginning to read, and, finally, why they want the information. It is not enough to say that they are clients. Your readers must be defined in terms that you can translate into guidelines. It is that information which enables you to judge how technical your explanations are to be.

Logical Charting

Writing is a process, a logical progression of ideas and information. Once you have a firmly established and well-defined goal, you can turn to a flow chart for direct help in determining intermediate objectives that will lead you in that logical progression to the goal. Such a diagram is, in fact, a generalized outline in graphic or chart form. It actually precedes outlining, since it helps you think out the problem and organize the basic phases and functions logically.

Designers of computer programs tend to draw their charts vertically, from top to bottom, while designers of equipment tend to draw charts horizontally, from left to right. I favor the second method, but you can use either, of course. Whichever method you use, begin with the one thing you know for sure, the final block, which represents the overall goal.

In this case I will assume that the publication is going to teach handyman TV service to the nontechnical person, and my goal is to enable the reader to do what is stated in the box below:

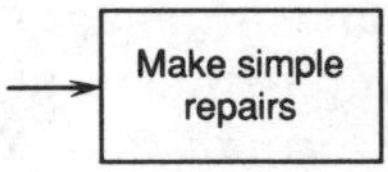

That established, I can begin to perceive the progression of things the reader must learn in order to reach that goal. The major steps in the process are these:

Observe symptoms
Analyze symptoms
Reach conclusion (diagnose)
Verify diagnosis
Make repair

The preliminary objective is that the reader gain an understanding of the basics of TV operation, enough at least to understand the simplified procedures to be presented. So my set of objectives is to teach the reader how to do the things illustrated in this logical block drawing:

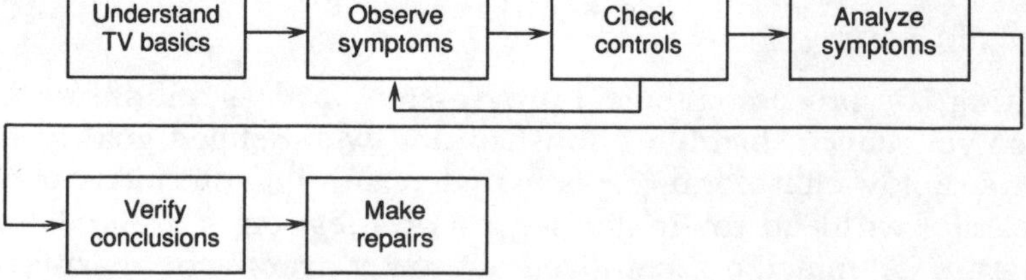

"Check controls" is added because that is part of observing and analyzing symptoms. Actually, many more details will be added in the full outline because each of these is a major topic that must be expanded in the outline. The outline must explain the implementation of each of these items, in fact.

Generally outlines and charts must pass through several revision stages before the writer is satisfied with the result. These are the stages in which to do the bulk of your drafting, rethinking, and revision—long before you attempt to do "serious" writing of draft text. The more you do here, the less editing, rewriting, and polishing you will have to do later and the better the later result will be.

Charting your thoughts as an initial step has three advantages. First, it compels you to think out the steps and the sequence. It is truly amazing how easily we can ramble on in writing, filling the paper but saying nothing of significance. Words are abstractions, of course, and for some uses, such as this one, they are not the best tools. But with charting, even with blocks containing those abstract symbols (words), evasion becomes quite difficult and visualization becomes much easier. Second, even a primitive chart makes it easier to perceive the logical flow, and thus the whole process of developing the full chart and subsequent detailed working outline is greatly facilitated. In fact, an excellent technique is to print the logical blocks on index cards and shuffle them around, seeking the most logical and most effective flow. Third, the chart itself usually becomes an asset you can use directly or via adaptation as an illustration in the written presentation, thereby simplifying the writing chore further.

You can easily verify the logic and validate your diagram by simply reading through the drawing in either direction. Reading the boxes from left to right reveals the "why" of the flow. And a feedback loop is provided from "check controls" to "observe symptoms" because checking the controls provides some of the symptomatic information. In fact, even this drawing is somewhat cursory, and many more blocks could be added as guidelines to the development of the working outline, which should be much more detailed than the diagram. The outline should answer the "how" of each block and of each transition from one block to the next. If it does not do so, the chart should be revised. Use the "why" and "how" questions to develop the chart as well as to validate it and generate the working outline.

Functional Divisions

Organization means separating the document into functional sections or groupings and presenting them in a consistently logical sequence. The size of such sections depends on the total size and nature of the end product.

For example, a document of 100 or more pages will need to be divided into chapters (whether they are or are not called chapters), each titled in a manner that identifies the focus of the chapter. (A flow chart for such a document might have each block identifying the focus of a separate chapter.) On the other hand, each division of a relatively brief report, article, or chapter of a book would normally be identified and introduced by a headline. Thus the divisions would be physically different, but functionally they would have the same needs and treatment. Each division (subject) would require an introduction at its beginning and a transition to the next division at the end.

RESEARCH AND DATA GATHERING

The quality of the research, which is often the key factor in the quality and success of the written product, is determined by the completeness of the research. Of course, there is the need for accuracy and selection of the most important material, but even these are linked closely to the completeness of the research, for that is the key to selecting the "best" data. And "best" is usually the information sought out and selected according to these guidelines:

The information that is most germane to your overall goal and the objectives you have established as the itinerary for reaching the targeted goal.

The information that appears to be most complete and most accurate or most reliable.

The information that appears to be most up-to-date.

The information that provides you, as a writer, with the greatest opportunities for drama, excitement, or other interest-arousing prospects.

You know your research is probably complete when the resulting information has become repetitious. This method is also a tool for judging accuracy. If most accounts agree, you have accurate information; but if there is serious disagreement among the sources, you are wise to search for ways to validate one source.

Despite all this, you are still faced with the need to rely largely on your own judgment, even when you have drawn information from official records. Court records, for example, may be legal truths, but they are still reflections of claims and opinions, and certainly not always factual.

Sources of Information

The biggest problem today is not how to *find* information, but how to *process* it—that is, how to compile, organize, filter, analyze, and otherwise assimilate and utilize it sensibly and efficiently. Among the many sources, most readily available, are the following:

Public libraries

Newspapers (modern libraries usually have microfiche copies of old ones, and actual copies of recent ones, but newspaper "morgues"—in-house libraries, that is—will often allow access to their files of back issues.

Other libraries, including those in government agencies, universities, civic nonprofit organizations, and even large corporations. Many of these will allow you access to their files.

Public information offices of all those organizations mentioned here.

Government agencies generally, especially those of the federal government.

Publications of the U.S. Government Printing Office (GPO). Usually you can quote directly from these and use illustrations and other material that is in them because most of the GPO publications are in the public domain, which means anyone can use the material in them. But there are exceptions. Some government publications include copyrighted material, for which permission to use has been granted the government; but that permission does not extend to anyone else. You must be sure that what you use is, indeed, in public domain.

Press clipping services. (These search many newspapers and other print media daily, clipping items on subjects you name, charging a fee for each clipping.)

Public databases you can access via your personal computer and modem. Recently these have become a particularly rich source; some can even help in selecting the specific data you seek. In one case I carried out a complete research job for a client by having such a service do my serch of their files, via computer, of course, and send me data via our telephone and modem link, which data I then needed merely to edit and print out to complete the task.

Historical societies

Foreign embassies, consulates, and tourism bureaus

Guidance in seeking out some of the offices and organizations suggested here is offered in Chapter 17, but the library and the telephone directory are also a great help when properly used. For example, if the information you want is industrial or technological, you may be able to get what you need from industrial or business firms. Moreover, you may even be able to get reproducible materials (e.g., news releases, specification sheets, tables, charts, and photographs) with permission to use these directly. You normally must promise attribution—a line acknowledging the source and identifying the product or process. You also should have written permission to use the material—a release form.

Some organizations and individuals, particularly in those cases where you seek permission to quote directly from copyrighted material, will require you to specify exactly what you wish to quote and may even demand the right to review your manuscript and approve or disapprove of your use. And some require payment, especially if the quotation is a lengthy one. I refuse to go along with giving the copyright owner the right to edit and approve or disapprove my work, so I generally drop the matter when that degree of control over my writing is demanded; it would be a most rare case where I could not get along well enough without the material.

Some organizations will include a letter granting permission to use their material (in the case of news releases and accompanying material, such as photographs, formal release is not necessary because the permission to reproduce is implicit), but it is more practical to supply a release form of your own. I use a rather simple one (see Figure 13–1); rarely have I found it necessary to use anything more elaborate than that. I do, however, send a courteous letter of request making it clear that I will use the material supplied objectively and will be scrupulously fair in any case where I find it necessary to make a critical comment. But I try to avoid the necessity for criticism, since I generally use materials to exemplify good practice.

RELEASE

Permission is hereby granted to Herman Holtz and his publishers to reproduce, cite, comment on, and/or quote briefly from material supplied herewith, with the understanding that full attribution will be made.

(Typed/printed name/title) (Signature)

(Company/division) (Date)

FIGURE 13.1. Simple release form.

WRITING THE DRAFT

Contrary to what other writers and lecturers on the subject of writing suggest, expert knowledge of grammar, punctuation, spelling, rhetoric, and other mechanics of usage is not *writing* any more than the ability to use a hammer and saw is cabinetmaking. They are the tools of writing, and you must have a reasonable mastery of them, but that mastery, no matter how great, will not of itself make you a writer.

Even if you have mastered the mechanics of writing and have thoroughly researched, planned, and prepared your document, you should expect to write a rough draft as a first step following outlining. Thorough planning greatly reduces the amount of revision you must do subsequently, but it does not eliminate the need for a first draft. Remember also that the more care you exercise with the draft, the less change you will have to make later and by far the less danger that something totally wrong will appear in the final document. In fact, with the convenience and encouragement of word processing to induce me to more self-editing and revision than I have ever done before, only a small proportion of what I finally print out now must be rewritten later, even after scrupulous editing by my publishers. It's a simple case of maximum prevention, resulting in minimum need for cure.

Introduction

Introduction, as applied to writing, is not a mysterious term, nor is it jargon. In fact, it is simplicity itself. It means merely telling the reader what you are going to discuss or reveal. Every subject and every functional division must be introduced. In a paragraph, the first sentence, or topic sentence, should be the introduction. In a chapter, the opening paragraph should introduce the chapter in the same way. Check the opening paragraphs of the chapters in this book for examples.

Transitions

Introductions to new material and new subjects, whether they are presented in new paragraphs or new chapters, are actually made or at least strongly suggested in the preceding paragraph or chapter. That is known as a *transition*, or a *bridge*. It is, quite simply, a clear clue to what is to come so that the new paragraph or subject does not come as a surprise.

Somehow, writing effective transitions appears to be a most difficult chore for many writers, and the ability to write smooth transitions is one characteristic of the accomplished professional writer. Writers develop an almost instinctual sensitivity to the need for smooth transitions and the ability to create them, but there are a few tips that will help anyone create transitions that work effectively.

One tip is to use key words as transitional links. That is, introduce a key word or topic at the end of a paragraph and use that same key word in introducing the next paragraph. Note, for example, the word *tip* so used in ending the last paragraph and introducing this one and the next one.

Another tip is to make sure to identify the next *theme* or *subject*, even if you do not use a key word to do so. For theme is very much a part of writing anything. My theme in this section of this chapter, for example, is that the mechanics of usage are the tools of writing, but they are not the art of writing, so becoming letter perfect in all those rules will not, of itself, make you a writer.

I did not set out immediately to prove that idea, but offered it as a theory, asking you to accept it on my authority as an experienced professional writer. And here, in this paragraph, I deliberately avoided using that word "theme" in making this transition because I wanted to demonstrate another means of making smooth transitions: I used another word—*idea*—instead of *theme*, knowing that since I was continuing the discussion you would have no trouble following the train of thought.

When you are concluding a discussion and preparing to set forth on an entirely different topic, you also need a transition to let the reader know that you are making a change. In some cases you need only an appropriate transitional word or phrase such as *however, on the other hand*, or *in comparison*. In other cases, such as when you are concluding a chapter and preparing to take up an unrelated subject, you might require an entire concluding paragraph to prepare the way for the introductory paragraph of the new chapter.

There are other methods for achieving good transitions, but all are based on the same idea. If the new subject continues a theme, guide the reader by linking the new subject directly to the subject you have just summarized. If the theme is new, alert the reader to the change of subject and provide an introductory orientation to the new subject or theme.

Readability

Readability is difficult to define because it means different things to different readers. On the one hand many people really mean *understandability* when they use the term. And there are no really good, scientific measures, despite many efforts to create standards.

One measure often used is grade level, with the *Reader's Digest* a de facto standard and nominally an eighth-grade level suitable for everything except possibly certain scientific and technical materials. Other ideas about readability concern the length and complexity of sentences and words, with some writers on the subject insisting that to be highly readable the words should never have more than two or three syllables.

The problem with all of these standards and guides is that there are too many exceptions for them to be truly useful. For example, there are many difficult or uncommon words that are quite short, while there are many common, easily understood words that are relatively long.

Sentence structure standards are also difficult to set. Contrary to some of what has been written on the subject, long sentences are not necessarily difficult, nor are short sentences easy to understand. However, the length of the sentence is not as important as the organization of information. If a sentence has one central idea, and the information is presented in a logical sequence, readers are not likely to have trouble with it. However, readers do have trouble with sentences that

Try to present more than one central idea
Fail to get to the point
Fail to make a clear and unequivocal statement
Use an irrational or illogical order of presentation
Evade the issue by using obscure euphemisms
Work hard at saying nothing

On the other hand, *readability* also refers to other aspects of written and printed materials having to do with format and related matters. Here are some tips on how to make your writing more readable in these respects:

Solid, unbroken blocks of text are formidable and may make unreasonable demands on the reader to retain large amounts of data before reaching a summary or conclusion. Keep paragraphs reasonably short and summarize key points often.

Use bulleted or otherwise listed items to make points.

Don't rely on text alone, especially when you want your reader to perceive an image. Even for presenting and explaining abstractions and broad concepts, analogies and drawings help. Readability is not concerned with words alone, but with total communication achieved by your writing.

In the end, you must be the judge as to what words, sentence structure, style, and organization will be most appropriate for and best understood by the readers for whom you are writing.

Imagery

Illustrations are not necessarily drawings or photographs; they can be verbal illustrations—that is, imagery or images drawn by words. Similes and metaphors are two of the most common types of imagery used to help readers (and listeners, in the case of oral presentations) grasp the concept. But simple word descriptions that help the reader or listener understand readily are also imagery.

In using imagery it is important to use comparisons that the reader is likely to be familiar with. It does not help to call something as complex as a "tracking equation" when the reader or listener is not likely to have any idea of what a tracking equation is, much less of how complex it is. The thing to which you refer as a simile or metaphor, or even as a simple comparison, must be something familiar to readers and listeners if it is to be at all effective as imagery.

Do-It-Yourself Artwork

It is not necessary to turn to professional illustrators for all artwork. Most modern art supply stores and office stationers can help you with templates, transfer (decal) type and drawing symbols, and clip art. Moreover, if you have a modern personal computer there are many desktop publishing programs that include clip art and various related capabilities to help you. Do-it-yourself illustrations are a reality.

Level of Detail

The amount of detail you should include in your writing should depend, logically, on two things: (1) the reader's need (and that should equate with the goals and objectives you are addressing in writing the material) and (2) the reader's ability to absorb, appreciate, and utilize the detail.

A most common problem in technical publications is offering readers far more detail than they need or can use, often more than they can understand, in fact. As a writer you do not need to report everything you know about the subject. Make an objective evaluation of what the reader needs and can use, and restrict yourself to that. And if you conclude that your reader needs technical detail but is not trained in even the rudiments of the technology concerned, there are still ways to provide a limited and almost painless education in the salient facts by providing tactful explanations as you go.

One problem, however, is that you often have a mixed audience or readership. Some are technical/professionals, while others are lay people. It is necessary to present the information so that both understand, and yet the technical/professional readers must not feel that they are being "talked down" to. Consider the following ways of explaining a multiplexed interface as an example of achieving this goal:

The interface is multiplexed, permitting the equipment to carry on concurrent exchanges of information with several dozen sources and destinations.

The interface is multiplexed, sampling each of several dozen inputs at 50-microsecond intervals in turn so that for practical purposes, several dozen transmissions are received concurrently.

The interface is characterized by multiplexing or the ability to handle a number of inputs and outputs in such rapid succession that it is virtually simultaneous.

The interface has a multiplex characteristic (the ability to handle a number of inputs and outputs in such rapid succession as to appear to be simultaneous.)

These are in a descending order of technical detail or an ascending order of technical explanation. Anyone can learn from this what multiplexing means, at least in a general sense. And yet no one should be offended, not even the knowledgeable engineer or technician who reads this.

USING WORD PROCESSING

Word processing is by far the most popular use of personal computers in both small and large offices, and even the principal reason for buying personal computers. Yet it is probably the most misunderstood and misused function of personal computers.

Far too many offices today have simply replaced the electric typewriter with the personal computer and word processor. Executives and professionals are still scrawling their copy on long yellow lined pads, and typists input the words. So very little has changed, except that the $800 to $1,000 typewriter has become the $2,000 to $4,000 computer/word processor!

Does this describe your office? Does this describe the way you work with a word processor? If word processing has not changed the way you write and especially if it has not greatly increased your efficiency and/or the quality of your writing, it is quite possible that you are not taking proper advantage of word processing. In fact, it is quite possible that you do not even understand what word processing is. It is not merely a more efficient way of typing and making corrections, it is a different and far better way of writing—a way of producing far better writing.

If you use a word processor but you still have not yet begun to enjoy these fruits of word processing, you are not alone. Unfortunately, a great many people who ought to know better regard word processing as an automatic typing and correction system—but those are only the least significant and least valuable of its capabilities and attractions.

Understand, first of all, that a word processor is not the machine—not hardware at all—but is the software program installed in the computer. This is significant because the machine can do many other useful things that are closely related to word processing.

A word processor, which is the software program not the hardware, enables you to create text, tables, and even a few simple sketches. It also enables you to delete, add to, and manipulate the text. And all of this on screen, before you print out a single word.

The word processor makes you more efficient because it allows you to review, edit, reorganize, revise, and rewrite on screen. It enhances the quality of your output simply because of the ease and speed with which all these things can be done—because once you begin to work this way you tend to do a great deal more self-editing, reorganizing, and rewriting. In fact, if you are one of those who hate to rewrite, this is for you; you are hardly conscious that you are rewriting because it is so simple.

However, you will probably have to learn new writing habits. Most of us write an entire manuscript in draft before attempting a rewrite, rather than rewriting every few pages. That's a hangover from typewriter production, in which we produce hard copy steadily as we go. Now we must learn to print out hard copy only when we have done all our reviewing and rewriting on screen and are satisfied that we have a final draft, ready for submittal.

Those injuctions I pressed on you earlier to edit and rewrite extensively, even continuously, were delivered with word processing aforethought. They are not at all burdensome when you learn to work this way, to take advantage of and to exploit the natural characteristics of computers and word processors. Quite the contrary, they make writing fun.

My own methods of working and using my own hardware and software system may not be the right one for you, but I will detail them for you to consider.

I work on one chapter at a time, making a separate file of each chapter. Most of my chapters run to about 20-30 pages, and I generally build them up with parcels of 5 to 10 pages at a time. That is, I "save"—transfer copy from memory to disk—every page or so, and then review and edit what I have. That means that by the time I have 5 to 10 pages composed I have edited and rewritten them several times.

When I am finally satisfied with the copy, I subject it to my spelling checker, make any corrections necessary, and print hard copy for that parcel. I continue this procedure for each parcel until the full chapter is complete.

It takes some self-training to learn to work on-screen. A page of copy is 55 lines long, 27 in double-spaced copy, but the screen displays only about 10 lines of double-spaced copy at a time. But you can learn to work with this. However, you can work with single-spaced copy on screen, if you prefer, because most programs will print the copy out single-spaced or double-spaced, at your option.

When you are comfortable with the computer, you should be ready for several other aids to word processing. These programs include spelling checkers (often more useful for proofreading assistance than for spelling assistance), grammar checkers, word counters, indexers, bibliographic programs, outliners, key redefiners, thesauri, footnoters, and others.

If you write books, your publishers will soon be asking for your disks and setting type from them. And one of the payoffs for using programs such as those just described is the effect on galleys and page proofs. If you use a spelling checker, you usually find very few typos in galleys and page proofs, which makes it easier to proofread them, as authors are usually required to do. Some programs, such as the new WordStar, have an internal thesaurus, enabling you to search for synonyms when the word you are using is not exactly the right one or when you can't think of the word you want. Even indexing becomes easier, especially if you rearrange your disks to agree with the page numbering of the final page proofs, a necessity if you are going to use an indexing program. But even without that special program the computer can help you with indexing; and at least you won't be struggling with hundreds of index cards.

I would suggest that you try this system and adapt it to your own work and preferences.

THE COMPUTER AS AN OFFICE MANAGER

Your computer not only helps with your writing skills, it performs other administrative tasks that will increase your efficiency and leave you more time for consulting. For example, I no longer keep a notebook containing names, addresses, and telephone numbers; those are on a list in the computer (literally *in* because they are on the hard disk) and are available to me with two simple key presses. My business diaries, logs, memos, appointments, and other such things are equally accessible. I even have a little alarm program to remind me of things to do! No more frantic searches for that scrap of paper with a number on it. No more searching among jumbled piles of paper for a memo. In fact, I even have programs that will search for information if I have forgotten where I stored it in the computer and tell me what file I need and where to find it in the computer! And, of course, the computer does not forget and never takes coffee breaks. If it does not increase your efficiency and make your life easier, you are almost surely not using it well.

14

Additional Profit Centers for Your Consulting Practice

Counseling clients on a one-to-one basis is not enough to constitute a successful practice. The successful independent consultant is well rounded in counseling as a writer, publisher, lecturer, teacher, and leader also.

"CONSULTING" MEANS DIFFERENT THINGS TO DIFFERENT CONSULTANTS

As do most enterprises, a consulting practice ultimately begins to assume a life of its own as it grows. In most cases the venture evolves gradually into an enterprise the entrepreneur never visualized. Among the major management consulting firms today, for example, many began not as consulting firms but as accounting or engineering firms. And many continue to operate in those original capacities, with consulting as a separate division.

But it is not only large firms who so evolve; even independent entrepreneurial ventures are overtaken by change and diversification. They become publishers, seminar producers, lecturers, and authors. Despite this, all are still consultants, still counseling and guiding clients. In fact, many carry on all the activities concurrently, as different aspects of their consulting services, rather than as specialists in one of the many ancillary activities open to the consultant.

Sometimes the diversification is unintentional, merely the result of circumstances; sometimes it is a deliberate business decision made to establish a firmer base of operations for the independent consulting practice. This type of deliberate diversification is the main topic of this chapter.

WHAT ARE "PROFIT CENTERS?"

Many corporations organize themselves into various departments or divisions, and reorganizations of these divisions take place periodically in the life of an organization, as circumstances inspire and often even dictate such changes.

There are many reasons for so structuring an organization. Different divisions often require entirely different talents, different resources, different marketing, and different management. In more than a few cases, many divisions are chronic losers of money, while one or two divisions are so profitable that they "carry" the entire corporation. It helps to keep those losers as separate entities so that they can either be made profitable or divested to stop the losses. However, the underlying thought is always that each division should be a profit center, a producer of income for the central organization. Establishing separate divisions facilitates managing them for profit.

The size of the organization has nothing to do with the philosophy of separate profit centers. Even an independent consultant, a one-person enterprise, can be so divided. Although all the activities are consulting services and are integral to your practice overall, each is or should be regarded as an entity, if you are to manage them well and derive maximum benefits from them. To do that, you should treat them in the following manner:

1. Establish each activity (e.g., newsletter, seminars, books, etc.) as a separate identifiable entity.
2. Set up separate accounting records for each such entity so that you can track all expenditures and income for each.
3. Operate each entity so that all become mutually supporting in sales (e.g., a newsletter promotes seminars, seminars promote book sales, etc.).
4. Make the activities share as many costs as possible, and reflect these shares in the accounting records of each.
5. Keep track of the activities so that you can also estimate, perhaps even measure, the benefit one derives from the other.

WHY ARE OTHER PROFIT CENTERS ESTABLISHED?

Some of the reasons for establishing separate profit centers include the following:

1. A suggestion is offered or an opportunity arises that interests you, and you act on these oportunities.
2. Individuals who are potential clients seek you out with specific requests (e.g., a seminar, a newsletter, a training program, a speech, etc.). This market demand inspires you to initiate an ancillary service.
3. You write or lecture, and discover that you enjoy it or that it is easier and more profitable than "straight" consulting.
4. You need additional sources of income.

You must diversify your practice if you are to survive as an independent consultant, especially in the early years. Consulting is typically a feast-or-famine enterprise. You may get several opportunities all at once, but you can usually handle only one at a time and must decline the others. And despite your best efforts to market effectively, between those bonanzas of opportunity there are lengthy periods when you have no work. And in the early years of your practice, you simply cannot charge high enough rates in peak seasons to build up profits that will see you through those lean times. To smooth these peaks and valleys of income you must develop other sources of income—other profit centers. That is why we find independent consultants becoming writers, lecturers, publishers, and otherwise diversifying the means and methods by which they serve clients' needs and see to their own.

The monetary need is not the only reason for diversification, however. Many jobs prove to be a disappointment to their practitioners, and they search for something with greater appeal. That, too, is one of the factors that leads consultants into other pastures.

THE COMMON DENOMINATOR

Consultants are specialists' specialists. They are specialists with rare specialities, specialists with unusually impressive records of achievement in their fields, specialists with outstanding talents and instincts. Consultancies have been founded and are based upon an almost infinite variety of technical/professional fields and, more often, on very special niches in those fields.

In many cases the consultant is also the practitioner of a specialized skill based on the knowledge, experience, or "talent" he or she possesses. The services provided to clients by such specialists may include actual performance—application of those special skills. A computer consultant, for example, may have a highly specialized trouble shooting or programming skill. In one case, where the client is a user of computers but has no computer technical skills, that knowledge can be put to work to solve a problem for the client only by actually doing the troubleshooting or programming. However, if the client is also a computer specialist (or has such specialists on staff), the consultant may be able to serve the client effectively by the classic consulting service of simply studying the problem and advising the client—recommending a method or procedure to pursue.

That is application-oriented information—truly a counseling or advising service that is the most basic and traditional of consulting generally. But there are many circumstances in which the client requires information that covers a specialized field but is still presented as general information on the subject. That would be the difference, for example, between calling on one to train a staff in telemarketing techniques generally.

If there is any common denominator among the many consulting practices, it is the existence of specialized knowledge gained through formal training and unique experiences. Consultants practice by utilizing this special knowledge in several ways, including:

1. Counseling a client with regard to a specific problem or need (the most basic consulting service).
2. Applying specific, specialized skills to *do* something for the client.
3. Providing general information—training—in some specialized field.

This last item, which opens the door to a variety of options for adding income-producing activities to broaden and solidify the base of your consulting practice, is implemented in two ways: writing and speaking.

WRITING FOR PROFIT

There are two basic ways in which you can earn income with your writing. One is by writing for publication by others, being paid for your writing. The other is by publishing your own writing, selling the written product. Which you choose to do depends in large part on your objectives and your preferences. However, that is something of an oversimplification; there is a great deal more to be said and a great many avenues to explore in even a brief treatment of the subject. Let's take a closer look at the subject and examine some rather well-known facts about it.

Writing for Publication by Others

Writing for publication by others as a means of generating income is a low-risk effort, as far as financial investment is concerned, since the chief investment is your time. However, earning money by writing for publication by others is by no means easy to do. Free-lance writing requires time and effort to study the markets thoroughly and to learn to write in a manner that meets the requirements and standards of commercial publications. Still, there are many consultants who do a considerable amount of profitable free-lance writing successfully, so a brief survey of the market is useful.

Writing for Periodicals

Periodicals (e.g., newspapers, newsletters, and magazines) represent a great market for free-lance writing because they cover a vast array of general and specialized topics. Let's examine the facts regarding free-lance writing for this periodical market:

1. Daily, "regular" newspapers buy relatively little of their material from free-lance writers. However, they do buy a number of feature stories, especially for Sunday supplements, and often these are "expert" pieces on technical subjects of interest to the public (e.g., diets, health, military positions of the nations, etc.).
2. By far the best rates for free-lance writing are paid by the publishers of those periodicals with the greatest circulation figures.

3. Not surprisingly, the most difficult to sell to are those magazines that pay the highest rates. That is partly the result of exacting demands by those publishers and partly the result of intense competition, most of it from experienced professional free lancers.
4. Equally without surprise, the trade journals pay far less and are far easier to sell to than are the popular magazines. Much of their material is bought from experts in various fields, such as yourself, who are not professional writers.
5. Many newsletters buy some free-lance material and so may be a good training ground for you to break into the profitable field of free-lance writing. However, the pay for newsletter writing is very low.

Writing for Syndicates

It is possible to write indirectly for periodicals by addressing your writing to syndicates. Most newspapers and some magazines get much of their material from these "middlemen" of free-lance writing. Syndicates distribute the work of writers as brokers on a commission basis, and many newspapers have come to depend on syndicates for most of their special features. The columnist sends his or her material to the syndicate, and the syndicate sends copies to all the newspapers and magazines to which it has sold the column. Commissions vary, according to circumstances, but the writer usually gets approximately one-half the revenue. In percentage terms, these commissions are much larger than those charged by literary agents. That is because syndicates do a great deal more work, including distribution of the material, whereas the literary agent's work is largely done, once the sale is made, although the agent continues to earn commissions from the royalties and other, subsidiary earnings.

Syndication offers the opportunity for quite substantial income if what you write proves popular, since syndicates generally sell the material on a nonexclusive basis—that is, the buyer, usually a newspaper with only local circulation, has the right to the piece exclusively in its own distribution area, but not elsewhere. So the syndicate may sell the item to many newspapers, as long as they are not published in the same city or area.

Any article you might sell to a magazine is likely to be of interest to a syndicate also. However, most newspapers do not like lengthy articles. They are more likely to want the shorter feature article of perhaps 1,000 to 2,000 words. Longer articles may be considered for inclusion in Sunday supplements.

Writing for Book Publishers

Writing for commercial book publishers represents, probably, your best opportunity to write for profit through publication by others. This is not to say that it is easy to succeed at this; you must still meet certain criteria to succeed at even getting your book published, much less at earning substantial income from it. These criteria include:

1. You must have something to say that is new, different, profound, or insightful. A recapitulation of what has already been published, widely circulated, and commonly accepted, is not "something to say."
2. It must be in a style that is not only literate but conveys its meanings with sufficient clarity so that it does not require excessive editing before it can be set in type. (That style and language depends, of course, on the reader for whom it is intended.)
3. It must have a wide enough appeal for potential readership that it is economically viable.

Of these requirements, the third is possibly the most critical, but that requirement depends in large part on satisfying the publisher that you can meet the first requirement.

Most publishers do not have an in-house expert on every subject on which you or some other expert might write a book. When a manuscript on a rather specialized subject is received and it appears to be literate enough and professional enough to merit serious consideration for publication, the publisher must seek an expert technical appraisal before going further. That is usually done by a consultant expert in the field, sought out and engaged by the publisher to validate the manuscript as technically accurate and worth reading. Your manuscript, if it is rather technical, will have to pass that test and satisfy the first requirement.

Even then there is no assurance that your book will be profitable. But most nonfiction best sellers have been written by authors who were not professional writers, but who were specialists of one kind or another and who wrote books that somehow appealed to the general public, not just other specialists. The book that does not have potential interest for the general public has little chance of gaining a spot on the published best-seller lists, although it may become a best seller within its genre. On the other hand, most popular best sellers are like novas: they flare briefly and then die rapidly. (There are occasional exceptions, such as best sellers that remain on the list for many months, and even years.) Many books that sell more modestly—several thousand copies each year, rather than each week—go on selling at that more modest rate for many years, and are ultimately more profitable than the best seller, as it pays royalties quietly and reliably, year after year, and is subject to less of a tax bite, as well.

But even this is speculation. By far the overwhelming majority of the 40,000 to 50,000 books published annually are only modest successes, if they succeed at all. But this should not deter you, if you have something to say and believe that it merits emergence as a book.

Miscellaneous Writing for Others

There are several other ways to write for publication or related use by others. This is, generally, writing on a contract basis. Over the years I have been paid flat fees many times to write a wide variety of materials about my special fields. These have included, for example, lecture guides, syllabi, manuals, storyboards and scripts for audiovisual presentations, brochures, and papers. Some were to be used in seminars and training programs, others were used for publicity and public information. In one case, I wrote a brochure on proposal writing for an association executive; his signature appeared on the cover as the author, while I was paid approximately $1,000 as the "ghost" author. In most of the cases of such contract writing, however, no one's name appeared as the author. I was simply paid a flat fee for my services, and the product appeared as the document of the organization.

This can be highly profitable writing, especially with today's computers, which enable you to store, revise, and otherwise utilize basic information. (I keep many "archive" files of basic data, charts, diagrams, tables, glossaries, and other materials I have developed, and I draw on these frequently in my writing.)

Rates of Pay

Writing, as an occupation in general, is most definitely not one of our higher paid professions. But that has not prevented a great many individuals from being exceptions and earning a great deal of money at the craft. You may very well be or become one of those exceptions. In fact, rates paid by commercial publishers vary enormously, especially with periodicals and even for a given publisher and/or publication. So it is not possible to do more than give approximations and examples.

Newsletters generally pay from about $5 per item to 3 to 5 cents per word. Some trade journals pay as little as that word rate also, but others may go to two or three times that amount. Many trade magazines pay by the printed page and generally range from about $75 to $150 per printed page. Popular magazines are more likely to pay from 25 to 50 cents per word, and even more in some cases. Newspapers and tabloids often pay for news items by the column inch.

Book publishers generally pay royalties (although they occasionally buy a book outright), usually starting at 10 percent of the publisher's dollar receipts from sales of the book and rising as high as 15 percent if the book sells well enough. There may or may not be a cash advance.

Contract writing is an entirely different matter. You name your price, usually on the basis of your hourly rate and the estimated number of hours required for the job, and possibly following negotiation with the client. Such tasks in my own experience have involved fees ranging from a few hundred dollars to approximately $25,000.

Payment by periodicals is generally offered either "on acceptance" or "on publication," with some offering to pay "after publication." Unfortunately, none of these necessarily represents prompt payment or even the strict truth. Even those who claim to pay on acceptance often take a long time to actually pay the author, and I have sometimes been forced to write a stern letter demanding payment. In one case the publisher advised me that he must have an invoice from me before he could process payment. And in another case, even that did not help; I never was paid by that prosperous trade journal. I suspect that with some of these publications it is a policy to never pay until pressed for payment, and even then taking as much time as possible. On the other hand, I do not wish to malign those honest publishers who do pay exactly as they represent themselves to do. The problems have been exceptions, not the rule, in my own experience. I generally avoid "pay on publication" periodicals because they can take many, many months to publish, and sometimes never do.

Tips on Selling to Periodicals

Remember always that you must "slant" your article to the periodical's own orientation. The requirements, rates of pay, and other details of most periodicals are reported regularly in monthly writers' magazines and annual writers' journals (see Chapter 17), but only sample copies of the periodical can give you the full flavor of the publication's special slant. Refer to the writer's guides for specific information about how to get sample copies and how to get the "Guidelines for Authors" that many periodicals will send you on request if you send a "SASE"—self-addressed stamped envelope. The more closely you can match the periodical's own slant, the better your chance of selling the piece and the better the rate of pay you are likely to get. Sometimes you simply get a check, with a statement that conveys rights to the publisher. But often the editor calls you to make an offer and may make the offer conditional on certain requested or suggested changes to your manuscript. Or you may receive a form to complete and sign, certifying that the work you are offering is original, your property, not previously published, and conveying rights to publication.

The common mistake of beginners in this field is that they offer their work to the inappropriate periodicals. The beginner may write a philosophical piece on marketing and send it to a periodical dedicated to ideas for home-based business. It is rare that an editor buys something totally different than the kinds of material he or she ordinarily uses.

Cold Turkey Versus Proposals

It is not always easy to anticipate an editor's probable interest. Perfectly good manuscripts might be rejected for reasons that have nothing to do with the worth of the manuscript and the quality of the writing. Therefore, only beginners today go "cold turkey"—that is, send unsolicited manuscripts out to editors they do not know and have not corresponded with. The professionals research the market, list the most likely prospects for whatever they have in mind to write, and send those editors queries, outlining their idea (before they invest time and money to write it) and asking for an expression of interest or even an assignment. *Query* is the popular term used, but I prefer the word *proposal* because it has a more powerful marketing psychology of offering and selling an idea, rather than the somewhat weak and negative idea of asking for an okay to go ahead.

Sending a proposal is by far the wisest procedure, even when it leads to an "on spec" agreement rather than an assignment. An assignment means that the editor has ordered the article written for some agreed-upon price, and if the editor subsequently cancels the agreement and does not take the piece, you get a "kill fee," usually about one-third of the agreed price. "On spec," however, means that the editor is speculating that you will produce an acceptable manuscript, and you are speculating that the editor will buy the article! It is a rare professional writer today who writes anything but proposals on spec.

It was once considered unethical to send a proposal to more than one editor at a time, but that worked a hardship on the writer, given the often slow pace at which editors responded. Today it is more common to make "multiple submissions," querying several editors at a time. So far, I have not run into any difficulty in doing this.

What Belongs in a Proposal?

A proposal for an article need not be elaborate. Here is general instruction and a checklist for proposals:

1. Explain your idea in summary form, preferably opening your proposal with the proposed lead of the article and following that with an outline or summary and explanation.
2. Avoid all the hyperbole—all the adjectives, in fact. Explain and describe your idea; don't appraise or evaluate it. Let the editor do that.
3. Explain your credentials vis-à-vis the subject—where the expertise and information will come from. That may be your own expert credentials or other sources. You may refer to an enclosure here if you have one that lists your credentials, bio, etc.
4. Explain your credentials as a writer. If you have had other things published, cite them and furnish a few clips as samples. Again, that may be in an enclosure.
5. Estimate the proposed length of the article.
6. Tell the editor how long it will take you to deliver the article after a go-ahead.

Opening your letter with the lead you propose for the article is probably the most important point. If you can do that well, you will in one paragraph demonstrate that your idea is an interesting one and that you can write well. This is especially important if you do not have much in the way of clips or citations of earlier work to demonstrate some credentials as a writer. A really good lead is itself an excellent credential.

Making it Pay

Since you are likely to be new to the field of writing for profit as a free lancer and, moreover, working in relatively low-pay markets, how can you make writing for publication by others pay you at all?

Most professionals agree that at the rates you earn for trade journals and similar markets you cannot afford to spend a great deal of time in extensive rewriting and polishing of language. Now that does not mean that you can get away with a crude and hasty rough draft. The writing must be of professional quality. Some professionals become skillful enough to write a draft that is acceptable for these markets without rewriting, but you should do at least one rewrite if you are not yet that skilled. Fortunately, if you are using a word processor that is not a difficult chore.

You also cannot afford to spend a great deal of time in research for an article that will pay you perhaps $150 to $200. Yet, you cannot get by with an inadequately researched article either; your article must be a complete and accurate presentation of the facts. The efficient professional approach to handling this is simple enough. Don't undertake articles (or books) in fields about which you know so little that it would be impractical to research them without the prospect of a large return. Another important tip is that you should not settle for only a single article (or book) from a research effort. Suppose that you are a computer expert, for example, and you plan an article on how to buy the right computer in today's market. Using the data gathered initially, you might write other articles on troubleshooting computer problems, finding software, and using public databases and electronic bulletin boards. Or you might write and rewrite the article for different readers—the accountant, the writer, the hobbyist, the executive, and others.

This idea works in writing books too. In writing a first book on selling to the federal government, I covered it all, from procurement regulations and practices, to solicitation and contract forms, to bids and proposals, to reference data. But soon after, I realized that I had remaining files of source data that I had not used and that chapters in the original book could easily be expanded into books themselves. There followed then a book on proposal writing, a directory of government purchasing offices, a book on selling computers and computer services to government agencies, and others. I wrote two books on proposal writing, in fact, one for defense contractors and others who write major proposals for government contracts and one for independent consultants, whose requirements are entirely different. The idea is to gain volume, by organizing the writing processes for efficiency.

The Lead

In a general sense, the lead is an introduction. To me, however, it is even more. It is an essential key to unlock my train of thought. It is my philosophical summation, the theme of my work, the road map to my destination. On occasion, when I have traveled many pages down the road and decided—that I was on the wrong road, I retraced my steps to the beginning and started over. I discarded the pages that represented my miles along that road, all the pages, as many as 50 of them. The lead is that important. There are many leads: (1) the first sentence of a paragraph, (2) the first page or paragraph of a chapter or article, and (3) the first chapter of a book.

The lead is, to me at least, thinking on paper. I doodle with words and ideas, thinking the matter out. What is my objective? Where am I trying to go? What do I wish to demonstrate? To point out? To explain? How can I best make my points? Do I really know what I am trying to do?

In my struggles for a lead I juggle words and sentences—ideas. I move words and sentences, even paragraphs, around. I cut and paste, cut and try. I go on, and I come back again, until I am satisfied. I manipulate the words until I *find* the lead. This process is immeasureably important to me and many other writers.

The lead is just as important to an editor. It tells the editor where you intend to go, how you intend to get there, what you intend to say along the way, even why you bring the whole subject up, and why the editor and the readers should be interested.

Most "bad" writing I have encountered has been so primarily because the writer had not done enough research or enough thinking. Writing a proper lead requires you to think. The lead is a reflection of the strategy you have decided on for the presentation. Consider, for example, these three different leads for a piece on selling to the government:

> The essence of government procurement is *competition*. The concept is that free and open competition results in the government being offered the best quality at the best prices.
>
> The chief difference between selling to private industry and selling to the government is that private sector organizations can buy where, when, and how they please, but government agencies are controlled by statute.
>
> Selling to government agencies is different from selling to private companies more in the size of the orders than in anything else.

Note the different themes and strategies of these three leads. The first focuses on competition as the underlying concept of government purchasing, the second wants to make the point that public laws and regulations control government spending, and the third says the difference is only of size not of kind. All are legitimate positions, but they are different positions. Each would have to proceed to prove or justify the premise of the lead. Each would then result in an entirely different argument, and a given publication might accept or reject your proposal entirely on the basis of their editorial policy, which might dictate agreement or disagreement with the premise of your lead.

What You Sell

When you sell your writing for publication in a periodical or book you usually sell the publisher certain rights, but not all rights. Most periodical publishers buy *first rights*, which allow him or her to publish your material first. But there are many *secondary rights* for reprinting/republishing, for publishing in foreign countries (with or without translation into foreign languages), for movie and TV rights, and others. Reprint rights may be valuable and have several possible applications. For example, you may wish later to collect all your published articles and have them reprinted and republished as a collection, perhaps as a book. You would probably do well to keep all secondary rights.

Some publishers insist on buying all rights, but will return all secondary rights after they have published the piece. This protects them against the exercise of secondary rights (e.g., the piece appearing in a rival magazine as a reprint) before they have been able to exercise the first rights to original publication.

The Ethics of Free-Lance Writing

Many editors stipulate that they do not object to simultaneous submissions provided they are advised that theirs is one of several submissions. The question is whether your ethical code should compel you to honor that request. My personal reaction is that you are not so compelled, and the editor's stipulation does not, in my opinion, place you under any obligation to honor it. On the other hand, there is the matter of ethical conduct should you get more than one offer. What do you do then?

I think it is unwise and will probably prove self-defeating in the end, if not unethical, to conduct an auction and try to get several editors bidding against each other. You are certainly entitled to listen to each offer and to try to negotiate, but once you have made a choice and accepted an offer, you must honor it even if someone else decides to make a better offer.

Twice I have been in a situation in which an editor suggested a book idea to me but took so long deciding about the proposal I prepared that I went out to other editors with my proposal and got other offers. In both cases, the first editor finally got back to me with an acceptance, and in both cases I rejected the other offers. My sense of fair play dictated my decision, and I think that it was the right one in each case.

Keep your promises. Stick to schedules, don't try to renegotiate an agreement, unless extraordinary circumstances dictate the need. Don't drop in on editors unexpectedly—they are busy people—and don't call them collect.

SELF-PUBLISHING YOUR BOOK

Many writers have published their own works. Edgar Allen Poe is one notable example, and Robert Ringer, author of the best seller *Winning Through Intimidation*, originally published the book himself, turning it over to an established publisher after he had demonstrated its success. Don Dible, author of *Up Your OWN Organization!* also self-published that book and has revised it periodically so that it remains in print after a number of years. Self-publishing a book is entirely honorable, with many respectable precedents, and is often greatly successful from a business standpoint as well.

Self-Publishing via Subsidy

Despite its precedents, self-publishing is greatly misunderstood by those not truly familiar with it. It is often confused with *subsidy publishing*, which is publishing by firms often referred to colloquially as the "vanity press." Subsidy publishers require that the author pay all costs, and the ability and willingness to do so are the chief prerequisites for "acceptance" of a book by subsidy publishers. The quality of the book and its prospects for commercial success appear to be matters of little concern here.

There are few success stories attached to subsidized book publishing. It is true that the subsidy publisher does take care of all the editing, typesetting, and printing, and does produce a professional-looking book, but it is a book without prestige. The fact that it was subsidized suggests that it was not worthy of normal commercial publication, and retail outlets will not normally handle the products of the vanity press. Moreover, the author does not even own the unsold copies but must buy them from the subsidy publisher!

True Self-Publishing

It is misleading, in my opinion, to even think of subsidy publishing as self-publishing. You do not need the vanity press to handle the production work; there are many printers who will typeset, print, and bind your book, and you can easily hire a specialist to handle the editorial chores efficiently if you need help with editing and formatting the book. In fact, there are large printing houses who will attend to even that for you, although that may cost you more than if you take the trouble to do some of the work yourself or, at least, arrange personally for contracting out each of the individual chores.

Nor do you need a subsidy publisher even to handle the remaining problem of "distribution" (a euphemism for marketing); you can undertake to see to that yourself. You can make arrangements to handle that through an established book publisher with existing marketing channels or through one of the several wholesale distributors of books. Or you may find it feasible to market your book directly, using mail order and other channels, such as "back-of-the-room sales" and PI/PO programs, which will be explained shortly.

In-House Production Resources

Setting type for your book is one of the major costs, if you have it done by a professional typesetter. It will probably cost you several thousand dollars for an average-sized book. However, today it is not necessary to go to that expense if you have a modern desktop computer and a modern printer, and especially if you have written your manuscript with a word processor. It is possible to produce good-quality final pages, ready for commercial printing and binding, using your word processor files. On the other hand, if your own system cannot do the job—if you do not have a good, letter-quality printer, for example—you can usually find someone to turn out the camera-ready copy from your own disks for far less than typesetting cost.

Binding is another costly item. Books are much less costly in *perfect* binding. That is the way paperbacks are usually bound, with individual pages and cover glued together. Conventional hard-cover binding usually includes sewn signatures, a more durable but more costly method.

Marketing Books

Established book publishers distribute through libraries, bookstores, book wholesalers, their own in-house mail order programs, and bulk sales to companies and associations (sometimes arranged through the influence of the author). They also distribute through various kinds of dealers (e.g., newsletter publishers) and through other dealerships and kinds of drop-shipping, which is an arrangement in which the seller does not stock the books but takes orders and forwards them to the publisher for fulfillment. Many of these methods and others are not the exclusive province of large businesses; they are also available to you too as a self-publisher of your own books.

Distribution to Bookstores

There are three ways to get your books into bookstores: (1) sell them directly to bookstore owners by personal calls and mail, (2) sell them through book wholesalers, and (3) make arrangements with an established publisher to distribute for you. (The *Literary Market*

Place, listed in Chapter 17, will furnish names and addresses of book wholesalers.) When you sell to bookstores and wholesale distributors, you must not only extend terms—that is, wait 30 or more days for payment—but you must accept returns of unsold books for full credit. But they are only one market.

Libraries are also a good market; they are usually given a discount of ten percent, and often not even that, and there is no question of returns, of course. Newsletter and other periodical publishers who run mail order bookstores (usually specialized along the lines of the slant of the periodical) generally want their orders drop-shipped, and therefore get a discount smaller than the usual 40 percent. (However, not all publishers allow 40 percent. Some of my own publishers allow discounts of only 25 percent.) Many self-publishers have also used the PO/PI type of promotion, some of them with great success.

PO/PI Programs

"PO" and "PI" mean *per order* and *per inquiry*, respectively. In the PO arrangement, the periodical agrees to run an advertisement, camera-ready copy which is usually supplied by the author/book publisher. The advertisement states that orders are to be sent, with payment, to the publisher of the periodical. The periodical publisher keeps the agreed-upon share of the money—40 to 60 percent, usually—and sends the remainder to the book publisher, along with a shipping label. The book publisher then drop-ships the book.

PI works somewhat similarly. The periodical runs advertising soliciting inquiries, to be sent to the periodical publisher, who forwards them to the book publisher with a bill, charging a rate per inquiry, such as $2 each.

This plan—gathering inquiries at a per-inquiry charge—is also used by other entrepreneurs, people who gather inquiries through means other than advertising in periodicals and make mailings of advertising literature to gather inquiries, so that the clients who pay for the inquiries can follow up with direct mail to the inquirers. This, like the per-order method, is a means readily available for selling books or, for that matter, for selling anything else that can be sold by mail.

Other Marketing Means

Of course, if you are publishing a newsletter of your own, you can sell your own books through your newsletter, which is usually an excellent medium for doing so. And if you are presenting seminars and/or lecturing, you can sell many books through that back-of-the-room sale which will be discussed in greater detail later.

OTHER PUBLISHING VENTURES

Many independent consultants publish newsletters, reports, and other specialty items. Unlike book publishing, the publishing of such materials is much more the province of very small businesses. And I use *very small* because the government's definition of small business is totally out of proportion to our discussions. According to the U.S. Small Business Administration, which is responsible for establishing the many different standards that define small business in different industries, the smallest of small business is one that employs not more than 500 people or has sales not greater than $3 million annually. That is hardly what we refer to here when we speak of small business. There are a few major publishers of such materials, but by far the majority of such publishers have annual sales of a great deal less than $3 million—or even $1 million. Probably that is because the very nature of specialty publishing is such that it does not require a great deal of capital to launch, and it can be run as an adjunct to a related profession or as a part-time enterprise.

Newsletter Publishing

Newsletter publishing is a growth industry. The ever-developing technologies and attendant complexities of life dictate the need for specialized media of communication as well as an ever-growing need for consultant specialists. The development of a newsletter by the independent consultant is a natural; the newsletter complements the consulting service. It is, in fact, itself a consulting service, one of the many a modern consultant should provide.

Consulting and newsletter publishing are based on the same concept—that is, a need for specialized knowledge and skills. Newsletters furnish information passed over by the popular press as not having interest for the general public. For example, the subject of superconductivity is important enough to merit many special articles in the general press explaining it generally to the public, but the engineers, physicists, and potential manufacturers and marketers of superconductive devices cannot depend on the popular press for information; they must subscribe to specialty publications, such as engineering trade journals, to keep up with developments in a field of great interest to them. Eventually they must seek a periodical that is even more specialized, a periodical devoted exclusively to the single subject of greatest interest. This medium will almost invariably be a newsletter.

A newsletter can spring into being almost overnight. It responds to needs of the moment and can be launched with modest investment and on short notice. When the federal govenment, in its wisdom, created the Occupational Safety and Health Administration, newsletters on the subject sprang out of the ground, just as the birth of the federal Consumer Product Safety Commission mandated the birth of newsletters on that subject. (Should these agencies vanish on Monday morning, the newsletters would vanish on Monday afternoon.)

Whatever your field, there are almost surely a few relevant newsletters being published in it, and there is probably room for one more—yours.

Newsletters are of a wide variety of configurations and concepts, and they provide many services, including:

Roundup summaries of relevant information drawn from a wide variety of other published sources.

News items only—personnel changes, new developments, etc.

Advisory service—answers to questions, general counseling, other such.

Interpretive discussions of events and developments.

Formats and Related Matters

The typical newsletter is in an 8-1/2-by-11-inch format, four or eight pages, composed by typewriter (or, more likely today, by desktop-computer printer), printed on white sulphite bond or offset paper, and published every month. There are many exceptions to that "standard," however. Some newsletters are of tabloid size, formally typeset, printed on newsprint or smooth calendered stock, on white or colored paper stock, published more or less frequently than monthly. Subscription rates vary quite widely, ranging from free subscriptions, to nominal rates, to quite extravagant rates, averaging, probably, from $24 to $60 annually.

The newsletter is a stern master. There are tight deadlines and potential problems with equipment, production, and printing. However, the newsletter is an asset in many ways:

1. It may become a valuable property in terms of the income it produces directly.
2. It may become valuable in terms of supporting your consulting practice generally, helping you gain clients and contracts for your services.
3. It may become an excellent medium for the sale of your books, reports, seminars, and/or other products and services you offer.

Even the newsletter that does not produce a direct profit is often a most valuable asset in these other benefits it delivers. In fact, there are marginal or unprofitable newsletters supported by the publishers—subsidized, in fact—because they are such excellent media for other ventures that are quite profitable.

Sources of Material

Newsletter readers do not pay the relatively high price of subscription to read for amusement; the appeal of a newsletter is its usefulness to the reader. And unlike the daily newspaper, the newsletter cannot base its appeal on different features for different readers; the reader expects to find all or nearly all the content to be relevant to his or her needs and desires. That is the very nature of a newsletter, specialized as it is, high priced as it is (relative to size and frequency of publication), and limited in size and number of pages as it is. The reader is paying for *information*, not writing style, and your editorial work must maximize both the quantity and quality of the information offered.

This is not an easy goal to reach. In fact, the newsletter is possibly the most difficult form of writing. Newsletters cannot be chatty and cannot waste space on trivia. Material must be scrupulously evaluated, and information not of direct use to readers must be ruthlessly discarded. Even that which is used must be condensed, boiled down to essentials, and even phrased in telegraphic style, which omits articles and conjunctions and keeps adjectives and adverbs to an absolute minimum.

Sources of raw material inevitably include other publications (e.g., periodicals, new books, other newsletters, press releases, etc.). You can obtain such information by sending out many complimentary copies of your own newsletter, especially to the publishers of other newsletters that cover matters relevant to yours. Most small newsletter publishers send out many complimentary copies, swapping "comp" subscriptions with others, often with mutual permission to copy each other's material (with attribution). Before long you will be getting press releases, several newsletters, some of the many free trade journals (many are free to "qualified" subscribers), and much other useful material.

Press releases are particularly useful when they are relevant and contain useful information. (A great many do not, unfortunately, because they are thinly veiled puffery.) They are relatively easy to edit and boil down to their essentials, so that they do not have to be rewritten as much as they need to be trimmed. (It is probably true, as alleged by one professional writer, that effective editing should eliminate about one-third of the original copy.)

In publishing a newsletter you must be concerned with copyright protection and plagiarism. Using *information* published elsewhere is not plagiarism; it is research. Copyright protection covers a given combination of words and phrases. It does not cover information itself. Plagiarism is, therefore, stealing another's writing. However, there is in the copyright law the doctrine of "fair usage," which allows you to quote published work briefly. The problem is that there is no definition of what is a "brief" quotation or citation under that doctrine. Caution is advised, and the safest course is to either get permission to quote or to rewrite, putting the information entirely into your own language.

Another source of material for your newsletter is soliciting work from other writers. To attract contributions from professional freelance writers, advise the editors of *Writer's Digest*, *The Writer*, and *Writers' Journal* that you are in the market for contributions, explaining just what you are looking for and what you are willing to pay. (Read sample issues of those periodicals for models of the kind of information they publish in such notices.)

It is also possible to get many free contributions from other professionals who will write material for the privilege of being published. Unfortunately, much of what you get in this fashion is not what you want or can use. You run the risk of offending the well-intentioned contributor when you do not use the material he or she has supplied. You can minimize this by asking for specific factual information only, such as personnel changes, news of new products, or other such items. The tendency of many contributors who are not professional writers is to editorialize, trying to use your vehicle as a medium for expressing their opinions publicly.

Whatever sources and information you use, remember that your subscribers have certain expectations. If you fail to meet them, the subscribers will be unlikely to renew their subscriptions. To ensure a successful newsletter, you must work constantly at discovering what appeals most to your readers and what appeals least to them and be governed by that. Take the time to read letters from your subscribers, and encourage them to write with their likes and dislikes. Let your readers tell you how to run your newsletter.

Publishing Other Specialties

There is no firm definition of the word *book*. Some publications referred to as books are often quite slender volumes, bound publications of less than 100 pages, while there are others that are massive tomes. In any case, many consultants who become publishers choose not to undertake the considerable labor and cost of producing formal books, even the relatively inexpensive paperback books. However, they do produce a variety of other publications, publications that are inexpensive and easy to produce, despite sometimes being of a size that might justify their publication as a book. These are usually publications with a quite limited investment required and a quite profitable return on investment. These are often referred to as "reports," "special reports," or "folios," perhaps for lack of a better name to identify the genre generally.

The key to these is that they rarely *look* like books; they look like internal reports or memoranda, typed (or computer printed) on ordinary white paper (sulphite bond or offset paper), bound with a corner staple or enclosed in a paper or plastic office binder. Most are small publications, marketed at a quite reasonable price, and highly profitable because they are inexpensive to produce. While fairly expensive to market, they do fetch a price that is high in relation to production costs.

The Economics of Specialty Publishing

Customers who buy books pay a great deal for the physical quality of the product. On the other hand, customers buying reports, newsletters, and similar specialty items are encouraged to ignore the aesthetic qualities of the physical product and to place the value of the product on the *information* it conveys. Your advertising must have that focus.

A handsomely bound book of 300 pages may sell for $19.95, while a simple, corner stapled report of 10 pages may bring $5. In fact, I developed over 30 such how-to reports, ranging from 2 to 20 pages, covering a wide variety of subjects related to my services, and had no difficulty in getting from $2 to $10 for them. I also developed a series of special reports on new federally funded public works projects, reports that merely identified the projects, their dollar value, and other such data, and I found a brisk market for these. Later I developed a series of three books on selling to the government, composed by Selectric typewriter and paperbound, and sold many of these as a package (via mail order and a newsletter I published) at $89.95. However, in retrospect I believe that the reports were more profitable and certainly less trouble than were the books.

Conventional wisdom in direct mail marketing dictates that you should set a selling price of not less than three times your product cost, and you should be prepared for selling costs of approximately one-half the selling price. That means that if the item costs you $5 to produce, you must ask at least $15 for it and be prepared to spend up to $7.50 in advertising and related costs to win the order. That leaves you with an approximate 16.66% gross profit—$2.50/$15.00 × 100—which is none too generous a margin. Therefore, even the 3 to 1 markup is rather thin, and it is wise to give yourself a wider margin if at all possible.

Fortunately, specialty publishing allows you that wide margin, which is why it is a relatively low-risk enterprise. The typical report can be produced at a cost of about 4 to 5 cents a page, and you can usually get about 50 cents per page without difficulty, giving you a gross profit of about 20 cents per page or 40 percent on investment.

You can see from such figures how it is possible to make PO deals in which you allow the other party to earn 50 percent of the selling price, while you still earn a substantial profit. If you sell your reports on such a basis, you get 25 cents per page, while the product costs you five cents, for a gross profit of 20 cents. Of course, you have the labor and cost of packaging and mailing the product, which, if you mail first class, can add about four cents more per page for postage alone, still leaving you an adequate margin to pay overhead costs and amortize your original development costs.

Of course, each time you fill an order you enclose advertising literature, offering your other publications and other services (e.g., seminars) as well as your regular consulting services. If you give good service and your reports contain good, useful information, you will find that you get repeat orders. You may lose money on first orders, since they are quite small and the cost of winning them is proportionately large, but the repeat business is quite profitable and more than compensates for the cost of first orders. Remember, the purpose of marketing is not to make sales; it is to make customers who return to buy again.

That consideration should dictate what you publish. You should think in terms of the interests of your typical customer and design your entire line of publications to be useful for that typical customer. Make the line of publications mutually supporting, offer a complete complement of information to encourage and stimulate repeat business.

Your publications and seminars should also be mutually supporting. You should use each to help sell the other. If first orders for publications can produce customers for buying other publications of yours, they can also produce customers for your seminars, a venture with a relatively high price tag and profit margin.

SPEAKING FOR PROFIT

Public speaking supports many individuals full time and provides extra income to many others. The "stars" of public speaking—referred to in the speaking profession as "celebrity speakers"—are well-known public figures, such as Barbara Walters, Henry Kissinger, and Art Buchwald, who earn as much as $25,000 for a lecture or speech. There are thousands of speakers who are not as well known and who earn far less than these celebrities do, but they still make comfortable wages for their speaking efforts, earning at least $500 for a speech, with fees of $1,000 to $5,000 not at all uncommon for well-rated speakers. Many are full-time professional speakers; others are part-time speakers from a variety of other fields—they are writers, scientists, engineers, executives, physicians, public officials, retired military officers, and specialists in many other fields. But many speakers are also consultants, and it is not always easy to determine whether one is a professional consultant who speaks frequently for fees or a professional speaker who consults often for fees!

There is a broad parallel to be drawn between writing for profit and speaking for profit. Both can be packaged as a product or even as a series of products to be sold to the general public, as a fee-paid standard package or series of packages to be sold to individual clients, or as a custom service for clients. This is especially true for seminars and other training programs. However, a great many professional speakers are also writers and self-publishers, earning much of their income through selling their self-published books to those attending their public presentations. The three professions and activities—consulting, writing, and speaking—are a commonly encountered combination.

THE PUBLIC SPEAKING INDUSTRY

Despite certain similarities, public speaking is quite different from free-lance writing. The professional writer, especially a writer of books, is quite likely to have a literary agent who represents the writer on an exclusive basis. Every book the writer produces is marketed by the agent, and all the writer's business dealings with publishers are handled by the agent. In the speaking industry, only the highest rated speakers, principally the celebrity speakers who are in heavy demand, are represented by an agent or manager. Other speakers do their own marketing, with some engagements arranged via lecture bureaus.

Lecture bureaus are nothing like literary agents, they are more like brokers. They do not represent the speaker at all; they represent the client who wants to engage a speaker. The client may request that the bureau arrange for the services of a specific individual or that the bureau supply candidates of a given type or to speak on a given subject. The lecture bureau provides a service to the client, but it is the speaker who actually pays the lecture bureau by permitting the lecture bureau to collect his or her fee and deduct a commission (usually from 25 to 40 percent of the fee, but often less when the speaker is in demand and commands a large fee).

There are no exclusive agreements between the lecture bureau and the client or the lecture bureau and the speaker. However, it is considered to be unethical for a speaker to arrange future engagements with a client originally booked via a lecture bureau without paying the lecture bureau a fee each time.

Most professional speakers obtain only a small percentage of their speaking engagements through lecture bureaus, they win most through their own marketing efforts. However, many lecture bureaus are the creations of the speakers, with the speaker as the principal, perhaps sole, speaker offered. Many speakers create their own lecture bureaus as a marketing device, a perfectly legitimate approach to this special market.

This does not mean that you should not register with as many lecture bureaus as possible; you certainly should. But do not expect to get the bulk of your bookings in this manner.

Who Are the Clients?

The clients for speakers are almost as varied as are the speakers, their subjects, and their presentations. They include colleges and universities, companies, government agencies, cruise ships, resorts, civic groups, unions, and associations.

Marketing Yourself as a Speaker

The basic marketing tools you require for speaking engagements are a brochure and some kind of audition tape. Today, many speakers have had videotapes made up for auditions, although an audiotape is generally still adequate for most needs (and even that is not always necessary, once you have become established). How you market yourself depends on many factors—that is, what kinds of presentations you make, who wants such presentations, and why they want such presentations. Here are just a few general types of speakers and presentations:

The famous
The infamous
Motivational speakers
Humorists
Entertainers
Experts

Curiosity probably explains the major appeal of the *famous* who are not especially gifted as speakers; many of the celebrity speakers are not especially good speakers, and many have nothing especially interesting to say. Very much the same considerations apply to the *infamous*, such as the former officials who took to the lecture circuit for handsome fees after they had served their time for Watergate crimes.

Many theologians and sales trainers are *motivational speakers* (sometimes referred to as "inspirational" speakers). They appeal to the emotions of the audience, preaching brotherhood, positive thinking, and other similar topics. They try to encourage certain helpful attitudes, to make listeners feel better about themselves and their lives, to inspire listeners to more lofty goals and thoughts. At the same time, many people find their messages entertaining, especially when they are such especially gifted presenters as Norman Vincent Peale or Art Linkletter.

Humorists and *entertainers* are also popular speakers. Probably the most famous American humorist of modern times was the late Will Rogers, who managed to perceive the humor in many well-known situations, especially those in the news. One who probably rivals him is Art Buchwald. However, there are many speakers who are humorists, albeit less well known than these two men.

There are also many speakers who are engaged primarily on the basis of their reputations as *experts* in some field, especially when an expert in that field is not easy to find. That, probably more than any great talent as a speaker, accounts for most of my own engagements. There are not a great many true experts in marketing to the government and writing proposals who are willing to lecture even briefly on the subject, let alone conduct an all-day seminar to train others.

These categories are admittedly somewhat arbitrary, for they often overlap each other, but the characterizations help to explain the different appeals of certain kinds of speakers, the different reasons for engaging a given speaker, and, consequently, they help to explain and delineate the markets for public speaking.

You will have to decide for yourself what you need in the way of materials to make yourself and your offer of public speaking known to prospective clients. You must identify your prospective clients and understand their needs and desires thoroughly, and then decide what it is that you can do for the prospective client. Of course, what you promise to do for the prospective client must correlate with the prospective client's needs and desires.

For example, I teach marketing to the government, including proposal writing, the critically essential key to winning government contracts. But I promise to help clients win contracts. I promise to help them get what they want as a *final result*, the *end*, not the means. Many marketing efforts fail, despite costly sales literature, simply because the consultant tries to sell the means and not the end. Clients always want to buy the result, not the means. My own clients do not care greatly whether I am an entertaining speaker or a trained orator; they care only whether I can produce the promised result of more success in pursuing government contracts.

But that promise, the *right* promise, is only half the battle for the order. The other half is proof, the evidence that you are what you say you are, can do for the prospect what you say you can do, and can deliver what you say you can deliver. Proof can be established by your audiotape or videotape, your printed literature, or testimonials and references.

THE SEMINAR BUSINESS

Attractive as the lecture circuit is, for many of us in the consulting field seminars offer distinct advantages, including:

1. You *create* something, packaging the seminar as a proprietary product and marketing it under your own total control, with options for profit that are not available to you as a presenter of a simple speech.
2. You create a seminar that is a unique product or program, thus gaining an important market advantage. (It is much more difficult to establish a speech as unique.)
3. You do not wait for a client to decide to want you as a speaker. You seize the initiative and present it as a program open to the general public—with open registration—something quite difficult to do today for a simple speech.
4. You also sell it to organizations as a custom service for substantial fees.

Seminar Subjects

Seminars are learning sessions that address highly specialized and perhaps little-known aspects of some field or topic, and are presented by a qualified expert. Often the subject is something rather new (e.g., a new kind of computer program or a new legal requirement), and sometimes it is new only in that it has never been presented as a seminar before.

Who Pays to Attend?

The two basic kinds of seminars are (1) those open to the public and (2) those presented on a custom basis for a client organization who will have certain individuals attend. For those seminars open to the public, the question of who will pay for the individual's registration and attendance must be studied to determine marketing strategy. Consider the following hypothetical seminar subjects:

1. Handling collection of delinquent accounts
2. More effective selling techniques
3. A weight-loss program
4. A stop-smoking program
5. Job-hunting tips and procedures.

Which of these do you believe employers would pay for? Which would attendees have to pay for themselves? Most employers would normally pay for seminars 1 and 2 but would not pay for seminars 3 and 4 since employers would not benefit from it (there are some employers who might be persuaded that such programs will benefit their employees' health enough to warrant the investment). Employers would probably not pay for seminar 5, although in some cases large corporations with substantial layoffs of employees might offer this kind of help.

In the case of my own seminars, most attendees were sent by their employers at company expense, but there were also numerous individuals, in business or planning to go into business, who paid their own way. But they attended as managers of their own businesses, not as consumers seeking to solve personal problems. That is a most significant point in marketing your seminar. It is basic in regard to understanding motivation, but it is even more critical in reaching your prospects with your advertising offer and appeal.

MARKETING THE SEMINAR

Sometimes you will find seminars advertised in the newspaper, usually in the business pages. Those are invariably seminars addressed to individual consumers, prospects who will attend for personal reasons and will pay for their own attendance. On the other hand, your name—the one you use for business—sooner or later finds its way onto many mailing lists, and your morning mail often includes brochures appealing to you to attend seminars of many kinds. By far the overwhelming majority of seminar promotions use the direct mail brochure.

Direct mail is the most effective way to market a seminar, and it is possible to find mailing lists of *businesses* of all kinds to use in your direct mail campaign. But it is difficult to find mailing lists of interested, local *individuals*—it is unlikely that individuals will travel great distances to attend the seminar. Thus advertising in the general public media, such as a newspaper, is usually the most practical way of marketing such a seminar, inefficient though it is.

By far the overwhelming majority of seminars are on business subjects and intended for businesses and thus direct mail efforts are the most productive. Business and industry represent the major market for seminars, and there are powerful arguments for designing seminars to appeal to employees rather than individuals.

1. An appeal to individuals to attend a seminar usually produces only single registrations; but it is not at all unusual to get several registrations from companies. I have had as many as six registrants from a single company, for example, so that even as few as 10 or 15 organizations responding can result in a well-attended seminar.
2. The business seminar can be sold as a custom, in-house seminar for organizations for adequate fees. There is rather little possibility of conducting seminars that appeal only to personal interests.

The appeal to employers should be designed to maximize the number of employees who might be sent to attend. A seminar on purchasing procedure might inspire employers to see the need to send only one employee, the purchasing agent, since that is the single individual who does all the purchasing in all but the largest organizations. But a seminar on more effective business writing is likely to inspire an employer to send a number of people because many people handle correspondence and other writing chores in most companies. This consideration alone, taken into account in conceiving and designing the seminar, may have an important influence on its success.

Marketing by Direct Mail

The principles of marketing by direct mail are not different from the principles of marketing in general, but the methods of implementation are quite different, taking advantage of what the medium offers. Here are four of those advantages:

1. Direct mail affords you an opportunity to target your prospects more closely than do other media. You can get mailing lists of many specific kinds of prospects—small businesses, appliance manufacturers, retail chains, and many other such characterizations at various levels of specialization. When using the more general public media—print and broadcast—the targeting is almost nonexistent.
2. In terms of cost per *qualified* prospect, direct mail is usually much less expensive than other media.
3. Testing offers and copy via direct mail are much more practical in terms of elapsed time and cost than it is in other media.
4. Direct mail affords you the opportunity to develop specialized, or premium, lists.

The Direct Mail Package

What has become the more or less traditional direct mail package includes at least a sales letter, a brochure, a "response device" (i.e., an order form), and a return envelope.

Direct mail experts maintain that including a return envelope, especially one that requires no postage (you pay the postage on each one delivered to you under the special permit for this kind of postal service), also increases response. They are undoubtedly right, as far as direct mail campaigns directed to individuals in their homes, since most people do not have envelopes and postage stamps conveniently at hand. However, when the direct mail literature is directed to business executives in their offices, that problem does not exist. To test this theory I included return envelopes in my earliest mailings promoting seminars. I found few of the registrations returned were in those envelopes. Almost all registrations were returned in the executives' own company envelopes. In my own subsequent mailings, therefore, I enclosed a sales letter and a brochure. One of the panels of the brochure was a registration form, perforated for easy separation. That was my "response device."

By now you may have noted that I did not use the conventional, self-mailer brochure. I thought this not the way to go when promoting seminars on a small scale because it was difficult to find the right mailing lists—lists of truly qualified prospects. That means that the brochures must be mailed to more generalized lists, which is a great waste of time and money. Couple that with the knowledge that a great many recipients discard what they recognize as advertising matter—"junk mail"—without even a glance, and you can see that the rate of response would be so small as to make the use of these brochures ineffective and wasteful. I decided to spend extra time compiling the right mailing lists and turned to the more conventional direct mail approach of a sales letter and brochure.

Mailing Lists and List Brokers

None of the foregoing explanations are intended to deride the existing mailing list services. There are a great many such services (see the list in Chapter 17) that meet most advertisers' needs. How we describe or characterize these services depends on our viewpoint. Those who rent mailing lists to users—and they are not sold but are rented for one or more uses, according to agreement—rent lists that are not their property, for the most part. Most own some "house" lists, but the bulk of the lists they rent out belong to publishers, large mail order dealers, and other business organizations. The list service is provided by a broker, earning a commission on the rentals. However, they prefer to be regarded by the owners of the lists as "list managers," attending to the interests of owners of the lists by organizing and marketing the lists.

With today's computers, most list brokers can retrieve lists according to a variety of classifications, and most will furnish you a catalog explaining their entire offering.

Compiling Your Own Lists

Mailing lists are valued in several ways. One way is in terms of accuracy, with certain guarantees regarding the maximum percentage of "nixies" (i.e., errors that make the item undeliverable). They are also valued by the demographic characteristics they display—high income, upwardly mobile, young marrieds, and/or other such indicators of qualifications as buyers. More important is the buying history of those on the list. Lists of "inquirers"—that is, those who respond to offers of information—are not as valuable as lists of buyers.

In this environment, the compiled list, which is derived from such sources as directories and membership lists, is of little value because it provides very limited information. Neither demographic data nor prior purchasing history are known.

I decided that in my own case I would do better with compiled lists, as long as I did my own compiling. I had the advantage of knowing my field well enough to be able to judge with a fair degree of accuracy which companies and other organizations (e.g., unions, associations, nonprofit corporations, and agencies of state and local governments who pursue federal contracts) would be suitable for my purposes. In many cases, I recognized the organization by name and knew a little about it; in other cases, their name or the circumstances in which I learned their name gave me a good clue. For example, I compiled many names and addresses from the help wanted sections of major daily newspapers, especially from the "professional opportunities" type of display advertising. The wording of the advertising itself furnished an excellent clue as to whether the advertiser was the type of organization that would be pursuing the negotiated type of government contract. However, I was also able to get a list of contractors from a Navy department, a list of minority-owned firms from the Small Business Administration, and a list of the subscribers to the *Commerce Business Daily*, the government's own publication that announces bid opportunities and contract awards.

It was a great deal of work, of course, but it paid off well. I achieved results others considered somewhat phenomenal in being able to win from 30 to 60 registrations from mailings of fewer than 5,000 pieces, often even from mailings of less than 3,000 pieces. I had, in fact, developed a *premium* list for my own needs. I chose to send the literature by first-class mail in a plain white business envelope that did not announce itself as advertising literature.

Copy and Ideas

Although advertising experts often stress the need to get attention first and then arouse interest, I consider these to be the same thing.

That is, getting attention should not be done through some unrelated gimmick, as it unfortunately is in some promotions, but should be directly related to the main promise of benefits. It should, in fact, *be* the main promise expressed as dramatically as possible.

Headline Copy

Consider the following headlines that get attention, arouse interest, and address the main promise:

THE *GRADUATE* COURSE IN WINNING CONTRACTS!
HOW TO WRITE WINNING PROPOSALS
BE A CONSULTANT. EARN $500 AND MORE A DAY
HOW TO BECOME INDEPENDENT

In many cases the headlines are made even more compelling by subheads or blurbs, and in some cases even require such additions to get their meaning across and complete their impact:

THE *GRADUATE* COURSE IN WINNING CONTRACTS
Secrets of the most successful professionals revealed!

HOW TO WRITE WINNING PROPOSALS
It's *Marketing* Strategy,
Not Writing Skill, That Makes the Difference

BE A CONSULTANT. EARN $500 AND MORE A DAY
Successful Consultants Earn at Least That Much

HOW TO BECOME INDEPENDENT
Here are dozens of ideas and reams of how-to information on
starting your business IN YOUR OWN HOME!

Figure 14–1 is the front panel of a brochure, sent out by one of the sponsors of my seminar programs.

Note the direct appeal of the headline, with its focus on secrets of success, followed by an entire series of subordinate headlines, summarizing the major points of the program. Note, too, the final item of the series, which promises "insider tips and secrets," repeating the main promise made in the headline.

United Business Institute

presents a marketing seminar

Secrets of Success in Winning Consulting Contracts with Federal, State, and Local Government Agencies

- **How government agencies buy**
- **How to sell to government agencies**
- **Finding the contract opportunities**
- **Writing winning proposals**
- **Beating the competition (under the new Competition in Contracting Law**
- **Benefiting from government budget cutbacks**
- **And many, many more insider tips and secrets**

Personally conducted by Herman Holtz.
author of the best-selling book:
"How to Succeed as an Independent Consultant"
Washington, D.C. **May 7, 1986**

FIGURE 14.1. Front panel of brochure illustrating headlines.

Body Copy

Once you have established the main promise—the major benefit which is your principal argument for registration and attendance—the rest of your literature must follow logically from that introduction. The body copy of your brochure should expand on the main promise, adding proof or evidence.

Figure 14–2, the second page of the brochure, indicates how that was done in this case, building the case primarily on the basis of the presenter's credentials as an expert, but also listing the names of some well-known organizations whose employees attended previous sessions. (In some cases, the brochure would quote former participants who recommended the seminar.)

How to Win Government Consulting Contracts

You can earn substantial dollars consulting with the federal, state and local governments. Government personnel cutbacks are creating a greater demand for consultants than ever before.

Key Benefits of Attendance:

- Hear one of the nation's most successful consultants tell you how to turn your present knowledge and experience into marketable skills.
- How government cutbacks benefit you.
- Find out how to penetrate the $200 billion market of federal contracts and billions of dollars in industrial and professional services.
- Get the facts from Herman on how to win contracts—he has won over $260 million in federal contracts alone.
- Learn how to write proposals that win.
- Find out why it is now easier for you as a consultant to penetrate the federal contracts market and win. The new law, "Competition in Federal Contracts Act," went into effect on April 1, 1985.
- Learn how to market your services with confidence.
- How to locate government markets.
- Understand the key to mastering sales and marketing skills.
- Leave armed with the tools you need to get started immediately—the knowledge and a seminar handbook, personally developed by Mr. Holtz.

"A large portion of those who enter into consulting services as a profession do not survive the first year, the chief reason being the failure to market their services effectively."—Herman Holtz.

The above quote is but a sample of the straight talk you will hear from Herman Holtz at this seminar. You will learn how to market your skills effectively and much more. That's why you can't afford to miss this opportunity to consult for a full day with Herman Holtz.

- How to turn your talents to profits
- How to inventory your technical assets and your talents
- How to cash in on trends
- Where the money is today

Some Previous Participants

Alcoa	Kenton
Bethlehem Steel	General Kinetics
Sikorsky Aircraft	Pitney Bowes
General Research	DSI Computer Services
Western Union	Dynamic Data Processing
Computer Sciences Corporation	Digital
Memorex	Marriott
Boeing Computer Services	Owens Corning Fiberglass
Bionetics	Sperry
Burroughs	Tele Sec Temporary Personnel
Raven Data Processing	AT&T
Finalco	Techplan
Tracor	Control Data Corporation
Watkins-Johnson	Color-Ad
Genasys Corporation	Systematic General
Illinois State OMBE	Scientific Applications
Flow General	The Maxima Corporation
Rolm Corporation	Battelle Memorial Institute

Seminar Leader

This seminar is personally conducted by Herman Holtz, the author of the best-selling book: "How to Succeed as an Independent Consultant."

Instructor
Herman Holtz

- Consultant
- Lecturer
- Author
- Seminar Leader
- Winner of over $260 million in government contracts

Herman Holtz can point to specifics—about $260 million—of success in marketing through his own direct efforts as a proposal specialist, director of marketing, and general manager of various organizations, and as a consultant to many companies. He has been employed by such major corporations as RCA, GE, and Philco-Ford, and has served many others—IBM, Control Data Corporation and Dun & Bradstreet, for example—as a consultant. As an independent consultant, he also lectures and conducts seminars on marketing, proposal writing, and a number of other subjects about which he has written extensively. And because of the great success of his book, *How to Succeed as an Independent Consultant*, he has been invited to speak frequently on that subject, as well to continue to write on the subject of consulting.

Herman Holtz is an independent consultant in Washington, DC and the author of several books including:

How to Succeed as an Independent Consultant, John Wiley & Sons, 1983.
Government Contracts: Proposalmanship and Winning Strategies, Plenum, 1979.
The $100 Billion Market: How to do Business with the U.S. Government, AMACOM (American Management Associations), 1980.
The Winning Proposal: How to Write It, McGraw-Hill, 1981.
Directory of Federal Purchasing Offices, John Wiley & Sons, 1982.
Profit from Your Money-Making Ideas: How to Build a New Business or Expand an Existing One, AMACOM, 1980.
Profit-Line Management: Managing a Growing Business Successfully, AMACOM, 1981.
The Secrets of Practical Marketing for Small Business, Prentice-Hall, 1982.
2001 Sources of Financing for Small Business, Arco, 1983.

Who Should Attend

Any man or woman with a marketable skill gained through education or experience—executives, managers, computer specialists, accountants, engineers, marketing reps, military, professors, grad students, entreprenuers, business planners, authors, real estate professionals, data processing specialists, computer scientists, lawyers, trainers, designers, personnel specialists, architects, psychologists, and anyone desiring to enter the consulting business.

Materials

Each participant will receive a personal copy of "Government Contracts—Proposalmanship," a seminar manual personally developed by Herman Holtz.

FIGURE 14.2. Body text on inside panel of brochure.

The evidence must demonstrate that yours is not an empty promise. It must show that you can and will deliver what you promise by revealing some details of your plan of presentation and of your own credentials as the presenter and expert. The brochure copy illustrates this principle. It and the accompanying sales letter suggested that attendees would learn some insider secrets. The literature included such startling claims as teaching attendees how to appear to be low bidders when they are not and how to gather the priceless and necessary marketing intelligence. These are the kinds of items that not only command attention and arouse interest, but virtually demand registering for the session. A detailed seminar outline (see Figure 14–3) lends great weight to this.

Persuasive Methods

The results of advertising are never completely predictable because the reaction of the public is never entirely predictable. However, some things work better than others.

1. The credibility of your claims and promises is in almost direct proportion to the amount or degree of detail you furnish in explaining them. The public senses instinctively that anyone can generalize, but only those who know what they are talking about can furnish the details of what they promise to do and how they will do it. But don't overdo it; too much becomes tedious. The art is in judging how much detail is just right.
2. Excessive hyperbole suggests vain boasting. Minimize your use of adjectives and use factual data, especially quantitative data, to impress the prospect (e.g., the $260 million in contracts won, cited in the brochure illustrated in Figure 14–2).
3. Prospects are usually strongly attracted by the words and ideas of *insider information*, *secrets*, and other promises of getting information not commonly available. Such words as *new*, *free*, *special*, and *sale* also never seem to wear out in their appeal.
4. The more appealing the promise, the stronger is the wish to believe it, but the more elaborate or dramatic the promise, the stronger the evidence backing it up must be. Sometimes it is better to downplay it, actually offering less than you believe you will deliver simply because the truth is sometimes difficult to believe and difficult to prove.

SEMINAR OUTLINE

I. The $600 Billion Market
- Understanding the market.
- What governments buy.
- How to sell to governments; federal, state and local.

II. Locating Sales Opportunities
- How to uncover selling opportunities.
- Getting on the appropriate bidder's list.
- How to use the *Commerce Business Daily* as an effective marketing tool.
- How to use the Freedom of Information Act to market.

III. Understanding the Marketing Process
- The three elements of marketing successfully
- Are your technical skills enough?
- Mastering market skills
- The elements of selling: Promise and Proof
- Mastering selling skills

IV. How to Market Your Consulting Services
- Instill confidence
- Gain prestige and build a professional image
- Develop the all-important leads
- Following up leads correctly

V. How to Win Government Contracts
- Understanding the public sector market
- How to sell to governments
- How to uncover selling opportunities
- The New Competition Act and how to benefit from it
- How to get on and stay on the bidder's list

VI. How to Benefit from Government Cutbacks
- How to determine where personnel shortages are most severe
- How to locate funding set aside for consultant services
- How to capture your share of the market

VII. Proposal Strategy Development
- Why proposals?
- What is a proposal?
- What does the customer want?
- What must the proposal do?
- What makes a winner?
- Why strategy makes the difference.

VIII. Persuasive Proposal Writing
- What is persuasion?
- The art of persuasive writing.
- What makes others agree?
- What turns them on? And off?

IX. How to Write a Winning Proposal
- Writing to communicate.
- Writing to sell.
- Writing to arouse and sustain interest.
- Your proposal should promise desirable end-results.
- Your proposal should, preferably, be a unique claim, one your competition can't match.
- Your proposal must be able to prove its validity.

X. Formats and Proposal Content
- Recommended format.
- Front matter and other elements.
- How to use format for best results.

XI. Broadening the Base of Your Consulting Practice
- Expand your profit center
- Write to sell
- Publish newsletters, reports, books, tapes, etc.
- Public speaking for profit

XII. How to Price Your Consulting Services
- Understanding costs
- The elements of a cost proposal
- Construction of the quote

XIII. Using Cost in Marketing
- Using prices as market tools.
- Bid/no bid.
- Parametric cost estimates.

XIV. Negotiating Basic Rates
- Labor rates.
- Overhead costs.
- Putting costs where they will do the most good.
- Negotiating with the auditors.

XV. Open Discussion

REGISTRATION FORM

United Business Institute
Oxon Hill Center, Box 448, Oxon Hill, MD 20745
(202) 822-3100

HOW TO WIN GOVERNMENT CONSULTING CONTRACTS

To ensure participation in this exclusive seminar we urge you to register in advance. You may reserve your space(s) by telephone and confirm by returning the form below. List your name and other data in the space below and enclose remittance now or call 822-3100 for reservations. Late payment may be made at the door with firm reservations.

Name ______________________
Organization ______________________
Address ______________________
City ____________ State ______ Zip ______
Telephone ( ) ______________________

Additional registrants from same organization:
Name ______________________
Name ______________________
Name ______________________
Name ______________________

Seminar Fee: $195.00 advance; $210.00 at door; $150.00 each additional registrant. Amount enclosed $ ____________

☐ Check ☐ Money Order ☐ MasterCard ☐ Visa Card No. ____________ Exp. Date ____________

Planned Date of Attendance: ____________

FIGURE 14.3

The Sales Letter

I am a believer in sales letters as the main element in a direct mail program. They furnish the opportunity for a chatty kind of communication with the prospect, in direct contrast to the formality of a printed brochure. In keeping with that idea, the sales letter should never be typeset, but always typed.

Figure 14–4 is one brief example of a letter, using a routing box suggesting the first addressee to whom the letter and accompanying brochure should be addressed.

A Few Special Promotional Ideas

One idea that paid dividends for me was a postscript to the sales letter along the following lines:

> In the event that you must miss this important event, there will be later opportunities. We will be pleased to put your name on a special list that will absolutely ensure your being advised of future sessions. In fact, I invite you to return the following brief form, suggesting times and locations that would be most convenient for you and your staff.
>
> ____
>
> Name & company
>
> ____
>
> Address, city, state, zip
>
> ____
>
> Preferred times & locations

Another successful idea was the inclusion of literature advertising a newsletter and special publications, offering the option of ordering individual items or ordering all in a special package deal. Many who did not register for the seminar forwarded checks and orders for the publications. In fact, the total of such orders usually produced enough income to cover all the initial expenses of the seminar, making it not only virtually risk-free, but profitable as well.

One thing that plagues seminar producers are the cancellations. Most seminar producers exact a penalty for last-minute cancellations, but even so they believe that they are impelled to guarantee refunds. I found it possible to avoid the problem of refunds entirely

EXCELSIOR ASSOCIATES
4722 Lincoln Drive
Pleasantville, OH 44444

Marketing Mgr____________________
____
____
____

HOW TO WIN [MORE] GOVERNMENT CONTRACTS

ANYONE CAN DO BUSINESS WITH THE GOVERNMENT--YOU, TOO!

The Federal government right now spends about $200 billion a year to buy just about every service and product known. The nearly 80,000 state and local government entities (that number comes from the U.S. Census Bureau) account, altogether, for more than twice as much, so the federal, state, and local governments of the United States spend over $600 billion a year--every year--buying almost every kind of goods and service known. Are you getting your share of this enormous market? If not, you are missing out on something you could easily share in.

There are several reasons that many marketing people shrink from approaching the government markets. The first reason is mythology: There are many false stories circulating, to the effect that the paperwork involved in doing business with the government is impossibly difficult, that you must "know someone" to win government contracts, that there is little or no profit in government contracting, that the government takes forever to pay its bills, and many other myths. Yes, myths, for most of these stories are totally untrue, at least for all practical purposes.

The simple fact is that you are as much entitled to pursue government business as anyone is, and the law clearly requires the governments to give you equal consideration with everyone else; public money--your taxes and mine --are being spent, and we all have a right to compete for a share of the business. The paperwork is no worse than you will encounter with any large organization, and many private-sector corporations take longer than the government to pay their bills.

How do I know this? I know it because I have over 25 years' experience in this field. I have won and managed many dozens of government contracts for former employers, for my own account, and for my many clients, organizations who have retained me to help them win government contracts.

Can I help you win a share of these billions of dollars? I am sure I can. Stay with me for a few more minutes and let me explain how the system works and what I can do to help you win your first government contracts or, if you are already doing some business with the government, how I can help you increase your volume of government business.

(MORE)

FIGURE 14.4. Sales letter with routing box.

through issuing "rain checks." I guaranteed anyone who canceled full credit for attendance at any future presentation of the seminar. That satisfied the registrant and eliminated refunds.

Fees and Costs

Most seminar producers charge a flat fee for attendance at a seminar, with a reduced fee for additional registrants from the same organization. Some, however, charge two kinds of fee, one for registration and one for attendance. The registration fee covers the organization; attendance fees are identical for as many participants as the organization wishes to send. And refunds are made of attendance fees only; registration fees are not refundable.

Most seminars carry a slightly higher fee for registration at the door than for prior registration and payment by check or credit card. Today, with telephone payments by credit card acceptable, it is a good idea to invite registration by telephone.

Typical seminar fees today are approximately $200 or more per day, although many independent consultants offer seminars at a somewhat lower fee. Usually that includes coffee and cakes in the morning and cold drinks in the afternoon. A few seminars include a lunch, often with a luncheon speaker, but that has become quite expensive. Most seminars include handout materials, including special seminar manuals. But some seminar producers also sell books, newsletter subscriptions, and tape cassette programs in back-of-the-room sales. That has become a rather common practice among professional speakers, especially those who publish their own books and other related materials. Many report that they derive as much income from the back-of-the-room sales as they do from speaking.

Best Days for Seminars

Mondays and Fridays are the worst days for attracting attendees. Those who must come from out of town to attend do not wish to travel on Sunday to attend a Monday session, nor do they wish to fight the Friday evening crush in most airports. Tuesday and Wednesday are the best days to present seminars. Summer is not a good time either because of travel difficulties and conflicting vacation schedules.

Presenting Custom Seminars

Many organizations will book you to present your seminar on a custom basis as an in-house event. I have been fortunate enough to present my seminars for many organizations and at various events throughout the United States. In some cases, you can generate a full fee plus all expenses. (I would suggest a minimum of $1,000 per day plus expenses.) However, in many cases it will be to your advantage to undertake such sessions even at very much reduced fees because they represent excellent PR opportunities that lead to highly profitable sessions.

The following are all potential opportunities:

Business and industrial corporations
Local community colleges
Special education programs at 4-year colleges and universities
Nonprofit corporations
Associations and annual conventions
Special schools and courses

15

Consulting and Computers

There is probably no item of equipment that can be of as much value to the typical independent consultant as the computer is. And yet the average independent consultant can probably benefit from some up-to-date knowledge and suggestions.

DESKTOP COMPUTERS

There has been no shortage of publications about the *personal computer,* also often referred to as the *microcomputer*. Few new developments have caught on as rapidly or developed as swiftly as has what I much prefer to refer to as the *desktop computer*. (It is "personal" only when so used, not inherently, and all computers and other electronic devices use microcircuits today.) Such computers are today almost as popular and as commonly found in offices, even the smallest ones, as typewriters are. So it is not my purpose to introduce you here to the desktop computer—it is likely you already have one in your office and have retired your electric typewriter in favor of the computer and word processor. But it is my intention to make suggestions for gaining the maximum benifits from it and to clear up some misunderstandings about the desktop computer.

Used properly, the computer is the greatest boon yet to office efficiency in general, especially in the small office, and especially if you have a reasonably modern machine. That adjective, "modern," has special meaning here.

The desktop computer has evolved and is still evolving so rapidly that I retired my first computer, vintage 1983, in 1986. It was still functioning well, but the newer machines offered many newer and greater capabilities. That first machine was a "CP/M" (commonly represented as referring to "control program/ microcomputers," but probably originally an abbreviation for "control program/monitor") machine, named for the CP/M operating system developed by Gary Kildall and for several years the *de facto* standard for desktop computer operating systems.

Unfortunately, many manufacturers devised their own variations on the CP/M theme, so most of the new computers were not compatible with the others, except on a most limited scale. But they were machines with only 64K memories, although that was a giant step from the earlier 4K, 16K, and other smaller memories. New machines offered memories starting at 128K, but soon ranging to 640K and even beyond that in a few cases. When IBM began using a new operating system, PC DOS ("personal computer disk operating system"), the market underwent revolutionary changes. The enormous market power of IBM was such that almost everyone except Apple Computer Company and a very few others soon abandoned their CP/M designs and began to produce machines that were nearly 100 percent compatible with IBM's PC computers.

The compatible machines were soon called *clones* because, with their MS DOS operating system, almost a double for IBM's PC DOS, they could do almost anything and everything that the IBM machines could do—frequently even more than the IBM computers—and they sold for considerably less money.

The original IBM PC soon evolved into an XT (extended technology) model and later into the AT (advanced technology) model. The industry settled, for a period, on IBM XT and AT models and XT and AT clones.

This history is important. If you are one of those using an earlier, CP/M model, you should know what is now available, what it should cost, and what it can do for you. If you own an XT or AT model (I own an XT clone) you should learn how you can gain maximum benefit from it, as I propose to explain here. You may have to reconfigure it or add to it, as I did, but you will find the relatively small investment required a completely worthwhile one.

One other major development came about, a development that is not linked to the operating systems (CP/M and PC DOS or MS DOS). The costly hard disk drives began to appear at much lower prices. Soon, the owner of a small computer who had been restricted to two 360K floppy disk drives, with all the disadvantages of the restriction, was in a position to buy systems with 10-, 20-, and 30-megabyte hard disk drives or add them to existing systems. That, too, made a great difference. The floppy disk drives that had been reasonably adequate in the 64K computer world were not adequate in a 640K world; hard disk drives were a must if we were to make good use of these new computers and the new software being generated for them.

SIGNIFICANT DIFFERENCES AND ADVANTAGES

The significant differences between those earlier CP/M-based machines and today's popular PC-DOS and MS-DOS machines are: (1) the larger memories (up to 640K) in today's popular XT and AT machines permit a great deal more sophistication in the software and the things of which the software is capable, and (2) the high degree of compatibility among these several million machines offers their owners a totally unprecedented and almost unbelievable volume and variety of usable software. Almost any software program that will run in one of these machines will run in all the others, regardless of who manufactured the machine. In short, the marketing power and market dominance of IBM brought about a high degree of standardization that was not possible with the earlier machines. Even hardware components are largely interchangeable, although hardware standardization did not become quite as great as that of software.

Despite the great success of Apple Computer Company, with its many models—especially the Macintosh models—the established base of Apple computers is not nearly as great as that of the IBM machines and its clones. The principal advantage of the Macintosh appears to be its specialized capabilities for use in graphics generation, display, and printout—there appears to be agreement that the Macintosh is considerably better adapted to desktop publishing, for example—but properly equipped DOS machines also have good capabilities for these things, and those capabilities are growing steadily. For me, the graphics capabilities is not a persuasive argument for sacrificing the many advantages I find in using an XT or AT. But perhaps the capabilities of a Macintosh would be more suitable to your needs. You will have to make that decision.

WORD PROCESSING

Word processing is widely recognized as the primary use of desktop computers. Every office, even the smallest one, can make good use of that function. A word processor, however, is not a computer. It is the software, the computer program, and any PC-DOS or MS-DOS word processor will work in all such systems.

WordStar dominated the word processor field for years, until it was unseated by WordPerfect as a result of the failure of producer MicroPro International Corporation to make more than cosmetic changes to update the program as more sophisticated machines arrived on the scene. Meanwhile, a newer firm of former MicroPro employees produced the more sophisticated WordStar-compatible NewWord. It was a great improvement over WordStar, but never achieved a breakthrough in the marketplace. MicroPro bought the little company and offered the market WordStar Professional Release 4, which makes good use of 640K memories and multimegabyte hard disk drives, with integral dictionary, thesaurus, indexing, and other programs that once had to be purchased separately and used separately. (Probably only a user of old and new systems can fully appreciate the enormous increases in speed and convenience—in sheer *capabilities*—these newer programs offer).

I am a WordStar fan (probably because I started with earlier versions of the program and came to know it) despite its many detractors. Probably WordPerfect and perhaps a number of other word processors are equal to and perhaps even superior to WordStar Professional Release 4, but I am delighted with it; it appears to me to do everything I could wish.

In any case, do not settle for anything less than the capabilities provided by WordStar Professional Release 4 and the latest version of WordPerfect (Version 5.1 at this moment). You shortchange yourself if you do.

DESKTOP PUBLISHING

"Desktop publishing" is a fairly recent concept, inspired in part, at least, by the advent of laser printers, but logically an extension of word processing. Desktop publishing programs offer special capabilities for creating newsletters and other publications (e.g., a variety of type fonts and facility in layouts, printing in multi column, justified type, generating and integrating graphics, etc.) There is a growing number of such programs and several periodicals on the subject of desktop publishing, as an indicator of the rapidly rising interest in this field.

As noted, the rise of desktop publishing appears to have coincided with the introduction of laser printers or to have followed immediately thereafter, for the laser printer provided true letter-quality printing without a daisy wheel or ball type element. It produced its characters, in fact, by converting the digital code to laser pulses that painted the electrostatic pattern on the transfer medium for transfer to paper, a la the conventional xerographic copier found in most offices today. It is a xerographic dot matrix, in fact, using a much denser population of dots and so achieving a much higher fidelity or resolution than the older 9-pin dot matrix printers. In its best implementation, the product approaches the quality of formal typesetting by the more conventional or traditional means.

Despite the quality of their output, laser printers do not dominate the field alone. Recently, a number of printer manufacturers have introduced 24-pin dot matrix printers, capable of true letter-quality printing and rivaling the quality of the laser printers when driven by high-quality software. And while the cost of laser printers is still high at this moment—generally from about $2,000 up—24-pin dot matrix printers are being offered at prices quite comparable with those of the earlier 9-pin printers, which had been available in many inexpensive models that performed quite well.

Graphics Developments

The desktop-publishing technology does not stop with improvements in the type reproduced. The new technology is applied also to graphics, which can be produced by both laser and dot matrix printers with a good degree of quality today. Even photographs are today scanned by electronic devices, "digitizing" them—that is, converting them into digital impulses that can be used to print them in very much the same way a photograph is reproduced as a "halftone" in conventional printing.

The new desktop-publishing technology has produced a new acronym, WYSIWYG, which stands for "what you see is what you get" and is pronounced "wissywig." It is a reference to the fact that modern desktop-publishing programs can display on the screen the full, composed page exactly as it will be printed.

Most of the advanced software that produces all of this requires a "graphics card," usually a CGA or color graphics card. Not everyone has a color monitor, however, nor would you necessarily want one, for unless you have the relatively costly enhanced graphics card, resolution on-screen is not nearly as good in color as it is in monochrome. However, most XT and AT models do come with a monochrome graphics card (a Hercules or Hercules-compatible graphics card). And it is possible to cause your computer to *simulate* a CGA and fool your desktop publishing software by using a simple simulation program. You then can run these programs in monochrome, as your printer will print them.

As I write this, all this is still a rather new technology but, given the speed at which new computer technology has unfolded in the past, it may very well be in widespread use in even small offices in the near future. Certainly, you should consider this in planning publishing operations of any kind.

THE COMPUTER AS A GENERAL AIDE

I am convinced that relatively few owners of desktop computers in small offices—especially in one-person offices—use their computers with anything even approaching true efficiency and effectiveness. For example, my own computer acts as my general assistant; an efficient secretary could not do a great deal more and could not do many of the chores nearly as quickly as the computer does. It is unlikely that any secretary or assistant could find an address, telephone number, or note as quickly as the computer does when properly organized and prompted. In my case, with the press of two keys, my telephone list is on the screen in alphabetical order. The same is true when I want to review my appointments, logs (diaries), correspondence, purchase orders, and other notes and lists I keep in various files. I have not quite achieved the paperless office, but I have made a great deal of progress toward it. I never have to search frantically through paper on my desk, looking for a note; it is in one of the several scratchpad files I keep.

Files, Disks, and Drives

Until I graduated from my original CP/M, two-floppy system to the one I now have, with its 20 megabyte hard disk, I kept a series of dedicated floppy disks. There was one dedicated to current correspondence, one kept for purchase orders, another for logs, and so on.

I had to find and install the proper floppy disk first to search out something I had filed, which was still troublesome and relatively slow. With an internal hard disk, however, that first step of finding the appropriate disk is eliminated; all files are literally *in* the computer, in sets known as *directories* in the PC-DOS or MS-DOS system. The hard disk, at least 20 megabytes large (although many today are using 30-megabyte and even 40-megabyte hard disks), is one of the two essentials necessary to maximize the use of your computer. The other necessity is a key redefiner, such as SmartKey, which is probably the oldest and best known one. (There are, of course, a number of others that do the same thing well enough, and some of the most modern word processors include such programs as integral elements, albeit often substantially more limited in capabilities than separate key redefiner programs.)

Key Redefiners

The concept underlying a key redefining program is simple. You, the user, can redefine a single key or combination of keys on your keyboard to represent a lengthy series of key presses or commands. Suppose, for example, that I am in the midst of writing something—I am in a word processor file, that is—and wish to look up a telephone number without taking the time and using the keystrokes necessary to close the word processor file, go to the other file, and then return to and open the word processor file. I can do this with about 20 keystrokes—*view c:\ltrs\tel.lst*—or I can use that special shorthand made possible by my SmartKey key redefiner and do exactly the same thing with only two keystrokes—the Alt key and the 7 key depressed simultaneously.

That speed in accessing a file is only one way to use a key redefiner effectively. You can also use it to set up definitions for various words, phrases, titles, standard paragraphs, and other items that you use frequently. For example, I have a two-key command that prints my letterhead, I have a command to view my personal dictionary—the words I add to the WordStar integral dictionary—and another to access it quickly to make special additions to it. I also have a number of such commands to type frequently used names and addresses, forms, and even brief form letters. (In some ways it is more efficient to store a form letter in this manner than to store it as an ordinary file.)

Secretarial Programs

There is a special kind of program designed to help you with secretarial chores—furnishing you a notepad, telephone list, telephone dialing service, and other such aids, and furnishing them spontaneously at the press of a key or two. Probably the best-known is SideKick. Many people use such programs and find them convenient. Personally, I prefer to use my key redefiners and organize my own such aids, but that is a matter of personal preference; you may find one of the commercial programs more suitable for your own needs.

Archives

One of the directories I keep on my hard disk is called ARC for *archives*. In that directory I keep materials I can use again and again in my work (especially in writing books), either directly or with suitable modification and adaptation. Here, to suggest such uses, are descriptions of a few of these files:

Trademarks and registered trademarks. The list, to which I add as the occasion arises, is a great time-saver for me.

Charts and graphs. Many of the charts and graphs I have developed rather laboriously can be adapted to new uses far more easily than new ones can be created, so I store many of these.

Glossaries of special terms. Like the other items, these can be adapted to new needs.

Bibliographic listings. Again, a file that is maintained and from which I draw what is appropriate for the occasion.

FINDING SOFTWARE

Software for the millions of XT and AT clones has become incredibly abundant, and with that growing abundance has come competition and more modest prices. But it is a complex market, with more than one kind of competition and more than one influence driving down prices.

Prices for commercial programs have long been discounted by retailers, so that "street prices" or "over-the-counter" prices are far lower than the list prices. A program for which the publisher lists a price of approximately $500 will usually be available "on the street" for not much more than one-half that list price. There are, however, increasing numbers of more modestly priced programs, ranging as low as $19. 95 for many, with the result that they are far less heavily discounted and frequently not discounted at all. The more modest list prices do not leave a great deal of room for discounting.

There is some public domain software (also sometimes referred to as "freeware"), programs written by individuals who generously donated these to the world at large. In many cases the author retained copyright but generously licensed everyone to use it for personal use—specifically not for commercial use—free of charge. That kind of software was particularly abundant for CP/M machines.

Today those individuals offer their software as "shareware." The author copyrights the program and makes it available to all on a trial basis, with the proviso that he or she—the author—expects payment for continued use of the program beyond a trial period. The payment is voluntary, of course, although the author suggests a specific figure (usually quite modest) for "registering" (and paying for) the program and promises some additional benefits, including a printed user's manual and free updating (providing a copy of subsequent revisions or updated versions of the program). Much of the shareware is of poor quality, much is highly specialized and of little interest to the average user, but much of it is quite good, perhaps even better than the expensive commercial versions. Most of the leading shareware communications programs are probably at least the equal of anything sold through regular commercial channels, for example, and there are many excellent "utility" programs (e.g., programs for copying files, displaying directories, and recovering accidentally erased files) One such program that I use displays the entire contents of my hard disk in one large directory of the directories, while another does an excellent job of copying all hard-disk files to floppies as "back-up" files. Such shareware is almost superabundant. The authors distribute it free to encourage trial by new users. Much of it is made available through the thousands of electronic bulletin boards, most of them operated by enthusiasts as a hobby, although many are sponsored by government agencies and private business firms too. Those equipped with modems and communications software can ring up such bulletin boards via telephone and "download" (i.e., have transmitted) the programs of interest. It is also possible to buy such programs from services who advertise in computer periodicals. They do not sell the software; the author's copyright specifically enjoins against this. But they sell the service and the disks on which they copy the programs, usually for about $3 to $5 per disk.

16

Business Ethics in Consulting

As a consultant, your image and reputation are among your greatest and most essential assets. Adherence to and maintenance of the highest ethical standards are necessary to first create and then safeguard those assets.

A BASIC STANDARD OF CONDUCT

We live in an increasingly cynical age, one that has had to invent the term "white collar crime" to identify criminal acts that represent a gross betrayal of trust by high-placed officials in government, business, and industry. In fact, in most of these cases it is that very position of trust that makes the criminal act possible.

By the very nature of your work as a consultant, it is almost inevitable that you are often entrusted with the proprietary and confidential information of your client's business affairs and perhaps even of his or her personal affairs. Even when the information is not specifically identified as confidential, you can usually easily recognize it as such. But even when that is not the case—when there is doubt in your mind as to the confidentiality of certain information you have become privy to in your consulting work—you should assume that the information is confidential. Perhaps you have gained information that can be directly profitable for you in a variety of ways (e.g., to guide investments or to make your services especially valuable to another client). Admittedly the temptation to profit, especially when business is in a lull, is great. But you must resist and hold the information in strictest confidence.

Even harmless gossip about a client is unwise, for clients are likely to infer from such gossip that you do not have professional integrity, that you are not to be completely trusted. The only safe course is to refrain completely from discussing a client with anyone. You must not only respect confidentially in fact, but you must not even *appear* to compromise it. It is the risk of appearing to be loose-lipped about a client's affairs that is most dangerous, and that is why you must go to extremes to avoid that appearance.

That creates something of a problem for you in citing a list of clients and types of projects you have handled, which is information that is essential for marketing purposes. The way around that problem is simple. Ask each client or former client for permission to cite the work you have done for them. Some clients may wish to review the specific citations you propose and edit them or comment on them, which means the client is not opposed to being named.

CONFLICTS OF INTEREST

Conflicts of interest are situations in which you find yourself with two interests, both of which are motivating but which cannot be reconciled with each other because they are in conflict. Here are five hypothetical cases that illustrate such conflicts:

1. You are supporting Client B who is a direct competitor of another client of yours, Client A. You can increase greatly the effectiveness and worth of your services by utilizing what you know about Client A, even without telling Client B what you know about Client A. Is it ethical to do so?
2. In the situation just described, Client B demands to know what you know about Client A. He or she will "fire" you—cancel your contract—if you don't come through with the information. It is a sizeable contract, and in general Client B is a much more profitable account than Client A is. Yielding to Client B's demands makes good business sense. Should you yield?
3. You meet an executive at a convention, and you discuss the executive's needs vis-à-vis your services—the possibility of becoming your client. The executive reveals information about his or her organization, but does not as yet retain you. Are you obliged to treat the information as confidential?

4. You are under annual retainer to a client company, giving them a priority call on your services. One day they call to ask your help with a project. But you have already begun work with a new client who is a direct competitor of the first company. Can you—should you attempt to—handle both assignments?
5. You are working with clients who are direct competitors of your former employer. You were in a relatively senior position in that company and in possession of confidential information about that company. Are you bound by any ethical considerations in using that information to achieve maximum success in your own enterprise?

The ethical issues of the first two cases are straightforward. Whether you disclose information about Client A directly to Client B or use that information in Client B's interest without disclosing the information or its use, the use of it is definitely a violation of confidentiality. The only safe course is to so compartmentalize your thinking that you can manage to forget, at least temporarily, the information concerning Client A. That is perhaps not easy to do, but it is necessary.

The third case is much more difficult. Inasmuch as you have not been retained or compensated in any way by the prospective client referred to, you are probably not legally and certainly not morally obligated in any way to that executive. Still, there are two serious considerations here, the more important of which is that your integrity should extend to all conversations with prospective clients as well as with actual clients. Prospects are unlikely to speak openly with you and discuss possible assignments unless they believe that the conversation is privileged.

The ethical issue in the fourth case is even more difficult. There is only one sensible thing to do here, and that is to avoid the problem entirely by pursuing a clear policy of prevention. If you have accepted an annual retainer or any other arrangement that provides a client priority rights to your services, you should recognize what this obligation means in its entirety. Morally, it means more than a priority right to call on you; it must be translated also as an obligation to anticipate possible and potential conflicts of interest and take preventive measures. That is, before agreeing to an assignment that may mean conflict of interest, you should have called the client who pays you a retainer and gotten his or her approval to undertake an assignment that might be in conflict. I do not mean by this that a retainer-paying client has the right to dictate your policies or actions. But such a client has the right to claim your services, usually, under such retainer agreements, and you should consider this in contemplating new assignments. For example, suppose that you are a marketing consultant and another client wants help in pursuing some important new contract, but that is the kind of contract your retainer-paying client might also pursue. You should not accept the new client without checking with your retainer-paying client to find out whether that client intends to pursue it and therefore wants your help. (In fact, I have had prospective clients inquire into my policies with regard to whether I would handle two clients competing for the same contract. Obviously, it is a concern of prospective clients, at least when they seek help in marketing, that you will not represent a competitor for the same contract.)

Case number 5 represents a rather typical situation, such as the case of former government executives becoming consultants to organizations seeking to do business with government agencies and sometimes even becoming consultants to the very agencies from which they have retired. These situations have become the subject of many mini-scandals despite the several legislative controls that have been established regarding them. Apparently many independent consultants believe that they owe nothing to former employers, especially private sector employers. But this ignores your obligation to yourself to maintain an ethical code and apply it without exception. It ignores the practical considerations that you must safeguard your reputation and that a former employer may become a client. The latter happens quite commonly and may happen to you if you nurture good relationships with former employers.

An Exception

There is at least one case in which it is perfectly ethical and honorable to use any information you have acquired in the course of earlier employment or in pursuing your consulting assignments. You may use all the information you acquire anywhere to benefit your enterprise in any way generally, provided that you keep the information itself in confidence and do not use it in any way that would embarrass, compromise, or injure your former employer or client. You might, subject to this qualification, use such information to

Compile a list of prospective clients.

Prioritize a list of prospective clients by arranging it in order of estimated probability of closing.

Compile information about prospective clients that will help you market successfully—that is win their agreement to retain you.

Develop marketing plans in general.

Formulate or identify specific consulting services, specialized or general, or modify your normal operating procedures to improve your practice in some way.

FEES AND RELATED ETHICAL CONSIDERATIONS

There are two different philosophies regarding standardizing fees. Those adhering to the first philosophy believe it is unethical, or at least unprofessional and unbusinesslike, to have different fees for different clients and different situations. The others believe that flexibility in setting fees is a practical necessity and certainly not dishonest, not reprehensible, and not unethical. A case can be made for both philosophies.

The Middle Road

I do not believe it to be unethical or dishonest to vary fees according to situations—in fact, I can find and will shortly present justification for it—but I think that it is a bad business practice to vary rates spontaneously or on the basis of expediency. That can lead to unethical and dishonest practices, such as misleading and deceiving clients about your fees. That sort of deceit is inevitably exposed, and it will destroy your credibility.

If you decide to have different rates for different circumstances, the rates should have a consistent basis and should be applied uniformly. Consultants must evaluate their circumstances and determine their own rate structures.

In my own case, my assignments tend to be short-term, from a few days to several weeks at most. I find it most practical to set my rates on a daily basis. However, I do not wish to keep a great many time records or to do complex calculating in making up invoices, so I charge a flat day rate. It is the same for an eight-hour day as it is for a twelve-hour day, and the same for Wednesday or Thursday as for Saturday or Sunday. I do not charge for overtime; I simply set my standard day rate large enough to permit me to work this way. (Occasionally it is necessary for me to charge an hourly rate. I have a fixed hourly rate that is less than my day rate divided by 8 because my day rate is not based on 8 hours. In fact, my hourly rate is my day-rate divided by 10.)

If I undertake a relatively large project, one that may occupy months of my time, I prepare an estimate for the entire job, based on rates that have nothing to do with daily or hourly rates. The estimate is based on direct labor, overhead, and profit, which is a much more realistic basis on which to estimate costs for a long-term project.

The nature and length of the assignments are so different that a single, fixed rate would be so impractical. So, though I have three different rate structures, I have a fixed and consistent policy, based on a rationale that I can explain to a client and that is unchanging. I recommend that you have your rate structure and rationale for it in some printed form that you can display to demonstrate to your clients that your rates are not arbitrary.

Personally, I have no hesitancy about explaining all of this to a client or prospective client. I have so far never found a client or prospective one resentful of my efforts to conduct business in a businesslike manner. I find that frankness about what I am doing and why I am doing so tends to make questions and objections fade rapidly. Clients tend strongly to be comforted and reassured by an objective and businesslike manner.

The Ethical Considerations in Billing

In my own practice, clients usually require me to furnish an estimate, often including a "not-to-exceed figure," before approving an assignment and issuing a contract or purchase order. It's usually rather difficult to make that estimate, and of course the tendency is to make the estimate and not-to-exceed figure as large as possible, yet not so large as to lose the contract. So it is not surprising that you often wind up needing more time than you estimated.

What do you do when you need another day or two? Ask the client for more time? Finish the job and then ask to be paid for the extra time? Finish the job and absorb the expense of the extra time yourself? Each situation dictates its own answer.

However, either the first or second alternative is correct for most cases. I have found that if you can justify the need for extra time—if you can demonstrate that it is not the result of a deliberate underestimate by you nor of an incompetent performance by you—clients will usually grant you the extra time. I have often asked for the time but indicated that while I thought I was justified in asking for it, I was prepared to accommodate the client by absorbing the cost. So far, I have never had to do so. I believe that reflects the typical clients' appreciation of being up front with them.

The one thing you should never do when you have exceeded an estimate or a not-to-exceed figure is to simply bill an overrun without explanation and especially without previous discussion with the client. That almost always leads to a dispute. In fact, even when the client is willing to pay for the extra time, your invoice often creates an administrative problem in that the invoice is for a different amount than that authorized by the purchase order. The purchase order must be voided and a new one written, the original purchase order must be amended, or an additional purchase order must be written. No client appreciates your making extra problems for them; the problem would have been minimized had you discussed it in advance with the client.

What do you do when you finish the project ahead of schedule? If you were authorized for 10 days and finished the job in nine days? Should you bill for ten days? For nine days? Should you talk to the client?

Of course, there is a temptation to bill for ten days, as authorized. It is not necessarily dishonest to do so, either. It depends on the contract you have with the client. If it is a fixed-price contract, one in which you guarantee to deliver for a fixed price and in which you must suffer the loss if you run over—you are clearly entitled to bill the full ten days. But if it was clearly based on a daily rate and your estimate of the time needed was ten days, you are not entitled to bill for more than nine days.

A RECOMMENDED CODE

I recommend the following code of ethics for your serious consideration:

Make no extravagant promises, verbal or written, that you would be unwilling or unable to live up to.

Do not withhold important facts or hype the truth to deliberately mislead the client, inducing him or her to believe something you did not explicitly say.

Be scrupulous in respecting the confidentiality of every client's proprietary information and what your business relationships with clients have been.

Make a strictly honest accounting of hours, when the contract calls for it, and be up front with all clients and prospective clients.

Refrain from denouncing or condemning competitors.

Make it a policy to deliver everything you promise a client.

Conduct yourself with professional dignity in all matters and at all times.

17

The Reference File

One benefit of education is learning how and where to seek out the information we need. This chapter will help you do just that.

A WORD OF INTRODUCTION

Within the confines of the pages available to me here I have tried to pass on what I know and have learned about consulting and, especially, what additional knowledge I have gained over the several years since I wrote the first edition of this book. It is not an easy task, for being an independent consultant is not easy; it requires you to be both specialist and generalist, master of some given discipline and yet highly competent in a dozen complementary disciplines. In this final chapter, I identify other sources (e.g., books, periodicals, computer programs, and services of many kinds) to help you cope successfully with all the many fields of knowledge that are essential to your success. These items and tips are certainly not all nor necessarily even the best information available. But I pass them on in good faith and I recommend them as at least a starter list.

BOOKS ON WRITING AND PUBLISHING

The Book Market, How to Write, Publish, and Market Your Book, Aron Mathieu, Andover Press, New York, 1981.

Business Writing, J. Harold Janis/Howard R. Dressner, Barnes & Noble Books, New York, 1956.

The Business Writing Problem Solver, Herman Holtz, Dow Jones-Irwin, Homewood, IL, 1987.

The Careful Writer, Theodore Bernstein, Atheneum, New York, 1965.

The Consultant's Guide to Proposal Writing, Herman Holtz, John Wiley & Sons, Inc., New York, 1986.

The Elements of Style, William Strunk, Jr. and E.B. White, Macmillan, New York, 1972.

How to Publish, Promote, and Sell Your Book, Joseph Goodman, Adams Press, Chicago, 1980.

How to Write Articles That Sell, L. Perry Wilbur, John Wiley & Sons, Inc., New York, 1981.

How to Write Books That Sell, L. Perry Wilbur, Contemporary Books, Chicago, 1979.

On Language, Edwin Newman, Warner Books, New York, 1980.

The Publish it Yourself Handbook, edited by Bill Henderson, Pushcart Press, Yonkers, 1973.

The Self-Publishing Manual, Dan Poynter, Parachuting Publications, Santa Barbara, 1979.

Word Processing for Business Publications, Herman Holtz, McGraw-Hill, 1984.

Writer's Guide to Book Publishing, Richard Balkin, Hawthorn Books, New York, 1977.

The Writer's Market, Writer's Digest Books, Cincinnati, published annually.

OTHER BOOKS OF INTEREST

Direct Mail Copy That Sells, Herschell Gordon Lewis, Prentice-Hall, Englewood Cliffs, 1984.

The Direct Marketer's Work Book, Herman Holtz, John Wiley & Sons, Inc., New York, 1986.

Literary Market Place, R.R. Bowker Co., New York, published annually.

Money Making Marketing, Dr. Jeffrey Lant, JLA Publications, Cambridge 1987.

The National Directory of Addresses and Telephone Numbers, Concord Reference Books, published annually.

The Secrets of Practical Marketing for Small Business, Herman Holtz, Prentice-Hall, Englewood Cliffs, 1983.

Speaking for Profit, Herman Holtz, John Wiley & Sons, Inc., New York, 1987.

Ulrich's International Periodicals Directory, R.R. Bowker Co., New York, published annually.

Writer's Resource Guide, edited by William Brohaugh, Writer's Digest Books, Cincinnati, 1979.

PERIODICALS OF INTEREST

Meeting News, Gralla Publications, 1515 Broadway, New York, NY 10036. This is a trade paper of hoteliers and others with an interest in business meetings and relevant conclaves of all types.

Corporate Meetings & Incentives, Harcourt Brace Jovanovich Publications, 1 East First Street, Duluth, MN 55802. This is also a publication for hotel operators and meeting planners.

Meetings & Conventions, Ziff-Davis, One Park Avenue, New York, NY 10016. This slick trade journal is published monthly.

Sharing Ideas!, published by Dottie Walters, P.O. Box 1120, Glendora, CA 91740. This is a bimonthly publication that generally runs about 30 pages. It is the bible of the public-speaking industry for many readers.

DM News, 19 West 21st Street, New York, NY 10010. This is a monthly tabloid on direct marketing, read by members of the industry.

Target Marketing 401 N. Broad Street, Philadelphia, PA 19108. This is a monthly slick paper trade magazine for marketers.

Personal SellingPower, published by Gerhard Gschwandtner, 1127 International Pkwy, Suite 102, P.O. Box 5467, Fredericksburg, VA 22405. This is a monthly tabloid for marketers.

Direct Response Specialist, P.O. Box 1075, Tarpon Springs, FL 34286-1075. This is a monthly newsletter of direct marketing ideas and guidance by direct-mail consultant Galen Stilson.

Writer's Digest, 9933 Alliance Road, Cincinnati, OH 45242. This monthly magazine is the bible for many professional writers. (I have been reading it since 1937.) You can find it on your newsstand.

Writer's Journal, Inkling Publications, Inc., Box 65798, St. Paul, MN 55165. A bimonthly periodical for writers.

The Writer's Yearbook. is published every spring, by the *Writer's Digest*. It is full of useful articles, guides, and directories.

BOOK WHOLESALERS AND DISTRIBUTORS

ACP Distributors, 105 Pine Road, Sewickley, PA 15143.

Atlantis Distributors, 1725 Carondelet, New Orleans, LA 70130.

Book Bus, Visual Studies Institute, 4 Elton Street, Rochester, NY 14607.

Bookpeople, 2940 7th Avenue, Berkeley, CA 94710.

Bookslinger, 2163 Ford Pkwy, St. Paul, MN 55116.

COSMEP/South, Box 209, Carrboro, NC 27510.

Distributors, 702 S. Michigan, South Bend, IN 46618.

Liberation Book Service, 16 E. 18th Street, New York, NY 10003.

New England Small Press Association, 45 Hillcrest Place, Amherst, MA 01002.

New York State Small Press Association, Box 1624, Radio City Station, New York, NY 10001.

Plains Distribution Service, Box 3112, Room 500, Block 6, 620 Main Street, Fargo, ND 58102.

SBD, 1636 Ocean View Avenue, Kensington, CA 94707.

Skylo Distribution, 1502 E. Olive Way, Seattle, WA 98112.

Small Press Traffic, 3841-B 24th Street, San Francisco, CA 94141.

Southwest Literary Express, 901 Pinon, Las Cruces, NM 77004.

Spring Church Book Co., Box 127, Spring Church, PA 15686.

These organizations distribute others' books. However, some established publishers will also undertake occasionally to distribute others' books. Hawthorn Books, Inc., Harper and Row, and Stein and Day have done so.

PEOPLE AND ORGANIZATIONS IN PUBLIC SPEAKING

Many successful consultants are also speakers, lecture agents, publishers, and trainers of speakers. Some conduct seminars for experienced speakers, where even these veterans of the platform can get guidance to help them become even more successful. The following sample includes many who offer products and/or services of one sort or another.

Lecture Bureaus and Trainers

Dottie Walters, 18825 Hicrest Road, Glendora, CA 91740, (818)335-8069.

Bob Montgomery, 12313 Michelle Circle, Burnsville, MN 55337, (612)894-1348.

Nido Qubein, CPAE, Creative Services, Inc., P.O. Box 6008, High Point, NC 27262.

Mike Frank, Speakers Unlimited, P.O. Box 27225, Columbus, OH 43227.

Lou Hampton, Hampton Communication Strategies, 4200 Wisconsin Avenue, Washington, DC 20016.

Plaza Three Talent Agency, 4343 N. 16th Street, Phoenix, AZ 85016.

Summit Enterprises, 3928 E. Corrine Drive, Phoenix, AZ 85032.

Sun Safari Tours, Inc., 7500 E. McCormick Pkwy, #33, Scottsdale, AZ 85258.

George Colouris Productions, 1782 West Lincoln, Suite J, Anaheim, CA 9280l.

A. Byron Perkins & Associates, Inc., 1201 W. Huntington Drive, Suite 102, Arcadia, CA 91006.

Bobbie Gee, Orange County Speakers Bureau, 31781 National Park Drive, Laguna Niguel, CA 92677.

SRI International, 333 Ravenswood Avenue, Menlo Park, CA 94025.

Masters of Ceremonies, P.O. Box 390, Monrovia, CA 91016.

Dean Howard, Success Seminars, 1539 Monrovia Avenue, Suite 14, Newport Beach, CA 92663.

Meeting Masters, Inc., 4000 MacArthur Blvd, Suite 3000, Newport Beach, CA 92660.

Virginia M. Thomas, West Coast Speakers Bureau, 3500 S. Figueroa, Suite 108, Los Angeles, CA 90007.

Darlene Oram, J.E.O. Marketing, Box 60719, Sacramento, CA 95819.

San Jacobi Star Productions, 4000 Mission Blvd, Suite 3, San Diego, CA 92109.

The Podium (women speakers only), Sandra Schrift & Jill Henderson, 3940 Hancock Street, Suite 207, San Diego, CA 92110.

Della Clark, D.L. Clark & Associates, 2295 N. Tustin, #4, Orange, CA 92665.

The Program Exchange, Sue Clark, 1245 E. Walnut Street, Suite 104, Pasadena, CA 91106.

David Belenzon Management, Box 15428, San Diego, CA 92115.

Samuel Westerman, 4062 Camintito Dehesa, San Diego, CA 92107.

McBride Speakers Bureau, 870 Quail Lake Circle, Suite 101, Colorado Springs, CO 80906.

Connecticut Speakers Bureau, 91 Reservoir Road, Newington, CT 06111.

Conference Management Corp, 17 Washington Street, Norwalk, CT 06854.

Master Talent, 993 Farmington Avenue, West Hartford, CT 06107.

Washington Speakers Bureau, Inc., 201 N. Fairfax Street, #11, Alexandria, VA 22314.

Wedgewood Productions, Inc., Box 440, Crownsville, MD 21032.

International Speakers Bureau, 100 Everett Street, Lakewood, CO 80226.

R. Joseph Advertising, Inc., 8201 Corporate Drive, Landover, MD 20785.

Alan L. Freed & Associates, Inc., Box 304, McLean, VA 22101.

Andres, P.O. Box 1093, Tappahannock, VA 22560.

American Society of Association Executives, 1101 16th Street, NW Washington, DC 20036.

Conference Speakers International, Inc., 1055 Thomas Jefferson Street, Suite 300, Washington, DC 20007.

Stull Lecture Bureau, National Press Building, Washington, DC 20045.

International Association of Professional Bureaucrats, 1032 National Press Building, Washington, DC 20045.

The Lobbyist Federation, 927 15th Street, NW, Washington, DC 20005.

Ida McGinniss Speakers Bureau, 2500 East Hallandale Beach Blvd., Hallandale, FL 33160.

Al Heydrick Associates, 2830 NE 29th Avenue, Lighthouse Point, FL 33064.

Bureau for Speakers & Seminars, P.O. Box 37, Maitland, FL 32751.

Potomac Speakers, 3001 Veazey Terrace, NW, #1625, Washington, DC 20008.

Freeds Speakers Bureau, National Press Building, Washington, DC 20045.

Gerry & Roland Tausch, 3530 Pine Valley Drive, Sarasota, FL 33579.

McCollum Management & Meetings, P.O. Box 10523, Tallahassee, FL 32302.

Jordan Enterprises, Success Leaders Speakers Service, Lenox Square, Box 18737, Atlanta, GA 30326.

Steve Brown, 4675 N. Shallowford Road, Suite 200, Atlanta, GA 30338.

Speakeasy, Inc., 1400 Colony Square, Suite 1130, Atlanta, GA 30361.

Ralph Andres, VP, International Association of Speakers & Sales Trainers, Box 3309, Augusta, GA 30904.

Convention Consultants of Savannah, Delta, Inc., 117 W. Perry, Savannah, GA 31401.

Convention & Conference Consultants, Box 313, Deerfield, IL 60015.

Convention Entertainment Productions, 1645 River Road, Suite 12, Des Plaines, IL 60018.

Programs Unlimited, 515 N. Main Street, Glen Ellyn, IL 60136.

Jane Marks, The Program People, Box 1426, Oak Brook, IL 60521.

Davis Marketing Group, Inc., 1550 N. Northwest Hwy, Suite 40, Park Ridge, IL 60068.

Bradley Barraks, Speakers Corner, 2018 29th Street, Rock Island, IL 61201.

ACA Atlantic Conventions, P.O. Box 891, Cherry Hill, NJ 08003.

Adelle Cox Convention Services & Consultants, P.O. Box 69-4770, Miami, FL 33169.

Sol Abrams Associates, 331 Webster Drive, New Milford, NJ 07646.

Ray Bloch Productions, Inc., 230 Peachtree Street, NW, Atlanta, GA 30303; and 1500 Broadway, New York, NY 10036.

California Association of Meeting Planners, 888 Airport Blvd, Burlingame, CA 94010.

California Leisure Consultants, Inc., 2760 E. El Presidio Street, Long Beach, CA 90810; and 3714 Fourth Street, San Diego, CA 92103.

CONVENTION MANAGERS AND PLANNERS

There are a great many convention planners, managers, consultants, and others who support such events. A small sampling is offered here.

A&B Businessworks, Inc., 529 Bay Avenue, Point Pleasant Beach, NJ 08742.

Atlantic Exhibit Services, 62 W. 45th Street, New York, NY 10036.

California Leisure Consultants, Inc., 2760 E. El Presidio Street, Long Beach, CA 90810; and 3714 Fourth Street, San Diego, CA 92103.

Convention & Conference Consultants, 644 Timber Lane, Lake Forest, IL 60045.

Details, 1750 Pennsylvania Avenue, NW, Suite 1208, Washington, DC 20006.

Harrison-Berkall Productions, Inc., 527 Madison Avenue, New York, NY 10022.

Audrey Hoffman Enterprises, 12 Prospect Terrace, Albany, NY 12208; McRand, Inc., 210 E. Westminster, Lake Forest, IL 60045.

The Meeting Market, 2025 Eye Street, NW, Suite 507, Washington, DC 20006.

Prince & Company, White Flint Mall, Kensington, MD 20895.

Professional Meeting Organizers, Inc., P.O. Box 141423, Coral Gables, FL 33114.

Promotional Planning, Inc., 502 Hulmeville Avenue, Langhorne Manor, PA 19047.

Gann Carter Convention Services, 261 E. Tahquitz, McCallum Way, Palm Springs, CA 92262.

City Welcome Corp., 100 Jericho Quadrangle, Suite 212, Jericho, NY 11753.

Conference Management Corp., 17 Washington Street, Norwalk, CT 06854.

Conference Resources, Inc., 1821 E. Fairmount Avenue, Baltimore, MD 21231.

Dr. Art Garner & Associates, 2519 Lovitt Drive, Memphis, TN 38138.

Meetings Unlimited, P.O. Box 5052, Westport, CT 06881.

Promotions for Industry, Inc., 6545 Carnegie Avenue, Cleveland, OH 44103.

Red Carpet Associates, Inc., 19 E. 57th Street, New York, NY 10022.

DeAnne Rosenberg, Inc., 28 Fifer Avenue, Lexington, MA 02173.

Round Hill-IVC, Inc., 89 Erickson Drive, Stamford, CT 06903.

Show Marketeers, Inc., Third Street, Suite 20, La Mesa, CA 92041.

SPEAKERS ASSOCIATIONS

There are a number of speakers associations. Here are three you should know about:

National Speakers Association (NSA), 5201 N. 7th Street, Suite 200, Phoenix, AZ 85014.

International Platform Association (IPA), 2564 Berkshire Road, Cleveland Heights, OH 44106.

Toastmasters International, Inc., P.O. Box 10400, Santa Ana, CA 92711.

MAILING LIST BROKERS

There is an abundance of mailing list brokers, and you can find them listed in the yellow pages, as well as in many other media. Here are just a few of them.

NCRI List Management, 30 East 42nd Street, New York, NY 10017.

Potentials in Marketing Magazine, 731 Hennepin Avenue, Minneapolis, MN 55403.

Names & Addresses, Inc., 3605 Woodhead Drive, Northbrook, IL 60062.

Qualified Lists Corp., 135 Bedford Rd, Armonk, NY 10504.

The List House, 130 Lyons Plain Road, Weston, CT 06883.

American List Counsel, Inc., 88 Orchard Road, Princeton, NJ 08540.

List Services Corp., 890 Ethan Allen Hwy, P.O. Box 2014, Ridgefield, CT 06877.

Hayden Direct Marketing Services, 10 Mulholland Drive, Hasbrouck Heights, NJ 07604.

The Kleid Company, Inc., 200 Park Avenue, New York, NY 10166.

Ed Burnett Consultants, 2 Park Avenue, New York, NY 10016.

R.L. Polk & Co., 3030 Holcomb Bridge Road, Suite F, Norcross, GA 30071.

Seminars, 525 N. Lake Street, Madison, WI 53703.

A Few Tips on Writing Direct Mail Copy

Here is a checklist for preparing direct mail copy:

1. Always make things as easy as possible for the customer.
   a. Make it easy to understand what you are saying. Use short words, short sentences, short paragraphs. Use one thought in a sentence, one subject and one main point in a paragraph. (Be sure that you fully understand the main point.)
   b. Make it easy for the customer to order, ask for more information, or otherwise reveal interest by providing a return card, telephone number, or other convenient means for responding.
   c. Make it easy for the customer to understand what you want him or her to do by *telling* the customer what to do.
2. A direct-mail cliche (which is nonetheless a truism) is "The more you tell the more you sell." Be sure to include a letter, a brochure or flyer of some sort, and a response device (envelope and/or order form) as an absolute minimum, and there is no harm in enclosing even more. The experts claim that three-

quarters of the response results from the letter, and that a good circular or brochure can increase response by as much as one-third. My own experience bears this out quite emphatically.

3. Don't tell it all in the letter. Split the copy up among the various enclosures, or at least provide additional details in the various enclosures. Make it clear that additional information are to be found elsewhere in the enclosures. Give the reader good reason to read everything, if you want maximum impact.
4. Geography makes a difference. Prospects who are nearby tend to respond better than those at a distance. Know nearby zip codes, and use these. But do test, for there are always exceptions. For example, when it comes to consulting and speaking services, there is some appeal, even a kind of mystique, to the expert from a distant place, especially if you are mailing from a major industrial or business center, such as New York, Chicago, Washington, or another major metropolitan area. If you are, take advantage of it, by giving it prominence in your copy.
5. If you use envelope copy—advertising and sales messages on the outside of the envelope—do two things:
   a. Use both sides of the envelope. If you are going to make a bulletin board of the envelope, you might as well get full use of it; copy on both sides pulls better than copy on one side only—if the copy is powerful.
   b. Now that you've served notice that the envelope contains advertising matter, why pay first-class postage? Save money by using bulk mail or, at least, something less expensive than first class.

ASSOCIATIONS OF CONSULTANTS

Many of those who belong to speakers' associations and to many other kinds of associations and professional societies are consultants. But there are also a number of consultants' associations, which are listed here:

American Association of Professional Consultants, 9140 Ward Parkway, Kansas City, MO 64114.

American Association of Hospital Consultants, 1235 Jefferson Davis Highway, Arlington, VA 22202.

American Association of Medico-Legal Consultants, 2200 Benjamin Franklin Parkway, Philadelphia, PA 19130.

American Association of Political Consultants, 444 N. Capitol Street, NW, Washington, DC 20001.

The American Consultants League, 2030 Clarendon Blvd, Suite 200, Arlington, VA 22201.

American Society of Agricultural Consultants, 8301 Greensboro Drive, McLean, VA 22101.

Association of Bridal Consultants, 29 Ferriss Estate, New Milford, CT 06776.

Association of Executive Search Consultants, 151 Railroad Avenue, Greenwich, CT 06830.

Association of Management Consultants, 500 N. Michigan Blvd, Chicago, IL 60611.

Independent Computer Consultants Association, Box 27412, St. Louis, MO 63141.

Society of Professional Business Consultants, 221 N. LaSalle Street, Chicago, IL 60601.

Society of Professional Management Consultants, 16 W. 56th Street, New York, NY 10019.

CONSULTANT LABOR CONTRACTORS

Many independent consultants with technical specialties in such fields as engineering, technical writing, and computer programming accept assignments through organizations that provide technical/professional temporaries, acting as brokers, in effect. Such firms advertise in the help-wanted columns, but a brief starter list of such brokers is offered here:

Consultants and Designers, 355 Lexington Avenue, New York, NY 10017.

GP Technology Corporation, 5615 Landover Road, Hyattsville, MD 20782.

H.L. Yoh Co., 210 W. 230th Street, New York, NY 10034.

Kidde Consultants, Inc., 1020 Cromwell Bridge Road, Baltimore, MD 21204.

Miles-Samuelson, Inc., 15 E. 26th Street, New York, NY 10010.

Tad Technical Corporation, Box 17012, Washington, DC 20041.

Volt Information Sciences, Inc., 101 Park Avenue, New York, NY. 10017.

A Few Seminar Tips

As one of the most important tools available to you to build your income base and market your services, seminar production deserves some thought, and for that reason a few tips and reminders are offered here for ready reference:

A typical day's session runs approximately six hours, three in the morning and three in the afternoon, with midmorning and midafternoon breaks of about 10 minutes. The lunch break is thus usually from 90 minutes to two hours.

Back-of-the-room sales may be conducted prior to the start of the morning session, during the lunch break, and after the close of the afternoon session.

Whether you sell books, tapes, or other materials, you should include handout materials as part of the seminar. These are often a major inducement to registration and attendance. It helps, from that viewpoint, if they are exclusively available to attendees. However, in many cases you can get excellent materials free of charge from government agencies, associations, community groups, large corporations, schools, and other sources.

Often visual aids are also available from such sources as those just named—movies, slides, film strips, transparencies, and posters of various kinds.

One rather profitable idea was the mini-seminar. I held these two- to three-hour sessions for 10 to 15 people in my offices on Saturday mornings, charging a modest fee of $25. If your offices are unsuitable for the purpose you can usually arrange to rent an inexpensive room somewhere.

A variant on that idea is to conduct two such sessions, one in the morning, another in the afternoon, enabling yourself to register twice the number of attendees for a single day. (The total cost is only slightly greater for two sessions, and the income is doubled.)

PROPOSAL DO'S AND DON'TS

In my opinion, nothing is more important to marketing your professional services that the proposal, used properly and with a few tips in mind:

Analyze the client's problem closely and be sure that you understand it fully before committing yourself to a plan of action. Don't rush to the word processor before you have done so.

Devise a specific strategy upon which to base your proposal.

Be highly specific in what you propose to do and furnish to the client.

Shun hyperbole. Stick with nouns and verbs, using adjectives and adverbs as sparingly as possible—especially avoiding superlatives.

Quantify as much as possible in providing details.

Avoid potential disputes by being sure to specify exactly what your quoted cost estimate covers.

Index